TOUGH GUYS AND TRUE BELIEVERS

The Routledge Series on Counseling and Psychotherapy With Boys and Men

SERIES EDITOR

Mark S. Kiselica
The College of New Jersey

ADVISORY BOARD

Deryl Bailey
University of Georgia

David Lisak
University of Massachusetts Boston

Chris Blazina
Tennessee State University

William M. Liu
University of Iowa

J. Manuel Casas
University of California, Santa Barbara

James O'Neil
University of Connecticut

Matt Englar-Carlson
California State University, Fullerton

Steve Wester
University of Wisconsin–Milwaukee

Ann Fischer
Southern Illinois University Carbondale

VOLUMES IN THIS SERIES

Volume 1: *Counseling Troubled Boys: A Guidebook for Professionals*
Mark S. Kiselica, Matt Englar-Carlson, and Arthur M. Horne, editors

Volume 2: *BAM! Boys Advocacy and Mentoring: A Leader's Guide to Facilitating Strengths-Based Groups for Boys – Helping Boys Make Better Contact by Making Better Contact With Them*
Peter Motorola, Howard Hiton, and Stephen Grant

Volume 3: *Counseling Fathers*
Chen Z. Oren and Dora Chase Oren, editors

Volume 4: *Counseling Boys and Men With ADHD*
George Kapalka

Volume 5: *Culturally Responsive Counseling With Asian American Men*
William M. Liu, Derek Kenji Iwamoto, and Mark H. Chae, editors

Volume 6: *Therapy With Young Men: 16–24 Year Olds in Treatment*
David A. Verhaagen

Volume 7: *An International Psychology of Men: Theoretical Advances, Case Studies, and Clinical Innovations*
Chris Blazina and David S. Shen Miller, editors

Volume 8: *Psychotherapy With Older Men*
Tammi Vacha-Haase, Stephen R. Wester, and Heidi Fowell Christianson

Volume 9: *Engaging Boys in Treatment: Creative Approaches to Formulating, Initiating, and Sustaining the Therapy Process*
Craig Haen, editor

Volume 10: *Dying to Be Men: Psychological, Social, and Behavioral Directions in Promoting Men's Health*
William Courtenay

Volume 11: *Working Successfully With Men in Couples Counseling*
David S. Shepard and Michelle Harway, editors

Volume 12: *Gender in the Therapy Hour: Voices of Female Clinicians Working With Men*
Holly Barlow Sweet, editor

Volume 13: *Tough Guys and True Believers: Managing Authoritarian Men in the Psychotherapy Room*
John M. Robertson

FORTHCOMING

Volume 14: *Men, Addiction, and Intimacy: Strengthening Recovery by Fostering the Emotional Development of Boys and Men*
Mark S. Woodford

Volume 15: *Resiliency, Achievement, and Manhood: Promoting the Healthy Development of African American Men*
Cyrus Marcellus Ellis and Jon Carlson, editors

Volume 16: *Project Gentlemen on the Move: Nurturing Excellence in African American Youth*
Deryl Bailey and Mary Bradbury-Bailey
Volume 17: *Counseling Widowers*
Jason Troyer

TOUGH GUYS AND TRUE BELIEVERS

MANAGING AUTHORITARIAN MEN
IN THE PSYCHOTHERAPY ROOM

JOHN M. ROBERTSON

Routledge
Taylor & Francis Group
New York   London

Scripture taken from the Holy Bible, New International Version®. Copyright © 1973, 1978, 1984 by International Bible Society. Used by permission of Zondervan Publishing House. All rights reserved.

Routledge
Taylor & Francis Group
711 Third Avenue
New York, NY 10017

Routledge
Taylor & Francis Group
27 Church Road
Hove, East Sussex BN3 2FA

© 2012 by Taylor & Francis Group, LLC
Routledge is an imprint of Taylor & Francis Group, an Informa business

Printed in the United States of America on acid-free paper
Version Date: 20120125

International Standard Book Number: 978-0-415-89042-7 (Hardback) 978-0-415-89043-4 (Paperback)

For permission to photocopy or use material electronically from this work, please access www.copyright.com (http://www.copyright.com/) or contact the Copyright Clearance Center, Inc. (CCC), 222 Rosewood Drive, Danvers, MA 01923, 978-750-8400. CCC is a not-for-profit organization that provides licenses and registration for a variety of users. For organizations that have been granted a photocopy license by the CCC, a separate system of payment has been arranged.

Trademark Notice: Product or corporate names may be trademarks or registered trademarks, and are used only for identification and explanation without intent to infringe.

Library of Congress Cataloging-in-Publication Data

Robertson, John M., 1949-
  Tough guys and true believers : managing authoritarian men in the psychotherapy room / John M. Robertson.
    p. cm.
  Includes bibliographical references and index.
  ISBN 978-0-415-89043-4 (pbk. : alk. paper) -- ISBN 978-0-415-89042-7 (hbk. : alk. paper)
  1. Authoritarianism (Personality trait) 2. Control (Psychology) 3. Men--Psychology. 4. Psychotherapist and patient. I. Title.

BF698.35.A87R63 2012
155.3'328232--dc23   2011050422

Visit the Taylor & Francis Web site at
http://www.taylorandfrancis.com

and the Routledge Web site at
http://www.routledgementalhealth.com

Contents

Series Editor's Foreword		ix
Preface		xiii
Acknowledgments		xix

SECTION I UNDERSTANDING AUTHORITARIAN MEN 1

1 *"Who Are These Men, Exactly?": Four Prototypical Faces* 3

2 *"He Always Has Been That Way": Authoritarian as Personality Type* 33

3 *"God Wants Him to Take Charge": Authoritarian as Divine Mandate* 55

4 *"He Is Only Doing What Comes Naturally": Authoritarian as Adaptive Strategy* 75

5 *"He Learned From the Best": Authoritarian as Social Construction* 93

Section I Summary 121

SECTION II MANAGING AUTHORITARIAN MEN IN THE PSYCHOTHERAPY ROOM 125

6 *"I Never Wanted to Be This Way": Up Close and Personal: Two Authoritarian Men* 127

7	*"What Does He Need the Most?": A Healing Relationship: Attunement and Empathy*	135
8	*"What Is Wrong With Him?": A Qualitative Assessment: Collaboration and Insight*	155
9	*"How Can He Be Helped?": A Multimodal Treatment: Self-Understanding and Self-Regulation*	193
10	*"Does an Authoritarian Man Really Change?": Human Change: The Processes and the Psychotherapists*	229
	Credits	261
	References	263
	Index	295

Series Editor's Foreword

During the late 1980s, I was employed as the principal clinical psychologist in an adult correctional facility for men while also participating in a number of community organizations that consisted of mainly male members. One of the immediate observations I had as I moved between these two worlds was that some of the men I met through my work in the community—men who viewed themselves as model citizens—were remarkably similar in many respects to the men I was treating in prison. Much like the incarcerated men, a handful of these "community leaders" were narcissistic, manipulative, deceitful, and domineering. They had to be the centers of attention and maintain control over others in all situations, and their ruthless ways were destructive to others, including their own family members. At times their disturbing behaviors overshadowed the presence and good work of the majority of the other community leaders, whose ways of relating to people were much more considerate and purely altruistic.

During this same period, I read a wonderful book, *Unmasking the Psychopath: Antisocial Personality and Related Syndromes* (Reid, Dorr, Walker, & Bonner, 1986), which I had purchased with the intention of enhancing my understanding of sociopathic men and learning methods for treating them in psychotherapy. Dr. Ethel Person, one of the contributors to *Unmasking the Psychopath* who is also a psychiatrist and analyst and, at the time, was director of the Columbia University Center for Psychoanalytic Training and Research, wrote a fascinating chapter titled "Manipulativeness in Entrepreneurs and Psychopaths." In this chapter she described the personal attributes of a subset of entrepreneurs who share many of the same qualities as psychopaths, including "characteristic ways of defending against anxiety, depression, and conflict. In particular, both groups employ sophisticated manipulative techniques both defensively and adaptively" (p. 259). I greatly appreciated Dr. Person's chapter because her cogent observations regarding the similarities between these two populations helped me to better understand both the men I served in the prison and the problematic men I had encountered in my work in the community.

Since reading Dr. Person's illuminating chapter, I have continued to work with antisocial men—both criminal offenders and non-offenders—in psychotherapy. I have remained concerned about the considerable harm they cause others, and have found it challenging to help them see the need to change their destructive, domineering ways. I also remain alarmed by the tendency of the non-offender group to use their religious beliefs or positions of power in the workplace and community as justification for manipulating and abusing other people, including their own children, girlfriends, wives, parents, siblings, friends, and coworkers. By talking with other clinicians about my experiences, I discovered that many of my colleagues share similar perspectives and have dealt with the same challenges in working with these two populations.

As I sought more ideas that could inform my clinical work with authoritarian, antisocial men, I had the pleasure of getting to know Dr. John Robertson, a gifted therapist, researcher, and writer whose work overlaps with that of Dr. Person, through our mutual participation in the Society for the Psychological Study of Men and Masculinity. When I first met Dr. Robertson in the early 1990s, he was the senior staff psychologist and coordinator of research at the Kansas State University Counseling Services, and he specialized in providing individual and group psychotherapy with men. More recently, he has been a staff psychologist with the Professional Renewal Center in Lawrence, Kansas, where he has worked with numerous authoritarian men who have engaged in disruptive behavior, professional sexual misconduct, boundary problems, compulsive behaviors, verbal and physical abuse, and substance abuse. Over the past 20 years as I followed Dr. Robertson's work and attended many of his presentations at the Annual Conventions of the American Psychological Association, I discovered that Dr. Robertson has remarkable insights into the psyches of authoritarian men; is keenly aware of the problems they cause in their communities, homes, and the workplace; empathizes with their hidden pain; and has numerous ideas for how to work with them in psychotherapy to make substantive, positive changes in their lives. In addition, he understands in a profound way the link between restrictive notions of masculinity and authoritarian behavior in men. Dr. Robertson also is an outstanding scientist/practitioner, writer, and presenter: He is adept at integrating current research findings into the therapeutic process and explaining that integration to others in an accessible, practical manner. So, when I launched the Routledge Series on Counseling and Psychotherapy With Boys and Men, I invited Dr. Robertson to write a book for the series. He responded by producing his outstanding volume, *Tough Guys and True Believers: Managing Authoritarian Men in the Psychotherapy Room*.

In *Tough Guys and True Believers*, Dr. Robertson describes four subgroups of authoritarian men: (1) the tough guy who is a workplace bully; (2) the tough guy who is an abusive partner; (3) the true believer who is a zealous follower; and (4) the true believer who sees himself as a messenger from God. He explains that all four types rely on power to get their ways and are highly controlling, very exploitive and manipulative, low on empathy, and low on egalitarianism. He draws from a diverse literature in psychology, sociology, men's studies, and neurobiology to hypothesize about how authoritarian men get to be this way, and he empathically demonstrates that these men are in emotional pain, even though they may appear on the surface to be pain-free. Acknowledging that getting authoritarian men to change is difficult, Dr. Robertson offers extensive practice advice about how to assess, engage, and treat this population. He also recommends numerous in-session strategies, as well as out-of-session, self-care activities that can help clinicians avoid being overwhelmed by authoritarian men. Thus, if you are a clinician and you have ever been afraid, intimidated, confused, and unsuccessful while working with authoritarian men, and if you want to help authoritarian men and the people who are adversely affected by their coercive ways, then *Tough Guys and True Believers* is the book for you.

I am indebted to Dr. Robertson for his fine work—this landmark contribution to the psychotherapy literature.

Mark S. Kiselica, Series Editor
The Routledge Series on Counseling and Psychotherapy With Boys and Men
The College of New Jersey

REFERENCES

Person, E. S. (1986). Manipulativeness in entrepreneurs and psychopaths. In W. H. Reid, W. H. Dorr, J. I. Walker, & J. W. Bonner (Eds.), *Unmasking the psychopath: Antisocial personality and related syndromes* (pp. 256–274). New York, NY: W. W. Norton & Company.

Reid, W. H., Dorr, D., Walker, J. I., & Bonner, J. W. (Eds.). (1986). *Unmasking the psychopath: Antisocial personality and related syndromes*. New York, NY: W. W. Norton & Company.

Preface

Some men are especially tough to manage in the psychotherapy room. They do not work well with *anyone* in their lives—work associates, family members, fellow believers, neighbors. These troubled and challenging men appear in many roles. Some are Tough Guys—workplace bullies, sexual harassers, abusive partners. Others are True Believers—zealous followers and messengers from God.

Does the idea of talking with these men in your psychotherapy room make you wince? Even a little? If so, you are not alone. These men are a challenge because of the traits they share. In a word, they are authoritarian. Over the last 60 years, researchers have developed a profile of these men. They are demanding, rigid, and overbearing. They tend to be chauvinistic toward women and prejudiced toward minorities. They support repressive causes and regimes. In so many ways, they harm others. Entire groups have become the target of their hate language, aggressive religious zeal, legislated inequalities, and worse.

Why treat *these* men? Aren't they incorrigible?

My answer has two parts. First, these men are worth writing about because the cost of their authoritarian behavior is so high. Helping one of them generates a ripple effect of benefits in society. Although they can be quite charming or charismatic, they also can become ridiculing, bullying, or attacking when they perceive threats. For both relational and social policy reasons, I believe it is critically important to understand their perspectives and inner landscapes.

Second, the behavior of authoritarian men can lead to their own suffering, as well. In treatment, most report lifelong struggles with isolation, neglect, and rejection. When they acknowledge that pain, they can be helped by trained and skillful psychotherapists. In these pages, I will offer evidence for this assertion. Empirical evidence exists and is persuasive. And I will report some personal stories, as well.

The first half of this book reviews four approaches to understanding these Tough Guys and True Believers. What makes them behave as they do?

- Is their authoritarian behavior an expression of a personality trait?
- Are they following a religious mandate that requires them to act as they do?
- Do their actions embody the evolutionary principle of sexual selection?
- Have they learned authoritarian traits in the context of social relationships?

Much scholarly thought and research has been devoted to these questions, and it is well worth thinking about this work as background for doing clinical work with them.

The second half of this volume offers specific assessment and treatment ideas that help these men. The most critical issue is the psychotherapeutic relationship itself. It is primary, and I will explain why. The clinical assessment begins to build that relationship, and I will suggest qualitative strategies that encourage that connection. Treatment forges that relationship, but it also teaches two sets of skills, self-awareness and self-regulation. Self-awareness helps them understand the sources of their maladaptive behavior, and self-regulation enables them to practice the skills of more adaptive behavior.

More than anything else, these men are in emotional pain. It is lifelong, and it is deep. They may be defensive and emotionally unskilled, but they also are distressed. When they are ready, most will admit to feeling puzzled and misunderstood. They are expected to be tough (durable, reliable, stoical), but they end up feeling devalued as burned out workaholics if they take that expectation too seriously. They try to live by religious teachings that seem to be Truth, but then are disparaged for being zealous, bigoted, or chauvinist. Emotionally, they are confused, alone, and very angry.

The central point of this book is that some authoritarian men *want* to change their thinking and behavior and they can do so. Their relational goals in life are not being met and they do not know why. But I have found that they *can* make changes when they step inside the psychotherapy room. These changes can be lasting. I will review research that supports this assertion and offer examples from my own experiences in working almost exclusively with this population as a clinician.

Clearly, this book addresses some large and controversial issues—sexual behavior, religious beliefs, evolutionary biology. I hope you will find my comments to be measured, fair, and respectful. You may disagree, but I hope not. At the outset, you have a right to know something about my background as a social scientist and my experiences with religiousness.

ACADEMIC GENEALOGY

An academic genealogy is a line of successive major professors that can be traced from the present time back to one of the founders of the

Preface

discipline. Out of curiosity, I have traced my own line of successive major professors of psychology back to Wilhelm Wundt. He is often regarded as the founder of modern scientific psychology because he founded the first psychological laboratory and edited the first psychology research journal. Below are the seven academic ancestors who connect me to Wundt. My degree was granted by the University of California at Santa Barbara in 1989 under Louise Fitzgerald, who got her degree under Samuel Osipow, and so on....

- Louise F. Fitzgerald, PhD (The Ohio State University, 1979)
- Samuel H. Osipow, PhD (Syracuse University, 1959)
- Francis J. Di Vesta, PhD (Cornell University, 1948)
- Asahel D. Woodruff, PhD (University of Chicago, 1941)
- Guy T. Buswell, PhD (University of Chicago, 1920)
- Charles H. Judd, PhD (University of Liepzig, 1896)
- Wilhelm Wundt, MD (University of Heidelberg, 1856)

Here is the reason I mention my academic genealogy. My recommendations for assessment and treatment of authoritarian men rest on concepts that have been passed down to me through seven generations of major professors. In another publication, I have traced these concepts in some detail (Robertson, 1994). Because these views have strongly influenced my writing of this book, I will summarize them briefly here.

Rule #1: Be empirical. Everyone on the above list conducted research. Lots of research. As a group, they published more than 2,000 monographs, articles, book chapters, and books. All seven of them developed psychological ideas and theories and tested and published them. Clearly, they believed in the scientific method. This approach to psychology was drilled into me during my own training, and I join them in believing that the social sciences must offer clinicians recommendations fortified by research. That is why the list of references at the end of this book is rather lengthy. If you wish to pursue any idea I discuss along the way, the reference list will provide at least an entry point for additional reading.

Rule #2: Be educational. All my academic ancestors have been interested in developing knowledge about how human beings learn. They have written about how we learn language and memorize (Di Vesta), how children learn to read (Buswell), how music and art are learned (Woodruff), how high school students learn (Judd), how students choose careers (Osipow), and how sexual harassment is perpetuated in the workplace (Fitzgerald). In this book, I summarize findings about how men *learn* to be authoritarian and how they can learn to think and behave differently. I will show how this learning occurs—in the context of cultural and religious ideas about how men should behave. Particularly relevant is the learning about life that takes place in their distressed families.

Rule #3: Be cognitive. Wundt proposed several theories about how humans think (Wundt, 1907). Wundt's student, Judd, thought the central task of psychology was to discover the principles of cognition (Judd, 1932). Woodruff (1962) began his textbook on concepts of teaching by listing 13 propositions about how students think. In the early days of the "cognitive revolution" in psychology, Di Vesta (1973) was among the first to introduce current cognitive theory to educators. Osipow (1990) argued that career decision-making is based more on people's thinking styles than on the facts and figures of various occupations. And Fitzgerald (2000) was deeply interested in the thinking (or myths) that perpetuate the sexual harassment of women. This book rests on the idea that men's cognitions matter. Authoritarian men *think* in certain ways, as I shall outline. Some struggle with basic rules of logic. This becomes an important clue in looking for treatment strategies that work.

Rule #4: Be developmental. Wundt (1916) believed that psychology should study cultural development—how social groups develop and adapt to their worlds. Judd (1910) argued that humans developed reading and writing skills to adapt to social problems. Di Vesta (1966) conducted investigations of children's development of semantic and connotative meaning. Osipow (1990) was interested in how people's career interests change at different developmental points in life as they respond to life's challenges. Fitzgerald's emphasis on how socialization processes affect the development of gender behavior is strongly developmental in tone. A primary assertion in this book is that authoritarian male behavior begins during the developmental years. Boys learn how to be authoritarian as they grow up in the context of families, ethnic groups, religious institutions, and nations. Because these behaviors are adaptive in origin, they are subject to change as new demands and expectations emerge.

Rule #5: Be generous. My academic line of psychologists has set a high standard for service back to the profession. They have served national governments as consultants, influenced military decisions, written widely used textbooks, edited major scientific journals, produced educational material for civic and religious groups, and been expert witnesses in major class-action court cases (Robertson, 1994). My own contributions have been meager by contrast. I have reviewed articles for scholarly journals, taught graduate school classes, served as a major professor, and held offices in state and national associations of psychologists. In large part, this book is motivated by service to my profession. I am past 60 years of age. My entire career in psychology has been devoted to understanding male psychology and treating men in the psychotherapy room. I want to share what I have learned about working with authoritarian men. I am hoping that at least some of this information may be useful to my peers who find working with this group of men to be confusing, frustrating, and at times, downright frightening.

Most social science scholars labor in obscurity. Their writing is dense, complex, and reinforced with detailed statistics. Findings are published in journals read mostly by other scholars. This is inevitable, perhaps,

Preface xvii

but also unfortunate, because it is the *lives* of scholars that motivate and enliven their work. I want to illustrate that connection in this book with a series of snapshots of scholars-as-people who study topics important in their own lives. Their stories appear in boxes located near my references to their work. Including their stories is consistent with an important treatment strategy emphasized in this book: helping a man find the multiple benefits of discovering and telling his own life story.

RELIGIOUS GENEALOGY

Most of my academic ancestors had experience with religiousness. Wilhelm Wundt's father was a university-educated Protestant minister. Charles Judd was born to missionary parents in northern India. Guy Buswell's father was a pastor in the United Brethren church in the United States. Ashahel Woodruff's great-grandfather was the fourth president of the Mormon Church. My point: Scientific research and philosophical inquiry tap similar human tendencies and curiosities. Both traditions are concerned with how we humans live and what can be done when life goes awry. These larger questions about life have been of interest to many in my academic tree. My own background may explain some of my interest.

Two state-established churches in Europe form the roots of my religious genealogy. For generations, my father's ancestors were associated with the Anglican Communion, both the Church of England and the Scottish Episcopal Church. My mother's ancestors belonged to the Church of Norway, which professes the Lutheran faith. When the immigrant men in my family left their generations-long traditions of coal mining and deep-sea fishing, they began new lives in the Pacific Northwest of the United States. Neither they nor their wives remained actively affiliated with their state-established churches. Curiously, all four of my grandparents were drawn to a small Christian denomination native to their new country. Two of them joined a Scandinavian congregation, and the other two joined or sympathized with an English-speaking congregation. Both my parents, then, were raised in this same fundamentalist denomination and attended schools operated by the group. They remained members of this faith community into the tenth decade of their lives.

This backstory means that I was raised in an atmosphere that fits the definition of fundamentalism offered later in this book. Scholars have found commonalities in fundamentalisms that cross religious and ethnic boundaries, and these findings are important in understanding some authoritarian men. Although I migrated out of that environment much earlier in life, I have first-hand knowledge of life inside such a group.

Because the evidence shows that membership in religious groups has benefits as well as costs, I hope my treatment of aspects of this topic will be seen as courteous rather than antagonistic. I want to acknowledge some of religion's benefits at the outset. There are many. Across centuries and cultures, all major faith communities have promoted codes of principled conduct, demanded compassion toward the weak and disadvantaged, provided a sense of community and social support, praised interpersonal gratitude and forgiveness, encouraged self-reflection, prayerfulness, and meditation, valued family life and commitments, and fostered hope for the future.

As an adult, my own religious curiosities have taken me through readings from the sacred texts and teachings of Judaism, Christianity, Islam, Hinduism, Buddhism, and many other smaller scale spiritual traditions. I have attended a wide variety of ceremonies and programs. Some of my curiosities were pursued more formally by completing a doctoral degree from a mainline Protestant school of theology (though I am not a member of the clergy). For most of my adult life, I have not been a formal member of any organized religious group or spiritual tradition, yet I have found my life enriched by the narratives, rituals, aesthetics, metaphors, reflections, and ethical exhortations that cross the boundaries of many communities of faith. Fellowship with like-minded seekers has been of great benefit to me.

At the same time, I am keenly aware of the horrendous damage done by those who have used religion as a brutal justification for naked expressions of greed, power, and aggression. Countless deaths have occurred. Tragically, these underbelly tendencies are not restricted to religious institutions and have found expression in virtually all human institutions—politics and government, education and science, even marriages and families. All human affiliations seem to have the potential of going heartbreakingly off track.

Finally, this book is about men, authoritarian men. I will review research examining what both scientists and religionists have to say about them, so this book is neither anti-science nor anti-religion. Instead, I offer insights from both traditions in confronting two basic questions: When an authoritarian man sits in front of a psychotherapist, how can he be understood? How can he be helped?

JMR

Acknowledgments

Truth is...many people have written this book. I admit to tapping the words onto my screen, but others have sparked the ideas that now appear as paragraphs in your hands. I have been raised, taught, and mentored by many.

My parents did much more than give me their two surnames—Martin and Robertson. They raised me with relational values I espouse to this day. From them, I learned compassion...even toward the disagreeable among us. I never heard my mother say a mean word about another person. I saw my father treat her with open affection and loyalty during 70 years of a compatible marriage. Though both disapproved of my ideas and behavior at times (sometimes strongly), they never rejected me. Implications for themes in this modest book are many. Celebrated author Willa Cather said it well, "I think that most of the basic material a writer works with is acquired before the age of fifteen. That's the important period: when one's not writing" (Cather, 1921, p. 214).

I have learned much from my adult family life, as well. My wife Janet has shown me that mindfulness and metta are wonderful ways to live together, not just ideals to consider. My children and grandchildren...oh, how much I have learned. Hours of reading them stories. Years of watching them create their own life stories. Thanks to you all: Marty, September, Georgia, and Griffin; Anna, Adam, and Aven; Scott, Dylan, and Evan.

Two high school teachers had more influence than they realized. My English teacher, Don Yost, inspired me to see language as art. Always, he drove me to write *every* phrase "with clarity and precision." My "philosophy of life" class teacher, Charles Teel, Jr., believed that conventional thought is only that—a familiar starting place for thinking. Over and over he asked, "Can you think outside the box on this one?"

I was fortunate to work for two of my college professors. Both shared a love of ideas and their power. My history professor, Gary Ross, taught me that human history is shaped mostly by concepts and the clash of ideas. Generals and kings can be entertaining, and sometimes horrific.

But it is the creative thinkers who have enduring humane impact—Locke, Galileo, Jefferson, Darwin, Freud, Einstein, and Gandhi. My professor Fritz Guy taught me that carefully reasoned philosophies can also evoke mystery and fascination... even a sense of the numinous.

My graduate school experience produced three mentors. Photos of all three appear in this book. Louise Fitzgerald demanded that I test an opinion with a carefully conceived dissertation that produced sheets of data. But the tedium of analyzing the numbers disappeared in her incisive wit and prescient optimism for the new field of men's studies. Glenn Good cochaired the dissertation, and became a lifelong friend. A true *mensch*—honorable, good, and kind. Michael Mahoney's psychotherapy classes pushed the edges of my spirituality and my understanding of what psychotherapy might accomplish. Those edges continue to expand.

Over the years, I have found much benefit from conversations with my colleagues and friends, many of whom I see in the Society for the Psychological Study of Men and Masculinity: Janet Bouley, Dan Berkow, Gary Brooks, Sam Cochran, Matt Englar-Carlson, Vic Frazao, Bob Freeman, Linda Gaffney, Brad Janey, Bill Hale, Vicky Hull, Mark Hurst, Mark Kiselica, Jim Kreider, Ron Levant, Jim Mahalik, Mike Maples, Clare McGinnis, Jim O'Neil, Peter Parks, Fred Rabinowitz, Aaron Rochlen, David Shepard, Ann and Doyle Shields, Mark Stevens, and Cia Verschelden.

Two psychologists decided to hire me. Fred Newton welcomed me into the world of university academics and clinical service. Betsy Williams gave me the opportunity to work with the men I describe in this book, and thereby to collaborate with colleagues I shall forever treasure: Supavan Khamphadky-Brown, Scott Campbell, Sid Frieswyk, and Randy Krehbiel.

Two editors have made this volume much easier to write. Series Editor Mark Kiselica's deep kindness and scholarly observations were invaluable. Behavioral Sciences Editor Dana Bliss shared his indispensable knowledge and experience with skill and grace. Several anonymous reviewers stimulated my thinking at the outset of this project with challenging reflections and penetrating questions. I thank each of you. Errors that remain are mine.

Finally and importantly, I acknowledge the authoritarian men I serve. They sit with me and open the vaults of their lives. I learn from their jokes and tears, their stories and silences, their poems and playfulness. Their self-reports of misusing power and domination grieve me. Their courage and resilience inspire me. Each new day, a man invites me to step with him into the ever-flowing rivers of his life. Heraclitus had it right: We never step into the same river twice. Change is constant. Even authoritarian men change. Actually, psychotherapy changes us both.

John Martin Robertson
Lawrence, Kansas

SECTION

I

Understanding Authoritarian Men

CHAPTER

1

"Who Are These Men, Exactly?"
Four Prototypical Faces

> Do not hold the delusion that your advancement is accomplished by crushing others.
> —Cicero, Roman politician, philosopher (106–43 BCE)
>
> Be kind, for everyone you meet is fighting a hard battle.
> —Plato, Greek philosopher, disciple of Socrates (428–348 BCE)

Exactly what *is* an Authoritarian Man? Here is an answer, both succinct and disturbing.

- He desires power for its own sake.
- He assumes dominance in all his relationships.
- He tends to be exploitive and manipulative.
- He is low on empathy.
- He rejects equality with others as an ideal.

This summary of authoritarian beliefs and practices is not entirely my own. It emerges from considerable research, much of which I shall summarize later (Adorno et al., 1950; Altemeyer, 2006; Asch, 1956; Duckitt, 1989; Feldman, 2003; Geary, 2010; Mahalik, 2000; Marty & Appleby, 1996; Norris, 2005; Rokeach, 1960; Sidanius & Pratto, 1999).

Two words begin our journey: *authoritative* and *authoritarian*. They look and sound similar, but the dictionary indicates the difference. Authorita*tive* men support ideas that are "substantiated or supported by documentary evidence and accepted by most authorities in a field." Therefore, they carry the "sanction or weight of authority" ("Authoritative," 2010a). This book will summarize much research generated by authoritative persons.

Authorita*rian* men are quite different. They come in two varieties, and in both versions they generate turmoil. Again, we go to the dictionary. Authoritarian *leaders* exercise "complete or almost complete control over the will of another or the will of others" and authoritarian *followers* "favor complete obedience or subjection to authority as opposed to individual freedom" ("Authoritarian," 2010b).

This chapter presents four prototypical faces of authoritarian men. I describe two of the faces as Tough Guys—the workplace bully and the domestic abuser. The other two can be called True Believers—the zealous follower and the "Messenger from God." Four faces, but a common set of behaviors. These four are not the only versions of authoritarian men, but they are among the most common. Other faces include the dictatorial coach, the brutal lieutenant, the entitled athlete, the ruthless politician, and... you can add to this list. In this chapter, I will summarize what we know about just four expressions of authoritarian behavior and recount the costs we all pay for their actions.

The word *prototype* deserves a brief explanation. Some concepts can be defined with precision, such as "grandfather," "plutonium," and "rectangle," and there are concepts that cannot. Take a term like *religious experience*. Long ago, William James wanted to write about this concept, but he decided he could not define it precisely. After trying common descriptors such as "solemnity, tenderness, and gravity," he gave up, concluding that the concept is "always misty and it is everywhere a question of amount and degree" (James, 1901/1958, p. 47, 48).

In the 1970s, Eleanor Rosch developed this notion of misty definitions further, and the idea became known as *prototype theory* (Rosch, 1973). A prototype is a "best example" of a concept. It is less a definition and more an illustration with hazy boundaries. Consider the botanical concept of fruit. A sample definition can sound precise—"ovary of a seed plant"—but the boundaries are blurry. Apples and tangerines would be excellent prototypes. But a coconut less so. Out on the indistinct edges of the concept, we find wheat grains and pine cones; they may be fruits in a technical sense, but not in the popular use of the term (Fehr & Russell, 1984).

In a human context, we use prototypes as a handy way to describe people. We can do this because human traits tend to be enduring, stable, and characteristic of a person. This is true in all cultures. The concept of "the intelligent man," for example, may include references to abstract reasoning, information processing, memory, and so forth. A given man might reveal *some* traits of the intelligent man, but not as many as other men.

Here is the point for our purposes. The Authoritarian Man is a concept that cannot be defined with exactitude. It is a continuous variable, not categorical. When measured, the concept produces high/low scores, not either/or groups. Some men demonstrate high levels of control, power, and manipulation, while others have little or none of these traits.

In this chapter, I offer four prototypes of this concept. Each prototype has its own particular collection of behaviors and attitudes that illustrate the concept. The following four sketches are brief and therefore incomplete. To compensate, I am including dozens of research references so you can take a closer look at these faces of authoritarianism if you wish.

SETTING THE STAGE: AUTHORITARIAN BOYS

> Every morning I wake up and ask why am I still here. I hate it (bullying). I wish I could be dead, the way some people talk to me and act towards me. It's continuous. It never stops. Every day, I get up and go to school knowing what will happen and it hurts to think about it. I can tell my dad or mom what happens at school, but every time I do they say you need to learn how to get along with others. They don't know what it is like for me. I have not tried suicide but I think that if these kids do not stop I will.
>
> —Dacia (2002, Washington state high school student)

Dacia recorded this comment from a fellow student in a school hallway and shared it with the Washington State House Education Committee (Dacia, 2002). She told the legislators, "It was easy to find these stories." This is an unpleasant topic—boys who control and bully others—but it provides a practical starting place for understanding the nature of adult male authoritarian behavior. As we shall see, many authoritarian men were bullied as boys. Many of them become bullies as well, and simply continue the behavior into their adult lives.

The Behavior of Authoritarian Boys

Scholars have developed precise descriptions of bully behavior. Dan Olweus is a professor of psychology at the University of Bergen in Norway and a widely acknowledged world authority on bullying. This topic has been the focus of his work since the early 1970s. He defines bullying as "negative actions":

> Negative actions can be carried out by words (verbally), for instance by threatening, taunting, teasing, and calling names. It is a negative action when somebody hits, pushes, kicks, pinches, or restrains another—by physical contact. It is also possible to carry out negative actions without the use of words or physical contact, such as by making faces or dirty gestures, intentionally excluding someone from a group, or refusing to comply with another person's wishes. (Olweus, 1993, p. 9)

We know that boys are more likely than girls to engage in this behavior (Olweus, 1993; Von Marees & Petermann, 2010). Who are these boys? Scholars have learned much about them. Here is a snapshot of their findings—the adolescent face of authoritarianism (Nansel et al., 2001; Olweus, 1993). The italicized words illustrate all five dimensions of the summary of authoritarian beliefs and practices noted earlier. These boy bullies:

- Are more *powerful* and physically stronger than their victims
- Use their strength to intimidate, *dominate*, and subdue others
- Show *little empathy* for their victims
- Are good at *manipulating* by talking their way out of situations
- Use fights and weapon to *control* others
- Score higher than their peers in reading emotions of others and use that information in *exploitative* ways
- Are typically diagnosed with conduct disorder or oppositional and defiant disorder

How big a problem is bullying for youth? It is *big*. Much bigger than most people might imagine.

- In the United States, a study of 15,686 students in grades 6 through 10 found that 29.9% of the students reported moderate or frequent involvement in bullying activity (Nansel et al., 2001).
- In Germany, a study of 550 primary school students classified 10% of the children as bullies (Von Marees & Petermann, 2010).
- A New Zealand study of texting as a form of bullying reported that 43% of 1,530 students had been subjected to at least one incident of text bullying, and 23% had experienced it more than once (Raskauskas, 2010).

These findings are typical, not unusual. A massive study of school bullying, involving nearly a quarter of a million students aged 13 to 15 in 66 countries, found the following averages: 32.1% were bullied at school at least once in the preceding two months, and 37.4% were bullied at least once in the previous 30 days (Due & Holstein, 2008).

The Impact of Authoritarian Boys

Fading Away

They had been
my friends before.
Suddenly they
acted like
they hadn't been.
They started to threaten me.
I felt like

> I was
> fading away
> from
> everything
> and everyone.
>
> —Monu Sachdeva, age 8, London
> (2006, U.K. Department of Education and Skills, p. 21)

After they leave school, many bullies become authoritarian men. One study showed that 60% of middle school bullies had at least one criminal conviction by the time they reached the age of 24, and about a third of them had three or more convictions (Olweus, 1993). They also are more likely to engage in partner violence as adults (Gullotta & McElhaney, 1999). Clearly, much damage is done by bullies—to themselves, to their victims, to the school environment, and to the communities in which they live after school.

Victim Impact

- A study of 6,094 Danish men born in 1953 found that those who were bullied in school had a greater risk of suffering depression at midlife (ages 31–51) than those who had not been bullied (Lund et al., 2009).
- A large study of 1,118 children aged 9–11 in the Netherlands showed that bully victims had significantly greater risks for headaches, sleep problems, abdominal pain, listlessness, skin problems, and bed-wetting (Fekkes, Pijpers, Fredriks, Vogels, & Verloove-Vanhorick, 2006).
- A large study of 9,938 students in the United States showed that compared with other students, students involved in bullying had significantly higher rates of self-inflicted injuries, accidental injuries, and abuse of over-the-counter medicines. They also were at greater risk for using weapons and being absent from school (Srabstein & Piazza, 2008).
- A review of several studies of children who were bullied found lifelong and increased risks for self-esteem problems, depression, loneliness, and making friends (Ferrell-Smith, 2009).
- A sample of 1,103 adolescents aged 12–18 in Australia found a significant relationship between bully-victim problems and suicidal ideation (Rigby & Slee, 1999).

Financial and Social Impact

- Bullying *increases medical, law enforcement, judicial, and incarceration costs* because of the criminal behavior that must be managed (Rigby, 2001).

- Bullies require *costly school and community interventions* to address problems associated with their behavior, such as low grades, increased use of cigarettes and alcohol, and engagement in criminal activities (Ferrell-Smith, 2009).
- Victims of bullies are four times more likely than other students to carry weapons to school, leading to a variety of *costly preventive and protective measures* by schools (DeVoe, Kaffenberger, & Chandler, 2001).
- Bullying is associated with *truancy*, necessitating costly responses by school districts and law enforcement (Gastic, 2008).
- Schools employ staff and *purchase the rights to use bully prevention programs* to reduce the scope of the problem (e.g., Newman-Carlson, Horne, & Bartolomucci, 2000).

These findings make it plain. Bullies are authoritarian. They exploit, manipulate, and dominate. They attack weak and vulnerable children. They threaten teachers and exasperate administrators. They challenge police, judges, jailors, and legislators who try to stop them. Randy Wiler trains teachers on how to reduce bullying in schools. He says it well: "It may take a village to raise a child . . . but a child who bullies can raze the village!" (Wiler, 2006).

Of course, bullying occurs in many settings, not just schools. Studies have examined bullying problems affecting nurses, prisoners, naval personnel, users of online social network sites, and many other groups of people. And that leads to a look at our first face of authoritarian men as adults.

FACE ONE: TOUGH GUY AS WORKPLACE BULLY

In the movie *Swimming With Sharks*, Buddy is cruel and callous toward his new assistant, treating him like a shark circling his prey. And Buddy is not alone. His clones appear in thousands of offices, assembly lines, and work crews.

In the 1990s, British journalist Emily Bass popularized a phrase that now describes the behavior of these men: workplace bullying (Bassman, 1992). She used strong language: "Bullying at work is like a malignant cancer. It creeps up on you long before you—or anyone else—are able to appreciate what it is that is making you feel the ill effects" (Bassman, 1992, p. 9). In the United States during the 1990s, Dilbert thrived in the cartoon pages with his satire of the Pointy Haired Boss. This man shocked people with electric belts and demanded they work 178 hours a week. Weeks only have 168 hours, so family members should fill in the gap (Adams, 1996, 2002). And then two psychologists, Ruth and Gary Naime, started an educational campaign to bring attention to abusive bosses and formed the Workplace Bullying Institute (Naime, 2003).

In this section, I will describe three versions of the Tough Guy as a workplace bully: the tyrannical boss, the disruptive professional, and the sexual harasser.

The Tyrannical Boss

Researchers have defined workplace bullying as requiring at least two factors: a power differential, such as a boss–subordinate link, and a pattern of harmful behavior that is pervasive, persistent, and repeated (Zapf & Einarsen, 2005).

The Behavior

Specifically, what behaviors are we talking about? Fox and Stallworth (2009) have developed a Workplace Bullying Checklist that describes examples of the behavior.

- Threats of demotion, punitive action, or violence
- Excessive criticism of job performance
- Insults and put-downs
- Spreading rumors
- Exclusion from work meetings
- Attacking another's plans, or misrepresenting them
- Destroying, stealing, or sabotaging work materials

Some countries have made workplace bullying illegal. Australia is an example. An interagency governmental group has targeted the following behaviors (Stop, 2008):

- Overloading a particular person with too much work or an unreasonable share of unpleasant jobs
- Unwarranted or unjustified constant checking of an employee's work quality, output, or whereabouts
- Humiliating a person through criticism, sarcasm, and/or insults, especially in front of other staff, customers, or clients
- Denying opportunities for training, promotion, interesting jobs, or assignments
- Deliberately withholding information necessary for a person to be able to perform work to the required standard
- Dangerous practical jokes or forms of ritual humiliation, including initiations

Most workplace bullies are men (Hauge, Skogstad, & Einarsen, 2009; Naime, 2003, 2007). In a sample of 1,000 persons, Namie (2003) found that men were more likely than women to engage in workplace bullying behavior, such as the following:

- Retaliating against a person after a complaint was filed
- Yelling, screaming, and throwing tantrums to humiliate a person
- Timing mistreatment to correspond with medical or psychological vulnerability
- Withholding resources for success, then blaming the target
- Interfering with paycheck or earned benefits
- Blocking access to equipment and resources
- Boasting about owning and having proficiency with a weapon

Are workplace tyrants authoritarian? Again, compare the above descriptions with our definition: Workplace tyrants thrive on their misuse of power; they tend to manipulate and exploit those under them; they dominate their relationships with others; empathy for their victims is absent; and they are more likely to target women and members of minority groups. Clearly, this workplace face of authoritarian behavior produces widespread damage in the lives of employees who feel trapped and unable to protest their abusive treatment.

How widespread is this behavior in the workplace? A 2007 survey of 7,740 workers across the United States found that 13% had been bullied at work during the previous year, and 37% said they were bullied at some time during their lifetimes (Naime, 2007). About 40% of those who said they were bullied never complained about it. An even higher figure was found in a British study in which half of more than 1,100 respondents reported some bullying during their lives at work (Raynor, 1997).

The Impact

Dealing with authoritarian behavior in the workplace is expensive. Employers must pay legal costs to defend lawsuits. Absenteeism reduces productivity. New workers must be recruited and trained because of turnover. A more subtle cost is "presenteeism," a term that refers to workers who are present but unable to focus or perform well because of abusive treatment (Kivimäki, Elovainio, & Vahtera, 2000). Researchers put these costs in the billions of dollars (Davenport, Distler, & Pursell, 1999).

Other costs employers must address include lower levels of job satisfaction, higher resignation and quitting rates, increases in plans to leave, lower individual commitments to the job, and a company reputation of being unjust and unfair. This latter cost is fueled by the fact that victims are more likely to leave the company than the abusive bosses who harm them (Tepper, 2000).

Victims experience much harm. Mental health costs include long-term anxiety and depression, impulsiveness, posttraumatic stress disorder, and fears of personal safety and job loss. Emotional distress includes resentment, embitterment, hostility, humiliation, withdrawal, and irritability. Conflict between work and family goes up, and so does the use of sleep-inducing drugs and sedatives. Measurable physical costs to victims include high blood pressure, cardiovascular disease, impaired immune system functioning, headaches, digestive problems, psychosomatic complaints, and disrupted sleep (Bassman, 1992; Brousse et al., 2008; Glozier & Grunstein, 2009; Naime, 2003; Tepper, 2000; Vartia, 2001).

The Disruptive Professional

This is another version of the workplace bully. For many years, I have worked in a treatment setting that serves men in the professions—mostly medicine, but also dentistry, mental health, religion, corporate administration, law, and athletics. Our team of clinicians at the Professional Renewal Center® (PRC) is trained in psychology, social work, psychiatry, psychiatric nursing, and psychophysiology (Robertson & Williams, 2010). About 90% of the clients are men, and most struggle with authoritarian tendencies. Rarely do they refer themselves for help. They are sent by their employers, colleagues, or professional licensing boards because their behavior in the workplace is no longer tolerable.

The Behavior

In the United States, the term "disruptive behavior" was given much attention in 2008 when it was used by the Joint Commission on Accreditation of Healthcare Organizations. This group accredits most healthcare organizations in the United States and now requires clinics and hospitals to follow protocols on responding to professionals whose behavior seriously disrupts medical care. Here is this accrediting body's definition of disruptive professional behavior:

> Overt actions such as verbal outbursts and physical threats, as well as passive activities such as refusing to perform assigned tasks or quietly exhibiting uncooperative attitudes during routine activities.... Such behaviors include reluctance or refusal to answer questions and return phone calls or pages; condescending language or voice intonation; and impatience with questions. (Joint Commission, 2008)

How common is this behavior in the medical profession? A survey of about 1,600 physician executives revealed that more than 95% see disruptive behavior on a regular basis, though 70% added that the behavior mostly involves the very same physician repeatedly. Somewhere between 3% and 5% of all physicians have been estimated to be disruptive (Leape & Fromson, 2006), and about 30% of all complaints filed with state medical societies deal with disruptive behavior (Wilhelm & Lampsley, 2000).

A particularly challenging cluster of problems to treat is related to boundary violations between professionals and clients or patients. This is a particularly repugnant expression of authoritarianism. In effect, physicians are saying to patients: "I have the power here. I will manipulate or coerce you into sexualized situations for my own benefit." These and similar exploitive behaviors are clearly prohibited in the ethical codes of all professionals (Dombeck 2006), not just physicians:

- No sexual relationships with those who seek their professional services
- No sexual harassment toward those who work for them or seek their professional expertise
- No financial, legal, supervisory, or other personal relationships with those they serve
- The responsibility for avoiding violations lies fully with the professional, not the victim

In spite of these ethical and legal prohibitions, some professionals do engage in these behaviors. Research suggests the prevalence rate for physicians may be between 3% and 10% (Swiggart & Starr, 2002). However, it may be higher, because many victims simply do not report violations to authorities (Sealy, 2002).

In the legal profession, similar attention has been given to ways in which lawyers may misuse their roles. Again, the underlying themes reflect a concern with restraining their use of power to dominate, control, exploit, or manipulate those who seek their services. The American Bar Association's Center for Professional Responsibility has produced a set of Model Rules of Professional Conduct. Included are many examples of behaviors that authoritarian lawyers might use in their work. (American Bar Association, 2010). Attorneys may not:

- Use harassment, intimidation, or misrepresentation
- Engage in sexual relations with clients
- Act adversely toward the disabled or incompetent
- Conceal or alter documents
- Engage in dilatory practices
- Use frivolous claims that harm others

Similar codes have been produced for other professionals, including psychologists, social workers, psychiatrists, counselors, clergy, researchers, music therapists, accountants, and more (Dombeck, 2006).

The Impact

The disruptive behavior of professionals produces many costs. In the medical profession, for example, Williams and Williams (2008) reviewed studies that demonstrate the widespread nature of the consequences in the workforce: more job dissatisfaction, higher turnover rates, increased levels of stress, greater risks for litigation, and reduced morale in workgroups. Disruptive behavior may also contribute to nursing shortages and nursing morale.

The impact of boundary violations is severe and far-reaching (Sealy, 2002). The victims are not the only ones harmed. The damage spreads to the families of victims and to the families of the violators when publicity leads to humiliation and disgrace. Also harmed is the professional's place of employment (financial and reputation costs), and the profession itself. The man's colleagues and friends are affected as well. But that is only the beginning. If complaints are filed with a licensing board or the news media covers the story, then more people become involved—attorneys, malpractice representatives, and courts. Men who face these problems typically are shocked by how far the ripple effect of their behavior spreads.

Similar consequences occur for victims of authoritarian behavior in other professions. The behavior can harm both mental and physical health and is often actionable. Attorneys can bring charges against professionals who create pain and suffering, impair their clients' earning capacities, and cause the need for medical care.

The Sexual Harasser

As a self-employed female vendor, my customers were car dealers. Until it happened to me, I never even thought about sexual harassment.... It started out of the blue at my best account by the used car manager in charge of authorizing my work. One day, he lowered his voice and started talking about us getting together (this man was married). At first, I was so numb that the only part I remember word for word was what he would always follow up with, and he would say "and you won't tell, would you?" This went on here and there for a period of several months. Then one day, I was in the key room collecting keys and he came in and physically tried to grab me. I was shocked.

—Jill (2010)

The Behavior

Sexual harassers are authoritarian. A definition of sexual harassment is offered by a support group dedicated to the memory of a female postal employee who committed suicide in 1995 after suffering persistent sexual harassment in her workplace. The organization is called Sexual Harasment Support, and it defines harassment in this way (boldface in the original):

Sexual harassment is not about sex—**at the core of the problem is the abuse of power or authority**.... The dynamics of sexual harassment usually involves an aggressor who holds a position of power over the victim. Most sexual harassment is perpetrated by men against women. Harassers often dismiss or show a lack of regard for the feelings of their victims, even when assertive attempts are made to put an end to the inappropriate behavior. When confronted about their inappropriate behavior, perpetrators of sexual harassment often act as if they are being victimized, or it is the victim who is at fault. This type of manipulation can make the victim feel guilty about trying to set limits or bringing a complaint against the harasser. ("Sexual Harassment," 2010)

Notice how closely this description matches the definition of authoritarian men offered at the beginning of this chapter: a man desiring power for its own sake, low on empathy, exploitive and manipulative, and dominating.

What about the scholars? How do they define sexual harassment? The most influential U.S. researcher of sexual harassment is my major professor, Louise Fitzgerald. She has described the beliefs of these men. They "subscribe to adversarial sexual beliefs, *authoritarianism, lack of empathy* [emphasis added], traditional sex role attitudes, and can be reliably identified by their behavior in a laboratory situation (Fitzgerald, 2000, p. 252).

Fitzgerald and her colleagues have developed a questionnaire (the Sexual Experiences Questionnaire) that operationalizes this face of authoritarian men (Fitzgerald et al., 1988; Fitzgerald, Gelfand, & Drasgow, 1995). The Sexual Experiences Questionnaire has been validated and used with multiple samples involving thousands of people in the military, the workplace, and academia. In effect, it has become the de facto psychological definition of sexual harassment (Reed, 2003). The instrument includes three empirically derived factors: gender harassment ("insulting, hostile, and degrading attitudes about women"); unwanted sexual attention ("repeated, nonreciprocal requests for dates, intrusive letters and phone calls; touching, grabbing, and cornering; and gross sexual imposition or assault"), and sexual coercion ("bribes and threats, whether explicit or subtle that condition some job-related benefit on sexual cooperation" (Gelfand, Fitzgerald, & Drasgow, 1995, p. 168).

Is sexual harassment authoritarian? Notice how the language in the Sexual Experiences Questionnaire reflects the coercive use of power, exploitation, and manipulation, and treats women as "less than." Egalitarian views do not govern their behavior. One study of 1,200 women in a workplace class action suit found a direct link between authoritarianism and the distress created by sexual harassment: the stronger the dominance, the deeper the distress (Collinsworth, Fitzgerald, & Drasgow, 2009).

How widespread is this problem? During the first decade of the 21st century, the U.S. Equal Employment Opportunity Commission (EEOC) received between 12,000 and 15,000 complaints of sexual harassment each year (EEOC, 2010). Estimates of the actual rates of harassment range from 17.5% to 53% of women in the workplace being affected (Dansky & Kilpatrick, 1997; Gutek, 1985).

MEET A SCHOLAR-CONSULTANT

LOUISE F. FITZGERALD

Louise Fitzgerald is a pioneer. Her authoritative research on sexual harassment has influenced public policy, courtroom decisions, and the lives of countless women. Her work has not been easy. Powerful forces (at times, authoritarian) have challenged her research and recommendations. But she has persisted.

How did her interest in sexual harassers begin? In 1970, she was married to a young lieutenant in Southeast Asia during the Vietnam War.

> (S)he was ensconced in a large villa in Bangkok, Thailand, complete with five servants, a daily round of bridge and luncheons with other expatriate wives, and a nagging sense that something was very wrong. Her visit to the military psychiatrist confirmed that sense, providing the "click" experience that propelled so many women into feminism in the 1970s. His reaction remains vivid for her today: "Jesus Christ, lady! Don't you know there's a war going on??? I've got more important things to do than spend my time on neurotic housewives!!" Humiliated and in tears, she told herself, "There's got to be a better way to do it than that... and I'm going to do it." (Fitzgerald, 2003, pp. 913–914)

And she did. One by one, she took on new roles: returning college student, graduate student, researcher, professor, mentor, consultant, and eventually... winner of major awards. Her career was capped with the prestigious Award for Distinguished Contributions to Research in Public Policy granted by the American Psychological Association. Reasons for the acclaim are many.

Dr. Fitzgerald essentially defined the concept of sexual harassment in the public arena. She developed the theory, collected the data, and constructed a research instrument to measure the concept. The Sexual Experiences Questionnaire remains the most widely used instrument to measure sexual harassment in the workplace. It has been translated into at least seven languages, and it has been used in hundreds of studies. Results from this research have been used to understand the scope of harassment in governmental agencies, educational institutions, the military, and corporations around the world. Interventions have been designed and public policy developed. She has been retained as a legal expert on more than 200 occasions (Fitzgerald, 2003).

Her work as a consultant illustrates the breadth of her impact. She has served as a consultant to several U.S. government institutions, including the Equal Employment Opportunity Commission, the Department of Defense, the Department of Justice, and the Internal Revenue Service. Her expertise has been sought by the U.S. Eighth Circuit Court for a taskforce that examined gender fairness in the courts. Within her profession of psychology, she has served for many years on the American Psychological Association's Taskforce on Male Violence Against Women.

Influential law schools in the United States now require students to read her writings as part of their training. In the controversial congressional hearings that approved Clarence Thomas for his post as a U.S. Supreme Court justice, Dr. Fitzgerald prepared testimony for the U.S. Senate that outlined the "state of the science" of sexual harassment at that point in history.

Louise was my major professor at the University of California at Santa Barbara. At the time, very few researchers were examining the impact of masculine ideology on personal and social problems. Gender research meant studying the damaging effects of socialized sexism on women. Louise encouraged the use of a wider lens, focusing on the experiences of men as men. She believed *both* men and women learn gender roles, and therefore research must examine the socialization of both genders. Public policy must use that research in developing regulations that change the very atmosphere of the workplace. Louise's classes and writing tutored an entire generation of female and male scholars who accepted her challenge and expanded our awareness of gender-based power and control and how it can be addressed in structural ways.

Person to person, Louise lives the values she teaches. I found her to be exacting and kind, a scholar with a clinician's heart, and a visionary with a keen eye for justice.

The Impact

> I had to see a doctor for meds for severe anxiety/depression. My blood pressure was high. I lost a lot of weight. My hair was falling out. I had trouble sleeping at night, and when I did sleep I had nightmares. Anytime I had to think about going to work I would shake uncontrollably. I felt like killing myself. I don't know how I lived through all of it. No self-respecting individual should have to tolerate that type of behavior. That's when I knew I would have to complain to EEOC to exercise my rights. My case is now pending, with, of course, the harassers denying everything.
>
> —Colleen (2009)

The impact of sexual harassment is severe. Some reports indicate that the damage to women can be at the same level as the effects of rape or sexual assault (Koss & Harvey, 1987). In the list below, I have organized the symptoms into categories of damage done.

- *Physical problems* include gastrointestinal disturbances, jaw tightness and teeth grinding, nervousness, binge eating, headaches, inability to sleep, tiredness, nausea, loss of appetite, weight loss, and crying spells (Gutek & Koss, 1993; Harned & Fitzgerald, 2002; Schneider, Swan, & Fitzgerald, 1997).
- *Emotional consequences* include anger, fear, irritability, lowered self-esteem, feelings of humiliation, alienation, helplessness and vulnerability, emotional numbing, hyperarousal, and problems trusting others (Gutek & Koss, 1993; Palmieri & Fitzgerald, 2005; Reed. 2005; Schneider et al., 1997).
- *Sexual and relational problems* often follow sexual harassment, including loss of desire, flashbacks during love-making, and emotional difficulties with partners, families, and significant others (Gutek & Koss, 1993; Schneider et al., 1997).
- *Psychiatric diagnoses* include depression, anxiety, eating disorders, posttraumatic stress disorder, and substance abuse disorders (Dansky & Kilpatrick, 1997; DeSouza & Cerqueira, 2009; Goodman, Koss, & Russo, 1993; Gradus, Street, Kelly, & Stafford, 2008; Gutek & Koss, 1993; Harned, 2000).
- *Suicide*: Sexual harassment of female physicians may exacerbate their likelihood of taking their own lives (Schernhammer, 2005).

Employers pay for sexual harassment in real dollars. This relationship is significant, even when controlling for the overall impact of occupational stress (Fitzgerald, 2000; Schneider et al., 1997). Costs appear on many lines of the expense side of the ledger and run into the hundreds of millions of dollars a year in the United States (Faley, Knapp, Kustis, Dubois, 1999; Fitzgerald, Drasgow, Hulin, Gelfand, & Magley, 1997; Laband & Lentz, 1998; Schneider et al., 1997).

- Merely reporting sexual harassment increases costs for employers.
- As departmental conflict regarding harassment goes up, productivity goes down.
- As job dissatisfaction among victims goes up, productivity goes down.
- When unhappy employees leave, productivity goes down while new employees are recruited and trained.
- When victims skip work to deal with symptoms of harassment, productivity goes down.
- Health care costs go up to treat victims.
- Morale goes down if supervisors minimize or ignore the harassment.
- If retaliation for reporting occurs, then turnover rates go up.
- If cases hit the media, image suffers and sales can be affected.
- Legal costs go up if complainants seek redress in the courts.

FACE TWO: TOUGH GUY AS ABUSIVE PARTNER

"Any man who will strike his wife has no manly principles," said Judge Menger in summing up the evidence in the Henry Parsons assault case. "In my opinion the lowest thing a man can do is to beat a woman. I will therefore fine the defendant $100 and costs."

—*Lawrence Daily Journal-World* (March 25, 1911)

I thought he was my soul mate and it was devastating to realize he was a manipulator and a control freak. My feelings never mattered to him. I was always being "too sensitive" and I needed to "lighten up."

—Anonymous (2008)

Those two comments were written nearly 100 years a part, but they address versions of the same issue: abusive partners. Megan Kruse tells about a case that introduces the nature of the problem.

I hadn't realized till then that Mark was the worst type of batterer—calculating, meticulous: the kind of man who would ride his bike several miles (and secretly break into his lover's house) to move a painting six inches, then thrill at the thought of his ex standing in the kitchen and wondering if she was losing her mind. (Kruse, 2010, p. 27)

These behaviors are a painful fact of life for countless women across all cultures. The control occurs anywhere—in stores, at work, on street corners, in moving cars, at home, in classrooms, and in the military.

The Behavior

In 1992, Patricia Evans wrote a book that gained much international attention. Her book was called *The Verbally Abusive Relationship*. Before writing the book, she interviewed 40 women who reported being controlled by their partners in verbally abusive ways for an average of 16 years. "Collectively, therefore, I have drawn upon more than 640 years of experience" with this problem (Evans, 2010, p. 16).

What did Evans find in her interviews? Her women respondents are surprised by his irritation or anger, feel hurt by his refusal to discuss problems, feel frustrated by an inability to get him to understand, and even wonder if he sees himself as a separate person (Evans, 2010, p. 22). She also offers several examples of behavior designed to *control* a partner: withholding, countering, discounting, diverting, blaming, judging, undermining, threatening, forgetting, and denial. (Evans, 2010, p. 81, 82).

The U.S. Department of Justice has a division called the Office on Violence Against Women. This organization's website offers a definition of domestic violence: "A pattern of abusive behavior in any relationship that is used by one partner *to gain or maintain power and control* [emphasis added] over another intimate partner" (Office on Violence Against Women, 2009). In addiction to physical and sexual abuse, the office defines other forms of authoritarian control.

- *Emotional abuse:* Undermining an individual's sense of self-worth and/or self-esteem. This may include, but is not limited to, constant criticism, diminishing one's abilities, name-calling, or damaging one's relationship with his or her children.
- *Economic abuse*: Making or attempting to make an individual financially dependent by maintaining total control over financial resources, withholding one's access to money, or forbidding one's attendance at school or employment.
- *Psychological abuse*: Causing fear by intimidation; threatening physical harm to self, partner, children, or partner's family or friends; destruction of pets and property; and forcing isolation from family, friends, or school and/or work.

The Indian Health Service is another U.S. government department that has devoted attention to this problem. Their website describes "warning signs" of abuser's controlling and manipulative behavior (Indian Health Service, 2005).

- Shows extreme jealousy and possessiveness
- In general, has a negative attitude about women
- His mistakes and failures are someone else's fault
- Shows extreme charm
- Is easily frustrated and has little flexibility
- Is selfish and has a need to always be right
- Grew up in a violent household

Again, we meet a version of our Authoritarian Man: pursuing power over their romantic partners, controlling and dominating them, engaging in manipulation, demonstrating little empathy, and not regarding them as equals. Every psychotherapist knows stories of the pain and destruction caused by this behavior.

Sometimes, women are blamed for choosing abusive partners. Or they are ridiculed for not leaving them. However:

> No one falls in love with an abuser. I'd said it on the crisis line over and over: "If someone were to hit you in the first date, you'd call the police." But weeks or months or years later, steeped in doubts, misunderstanding, and hurt, it's hard to say clearly what has happened. We fall in love with a person believing we know who he or she is. How terrible it must be to be proven so wrong.
>
> —Megan Kruse (2010, "Constellation," *The Sun*, p. 26)

The Impact

Victims pay the highest costs, in both physical and psychological harm. Here is what researchers have found:

- *Physical consequences* include an increased risk for physical injuries, sexually transmitted diseases, unwanted pregnancies, miscarriages, and substance use disorders (Ely & Flaherty, 2009).
- *Psychological consequences* include increased learned helplessness, deficits in problem-solving skills and coping abilities, self-blame, mood problems, addictions, posttraumatic stress, and the Stockholm syndrome (Lundberg-Love & Wilkerson, 2006).

Family members and friends also experience the consequences, as they witness the coercion and feel helpless to stop it. Friends are called in to offer support or protection, and coworkers must fill in for absences when persons are injured or emotionally unable to work. Those most dramatically affected are the children trapped in situations they can neither understand nor escape. Children learn by observation. Force, coercion, and control become normal. These lessons make children more likely to perpetuate the pattern into the next generation. There is evidence that children of parents who display coercive violence are more likely to become aggressive themselves (Salzinger, Rosario, Feldman, & Ng-Mak, 2008).

Costs are high even for the man who explodes with physical aggression toward those he says he loves. His risks increase for heart disease, stroke, hypertension, diabetes, arthritis, neck and back pain, ulcers, and chronic pain (McCloskey, Kleabir, Berman, Chen, & Coccaro, 2010).

Economic costs are borne by all of us. But grasping the true breadth of the cost is exceedingly difficult, and researchers have found no reliable approach to calculating the cost has been devised. Many agencies and groups are involved, all of them with budgets. Think for a moment about the scope of interested groups: health service providers, civil justice courts, criminal justice officials, social services, community and public housing organizations, women's refuge services and safe homes, advice and advocacy groups, and employer benefits programs that administer medical, disability, psychological, and family leave programs (Crisp & Stanko, 2000). The true cost has not yet been calculated in the literature.

FACE THREE: TRUE BELIEVER AS ZEALOUS FOLLOWER

Be forewarned. The following words are harsh and bellicose.

> I want you to just let a wave of intolerance wash over you. I want you to let a wave of hatred wash over you. Yes, hate is good.... Our goal is a Christian nation. We have a Biblical duty, we are called by God, to conquer this country. We don't want equal time. We don't want pluralism.
>
> —**Randall Terry (1993, founder of Operation Rescue)**

> Those who know nothing of Islam pretend that Islam counsels against war. Those [who say this] are witless.... People cannot be made obedient except with the sword. The sword is the key to paradise, which can be opened only for holy warriors.
>
> —**Ayatollah Ruhollah Khomeini (1942, *Islam Is Not a Religion of Pacifists*, p. 242)**

Statements like these—extreme though they may be to most people—do attract followers. However, it would be a mistake to conclude that such voices represent the sentiments of most religious authoritarians. Most religious invitations to potential followers are not belligerent. In Chapter 3, I will summarize research that reviews in detail the thinking and practices of True Believers. For now, I want to preview those findings by describing another prototype.

The Behavior

Bob Altemeyer at the University of Manitoba in Canada has devoted most of his academic career to studying authoritarian behavior. He has identified three principle characteristics: Authoritarian followers are *highly conventional* in their social behavior, *highly submissive* to the "established and legitimate" authorities in their societies, and *highly aggressive* in the name of these authorities (Altemeyer, 1996, p. 6; 2006). That is the core of it. Altemeyer has developed a reliable and valid scale that measures these variables. Just three items from his 22-item scale illustrate their inner worlds (Altemeyer, 2006, pp. 17–18). Authoritarian followers tend to *agree* with statements such as the following:

- The established authorities generally turn out to be right about things, while the radicals and protestors are usually just "loud mouths" showing off their ignorance.
- Our country will be great if we honor the ways of our forefathers, do what the authorities tell us to do, and get rid of the "rotten apples" who are ruining everything.
- The "old-fashioned ways" and the "old-fashioned values" still show the best way to live.

It is helpful to look more closely at these three traits of authoritarian followers.

Conventional. A Russian researcher—Andre Kamenshikov—surveyed students at Moscow State University following Gorbachev's loosening of restrictions on conducting research in the Soviet Union. He was interested in what students thought about the Cold War. Simultaneously, Bob Altemeyer asked the same questions of American students on three campuses. They identified students in both countries who supported their own country's version of the Cold War. Who were these students? In both countries, the answer was the same: They were authoritarian followers. Politically, the views of the Russian and American students were exactly opposite each other. But, psychologically, they reached their views in the same way. Those who scored high on the authoritarianism scale in both groups more readily accepted the conventional views of their respective governments (Altemeyer & Kamenshikov, 1991).

Similar results were found among Jewish and Palestinian students. Those with most conventional views in both groups—beliefs of the religiously orthodox—were the most resistant to peaceful solutions to the intense conflicts in the Middle East (Rubinstein, 1996).

It appears that authoritarian followers strongly support values that are conventional in the groups to which they belong. And religious views are a rich source of what is conventional. These views are not only more comfortable to authoritarian followers; they are preferable to other views and must be defended, sometimes aggressively.

Submissive. People in every culture find themselves submitting to authorities and laws. Generally, some submission to community needs is essential, or else a society cannot function. Someone needs to govern. Authoritarian followers, however, take these needs to an extreme and are more likely to support a leader no matter what that person does or says. Altemeyer's own research over many years has illustrated how far authoritarian followers will go. They will tolerate illegal or unjust behavior long after others have decried it.

As we shall see in the next chapter, their loyalty to authoritarian leaders can permit them to turning of a "blind eye" to violation of laws designed to protect minority views—that is, the views of those with whom they disagree. They believe those in power know best how to deal with rebels, dissenters, radicals, and gadflies. If laws need to be bent to deal with them, so be it.

True Believers carry this submissive attitude into their religious lives. Their leaders know the truth. Always, they are correct in what they say. They must be served.

Aggressive. Does might make right? Religious pacifists say no. An example in the United States is the Reverend Adin Ballou. In the years leading up to the U.S. Civil War, he argued that pacifism was the best challenge to slavery in the States. He suggested replacing "might makes right" with the opposite view: "Evil can be overcome only with good." He encouraged religiously motivated abolitionists to "resist not injury with injury" (Ballou, 1846, pp. 32–33).

True Believers would disagree. For them, established might makes right. Bob Altemeyer and his colleagues found that authoritarian followers define "right" as views "endorsed by established authority" (Altemeyer, 2006, p. 21), and that "might" means authorities have the power to enforce the proper views. These right views typically include positive opinions of their own groups and negative views of others. His studies have shown that True Believer followers are likely to agree with stereotypical views of minorities as being inferior to themselves (e.g., more violent, primitive, dishonest, lawless, cruel, etc.) (Altemeyer, 2003, 2004).

One result is a True Believer's tendency to support aggression against weaker persons: "Women, children, and others unable to defend themselves are typical victims" (Altemeyer, 2006, p. 21). There is no guilt in True Believers for their support of aggressive actions because they possess the moral upper hand. They are defending truth and attacking error. For them, aggression in support of their moral views can be a good thing. In a series of studies, Altemeyer found that authoritarian followers support much stronger prison sentences for crimes and strongly support the use of capital punishment. They are also more willing to deliver shocks to people who made mistakes while trying to memorize nonsense syllables (Altemeyer, 2006).

Again, notice how these beliefs and behaviors illustrate our summary of the beliefs and practices of authoritarian men. True Believers support the use of power to enforce conformity to their truths, show little empathy for those who disagree, and reject egalitarianism as an ideal.

FACE FOUR: TRUE BELIEVER AS MESSENGER FROM GOD

We signed over all our property. We wrote and signed false, self-incriminating statements.... We were so frightened of him and his power that we would have sworn to anything he asked.... It is impossible to explain the effect.... We do know that it took months after we left to be able to think and act as normal, reasonable people.

—Jeannie Mills (1979, *Six Years With God*)

This face is an extreme version of the True Believer—the man who claims the weighty title of Messenger from God. I capitalize the phrase to reinforce its boldness. Responses to this claim have varied, of course. Only a few Messengers have been so widely accepted that their words have transcended cultural origins and become honored by people across millennia. The words of Moses, Buddha, Jesus, and Muhammad have been revered by billions of people and sparked the beginning of new and enduring spiritual communities. Today, their teachings are highly valued by more than half (54%) of the world's current population (Adherents, 2011).

It is useful to again recall the difference between authoritative and authoritarian. Many who belong to these centuries-old religious groups view the teachings of their Messengers from God as authoritative. The conceptual, ethical, social, and ritual dimensions are experienced as helpful, reliable, and useful. The appeal is in the content of those messages, with leaders appearing in succession over the centuries.

Other groups, however, are led by authoritarian—not authoritative—men. These modern groups are often much smaller in membership, and members are drawn to the charisma of the Messengers themselves. In the last 100 years, many of these groups have come and gone. When the charismatic leader dies, membership dwindles. But while active, some Messengers take their roles very seriously and expect their followers to subject themselves to their rule. These leaders, most often men, become authoritarian in their treatment of members. It is the behavior of these men that is relevant to the purpose of this book because their (former) adherents do appear in psychotherapy rooms.

The Behavior

Scholarly observers suggest authoritarian leaders have two characteristics in common. One is totalism: Members are obligated to follow the teachings of the group (the total truth) and to follow unerringly all the rules of the group (total social control) (Lifton, 1961/1989). The other trait is separatism: Members are expected to withdraw from others in the larger society. Here is one scholar's description of the groups spawned by these authoritarian leaders:

> ...A sharply bounded social group or a diffusely bounded social movement held together through shared commitment to a charismatic leader. It upholds a transcendent ideology... and requires a high level of personal commitment from its members in words and deeds. (Lalich, 2004, p. 5)

The thought processes inside these authoritarian groups have fascinated many observers. One of the most thorough reviews of authoritarian cognitive patterns was published by psychiatrist Robert Jay Lifton, who taught at Harvard, Yale, and the City University of New York. In a work that has become a widely read and influential classic, he identified what he called the Eight Criteria for Thought Reform (Lifton, 1961/1987). Originally developed as a description of political authoritarianism, his theory has been adapted and applied to religious groups as well (e.g., Hassan, 1988). Here are the eight descriptors.

Milieu control. Authoritarian religious leaders take total control of the information available to members. That includes information coming from sources outside the group (news reports, communication from families, etc.), as well as information exchanged among members themselves in everyday conversation. Even silent and internal thoughts must meet the requirements of the group. This process naturally results in isolation in the larger society. Members know less and less about the world around them.

Mystical manipulation. Thoughts, emotions, and actions are manipulated in many ways. History, scripture, and personal experiences are interpreted in ways that reinforce the central messages of the leader. The Messenger from God brings divine mandates to members. Their actions might fail to meet community standards of decency, equality, and human rights, but that is not problematic. The expectation is that members submit everything to the divine mandates that govern their lives.

Demand for purity. Messengers of God typically view the world in binary terms, with every idea labeled right or wrong. The Messenger, of course, knows which is which. This means that all "impure" thoughts, objects, friendships, and habits must be identified and eliminated. The immediate psychological consequence of this forced dichotomy is guilt for violating the norms and shame for being a flawed person. People don't just make mistakes; they *sin*. They don't simply err; they *shame* themselves and the group.

Confession. Although the demand for perfect purity can never be met, guilt can be expiated by confessions. These confessions typically are intense, public, and often humiliating. The purpose of these confessions is not only to provide inner peace and forgiveness. It also is to exploit a person's vulnerabilities for the purpose of increasing loyalty. Confessions of even private thoughts are normative and mandatory. The distinction between private and public becomes blurred.

Sacred science. Because the Messenger's words come from God, they are sacred, logical, and even scientific. They are Truth. How can they be anything else? The emotional impact of thinking this way is the promise of feeling secure and eternally safe. This combination creates a strong hold on members. Truth not only *feels* right; it also is *rational*.

Loading the language. Messengers often reduce complex ideas to brief phrases and terms. These clichés function like internal code words for members. Outsiders may not understand the language, but believers see them only as Truth. The specialized lingo has a strong appeal. A person can be "in the know" of divine secrets and be able to express insights that are both correct and necessary. Again, the psychological consequences can be pronounced.

Doctrine over person. The Messenger's teachings come to be valued as more important than any person the adherent knows. That is because individual identities are submerged into the group mold. A person's own skills and inclinations disappear into the larger Truth. The assumption is clear: The dogma must be regarded as superior to any human trait or experience. Every aspect of human life is understood in light of the overarching doctrinal structure. Any other approach is deviant, impure, sinful, and the like.

Dispensing of existence. The final characteristic flows inevitably from the preceding ideas. The Messengers have final say on matters of personal existence. Put more bluntly, they point the way to ultimate life or eternal death. In the words of Jean Paul Sartre (1943/1992), the choice is between "being and nothingness." The leader knows the true path to bliss and holds the guarantee of entrance into an even better life at death. The Messenger knows the entrance criteria and decides who meets them. The rest of the world is outside the fold, unsaved, unenlightened, and doomed. If they do not accept the Messenger, then believers are obligated to reject them.

Finally, Lifton offers two observations about his eight-part schema. First, the descriptors of totalism are a continuum, not a categorical variable. No religious group is completely totalist, and many groups show only modest levels of totalism. And second, Lifton, as a psychiatrist, offers an analysis of the sources of totalism's appeal that we shall revisit later in this book:

> The degree of individual totalism involved depends greatly upon factors in one's personal history: early lack of trust, extreme environmental chaos, total domination by a parent or parent-representative, intolerable burdens of guilt, and severe crises of identity. Thus, an early sense of confusion and dislocation, or an early experience of unusually intense family milieu control, can produce a later complete intolerance for confusion and dislocation, and a longing for the reinstatement of milieu control. (Lifton, 1961/1989, pp. 435, 436)

We shall visit this concept in more detail in Part II of this book. But for now, notice our definition of the Authoritarian Man in Lifton's summary of totalism: power, control, manipulation, exploitation, a lack of empathy, and rejection of all outside groups as inferior. These ideas in a religious context create an environment in which authoritarianism can flourish.

The Impact

> Men never do evil so completely and cheerfully as when they do it from religious conviction.
>
> —Blaise Pascal (1669/1958, *Pensées* # 894, p. 265)

The most evocative way to consider the impact of radical authoritarian religious leaders is to listen to those who know about it first hand.

You likely remember the sensational headlines about Jim Jones, who led more than 900 people to their murder/suicides in Jonestown, British Guyana, in 1978. Jeannie Mills, who defected from Jones's group in 1975, wrote a book about her experiences and later was murdered in her home with her husband and daughter. After the Jonestown tragedy, she warned:

> When you meet the friendliest people you have ever known, who introduce you to the most loving group of people you've ever encountered, and you find the leader to be the most inspired, caring, compassionate and understanding person you've ever met, and then you learn the cause of the group is something you never dared hope could be accomplished, and all of this sounds too good to be true—it probably is too good to be true! Don't give up your education, your hopes and ambitions to follow a rainbow. (Mills, 1979)

Those who leave such groups report problems with alienation, confusion about gender roles, limited friendships, sexual problems, a lack of education or job experience, and health concerns (Boeri, 2002). Others report depression, loneliness, trouble with dissociation, obsessiveness, and other patterns similar to those who divorce (Wright, 1991). The costs come alive in the words of those who have experienced them.

> When your own thoughts are forbidden, when your questions are not allowed and our doubts are punished, when contacts with friendships outside of the organization are censored, we are being abused for the ends never justify the means.... When we consider staying in a group because we cannot bear the loss, disappointment and sorrow our leaving will cause for ourselves and those we have come to love, we are in a cult.... If there is any lesson to be learned it is that an ideal can never be brought about by fear, abuse, and the threat of retribution. When family and friends are used as a weapon in order to force us to stay in an organization, something has gone terribly wrong. (Layton, 1998, p. 299)

SUMMARY: THE AUTHORITARIAN MAN

This topic is heavy, even depressing. But there is good news in the second half of this book. Authoritarian men can change. They really can. But for now, here is a summative answer to the question that opened this chapter. Who are these authoritarian men, exactly?

High on Power. Authoritarian power is a power-over. It is not just a capacity to exercise power; it is the actual exercise *of* the power. Max Weber, the renowned German sociologist and economist, put it well: power is "the probability that one actor within a social relationship will be in a position to carry out his own will despite resistance..." (Weber, 1978, p. 53).

Authoritarian men rely on power to get their way. Whatever power they have, they use—personal strength, supervisory power, romantic appeal, political influence, and religious authority. As boys on the playground, they find weaker children to bully. In the workplace, they look for inept subordinates to mistreat or women to sexually harass. When they look for romantic partners, they find women who are vulnerable and uncertain of their own power. And in religious settings, they invoke God or Truth to force compliance with their views or wishes. They rely on their power to push, prod, coerce, and demand.

Several concepts explain this expectation of submission to power:

- Proper behavior is clearly defined: the conventional, the long-standing, the familiar.
- These traditional behaviors are moral standards that must be enforced.
- Social conformity is valued, in and of itself.
- Obedience to authority (male or religious) is a duty.
- Autonomy is minimized or disregarded.
- People who emphasize freedom of choice and behave permissively must be penalized.
- Disagreement is viewed as defiance or rebellion.
- Upholding conventional law is a higher value than extending human rights to those who differ.

Those who exercise this sort of power are authoritarian leaders. Those who readily and unquestioningly accept this use of power are authoritarian followers.

High on Dominance. Dominance is about the control of others. Strong boys dominate weak boys, men dominate women, locals dominate foreigners, and the righteous dominate sinners, unbelievers, or apostates.

In relationships, authoritarian men justify their dominance in various ways. They may appeal to their personality strengths ("I am a good person; you owe me"), they can rely on religious grounds ("God made me responsible for your welfare"), or they may cite evolutionary theory ("Men are naturally stronger").

Authoritarians are also more likely to support the domination of certain social groups by other groups. As we shall see, they look to control every relationship and interaction they have. They feel compelled to be regarded as the most important, the most influential, the man in charge. As boys, they seek to control children who are small, anxious, or different. As men, they seek to control their female partners, their children, their employees, their followers, or inferior social groups.

High on Exploitation and Manipulation. Alan Wertheimer reviewed 16 definitions of exploitation by philosophers and drew this conclusion: "All these accounts are compatible with the view that 'A wrongfully exploits B when A takes unfair advantage of B'" (Wertheimer, 2008). Yes, indeed. All the prototypes of authoritarian behavior in this chapter take unfair advantage of others—they are exploitative. How is this accomplished? Often, by being manipulative. The core of manipulative behavior is quite simple. It consists of if–then transactions. If you do what I want, then I will treat you well. If you don't do what I want, then I will make your life difficult.

To this end, authoritarian men continue to pursue what they want from others even when the first response is "No." They select from a long menu of strategies to make this happen. They mislead. They cajole. They argue. They threaten. They induce guilt. They use sympathy and "woe is me" comments to induce others to feel sorry for them and meet their needs. They may engage in any of these behaviors while emphasizing the "free choice" they are giving others to make up their own minds. These efforts can be smooth, glib, and persuasive. But their intent remains clear: Their own opinions and needs are realities that others must acknowledge. Others may complain that they seem to get away with not meeting their responsibilities, and often they do. Authoritarian men who exploit and manipulate seem to get their way, over and over and over.

Low on Empathy. Psychologists have defined empathy in several ways and measured it with the development of various instruments. One widely used instrument includes four components (Davis, 1996, pp. 55–57):

- Perspective taking: the tendency to spontaneously adopt the psychological view of others in everyday life"
- Empathic concern: the tendency to experience feelings of sympathy or compassion for unfortunate others");
- Personal distress: the tendency to experience distress or discomfort in response to extreme distress in others"; and
- Fantasy: the tendency to imaginatively transpose oneself into fictional situations").

These experiences are foreign to authoritarian men. They are not in the habit of paying much attention to the thoughts and feelings of others. Nor are they too interested in the negative impact their behavior may be having on others. Unless it threatens their intentions, they do not particularly care how they are perceived. One study has shown this explicitly: The higher the authoritarian scores, the lower the empathy scores (McFarland, 2010). In Part II of this book, we'll look at the question of whether or not empathy training works (the news is encouraging). The prototypical faces portrayed in this chapter are keenly interested in their own needs and desires. When they do pay attention to the words and feelings of others, it is typically for the purpose of using that information to further their own ends.

Low on Egalitarianism. Since the American and French Revolutions, Western democracies have espoused equality of treatment as an ideal. This ideal generally means that all persons must be given equal dignity, worth, and respect. It therefore becomes a political, if not moral, duty to treat others as equals in terms of rights and duties. All persons must be given the same opportunities to achieve desired jobs and positions in society.

Nice as an ideal, but authoritarian men tend to disagree with this concept. In true Orwellian fashion, they regard themselves as more equal than others. The inequality can be based on differences in social status, gender, age, ethnicity, sexual orientation, religious affiliation, and other identifying descriptors. This authoritarian characteristic is an idea, a way of thinking about self in relation to others. Following are examples of nonegalitarian thinking abound.

- Men are inherently more skilled than women.
- Men are divinely ordained to take charge of their families.
- Some ethnic groups are demonstrably superior to others.
- Our country is entrusted with moral responsibilities to regulate your behavior.
- Our theocracy is superior to your democracy.
- Your group is inherently undeserving because of your laziness, disbelief, or sinfulness.

Put in personal terms, authoritarian men believe their own needs and views are preeminent. They expect privilege and entitlement. Others are naturally destined to serve them, or even cower to them. They believe their own characteristics identify them as superior—sex, ethnicity, nationality, religion. Equality of treatment is not a value that authoritarian men live by.

Clearly, this five-part summary does *not* include many pro-social traits. It is worth noting some of the traits authoritarians do not have. They do not collaborate well with others. They do not easily acknowledge their behavior as harmful. Nor do they subscribe to such concepts as being mutually respectful, finding common ground, compromising with others, or being emotionally vulnerable.

A man in one of my psychotherapy groups (he was an internationally prominent medical researcher) came to treatment because his workplace was tired of his tyrannical domination of other employees. After dominating a 90-minute group session with comments that were frequent, lengthy, and directive, he said with a big and satisfied grin, "This has been the Me Show!" His views of his own fame and occupational status permitted him to dominate conversations with his fellow professionals. They were merely private practitioners.

LOOKING AHEAD

Given this definition of authoritarian men, two questions follow.

How did they get this way? The rest of Part I reviews four perspectives on this question. Some view authoritarianism as a personality variable (Chapter 2). Others emphasize the influence of religious ideology (Chapter 3), the realities of biological adaptation (Chapter 4), and the power of social and cultural influences (Chapter 5). All these perspectives add substance to our understanding.

Can authoritarian men be helped? The answer is yes, and that's the real reason for this book: to offer therapeutic ideas and tools based on both research and experience. To make this clinical information as useful as I can, I introduce two authoritarian men in Chapter 6. Their cases are followed in the chapters that follow. Chapter 7 focuses on the critical role of the therapeutic relationship in working with these men. Chapter 8 outlines qualitative methods for assessing their situations. Chapter 9 describes treatment strategies that have been shown to be effective. And finally, Chapter 10 addresses outcome issues: Do authoritarian men really change, and does it endure?

CHAPTER
2
"He Always Has Been That Way"
Authoritarian as Personality Type

> Once we understand...how the war experience may in some cases have strengthened personality traits predisposed to group hatred, the educational remedies may follow logically. Similarly, to expose the psychological tricks in the arsenal of the agitator may help to immunize his prospective victims against them.
>
> —Theodor W. Adorno and colleagues (1950, *The Authoritarian Personality*, p. vii)

DEFINING THE AUTHORITARIAN PERSONALITY

How are we alike, you and I? How are we different? These questions have been asked for millennia and still fascinate us. We humans sort ourselves in many ways: talents, interests, drives, values, self-concepts, and, especially, personalities. Considerable energy has gone into developing theories about our personality differences. Centuries ago, for example, Greeks and Romans discussed the model proposed by Galen, a prominent physician who provided health care to three Roman emperors. Galen named four personality types: choleric (enthusiastic and easily angered), sanguine (cheerful and pleasant), melancholic (somber and sad), and phlegmatic (cool and calm).

Today, we still ask each other about our personality traits. Newer theories have produced lengthy questionnaires for psychotherapists to use in understanding a man's personality. Currently, the most prominent is the Five Factor Model, which holds that each person has varying amounts of five basic personality dimensions: neurotic (stressed and unsettled versus secure and confident); extraverted (social and energetic versus reserved and solitary); open (imaginative and curious versus closed and cautious); agreeable (pleasant and cooperative versus disagreeable and competitive); and conscientious (dutiful and organized versus easy-going and hasty) (Costa & McCrae, 1992).

A "minimalist" definition of personality that captures the essence of most current theories is offered by Amy Heim and Drew Westen (2009): "Personality refers to enduring patterns of cognition, emotion, motivation, and behavior that are activated in particular circumstances" (p. 13). Together, these factors define a person's characteristic and enduring patterns of response to the world. Much research demonstrates that personality traits are rooted in both biological and socially learned factors (e.g., Bouchard & McGue, 2003).

Two notions have particular relevance for our inquiry. One is the idea that personality traits are dimensional; that is, a person can have more or less amounts of many traits, such as conscientiousness, self-confidence, and protectiveness (cf., Oldham & Morris, 1990). The most prominent example of this approach is the Five Factor Model noted above. The other idea is that personality differences are best understood as categorical. Each personality type is hypothesized, named, defined, and tested. In the end, a man can be diagnosed as fitting a category, such as obsessive, narcissistic, histrionic, or defensive. This approach is best illustrated in the diagnostic manuals used to assess personality difficulties, especially the *Diagnostic and Statistical Manual* series published by the American Psychiatric Association. In the last chapter, I suggested that authoritarian traits are best understood as dimensional—any given man has more or less of them. However, in the diagnostic world of some Western countries, it has become necessary to identify categories (disorders) to obtain payment for treatment. A person is either obsessive, or he is not.

What about authoritarian behavior? Is it a personality variable? This possibility is worth reviewing because it adds to our understanding of authoritarian male behavior.

"The Authoritarian Personality" (Theodor Adorno)

In May of 1944, exactly one year before the war in Europe ended, Theodor Adorno was invited to a 2-day conference sponsored by the American Jewish Committee in New York City. A group of prominent scholars met to establish an extensive research program on the problem of "religious and racial prejudice" (Adorno, Frenkel-Brunswik, Levinson, & Sanford, 1950, p. v). The project was jointly administered by the Berkeley Public Opinion Study (University of California at Berkeley) and the Institute of Social Research (Columbia University).

MEET A SCHOLAR

THEODOR W. ADORNO

For Theodor Adorno, authoritarianism was personal. He was fired from his job as a professor of sociology in Germany in 1933 for two reasons: His father was Jewish, and his academic interests threatened the Nazis. He worked at the Institute for Social Research, where the stated purpose was to investigate "knowledge and discovery of social life in its whole entirety" from a socially liberal perspective (Society for Social Research, 1925, p. 12).

Adorno fled Germany for his life. He escaped to England in 1934, and then to New York City, where the institute continued functioning during World War II (Martin, 1984). All along, Adorno was keenly interested in authoritarian oppression. Following the horrific events of World War II, he combined his personal experiences and academic expertise in a project that received much attention. He was principal investigator for the Authoritarian Personality, the now-classic initial study of the psychology of authoritarianism. The topic affected him profoundly: "After Auschwitz no further poems are possible, except on the foundation of Auschwitz itself" (Adorno, 1970/1997, p. 330).

Adorno was an only child, born to a wine merchant and an opera singer. He demonstrated an exceptional musical talent—both as an accomplished pianist and as an avant-garde composer. As a young man in his 20s, he studied with some of the major composers of the 20th century, including Anton Weber and Arnold

Schoenberg. He also took lessons from the piano teacher who taught Paul Hindemith. Adorno's own 12-tome work, *Studies for String Quartet*, is still commercially available. His musical interests led to a lifelong and professional interest in the interaction of music and culture (e.g., Adorno, 1938/1982, 2002).

During his stay in New York during World War II, he became musical director of the Radio Project at Princeton University. The purpose of this effort was to examine the impact of mass media on society. Adorno believed that the "culture industry" in Western society had invented technologies that make it easy for authoritarian leaders to control individual consciousness. Radio, for example, forces many people to listen to exactly the same programming, and thereby influences the thinking of an entire culture.

Adorno also was a philosopher who tried to make sense of human suffering. As a graduate student, he was encouraged by Paul Tillich, who supervised Theodor's doctoral thesis on *Kierkegaard: Construction of the Aesthetic*. After World War II, he became a key figure in the development of Critical Theory. He argued that authoritarian leaders create oppression in several ways. They control not only the politics and economics of a society but also the popular culture.

This philosophical view led him to praise the music of serious composers as "true art," but also to condemn popular music as passive and apathetic. He criticized, for example, the war protest music of Joan Baez during the Vietnam War for "taking the horrendous and making it somehow consumable" (Adorno, 2011). The evocative impact of her music was highly problematic for him, as it served mostly to sustain authoritarian power: "Emotional music has become the image of the mother who says, 'Come and weep, my child.' It is catharsis for the masses, but catharsis which keeps them all the more firmly in line...." (Adorno, 1991, pp. 313–314). Most of his philosophical writing was produced while he was in the United States, holding academic posts not only at Princeton University but also at Columbia University and the University of California at Berkeley.

Theodor Adorno was a true "renaissance man" of the 20th century. His brilliance appeared in several roles: sociologist, pianist and composer, music critic, philosopher, and social essayist. He died at the age of 65 after suffering a heart attack while on vacation in Switzerland. He had ignored warnings by his doctor and climbed a nearly 10,000-foot mountain. Today, the prestigious Theodor W. Adorno Award is given in Germany to outstanding achievement in philosophy, theater, music, and film. The award is announced every 3 years on his birthday, September 11.

As the scope of the Holocaust became clear, the questions before this scholarly group were urgent. What had just happened in Europe? How could an entire society become so authoritarian that millions could be killed on ethnic and religious grounds? How could "the irrational remnants of ancient racial and religious hatreds" appear in a society that valued "law, order, and reason"? More to the point for this group of researchers: Are there personality traits that drive people to join movements that foster "attitudes and acts of destruction" (Adorno et al., 1950, p. v)?

In 1950, just 5 years after World War II, this research group offered an extended answer to these questions in a five-volume publication of nearly 1,000 pages. Adorno was the lead author of the report called *The Authoritarian Personality* (Adorno et al., 1950). Their findings are worth noting, as they comprise the first extended look at authoritarianism in modern scholarship.

The group's research moved through several steps. First, they reviewed previous empirical and theoretical literature on anti-Semitism and fascism. Then they identified 2,000 people living in California and Oregon for their study. These participants came from all walks of life: college students, teachers, social workers, nurses, merchant marine officers, men in service clubs, war veterans, prison inmates, and clinical patients in treatment.

The research team gathered data from this group in many ways—assigned essays, structured interviews, scales that measured attitudes and beliefs, and psychological findings from the Thematic Apperception Test. Ultimately, this mountain of information led to the development of a scale that conveyed their definition of authoritarianism. Nine traits of "the authoritarian personality" were described (Adorno et al., 1950, p. 228):

- *Conventionalism*: rigid adherence to conventional middle-class values
- *Authoritarian submission*: submissive, uncritical attitude toward idealized moral authorities in the ingroup
- *Authoritarian aggression*: tendency to be on the lookout for and to condemn, reject, and punish people who violate conventional values
- *Anti-intraception*: opposition to the subjective, the imaginative, the tender-minded
- *Superstition and stereotypy*: the belief in mystical determinants of the individual's fate; the disposition to think in rigid categories
- *Power and toughness*: preoccupation with the dominance-submission, strong-weak, leader-follower dimension; identification with the power figures, exaggerated assertion of strength and toughness
- *Destructiveness and cynicism*: generalized hostility, vilification of the human

- *Projectivity*: the disposition to believe that wild and dangerous things go on in the world; the projection outwards of unconscious emotional impulses
- *Sex:* exaggerated concern with sexual "goings-on"

Notice traits we identified in Chapter 1 as descriptive of the Authoritarian Man: "identification with ... power," "dominance-submission," and a "rejection" of "people who violate conventional values." Note also the distinction between some authoritarians who take a "restricted, conventional" approach toward others (authoritarian followers) and others who take "a ruthless manipulative approach" (authoritarian leaders) (Adorno et al., 1950, p. 475).

The philosophical underpinning of this portrait of the authoritarian personality was psychodynamic theory, highly influential in the late 1940s. Prejudiced men were said to project onto others the traits they cannot accept as their own. In a later work, Adorno put it this way: "In the end the tough guys are the truly effeminate ones, who need the weaklings as their victims in order not to admit that they are like them" (Adorno, 1951/1974, p. 46). The Berkeley report defined several such traits: "fear, weakness, passivity, sex impulses, and aggressive feelings against authoritative figures, especially the parents." In this way, "it is not oneself but others that are seen as hostile and threatening." Rather than acknowledge these disagreeable traits in themselves, they focus on incorporating the opposite: a "drive for power, strength, success, and self-determination." With regard to others, they develop a "sharp ingroup–outgroup dichotomy" and then place their unwanted impulses on the "weak outgroups from whom no retaliation need be feared" (Adorno et al., 1950, p. 474, 480). We shall return to this theory in the next chapter.

"The Authoritarians" (Bob Altemeyer)

Not surprisingly, the Berkeley project sparked additional research on authoritarianism. One scholar in particular was inspired to make this topic the focus of his entire academic career. His name is Bob Altemeyer from the University of Manitoba in Canada. "I never would have found anything about authoritarianism, or even gotten interested in the area, if it had not been for the Berkeley researchers" (Altemeyer, 1996, p. 45). Here is how it happened for Bob:

> When I took the exams for getting a PhD at Carnegie-Mellon University in Pittsburgh in 1965, I failed a question about a famous early effort to understand the authoritarian personality. I had to write a paper to prove I could learn at least something about this research.... Thus, I didn't start studying authoritarianism because I am a left winger (I think I'm a moderate on most issues).... I got into it because it presented a long series of puzzles to be solved, and I love a good mystery. (Altemeyer, 2006, p. 1)

Thirty years later, Altemeyer's conclusions supported some of the findings of the Adorno group, but not all. In brief, he found support for the first three of the nine traits outlined in 1950: conventionalism, submission, and aggression. However, Altemeyer's work does more than that; it advances the theory of an authoritarian personality in other ways. He has developed a detailed measurement that is valid, reliable, and widely used. He emphasizes more the social learning tradition than the psychoanalytic tradition used by the Berkeley group. And the targets of authoritarian attacks are defined much more broadly—not just those who violate conventional behavior, but virtually anyone who belongs to a different group. In the previous chapter, we mentioned some of the beliefs Altemeyer has found common in authoritarians. The complete list is found in his measurement instrument that contains 22 items (Altemeyer, 2006, pp. 11–12). Here are three more items:

- This country would work a lot better if certain groups of troublemakers would just shut up and accept their group's traditional place in society.
- The only way our country can get through the crisis ahead is to get back to our traditional values, put some tough leaders in power, and silence the troublemakers spreading bad ideas.
- Our country will be destroyed someday if we do not smash the perversions eating away at our moral fiber and traditional beliefs.

Notice the three ideas behind those three statements. An authoritarian man (1) is *conventional* in his social and political views, (2) believes that people must be *submissive* to established authorities, and (3) is likely to be *aggressive* in his support of those views. Altemeyer called this perspective "*right* wing authoritarianism," not because it refers to conservative political views, but because it highlights the word's origin; "right" is that which is "lawful, proper, and correct, doing what the authorities said" (Altemeyer, 2006, p. 15). Altemeyer conducted dozens of studies that demonstrated these three findings.

Conventionalism. In the previous chapter, I summarized the study of students in Russia and the United States, following Gorbachev's introduction of Glasnost in the 1980s. Altemeyer and his Russian coinvestigator found that students scoring high on authoritarianism in *both* countries took their own government's views of the Cold War more than those who scored lower on authoritarianism (Altemeyer & Kamenshikov, 1991). Altemeyer summarizes this in his characteristically stark language: "... it means the most cock-sure belligerents in the populations on each side of the Cold War, the ones who blamed each other the most, were in fact the same people, psychologically" (Altemeyer, 2006, p. 28). Translation: they were conventional. They were authoritarian followers.

Submission. In 1974 during the Watergate era in the United States, college students on five U.S. university campuses were given a question about an imaginary situation. Researchers framed a press report that the Federal Bureau of Investigation (FBI) had set up illegal wiretaps of 60 people who were "sympathetic toward radical political organizations." Contrary to law, the FBI was said to have avoided asking for court approval (as the law requires) because "they believed the case was too weak and the courts would deny" the wiretaps. The scenario had the FBI denying entirely that the wiretaps even existed (Altemeyer, 2006, p. 17).

Students were asked how serious they thought this situation was. Altemeyer found that students who scored high on a measure of authoritarianism were not much bothered by the illegal wiretaps. Nor were they troubled by the FBI lying about the wiretaps. Students were willing to submit to the idea that the FBI knows best, and if rules needed to be bent in harnessing 60 radicals, so be it. It was for a good cause.

Altemeyer ran similar experiments for other illegal behavior conducted by authorities, such as police burglaries to retrieve confidential information, drug raids without appropriate search warrants, burning down buildings of radical organizations, unauthorized opening of private mail, and more. Always, those scoring high on authoritarian attitudes were quite willing to support such actions. Why? Because they are submissive—they believe those in charge know best and must be trusted.

Aggression. Highly authoritarian people are more punitive than most when it comes to dealing with people who belong to groups they do not like. They may be willing to go easy on authorities who break the law, but they are quite willing to go overboard on ordinary folks. Misbehavior must be dealt with harshly.

In a series of studies between 1982 and 1990, Altemeyer studied attitudes of authoritarians toward several unpopular groups. He wanted to know how aggressive authoritarians might be in dealing these minorities. Each study examined a different group—a religious cult, homosexuals, abortionists, Ku Klux Klan, radical journalists, even other authoritarians. But the question always was the same. How would you respond if the government passed a law outlawing this group? Participants could choose from a set of six options (Altemeyer, 1996, p. 25):

1. I would tell my friends and neighbors it was a good law.
2. I would tell the police about any radicals I knew.
3. If asked by the police, I would help hunt down and arrest members of radical groups.
4. I would participate in attacks on radical group's meeting places if organized by the proper authorities.
5. I would support the use of physical force to make radical group members reveal the identity of other radicals.
6. I would support the execution of radical group leaders if the government insisted it was necessary to protect the country.

How do you suppose students who scored high as authoritarian followers responded to these six aggressive actions? They did not find them abhorrent. Instead, they rated these actions as only slightly or moderately untrue of them. The conclusion was clear: Authoritarian followers are prone to support aggressive behavior toward groups different from their own—liberal or conservative does not matter.

Altemeyer's work has spawned much research. At the time of this writing, the actual name of his measurement instrument (the Right-Wing Authoritarianism Scale) has been in the title of more than 100 articles and books. Sample populations have been studied in Italy, Poland, Taiwan, Canada, Switzerland, Australia, Sweden, and other countries. The instrument is not only reliable and valid but also demonstrates the connection between these three authoritarian personality traits and the specific components of our Authoritarian Man (acceptance of power, control, and exploitation; absence of empathy and equality).

Altemeyer also studied authoritarian dominators. He reported findings from more than 6,500 college students and their parents. Here is his conclusion:

> (D)ominating authoritarians are among the most prejudiced persons in society. Furthermore, they seem to combine the worst elements of each kind of personality, being power-hungry, unsupportive of equality, manipulative, and amoral, as social dominators are in general, while also being religiously ethnocentric and dogmatic, as right-wing authoritarians tend to be. (Altemeyer, 2004, p. 421)

And that comment brings us to the work of Sidanius and Pratto.

"Social Dominators" (Jim Sidanius and Felicia Pratto)

> However sugarcoated and ambiguous, every form of authoritarianism must start with a belief in some group's greater right to power, whether that right is justified by sex, race, class, religion, or all four. However far it may expand, the progression inevitably rests on unequal power and airtight roles within the family.
>
> —Gloria Steinem (1983, *Outrageous Acts and Everyday Rebellions*, p. 347)

In the preceding section, we looked at authoritarian followers. Now we consider authoritarian leaders, or dominators as they are often called. What do we know about authoritarians who minimize, disparage, or persecute entire groups of people?

Two U.S. researchers devoted 25 years to this topic. Jim Sidanius worked at the University of California at Los Angeles (UCLA), and Felicia Pratto at the University of Connecticut. They sought to capture something different from Altemeyer's notion of authoritarian followers. They were not interested in interpersonal dominance. Instead, they were curious about the larger picture—how does authoritarian behavior become societal so that a person justifies the domination of entire groups of people?

They carefully developed an answer to this question. Their theory is called Social Dominance Orientation (SDO) (Sidanius & Pratto, 1999). They concluded that this orientation is "a personality variable" that could predict various social and political attitudes consistent with our definition of authoritarianism (Pratto, Sidanius, Stallworth, & Malle, 1994).

Because the theory has been studied widely by scholars in many cultures, it is worth considering for a few moments. They begin with the observation that virtually all societies develop group-based hierarchies, with one group dominant over others. The dominant group demands a disproportionately large share of the society's resources. Some group divisions are based on age (old versus young). Others are based on sex (male versus female). But most are based on what they call *arbitrary-set systems*. With this term, they refer to group differences based on ethnicity, social class, or religion. In each case, one group pursues the domination of other groups deemed inferior.

Within a culture, some ideas and institutions reinforce these group disparities, while others try to weaken it. The two researchers call these ideas "legitimizing myths" (Sidanius & Pratto, 1999, p. 45). Some of these concepts promote authoritarian inequalities (racism, sexism, conservatism), while others promote group equality (universal rights, feminism, and socialism).

Social dominance, then, is given a dimensional definition: "the degree to which individuals desire and support group-based hierarchy and the domination of 'inferior' groups by 'superior' groups" (Sidanius & Pratto, 1999, p. 48).

Over many years, an instrument was developed to measure SDO in valid and reliable ways. The instrument was tested on 45 samples of 18,741 people living in 11 countries (Sidanius & Pratto, 1999, p. 67). Some items from this measure illustrate our five-part definition of the Authoritarian Man:

- *Pursuit of Power:* "In getting what you want, it is sometimes necessary to use force against other groups."
- *Control and Domination of Others*: "Sometimes other groups must be kept in their place."
- *Exploitation:* "It is probably a good thing that certain groups are at the top and others are at the bottom."
- *Non-Empathic*: SDO is inversely related to empathy, concern, communality, and tolerance (Pratto et al., 1994).
- *Anti-Egalitarianism:* "Some groups of people are simply inferior to other groups."

High SDO scores predict attitudes toward numerous racial, sexual, religious, and ethnic groups. Social settings where these views are enacted include housing, retail markets, labor, education, health care, and the criminal justice system. Apropos to our interests, it should be noted that SDO is theoretically and psychometrically distinct from Altemeyer's theory of the authoritarian personality (Altemeyer, 2006; Pratto et al., 1994). That is, they tap different dimensions of personality. Also important, men show more social dominance than women (Pratto et al., 1994).

So far in this chapter, we have reviewed evidence for the suggestion that authoritarianism is a dimensional personality trait; that is, any authoritarian follower can be more or less conventional, submissive to authority, and aggressively supportive of authority. And authoritarian dominators are variable regarding their use of power, control, exploitation, empathy, and egalitarianism.

The next question is ready to be addressed. How do these authoritarian traits fit into the larger system of personality dimensions outlined in the Five Factor Model?

THE "FIVE FACTOR MODEL" (PAUL COSTA & ROBERT McCRAE)

The Five Factor Model (FFM) of personality structure has become dominant in the dimensional approach to understanding personality. The undergirding research is solid and began with a series of lexical studies of the words we humans use to describe each other. Statistical procedures clumped together various English words that describe people until it became clear that most people assess others along five dimensions. Researchers then took the same approach to other languages and found the same five dimensions in German, Dutch, Czech, Polish, Russian, Italian, Spanish, Hebrew, Hungarian, Turkish, Korean, and Filipino. Additional research using other strategies has confirmed these five dimensions as central to our understanding of personality.

These dimensions are measurable with the NEO Personality Inventory and the NEO Five-Factor Inventory (Costa & McCrae, 1992), and with the shorter Big Five Inventory (John & Srivastava, 1999). Costa and McCrae (1992, pp. 9–16) provide descriptions of each of the five dimensions that include neurotic (how people manage their emotions), extraverted (moving toward others, or away from them), open (how imaginative versus conventional), agreeable (cooperative versus antagonistic), and conscientious (organized versus careless).

How are the Five Factors (and their 30 components, called facets) related to authoritarianism? Two researchers in Sweden published a study that addresses this question (Akrami & Ekehammar, 2006). They gave 332 people the three instruments we have just described—the authoritarian measure (Altemeyer), the social dominance measure (Pratto & Sidanius), and the Five-Factor instrument (Costa & McCrae, 1992).

Findings provide more detail to our understanding of authoritarian men. There were significant correlations on many of the 30 facets, all at the <.01 level or greater (Akrami & Ekehammar, 2006, p. 119).

Authoritarian followers and dominators share the following FFM traits:

- *Low on openness*: They are conventional, conservative, prefer the familiar, and are muted emotionally.
- *Low on openness/fantasy*: They do not think it is productive to use their imaginations to create rich inner lives. They prefer to keep their focus on tasks that are in front of them at the moment.
- *Low on openness/aesthetics*: They are largely uninterested and unmoved by the arts, and their knowledge and appreciation of art is lower than the average.
- *Low on openness/feelings*: They do not believe that feeling states have much value, and they are not particularly interested in their own inner feelings and emotions.
- *Low on openness/actions*: They are not likely to be seen trying new activities. They prefer the familiar and the routine.
- *Low on openness/values*: They accept authorities in various fields, often without much skepticism, so their views on social, political, and religious values tend to be conservative, if not dogmatic.
- *Low on agreeableness/trust*: They do not trust easily, and they tend to believe that others are not likely to be honest or well-intentioned and actually may be dangerous.
- *Low on agreeableness/tender-mindedness*: They are hard-headed, rational, and value cold logic rather than concern or empathy for others.

In addition, authoritarian followers (but not dominators) were correlated with two other FFM facets:

- *Low on neuroticism/impulsiveness*: Followers have a high tolerance for frustration and can control many of their cravings and urges.
- *Low openness/ideas*: They are unwilling to consider new and unconventional ideas and do not enjoy playing with new intellectual concepts. They may be highly intelligent, but they prefer to pay attention to a limited set of topics.

And finally, authoritarian dominators (but not followers) were associated with four other facets:

- *Low on extraversion/warmth*: Dominators are formal, reserved, and distant in their relations to others and are unlikely to be seen as warm, affectionate, friendly, and closely attached to others.
- *Low on agreeableness/straightforwardness*: They are more willing to manipulate others using flattery or deception. They see these traits as useful social skills and think of more straightforward people as naïve.

- *Low on agreeableness/altruism*: They are self-centered and reluctant to get involved in helping others. They are not known for being generous and considerate of others.
- *Low on agreeableness/compliance*: They are aggressive, competitive, and prone to express anger easily. They do not defer to others and do not forgive and forget.

Many other studies have reported similar results. A review of 71 separate studies involving 22,068 people found that authoritarian followers are closed to new experience and highly conscientious, while authoritarian dominators are closed to new experience and antagonistic. These findings "were robust and consistent across samples" (Sibley & Duckitt, 2008, p. 248).

Followers and leaders are distinct, yet they both cause much human suffering. Person-to-person, authoritarians become workplace bullies, sexual harassers, and domestic abusers. Group-to-group, authoritarian dominators produce divisions, power struggles, and more. The combination of the two sets of traits (followers and dominators) is deadly (Son Hing, Bobocel, & Zanna, 2007). Altemeyer's description is a chilling reminder of what can happen (2006):

> This is now called the "lethal union" in this field of research. When social dominators are in the driver's seat, and right-wing authoritarians stand at their beck and call, unethical things appear much more likely to happen. True, sufficiently skilled social dominators served by dedicated followers can make the trains run on time. But you have to worry about what the trains may be hauling when dominators call the shots and (authoritarian followers) do the shooting. The trains may be loaded with people crammed into boxcars heading for death camps. (p. 182)

Summary: Authoritarian Personality Traits

So, what can we learn from comparing the research findings on authoritarianism (Altemeyer), social dominance (Sidanius and Pratto), and the Five Factor Model (Costa and McCrae)? Three conclusions:

1. Authoritarian followers *and* dominators share many personality traits. They devalue imagination, aesthetics, emotions, new experiences and ideas, interpersonal trust, and tender-mindedness.
2. Authoritarian *followers* also have a high tolerance for frustration, pursue conventional and limited interests, are conscientious, and see themselves as purposeful and well-prepared to deal with their lives.
3. Authoritarian *dominators* are also emotionally distant, manipulative, self-centered, inconsiderate, aggressive, and anger-prone.

A final note about defining authoritarian attributes as personality traits. Both right-wing authoritarianism and social dominance have been presented by their creators as personality theories. Not all scholars agree. Some prefer to see these variables more as social attitudes or social beliefs than personality characteristics (e.g., Duckitt, Wagner, Du Plessis, & Birum, 2002). We'll develop these ideas further in Chapter 5. For now, the central point is that authoritarianism is an identifiable pattern of human behavior. The FFM enriches our understanding of the authoritarian personalities identified by Bob Altemeyer, Jim Sidanius, and Felicia Pratto.

DIAGNOSING AN AUTHORITARIAN MAN

How does the authoritarian personality—follower or leader—get diagnosed? At the present time, mental health professionals have three options when it comes to diagnosing personality problems. The first manual is the long-running series in the United States, the *Diagnostic and Statistical Manual of Mental Disorders* (DSM) (American Psychiatric Association, 1952, 1968, 1987, 1994, 2000). A second classification system is the *International Classification of Diseases* (ICD) (Commission, 1968, 1986, 1991), which has become the international standard for diagnosing the full range of human diseases. The third option is much newer and not widely used at present. It is called the *Psychodynamic Diagnostic Manual* (PDM Task Force, 2006), and it defines both healthy and unhealthy personality capacities. All three of these classification systems make one thing abundantly clear: Diagnosing a man with a personality disorder is serious business. It marks him as impaired in ways that are distressing to him, disruptive to others, and likely to last a lifetime.

Diagnostic Impression: The Authoritarian Triad (Plus One)

In the center where I work, we diagnose most authoritarian men with a personality disorder. We have identified a pattern in our use of diagnostic categories. Over the years, we have used several personality assessment instruments, including the *Personality Assessment Inventory* (PAI), the *Millon Clinical Multiaxial Inventory* (MCMI), and the *Minnesota Multiphasic Personality Inventory* (MMPI). When reporting findings from our assessments, we typically use the DSM series. We have found that three personality trait clusters are so common that we use an informal name for them: "the disruptive triad." In addition, the MCMI subscale of Desirability consistently is very high, as well; hence, the Plus One. Here are the three personality traits of what we have found in the "disruptive professional," described in Chapter 1 as one of the prototypical faces of authoritarian men:

1. *Narcissistic.* He has a strong sense of entitlement, is interpersonally exploitive, lacks empathy, is arrogant in word and deed, has grandiose views of himself, thinks he is special, and requires much admiration from others.
2. *Obsessive.* He is rigid and stubborn, works hard in single-minded ways, always thinks he knows the right way to do things, believes in perfection for himself and others, can get lost in the details of situations, is preoccupied with doing things perfectly, and is inflexible about his moral and ethical values.
3. *Histrionic.* He seeks to be the center of attention, engages in behavior that others find seductive or provocative, experiences moods and emotions that are intense and shift quickly, can act quickly and impulsively, requires much praise, is suggestible, and misunderstands the closeness or intimacy of his relationships with others.

(Plus One) To rank high on the Desirability Scale, he must be heavily invested in "looking good" to others. This man pays much attention to his appearance and reputation, and he minimizes the presence of any psychological or emotional problems. He wants to appear confident, sociable, and cooperative. He professes a strong belief in following the rules of society and respecting proper authorities. As such, this variable is not technically a personality trait, but a prominent tendency.

This is our diagnostic impression of authoritarian men. The traits are dimensional. A man may not reach criteria for a personality disorder in all four components. Some traits will be higher than others, and some authoritarians have prominent amounts of borderline, antisocial, or paranoid traits. But the above four traits consistently produce the highest scores, and thus are exemplars of our authoritarian man. Other mood and behavioral diagnoses are frequently used as well, including impulse control, mood dysregulation, substance use disorders, and unaddressed trauma.

The trauma diagnosis is especially important and signals a focus for treatment. In our center, we have found the still-developing description of Complex Posttraumatic Stress Disorder (C-PTSD) to be especially helpful. Judith Herman identified and defined this version of PTSD in the early 1990s (Herman, 1992). Rather than describe a singular traumatic incident (war, natural disaster, assault, rape), C-PTSD refers to a pattern of repeated trauma that lasts for years. The symptoms are more "complex, diffuse, and tenacious than simple PTSD," and they lead to personality disorders involving "relatedness and identity." They remain vulnerable to self-harm for decades (Herman, 1992, p. 379). These realities are a sad component of the diagnostic picture for the vast majority of authoritarian men we treat.

The DSM-V promises to provide broader and more detailed language in defining personality disorders. The new definitions are a hybrid of the dimensional and categorical perspectives of understanding personality.

How this approach will play out in the clinical setting for authoritarian men remains to be seen, but some of the proposed language is highly relevant for our purposes. Here, I select phrases from these descriptions that are consistent with what we have found in using the DSM-IV-TR at our center (American Psychiatric Association, 2011). Time and research will tell if the following hypotheses hold up.

Tough Guy authoritarians may be more likely to be diagnosed with traits that appear in the new antisocial/psychopathic type:

- *Callousness*: lack of empathy or concern for others' feelings or problems, exploitativeness
- *Aggression*: using dominance and intimidation to control others
- *Manipulativeness*: use of cunning, craft, or subterfuge to influence or control others; casual use of others to one's own advantage; use of seduction, charm, glibness, or ingratiation to achieve one's own end
- *Narcissism*: vanity, boastfulness, exaggeration of one's achievements and abilities; self-centeredness; feeling and acting entitled, believing that one deserves only the best

True Believer authoritarians seem more likely to be described as Obsessive–Compulsive Types. These characteristics will be developed further in the next chapter.

- *Perfectionism*: insistence on everything being flawless, without errors or faults, including one's own and others' performance; conviction that reality should conform to one's own ideal vision
- *Rigidity*: being rule- and habit-governed; belief that there is only one right way to do things; difficulty adapting behaviors to changing circumstances; processing of information on the basis of fixed ideas and expectations; difficulty changing ideas and/or viewpoints, even with overwhelming contrary evidence

We can review our Authoritarian Triad of personality disorder traits in more detail by comparing them with facets of the Five Factor Model. The FFM is divided into 30 "facets" that highlight various aspects of each of the five factors. One study of people aged 18 to 45 found several connections between our three authoritarian personality traits and the facets of the FFM (O'Connor & Dyce, 2002).

- *Narcissistic personality disorder* demonstrated a positive correlation with the Extraversion facet of assertiveness. Negative correlations were found for the Agreeableness facets of trust, straightforwardness, altruism, compliance, and modesty.
- *Obsessive–compulsive personality disorder* exhibited a positive correlation with three Agreeableness facets (straightforwardness, altruism, and compliance) and with six Conscientiousness facets (competence, order, dutifulness, achievement striving,

self-discipline, and deliberation). It revealed a negative correlation with Neuroticism (impulsiveness and vulnerability).
- *Histrionic personality disorder* showed positive correlations with all six Extraversion facets (warmth, gregariousness, assertiveness, activity, excitement seeking, and positive emotions), with two Openness to Experience facets (feelings and actions), and with the Agreeableness facet of trust. Negative correlations were found with four Neuroticism facets (anxiety, depression, self-consciousness, and vulnerability) and with the Agreeableness facet of modesty.

Personality Diagnoses for Our Authoritarian Prototypes

In Chapter 1, we reviewed prototypes of the Authoritarian Man. We can revisit those prototypes now, with a look at what we know about their personalities.

Workplace Bullies

Two scholars in Britain generated considerable publicity in 2005 for a study that examined workplace managers. Belinda Board and Katarina Fritzon, based at Surrey University, posed a provocative question: Is there any similarity in the personalities of high-level business managers and criminal psychiatric patients? Their findings are striking, because their answer is yes (Board & Fritzon, 2005).

Their sample included 39 successful British executives and 317 criminals and psychiatric patients at Broadmoor Hospital, a high security psychiatric facility. They compared levels of personality variables in the groups, using the *Minnesota Multiphasic Personality Inventory Scales for DSM-III Personality Disorders*. The researchers discovered that their group of successful senior British managers scored higher on 3 of 11 personality disorders than the disturbed criminals. Which three? The now-familiar facets of our authoritarian personality. These workplace bosses were

- *Narcissistic.* They were more grandiose, self-focused, exploitive, and independent than the psychiatric criminals, and they were higher on independence.
- *Obsessive–compulsive.* The managers also were highly perfectionist, excessively devoted to work, rigid and stubborn, and showed more domineering tendencies than their counterparts.
- *Histrionic.* They showed more superficial insincerity, egotism, and manipulativeness than the criminal psychiatric patients.

One of the researchers, Belinda Board, later wrote an op-ed piece for the *New York Times* (Board, 2005). Her words underline the dimensional nature of authoritarian personalities.

Take a basic characteristic like influence, and it's an asset in business. Add to that a smattering of egocentricity, a soupçon of grandiosity, a smidgen of manipulativeness and lack of empathy, and you have someone who can climb the corporate ladder and stay on the right side of the law, but still be a horror to work with. Add a bit more of those characteristics plus lack of remorse and physical aggression, and you have someone who ends up behind bars.

Partner Abusers

Two researchers at the University of Oklahoma—Ron Beasley and Cal Stoltenberg—wanted to identify personality characteristics of men who abuse their partners. So they formed two groups, one with 35 nonbattering men, the other with 49 abusive men in treatment. To get into the abusive group, men had to admit they had at least pushed or shoved their partners (Beasley & Stoltenberg, 1992).

Both groups answered standardized questions about their personalities, their anger, and their early life parental relationships. Like the diagnostic profiles we have been describing, this study did not find that a single personality disorder diagnosed abusers. Rather, abusers scored higher than nonabusers on several scales. Here are a few of their statistically significant findings:

- Abusive men scored higher than nonabusive men on 18 of the 20 scales that form the *Millon Clinical Multiaxial Inventory*. The level of disruption in the abuser's lives was both chronic and moderately severe.
- Abusers with high narcissistic scores also reported stronger endorsement of a subscale called Exploitiveness/Entitlement.
- Abusers scored higher on both State Anger (situational responses) and Trait Anger (a personality variable) measures.
- Abusers also witnessed more verbal aggression and physical violence in their families of origin.

Again, elements of our Authoritarian Man are evident. Men in this study reported the traits we have been identifying all along—narcissism, aggressiveness, exploitiveness, entitlement, and (as we shall see later) early life maltreatment.

Similar findings for partner abusers have been found in other studies of abusive men, who generally have been diagnosed with narcissistic personality disorder (Hamberger & Hastings, 1986, 1988), histrionic personality disorder, and sociopathic personality disorder (Faulkner & Stoltenberg, 1988).

Zealous Followers

Studies have found a positive correlation between authoritarianism (conventionality, submission, and aggression) and religious fundamentalism (Altemeyer & Hunsberger, 1992; Hunsberger, 1995; Laythe, Finkel, & Kirkpatrick, 2001; Mavor, Macleod, Boal, & Louis, 2009) (Note: We'll look at this term *fundamentalism* in depth in the next chapter).

Let's take just one of these studies and see how this connection has been made. Bob Altemeyer and his late fellow researcher Bruce Hunsberger developed a scale to measure *attitudes* toward religious fundamentalism. Notice they did not measure fundamentalist beliefs themselves, but attitudes toward those beliefs (Altemeyer & Hunsberger, 1992). People who scored high on their Religious Fundamentalism scale *agreed* with statements like these:

- God has given humanity a complete, unfailing guide to happiness and salvation, which must be totally followed.
- To lead the best, most meaningful life, one must belong to the one fundamentally true religion.

And they *disagreed* with statements like these:

- No single book of religious teachings contains all the intrinsic, fundamental truths about life.
- It is more important to be a good person than to believe in God and the right religion.

The idea for the instrument was to write statements that would describe fundamentalists of various religious persuasions, such as Jewish, Hindu, or Christian. Altemeyer and Husberger conducted five studies of university students ($n = 701$) and parents ($n = 726$). The group included members of many different religious groups. The researchers gave these participants the authoritarian measure noted earlier and the Religious Fundamentalism scale.

The findings? Those who scored high on Religious Fundamentalism also scored high on the authoritarian scale that measures agreement with statements about conventionality, submission, and aggressiveness. The two go together. The correlation was .68, significant at the <.01 level. Another study has reinforced this connection between fundamentalism and authoritarianism and also identified mediating beliefs (Hathcoat & Barnes, 2010).

Narcissus, Then and Now

You remember the central scene in the story. The mother of Narcissus is told by an oracle that she must never let Narcissus know himself. If he can remain unaware, then Narcissus will live to a ripe old age. But one day, poor Narcissus bends low over a spring of water and sees his own beauty for the first time. He reaches out to kiss or grasp this figure. But every time he tries, the figure flees, only to return again and repeat the rejection. He becomes so obsessed that he cannot take his eyes off his own image. He is unable to stop to eat or drink, and he wastes away to his own death.

This metaphor still lives. One man in my clinical practice told me, "You know how you see yourself in the storefront glass when you walk down the street? I sometimes wave at my image, just to see someone noticing me." Another man saw this image on a Rorschach card: "I see a lipstick image of me kissing a mirror in my bathroom." A physically healthy man in his 60s proudly announced he already owned his own headstone for his grave. A large photo of himself was embedded into the stone, "so that my image will last longer than I do."

It is tough to be empathic and egalitarian when even store windows, inkblots, and headstones become adoring objects. The narcissistic myth makes a timeless point: Too much self-love is not good for a man's soul... or for other living creatures he knows. It is a hollow life, indeed.

> Narcissus so loved himself, himself forsook,
> And died to kiss his shadow in the brook.
>
> —William Shakespeare
> (1593, *Venus and Adonis*, Lines 161, 162)

SUMMARY

Is authoritarian behavior a personality trait? This question was electric in the aftermath of World War II, when authoritarian behavior led to the deaths of millions of people. Theodor Adorno and a group of scholars devoted 4 years to this problem and announced their answer in 1950: The "authoritarian personality" is a set of nine traits. That set of nine suggestions has not held up well in subsequent research, but the Adorno group's work sparked additional research that has revealed much. We now know that authoritarians come in two versions: most are followers, and some are dominators. The personalities of the two versions are mostly similar, but there are some differences.

Authoritarian followers were the professional focus of Bob Altemeyer for three decades. Dozens of studies helped him discover three traits. They are *conventional* in thought and behavior, *submissive* to established authorities, and *aggressive* in their support of those authorities.

Authoritarian leaders have been called Social Dominators by Jim Sidanius and Felicia Pratto. This team spent 25 years studying these folks and identified a core belief they all share. For them, the world divides into groups: their own and all the rest. Theirs is superior. Others are inferior. This finding holds up, regardless of the dominator's cultural,

"He Always Has Been That Way" 53

religious, or ethnic group identity. In a word, authoritarian leaders are nonegalitarian. That core belief expands readily. If our group is better than yours, then we have a duty to take charge of yours. It is for your own good. To enforce group dominance, then, these men become exploitive, coercive, and aggressive.

Authoritarian personality traits have been identified in the Five Factor Model of personality. Research has shown:

- *Both* followers and dominators are more closed to new experiences than open and more antagonistic than agreeable. They do not trust, expecting others to be dangerous. They are stubborn and rigid, value their rationality, and are not much interested in empathy.
- Authoritarian *followers* (but not leaders) have a high tolerance for frustration, narrow their interests to conventional and limited pursuits, are conscientiousness, and see themselves as dedicated and prepared to face life.
- Authoritarian *leaders* (but not followers) are distant, unfriendly, and detached. Because they see others as naïve and inferior, they readily use manipulation, flattery, or deception to get what they want. They are angry men, competitive and aggressive. They do not forget slights, and forgiveness is unappealing. They do not defer; they take control. They are in charge.

Diagnostically, authoritarians show several problematic personality traits. They score high on measures of personality disorders, especially on narcissistic, obsessive, and histrionic dimensions. They also are highly defensive. Support for the link between these personality patterns and authoritarianism is found in studies that examine personalities of both Tough Guys (workplace bullies and disruptive professionals) and True Believers (zealous followers).

How do these personality traits develop? What turns a man into an authoritarian? Part of the answer is biological (Chapter 4), and part clearly is social (Chapter 5). But first, another important factor: the relationship between religious fundamentalism and authoritarianism.

CHAPTER
3

"God Wants Him to Take Charge"
Authoritarian as Divine Mandate

> What is objectionable, what is dangerous, about extremists is not that they are extreme, but that they are intolerant. The evil is not what they say about their cause, but what they say about their opponents.
>
> —Robert Kennedy (1964, *The Pursuit of Justice,* p. 69)

While the scholars at the University of California at Berkeley were thinking about "the authoritarian personality" as an explanation for the mass appeal of dictatorial governments in World War II (see Chapter 2), another man was puzzling over the same questions. He was not a scholar. In fact, he had virtually no formal schooling at all. Orphaned by both parents before he was 20 years old, he spent the next 20 years living on his own as a migrant worker in California. He educated himself, spending countless hours in local libraries. By the time World War II came along, he had gotten a job loading and unloading cargo ships in San Francisco, just across the bay from the Berkeley professors. When he wasn't working, this unmarried and rather isolated man struggled to understand the events of World War II. How do entire nations become authoritarian? What motivates people to give up so much of their own lives to join mass movements of any kind? This longshoreman's name was Eric Hoffer (Tomkins, 1968), and his answer to these troublesome questions was published in 1951, less than a year after the Berkeley scholars published their theories and research on the same questions.

Hoffer's book is called, *True Believers: Thoughts on the Nature of Mass Movements* (Hoffer, 1951). He was nearly 50 years old at the time, and unpublished. But the book was a sensation and best seller. President Eisenhower praised the book so frequently that *Look* magazine called Hoffer "Ike's Favorite Author" ("Ike's Favorite Author," *Look*, 1956).

Hoffer defined a True Believer as a person "of fanatical faith who is ready to sacrifice his life for a holy cause" (Hoffer, 1951, p. xii). He argued that although "there are vast differences in the contents of holy causes and doctrines," these mass movements share "a certain uniformity in the factors which make them effective" (Hoffer, 1951, p. xii). He noticed a common pattern. Charismatic leaders identify a set of current problems in society, such as poverty, unemployment, and religious or ethnic oppression. Then certain ideas or groups are targeted as being responsible for the problems. Leaders next recruit members from groups Hoffer describes as misfits, the overly selfish, the burdened minorities, the poor, the bored, and the sinners (Hoffer, 1951, p. 24–57). Adherents are told they must sacrifice their own interests for the larger cause that will solve the identified religious or social problems. The promised result is a brighter and better future for everyone.

The term "true believer" is now in modern English dictionaries. The term refers to someone "who professes absolute belief in something," or who is "a zealous supporter of a particular cause" ("True Believer," 2010). These folks are completely convinced that a particular idea, cause, or movement holds the absolute answer to identified social problems.

In religious contexts, some True Believers are now called fundamentalists, regardless of ethnicity or culture. Because these groups typically emphasize authoritarian perspectives and practices, I believe it is necessary for psychotherapists to understand the thought worlds of fundamentalists. It never hurts to spend a little time seeing the world through the eyes of someone we are trying to help.

We can begin our discussion with a look at the word itself, which is a problem because of its elasticity. It has been stretched into definitions by experts in politics, religion, history, psychology, anthropology, philology, and more. Historically, the *Oxford English Dictionary* (1971) traces the word *fundamentalist* back to the 13th century. The root of the word is "fundament," and it referred to "the lower part of the body on which one sits, the buttocks," as well the base of a wall, a surface on which to stand, or the act of founding an institution (Oxford, 1971, p. 1095).

The current use of "fundamentalism" as a distinctly religious term goes back only a hundred years. In the 1910s, two Christian oil millionaires in the United States (Lyman and Milton Stewart) were dismayed by the work of scholars who were investigating the historical and linguistic origins of the Bible, thereby casting doubt on its divine authorship. In 1908, they founded the Bible College of Los Angeles to combat these teachings (Armstrong, 2000). The next year, they funded the production of a series of pamphlets called *The Fundamentals: A Testimony to the Truth*. These essays were designed to counter perceived attacks by theologians who had noticed historical inaccuracies in the Bible, traced changes in scriptural texts over time, and offered interpretations of Biblical texts that reflected these findings. The authors of *The Fundamentals* argued that the Bible has no errors of any kind because it records the original and actual words of God. This meant that correct Christian doctrines must be based on a literal reading of those words. Three million copies of the first round of these pamphlets were published and given away free (Armstrong, 2000). The group eventually published four volumes of polemical essays that criticized evolution, socialism, and spiritualism, and also condemned the teachings of other Christian churches: Roman Catholic, Church of Latter-Day Saints, and members of the Christian Science faith community (Torrey et al., 1917, 1996).

The term *fundamentalist* was given more force in July of 1920. A doctrinal conflict had developed between two groups inside the Northern Baptist Convention. The editor of a publication called *The Watchman Examiner* decided that folks on the conservative side of the debate needed a name: "We suggest that those who still cling to the great fundamentals and who mean to do battle royal for the fundamentals shall be called 'Fundamentalists'" (cited in Pettegrew, 1982, pp. 1–2). The notion of being in a "battle" with perceived opponents has stuck with fundamentalists ever since.

Some observers have found it useful to make a connotative distinction between fundamentalism and orthodoxy. The focus of orthodoxy is on the *content* of a set of beliefs. Fundamentalism conveys more of an *attitude* toward one's beliefs. The attitude is combative. Truth must be vigorously and (at times) aggressively defended against assault. Perceived adversaries are given pejorative names, such as infidels, unbelievers, liberals, secularists, apostates, satans, and so forth (Altemeyer, 1996).

FUNDAMENTALISM: THE SCHOLAR'S VIEW

The most weighty modern attempt to understand fundamentalism was published in five lengthy volumes over about a decade beginning in the 1990s. The series is called *The Fundamentalism Project* (Marty & Appleby, 1991, 1993, 1996, 2002, 2004a, 2004b). The two principal editors held academic posts at the University of Chicago (Martin E. Marty) and the University of Notre Dame (R. Scott Appleby). They assembled a cast of about 75 scholars who produced nearly 4,000 pages of extraordinarily detailed and thoughtful information about the nature, teachings, and functions of religious movements often identified as fundamentalist. Academically, the contributors were trained mostly in the social sciences: anthropology, philosophy, religious studies, history, sociology, economics, Oriental languages, English literature, religious history, Asian studies, and international relations. They were based in universities located in Argentina, Australia, Canada, Ecuador, England, Germany, Hawaii, India, Iran, Israel, Pakistan, Switzerland, and the

MEET A SCHOLAR

MARTIN E. MARTY

Martin E. Marty is an extraordinary scholar. A professor at the University of Chicago since 1963, he has produced more than 50 books and 5,000 (not a misprint) articles and essays. Fellow scholars have noticed the quality of his work—universities have given him 75 honorary doctorates. Other writers have been impressed—he won the prestigious National Book Award for *Righteous Empire*, a 1970 analysis of the U.S. Protestant concept of a national righteousness. Even politicians have noticed Marty's wisdom—he served on two U.S. Presidential Commissions addressing the health, educational, and artistic needs of children.

Marty is a realist. Though a Lutheran pastor, his scholarship candidly acknowledges the dark side of religious history: "The collisions of peoples of faith are among the most threatening conflicts around the world.... They grow more ominous and even lethal every season" (Marty, 2005, p. 1). The title of one of his university seminars illustrates his concerns in this regard: *Violence in American Culture*. He begins his book *When Faiths Collide* with a blunt description of religious strife and killings in many countries, then writes: "Religion inspires, exacerbates, or justifies conflicts that often also involve ethnicity, territory, revenge, and political ideology" (Marty, 2010, p. 2).

Yet Marty also writes about hope—realistic and personal. The only basis for constructive responses to religious authoritarianism, he argues, is a society that is just, humane, and respectful. Not

> passively tolerant, but active and curious. Be hospitable to religious strangers, he urges. Converse with them. Build cultures of trust. Get to know people who are truly different (Marty, 2005, 2010).
>
> He concedes that authoritarian forces must be confronted with a strong defense when necessary. But he also contends that authoritarian attitudes can be undermined by personal relationships that cross boundaries. These ideas are not merely philosophical for Marty. He joined Martin Luther King, Jr. in the pivotal civil rights march in the U.S. from Selma to Montgomery in Alabama in 1965. He also is the Mohandas M. K. Gandhi Fellow of the American Academy of Political and Social Sciences.
>
> Near the age of 80, Marty wrote *The Mystery of the Child* (2007a). In a televised conversation with Bill Moyers about the book, Marty agreed that children share certain traits: "Receptive. Responsive. Amendable. Simple. Teachable. Relatively helpless. Insignificant. Unimposing. Lacking status" (Marty, 2007b). He continues, "Men see the world in terms of power. Big events. Wars, treaties who gets elected—who tromps on whom. That's basically the plot of most history." But children see the world differently.
>
> This contrast is not theoretical for Marty. He is father to seven children, including two foster children from another country. He knows children, and he takes seriously the saying of Jesus of Nazareth: "Truly I tell you, unless you change and become like little children, you will never enter the kingdom of heaven" (Matthew 18:2, New International Version). Dr. Marty's take on that famous comment: "I think the notion that you spend your life finding ways to change and become like a little child means you will be more open to mystery, more responsive to others, more receptive" (Marty, 2007b).
>
> Ultimately, that open spirit widens the possibility of understanding... even of religious authoritarians. "Whatever is mysterious about the child is something we can constantly keep changing to be replenished by. And so we don't give up on people." He captures this openness within a definition of a deeply religious word: "Soul is not a ghost in a machine. Soul is not a pilot on a ship. Soul is not a thing. Soul... is the integrated, vital power of any organic body open to possibility and future" (Marty, 2007b).

United States. This multicultural panel of scholars investigated numerous fundamentalist religious groups and movements around the world in the 20th century—Christian, Islamic, Jewish, Hindu, Confucian, Sikh, and Buddhist.

Nine "properties" of fundamentalist movements were identified by this international and multidisciplinary team of scholars (Almond,

Sivan, & Appleby, 2004a). These markers are summarized here because they form an ideological and organizational context for the development of religious authoritarianism, which in turn draws and reinforces authoritarian men.

Reactivity

> How can there be peace when drunkards, drug dealers, communists, atheists, New Age worshipers of Satan, secular humanists, oppressive dictators, greedy money changers, revolutionary assassins, adulterers, and homosexuals are on top?
>
> —Pat Robertson (1991, *The New World Order*, p. 227)

A starting point for understanding fundamentalist thought is to recognize its oppositional stance toward the modern world. In many ways, this is the defining characteristic of fundamentalist movements, regardless of their heritage: ethnic, national, or religious. They organize to fight the waves of modernism that are washing through their cultures. Charismatic and forceful leaders emerge who call the disaffected to ideological arms. For those who join, the cost is high. Certain ideas must be accepted (orthodoxy). Specified behaviors must be seen as moral and therefore required (orthopraxy). And certain attitudes toward these ideas and behaviors must be held (fundamentalist).

Fundamentalist groups react strongly to trends that weaken the true religion as they understand it. The offending trends are found in three sources: in the wayward practices of their own religion (watering down historic truths), in the sinful practices of the secular state (pluralism, divorce, etc.), and in the behavior of unbelievers (gambling, wearing "revealing" clothing, seeing popular films, etc.) (Almond et al., 2004a).

Fundamentalist groups react to these perceived offenses in one of four ways (Almond, Sivan, & Appleby, 2004b). One reaction is to try to *conquer the world* by taking charge of the structures of society: the media, the government, the educational system, and law enforcement. A second reaction is to *transform the world* through skillful political actions, legal challenges, lobbying, proselytizing, public relations efforts, and the use of media to condemn unwanted cultural practices. A third approach is to *create a separate community* within the larger world by developing their own structures, publishing outlets, musical groups, educational systems, clothing practices, etc. And finally, fundamentalists can react by *living in the world, but renouncing it* at the same time. The energy of this latter group is neither turned outward with a conquering attitude nor inward by escaping into a separate community, but rather toward an uneasy coexistence with the world.

Selectivity

In order to promote their larger goals in society, fundamentalist groups are highly selective in their use of scriptural texts, modern conveniences, and political targets (Almond, Sivan, & Appleby, 2004c). Certain scriptural texts are selected for emphasis because they describe or justify the group's existence, highlight distinctive teachings and rituals, or condemn current practices regarded as sinful or subversive. Academic scholars of religious literature may find these scriptural texts to be apocalyptic, figurative, or metaphorical, but fundamentalist interpreters do not. Instead, they apply these verses to modern ideas they regard as central to their self-understanding or work. Examples are readily available: From the Christian perspective, Revelation 13:1 was once selected to predict the existence of the European Union (Lindsey, 1970); from the Islamic faith community, the invention of air travel is said to be predicted in Qur'an 34:12 (cf., Yahya, 2001); and some members of the Jewish community select texts that justify political views about the expansion of Jewish-controlled territory in the Middle East (Hirst, 2003; Shabak & Mezvinsky, 1999).

Fundamentalists are also selective as to which modern practices to oppose and which to use. They may object to one particular medical practice, but not all medical procedures, one line of research, but not all scientific findings, or one social program, but not all governmental social policies.

These selective stances are intertwined. Selected texts address selected problems in the social or religious culture, and selected communication techniques are used to promulgate the messages of concern.

Dualism

> My father was a Baptist minister. I'm a Christian man. I have problems with people who don't believe in God.
>
> **—H. K. Edgerton (December 7, 2009, *Ashville Citizen-Times*)**

H. K. Edgerton was outraged that his city of Ashville, North Carolina, had elected an atheist to the city council. He threatened to sue, citing an 1868 North Carolina statute that outlaws all officeholders "who shall deny the being of Almighty God" (Patterson, 2009). For Edgerton, there are only two categories of people: believers and atheists. And only believers should hold office.

A common fundamentalist perspective is the division of ideas and people into just two categories: good and evil. All thinking and behavior is subject to being judged right or wrong, moral or immoral, holy or sinful. For those on the inside, of course, the "outside world" is thoroughly degraded, wicked, and doomed to destruction. The insiders are the pure, the specially selected ones.

Fundamentalist groups cite scriptural texts to portray the reality of this dualism, often in metaphorical language. The Christian New Testament speaks of the "cup of the Lord and the cup of demons" (I Corinthians 10:21, New International Version, 1984). The Jewish Torah refers to God creating light and darkness: "I form light, and create darkness" (Isaiah 45:7, Jewish Publication Society, 2000). The Qur'an (2:24, 25) predicts fires for disbelievers and gardens for believers (Pickthall, 1953).

Contemporary versions of this binary cosmology thrive today in many different fundamentalist groups.

Messianism

Messianism follows naturally from dualism and is a forward-looking aspect of fundamentalism. Eventually, good will defeat evil. In the final analysis, when human history ends, the good will be rewarded with immortality, and the evil will be punished with eternal finality. Most fundamentalist groups describe events that will precede the final denouement, sometimes in great detail. The central theme in these predictions is that although the righteous will suffer greatly, they eventually will be honored, rescued, or translated by a messianic figure. Victory over evil is assured.

Long ago (6th century, BCE), Zoroastrian beliefs predicted the arrival of Saoshyant, who would lead the final and dramatic battle against evil (Boyce, 2001). All the metal in the mountains would melt, creating a glowing molten river around the world. The dead were to rise and join the living in walking through the river. To the righteous, the molten river would feel like milk, but to the wicked, it would be fire. Thus, everyone would be rewarded or punished, with the righteous living on eternally (Harris & Levey, 1975, p. 3049).

Today, similar approaches to messianism are easily found in modern fundamentalisms. For Christians, the righteous will be rescued when Christ comes to the earth from the heavens for a second time. Many predict this kingdom will last 1,000 years (LaHaye & Jenkins, 1999; Pentecost, 1976).

Hirst (2003) cites the prediction that a Jewish Kingdom will arise under God's total sovereignty, and be governed by the Halakkah, the collection of ancient Jewish laws. Rabbis will issue authoritative interpretations of the law, and civil officials will enforce it. Though Jewish fundamentalists come in many sects, "all are agreed on this basic eschatological truth" that the Messiah will come and "the Jewish Kingdom will arise" (Hirst, 2003, p. 82).

Historically, some schools of Buddhism have expected a fifth and final successor to its founder, Gautama Buddha. This Buddha is called Maitreya, and he is to arrive at a time when the teachings of the original Buddha have been forgotten on the earth. The promise is that this successor will achieve pure enlightenment, then rule over Ketumati Pure Land, a paradise on earth (Diener, Erhard, & Fischer-Schreiber, 1991).

Many Hindus believe that the end of the present age of darkness will come when Kalki Avatar arrives as the tenth and final incarnation of Lord Vishnu. "At this time the rulers of the earth will have degenerated into plunderers" (Bhag. 1.3.25). Kalki will set things right and make sure that harmony, righteousness, and truth will prevail.

In the Baha'i faith, the messianic age has already begun. A 1,000-year period is believed to have started in 1863 when Baha'u'llah, the founder of Baha'i, issued a "declaration" in which he claimed to be the symbolic fulfillment of the messianic expectations of Christianity, Judaism, Zoroastrianism, Islam, and Babism (Buck, 2004; Declaration of Baha'u'llah, 2010).

In Islam, believers look to the coming of the Hidden Imam, who will arrive shortly before the Day of Judgment.

> The Imam Mahdi will lead the forces of righteousness against the forces of evil in one final apocalyptic battle in which the enemies of the Imam will be defeated. The Imam Mahdi will rule for a number of years.... The Mahdi will fill the earth with justice after it has been filled with injustice and tyranny. (Momen, 1985, p. 166)

What all of these messianic stories have in common is a belief that the state of the world is hopelessly flawed and evil. No normal human powers can correct or rescue it. Intervention from outside is the only solution, and believers are encouraged to anticipate this event when all wrongs will be corrected.

Boundaries

Following the tsunami in 2004 that killed 226,000 people in South Asia, syndicated radio host Michael Savage (2005) opposed Western efforts to provide assistance to the victims, and he made this comment on the air: "Many of the countries... that were hit by these tidal waves were hotbeds of radical Islam. Why should we be helping them destroy us? I think what we're doing is feeding our own demise." Another outgrowth of dualism is the concept that righteous and unrighteous are incompatible concepts. A clear boundary must separate people into these two categories. The line of demarcation can be drawn between an entire religious community and the larger society around it. Or it may be drawn *within* a religion's group, separating true believers from those regarded as lax in their faith.

When the boundary separates true believers from other believers, the dividing line can be doctrinal, behavioral, or cultural. Fundamentalists believe it is their duty to correct wayward brothers and sisters who have become too worldly. If appropriate changes are not made, campaigns may be undertaken to define the boundaries. Letters of protest are written. Groups are organized, and leaders are challenged. These battles can become intense and quite personal. Fundamentalists see these conflicts as a fight for truth, not a struggle for power. Their mission is sacred, not secular. Religious history provides countless examples of what happens next.

If the target is internal, then the boundary can become structural. Believers can break away, split, or secede. At that point, the boundary is no longer ideological; it is organizational.

When the target is secular society, believers can make the boundary geographical. They cluster together in enclaves, communities, or regions. Utah is known for the size of its Mormon population. A large community of Seventh-day Adventists lives in Loma Linda, California. Amish communities have formed throughout the Midwest. Or monasteries and nunneries can provide a nearly complete boundary between the professionally religious and the outside world.

Boundaries become more visual, of course, when a person belongs to a group that requires special clothing: headscarves, robes, veils, etc.

Inerrancy

Fundamentalist groups regard scriptures, canons, or sets of writings as absolutely definitive, flawless, and truthful in every detail.

In Islam, many believe the original Arabic text of the Qur'an to be a revelation from God to the Prophet Muhammad, revealed over the span of more than 20 years by an angel named Gabriel. The word Qur'an itself means "he recited." Some believe that any translation from the classical Arabic is a sacrilege (Harris & Levey, 1975), because the Qur'an itself seems to report that it is the literal word of God (Qur'an 2:23–24). For this reason, it is highly blasphemous to many Muslims to treat a copy of the Qur'an with disrespect by recycling old copies or discarding them. Instead, they must be burned or buried in respectful ways. The Qur'an itself argues for its own inerrancy (Qur'an 4.82, Shakir, 1983).

In Judaism, some in the Orthodox tradition regard all the faith's foundational writings in a similar way (e.g., Guttman, 2008). This conviction is prominent in connection with the Halakhah, the collection of laws regarded as the revealed or actual will of God. But it can also extend for some to the whole of the written Torah (the laws, the prophets, and the writings). The oral Torah (the Talmud) may be given an authoritative role, as well.

Within both Catholicism and Protestantism, groups of Christians regard their scriptures as inerrant (Bacote, Miguelez, & Okholm, 2004). Roman Catholics find this view in a document endorsed in 1965 by Pope Paul VI. In part, it states: "...the books of Scripture must be acknowledged as teaching solidly, faithfully and *without error* [emphasis added] that truth which God wanted put into sacred writings" (Paul VI, 1965, III, 11). Conservative Protestants agree with a document produced by a conference of hundreds of evangelical leaders in 1978. The statement was called *The Chicago Statement on Biblical Inerrancy*. Their declaration included this statement: "Being wholly and verbally

God-given, Scripture is *without error or fault* [emphasis added] in all its teaching.... The authority of Scripture is inescapably impaired if this *total divine inerrancy* [emphasis added] is in any way limited or disregarded, or made relative to a view of truth contrary to the Bible's" (Chicago Statement, 1978, I, 4, 5).

Some conservative Christians who are uncomfortable with the idea that every single word of Scripture came directly from God (inerrancy) have added a different word to the discussion: infallible. They suggest infallible describes the truths behind the words of scripture, while inerrant describes the more narrowly defined view that the very words are without error. This approach is also taken in some Buddhist and Hindu writings that cite the comments of founders and leaders. The emphasis typically is on the ideas or theories being discussed, not the flawless or normative language of the writings, per se.

Chosen

Fundamentalists give true believers special status. The chosen ones have been called the "faithful," the "remnant," the "last outpost," the "Covenant keepers," those who "bear witness," "who walk with the Lord," and the like (Almond et al., 2004c, pp. 407–408). Support for these self-perceptions come directly from writings regarded as sacred or biblical. A few illustrations give life to this concept.

For millennia, an important part of Jewish identity has been the concept of having been chosen by God. This theme is repeated in the Pentateuch, the Writings, and the Prophets (Deuteronomy 7:6; Psalm 33:12; Isaiah 41:8–9). Christians also cite scriptural language that identifies them as chosen by God. The New Testament repeats this theme multiple times. The Apostle Paul refers to believers as "a remnant according to God's gracious choice" (Romans 11:5). The Apostle Peter uses the phrase "chosen of God" (Colossians 3:12, New American Standard Bible, 1995).

Centuries later, in the modern context, fundamentalist Christian churches continue to describe themselves as chosen, elect, and the remnant. To illustrate, here is a quotation from one group's official statement of beliefs:

> The universal church is composed of all who truly believe in Christ, but in the last days, a time of widespread apostasy, a *remnant has been called out* [emphasis added] to keep the commandments of God and the faith of Jesus. *This remnant announces* [emphasis added] the arrival of the judgment hour, proclaims salvation through Christ, and heralds the approach of His second advent. (General Conference, 2009)

Behavior Codes

In general, behavioral codes found in the scriptures of major world religions are written broadly, at the level of principles and guidelines. In their original forms, these scriptural codes of conduct are brief and succinct. Some behaviors are prescribed as beneficial, and others are proscribed as harmful. When the codes of major world religions are compared, the similarities are quite striking.

Believers in all three Abrahamic traditions are prohibited from lying, killing, stealing, coveting, and lusting. They are required to honor their parents and care for the needy (Torah, Exodus 20:2–17; New Testament, Matthew 5:21–48; Islam, Qu'ran, 17:22–39).

Buddhist philosophy defines similar ethical norms in the well-known Eightfold Path (Buddha, 1995a). Three of the eight components of the Path directly address ethical conduct. Right Speech is abstaining from false, malicious, harsh, and idle comments. Right Action is abstaining from killing, stealing, and sensual misconduct (Buddha, 1995a, p. 1, 101). Right Livelihood is making a living in occupations that do not harm others or involve manufacturing lethal weapons, making intoxicants, or engaging in cheating (Rahula, 1974, p. 46).

Hinduism's code of conduct has twenty requirements. Ten rules (yamas) regulate personal behavior, such as truthfulness, nonstealing, faithfulness in marriage, patience, compassion, and following health practices (*Hinduism Today* editors, 2007, pp. 338–340).

Notice the general and expansive sweep of these codes of conduct. Adherents of the five religions just cited include 78% of the human population of the earth. It almost goes without saying that if that many people complied with these codes, the nature of international and personal relations would improve dramatically.

And this is where fundamentalists appear to have found a niche. Although they view the ethical codes as absolutes rather than idealistic principles, they also have devoted considerable effort to reifying much longer lists of requirements based on their interpretations of the scriptural codes. These behavioral rules can extend to how members dress, eat, sing, speak, proselytize, parent, read, date, drink, and engage in sexual activity.

In one contemporary Christian church, members are given rules on how to observe a weekly Sabbath: "You should refrain from shopping or participating in other commercial and sporting activities that now commonly desecrate the Sabbath" (*The Commandments*, 2010). Other Christian groups require members to refrain from dancing, playing cards, watching movies, using narcotics, dressing immodestly, listening to rock music, and (for men) not wearing their hair long (Garrett, Hinson, & Tull, 1983). In fundamentalist Judaism, Haredi authorities forbid the use of television and films or the reading of secular newspapers. Regulations are asserted for the use of the Internet. It is forbidden to publish or view photographs of women. One newspaper recently digitally changed a photograph of the Israeli cabinet so that two pictures of female cabinet ministers were replaced with photos of men; another newspaper simply blanked out the women (Papers Alter, 2009).

Here's the point of paying attention to behavioral codes. Fundamentalists in all religious traditions carry a sense of obligation about these detailed expectations regarding their behavior. To understand True Believers, it is not enough to have a general understanding of the Ten Commandments or the Eightfold Path. These codes can be applied in countless ways and enforced with a strong sense of sacred duty. Not knowing some of these details can limit a psychotherapist's awareness of the world in which an authoritarian man lives.

Authoritarian Male Leaders

Religious leaders are often men: emir, bishop, father, imam, pope, and priest. Within fundamentalist groups, the leaders are almost always men. Typically, these men are magnetic, forceful, and solely in charge. They are given high status and have special access to the Divine. They are assumed to have special rights and knowledge. They make important rulings and judgments—on admitting new members, defining proper behavior, and writing statements of truth.

In 1946, just after World War II, sociologist Max Weber emphasized the crucial role of the authoritarian leader as a Messenger from God. He must "personally and actually be the God-willed master" (Weber, 1946, p. 239). It is this perspective that makes the following behaviors more likely (Lalich, 1997; Martin, 2003). Think about what it must be like to *be* an authoritarian man in this context, or to follow one.

- Leaders frequently speak of their own authority and status as Messengers from God, thus claiming the right to command their followers. Loyalty, therefore, is expected. Members may be expected to meet the personal requirements of the leader, such as meeting his financial, emotional, and power needs.
- The claims of divine authority are often supported by unusual or idiosyncratic interpretations of obscure scriptural texts.
- Leaders are final authority on topics of dogma, policy, and behavior. These teachings are not open for discussion or debate. Members who complain about decisions or policies of the leader are identified as problems themselves.
- Secrecy with regard to certain practices, rituals, and teachings may be required.
- Some male leaders coerce sexual activity with female members or force marriages.
- Leaders often try to isolate members from others who do not believe as they do. Opponents are condemned as prejudiced, ignorant, or satanic. Contact with these outsiders is discouraged or forbidden. Violators are subject to punishment or expulsion.

- Doubting members who transgress the rules are dismissed from membership. Family members who remain in the group may be forbidden from contacting the ousted member. This ban may even include speaking at a funeral for a family member who has been expelled (e.g., Watchtower Bible, 1991, p. 103).

Two Caveats

Stepping back from these nine characteristics for a moment: Any fundamentalist group may emphasize some of these characteristics more than others. Editors of *The Fundamentalism Project* have suggested, for example, that the same group can be high in reactivity, selectivity, and dualism, low on messianism, and not include inerrancy. A table of these ratings appears in Almond, Sivan, and Appleby's summary of the project's work (2004b, pp. 414–415). Virtually any combination seems possible, though groupings of markers within the nine characteristics do appear to occur.

Another caveat is the obvious distinction between a man and the group to which he belongs. Just because a man reports that he belongs to a known fundamentalist group does not mean he shares all the beliefs and attitudes of the group. In fact, research shows that men from fundamentalist groups who appear in counselors' offices often have some doubts about their religion's teachings. We'll look more at this reality in the section on therapeutic strategies useful in working with men who are true believers.

AUTHORITARIAN MEN: THE DIVINE APPROVAL

> My Grandmother always told me to make friends with those who search for the truth, but to run for the hills when you meet those who have found it.
>
> —Karen Dawson, (2009, quoted in *An Invitation to Social Construction*, p. 161)

Is there any connection between religious fundamentalism and authoritarianism? Some evidence suggests there is. One study (which defined authoritarianism as the expectation of strict obedience to authority) found a positive correlation between religious orthodoxy and authoritarianism (Beit-Hallahmi & Nevo, 1987). Fundamentalism also has been shown to have associations with other traits consistent with our definition of authoritarianism: dogmatic thinking, the inability to handle ambiguity, and a generally rigid approach to life (Hassan & Khalique, 1981; McNeel & Thorsen, 1985).

More generally, large proportions of men hold distinctly religious views. One carefully administered survey of men in the United States

(Davis & Smith, 2004) reported high levels of agreement with the following statements:

- I find comfort in my religion or spirituality (83.3%).
- I feel guided by God in the midst of daily activities (82.3%).
- I feel God's presence (81.1%).
- I feel God's love for me, directly (77.4%).
- I pray at least once a week (68.8%) or daily (45%).

Another study found that 36.9% of men in North America personally read from the Bible, Qur'an, or Torah at least once a month (Bader, Froese, Johnson, Mencken, & Stark, 2005). More importantly for our purposes, another study reported that many men (38.4%) view these holy books as "the actual word of God" and that they are "to be taken literally, word for word" (Greenberg & Berktold, 2005).

Some of these beliefs you will notice as consistent with the nine traits noted in the first part of this chapter. Of course, accepting these concepts does not make a man guilty of authoritarian behavior toward others. Rather, these views illustrate how acceptance of certain religious teachings *can* serve as a context in which authoritarian ideas can emerge. If a man believes his scripture's words are the actual words of God, then he is more likely to interpret those statements literally and to regard others who see the language as figurative or metaphorical as apostates.

The following ideas illustrate some of these potential connections.

Control: Men Must Take Charge

The first example is the idea that fathers are authorized to take charge of their families. Fully 70% of US men regard themselves in this way, as "heads" of their families (Greenberg & Berktold, 2005). This head-of-household idea evokes the religious metaphor of God being like a father. High percentages of both US men (70.7%) and women (80.1%) say that "father" describes their view of God either very well or somewhat well (Bader et al., 2005). A connection between fatherhood and Godhood is found in both Jewish (Jeremiah 31:9) and Christian (Romans 1:7) scriptures.

Translated, this means that many religious men may view themselves as the rightful heads of their families, just as God is seen as the head of the universe. It can then be a short step to the conclusion that they must have "the final word" in family matters. This link was examined explicitly by one study of 11 religious groups, which reported that this particular view of family roles was affirmed by notable percentages of both men (16.6%) and women (15.4%) (Benson, Williams, and Johnson, 1987).

It is important to note, however, that not all members of major religious traditions view family roles in authoritarian ways. Large numbers take quite different views of fathering roles, emphasizing the equality of rights and responsibilities between parents, and more collaborative styles of family management. Examples are readily available in Jewish thought (Berke, 1996), Christian writing (Van Leeuwen, 2004), and Islamic commentary (Burns, 2007), among others.

Nonegalitarian Views of Women

The scriptures of major faith communities do contain statements that suggest that men and women are not regarded as equal. Though many adherents in these religions interpret these ideas as culturally bound and no longer normative, the words nevertheless appear to support subordination of women.

- *Judaism:* "When you go to war... and you take captives, if you notice among the captives a beautiful woman and are attracted to her, you may take her as your wife" (Deuteronomy 21:10–12).
- *Christianity*: "For the husband is the head of the wife... wives should submit to their husbands in everything" (Ephesians 5:23–25).
- *Islam:* "Men are in charge of women, because Allah hath made the one of them to excel the other, and because they spend of their property for the support of women" (Qur'an IV:34).
- *Hinduism*: "Those who take shelter in Me (Lord Sri Krishna), though they be of lower birth—women, merchants, as well as workers—can approach the supreme destination" (Bhagavad-Gita, Yoga of Mysticism 9:32).

What are we to make of these statements? If a man believes these scriptural words are the literal word of God and without error of any kind, then subordination of women becomes possible. Mistreatment, then, is only an argument away.

Of course, different interpretations of these texts are possible. Nevia Beth Skovill (2011) has shown that all four of these historic religions have developed broader understandings of these comments. She notes the following:

- In Judaism, most precepts in the Torah apply equally to both men and women. Further, the Torah approves of women who do the right thing without male approval. One notable example is the three women who acted heroically when Moses was born—hiding him, getting him adopted, and finding a nursemaid.
- The Christian New Testament also portrays women in prominent roles. Jesus invited women to join his movement, and women are frequently mentioned in the Gospels and Epistles as leaders. One prominent example is the support Jesus gives to Mary, who wanted to study with him rather than assume the traditionally female duties of cooking and serving food (Luke 10:38–42).

- Muslims believe that both men and women are to follow the Five Pillars of their faith, such as praying five times a day, giving to the poor, and fasting during Ramadan. The Qur'an explicitly prohibits killing female infants, gives women the right to inherit, and protects them in marriage. It also declares that men and women are to protect each other (Surah 9:71).
- Many Hindus believe that their faith teaches the equality of men and women. To subordinate women, men would have to deny the unity of all things. Male and female are complementary contributors to the creation of the universe. From this perspective, there is no subordination, no distinction. Rather, there is complementarity.

These latter interpretations do not subordinate women, but present an egalitarian ideal. Although authoritarian men may cite sacred verses that endorse the subordinate treatment of women, their views may be weakened by the broader ideals that appear in those same scriptures.

Power: Men Can Hit Children

How should children be treated when they err? Some fathers believe in the use of pain as a punishment. Most men would deny they are deliberately injuring their children, arguing that their purpose is to teach a lesson, not to harm. But that line can be blurred. Given the above review of nine traits of fundamentalism, it may not be surprising that several studies have found that fundamentalists are more likely than others to use corporal punishment (e.g., Ellison, Bartkowski, & Segal, 1996).

Taking a literalist view of scriptures appears to be the variable most likely to justify corporal punishment (Grasmick, Bursik, & Kimpel, 1991). Certain quotations are interpreted quite literally by Jews (e.g., Proverbs 13:24), and by Christians (Proverbs 13:24; Hebrews 12:6–7). Also influential is the view that parenting is a spiritual role. Those who accept that view are also more likely to engage in the use of corporal punishment (Murray-Swank, Mahoney, & Pargament, 2006). The fact that corporal punishment is largely rejected by social science research is irrelevant to them (Donnelly & Straus, 2005; Schwartz, Hage, Bush, & Burns, 2006).

These ideas—the father is in charge of women, and he can use pain to punish children—are consistent with our concept of the Authoritarian Man. These views encourage the use of power, control, and domination, and explicitly reject egalitarianism.

Counterpoint: Religious Empathy

We shall return to this idea in Chapter 9, but it is useful to note briefly the vast sacred literature that undermines authoritarian behavior. David Lundberg has collected an entire book filled with religiously inspired statements from founders and revered figures in Christianity, Islam,

Judaism, Hinduism, Buddhism, Taoism, and Confucianism. To illustrate, consider statements on the concept of nonjudgmental empathy, a practice not common in authoritarian men (Lundberg, 2010, pp. 287–294):

- Jesus, founder of Christianity: "Why do you look at the speck of sawdust in your brother's eye and pay no attention to the plank in your own eye?... You hypocrite, first take the plank out of your own eye, and then you will see clearly to remove the speck from your brother's eye" (Matthew 7:3–5, New International Version).
- Rabbi Hillel, Judaism, first century, BCE: "Do not judge another until you are in the same position" (Mishnah, Pirklei Abot 2:5).
- Garuda Purana, Hinduism, third to fifth century, CE: "The vicious and the mean observe other's faults, be they so little as the mustard seeds. They see but pretend not to see their own faults as big as bilva fruits" (about the size of a grapefruit) (Garuda Purana 113:57).
- The Buddha, fifth century, BCE: "It is easy to see the flaws of others, hard to see one's own. One exposes the flaws of others as one winnows the chaff, yet hides one's own faults as a cunning fowler [bird hunter] who covers himself" (Dhammapada 18:18).
- Islam, Iman An-Nawawi: "Let him who finds good praise Allah, and let him who finds other than that blame no one but himself" (Forty Hadiths, #23).
- Confucius, Analects, sixth century, BCE: "The gentleman calls attention to the good points in others; he does not call attention to their defects. The small man does just the reverse of this" (Analects 12:16).
- African Traditional Religion, Nigeria, Buji Proverb: "A man holding a basket of eggs does not dance on stones."

Though it is not useful to challenge outright a man who is using religious concepts to justify his authoritarian treatment of others, it can be helpful to know that other views exist within all major faith communities. Sometimes, these ideas can be discussed directly in the psychotherapy room. A man who is struggling with the consequences of concepts he has espoused in his life may be more open to considering additional ideas and texts from his tradition. Consultation with appropriate clergy is crucial.

SUMMARY

The religious ideas summarized in the first section of this chapter range into all domains of human life, including science and technology, education and communications, politics and law, economics, and social life (Marty & Appleby, 1993, 1996). For fundamentalists, views on these matters are not negotiable. They are the truth, the whole truth, and nothing but the truth. New members must accept the teachings, engage in correct behavior, and risk their all for the cause. In so doing, they become True Believers.

Here is the uncomfortable question. Do these nine religious ideas foster authoritarian behavior by men? Consider the concepts, one more time:

1. Things modern and secular must be opposed.
2. Scriptural texts can be used to promote social and political agendas.
3. All persons, behaviors, and ideas are either good or evil.
4. In a messianic way, good must ultimately defeat evil.
5. It is the duty of the good to correct the evil.
6. Every biblical word is a flawless utterance from God.
7. Good people are chosen by God for a special relationship.
8. Interpretations of scriptural ethical codes must be normative for all people.
9. God gives men special powers, rights, and responsibilities.

I hope it is clear how easily these ideas can be (mis)used to justify authoritarian behavior by a man in any religious fundamentalism. An empathic look at this man is useful. Imagine what it must be like for him to believe that God wants him to take charge of his family, to control his children by hitting them (calling it a spanking), and to assume responsibility for the behavior of everyone in his family. Think of the pressures that come with believing that people who disagree with him are evil. Or that he must sign petitions that would turn his scriptural views into governmental law. Or that he must feel unconcerned about the condition of the planet because it faces a messianic ending. These pressures are real and can be used to justify the authoritarian behavior we have been considering. I know this is true. In my psychotherapy room, I have heard men use these very ideas to justify the authoritarian treatment of their wives and children.

These ideas, of course, can divide families. James Naismith is buried near my home. Basketball fans will recognize him as the inventor of the game in 1891. As a young adult, Naismith planned to become a Christian minister and attended a Presbyterian seminary in Canada. But he decided that he could "minister" to young people more effectively through sports, so he went to the YMCA International Training School in Springfield, Massachusetts, to prepare for a career in physical education.

While there, he invented the game of "Basket Ball" to give young men an indoor game to keep them occupied during the winter. From 1898 until his death in 1939, Naismith served the University of Kansas as athletic director, campus chaplain, exercise researcher, and head of the physical education department. Though he remained an active Christian all his life, his decision to leave the ministry created a permanent and sad rift with his sister:

A few years ago, on a visit to my only sister I asked her if she had ever forgiven me for leaving the ministry. She looked seriously at me, shook her head and said, "No Jim, you put your hand to the plow and then turned back." As long as she lived she never witnessed a basketball game, and I believe she was a little ashamed to think that I had been the originator of the game. My sister was very religious.... (Naismith, 1941, p. 129)

Alternatives to the views of Naismith's sister have long been expressed in the arts. Many writers and musicians have decried the use of religious power and domination, and prayed for more religious empathy and egalitarianism. One example closes this chapter: *Parable*, a symphonic oratorio written in 2009. The words and music examine the problem of tolerance faced by all religious faiths. Composed by Robert Aldridge with text by Herschel Garfein, this recent work includes six simple lines that appeal to the empathic and tolerant spirit:

Faith! Faith!
Faith must be stripped of triumph.
Belief must not defeat belief.
When faith is stripped of triumph
We will hear the God of Others speak.
Speak. Speak.
(Aldridge & Garfein, 2010, p. C-24)

CHAPTER
4

"He Is Only Doing What Comes Naturally"
Authoritarian as Adaptive Strategy

> That your Sex are Naturally Tyrannical is a Truth so thoroughly established as to admit of no dispute.
>
> —Abigail Adams, letter to John Adams (March 31, 1776)

MALES AND FEMALES: HOW (OR) DO THEY DIFFER?

Abigail Adams was far more than a wife and mother (wife to the second U.S. president, and mother of the sixth). Though some of her ideas were unorthodox at the time, she made substantial contributions to discussions about the development of the Constitution of the United States. A remarkably forward-looking woman, she wrote carefully reasoned letters to her husband and others, decrying the natural tendencies of men to be authoritarian ("to be tyrants"). While these men were busy designing the new constitution, called the Articles of Confederation, she wrote them a bold letter asking them to set aside their natural tendencies to control and dominate, and instead give property and educational rights to women:

And by the way, in the new code of Laws which I suppose it will be necessary for you to make, I desire you would remember the Ladies, and be more generous and favorable to them than your ancestors. Do not put such unlimited power into the hands of the Husbands. *Remember all Men would be tyrants if they could* [emphasis added]. If particular care and attention is not paid to the Ladies we are determined to foment a Rebellion, and will not hold ourselves bound by any Laws in which we have no voice, or Representation. (Adams, 2004, p. 91)

Abigail Adams's views of males are shared by many: Men are naturally tyrannical. Some researchers believe men have pursued "unlimited power" for a reason. According to these scholars, an explanation for this trait is found in the evolutionary concepts of natural selection and sexual selection. This view deserves significant attention in our quest to understand authoritarian men. We begin with a brief reminder about two striking differences between men and women in our time.

MEET A SCHOLAR

ABIGAIL ADAMS

Men are "naturally tyrannical." So wrote Abigail Adams in a letter to her husband in 1776. What did this eventual wife of a U.S. president mean? The *Oxford English Dictionary* offers clues of how those two words were used in her era. "Naturally" often meant "by the operation of natural laws," such as when "good ground naturally brings forth thistles" (*Oxford*, 1971, p. 1900). And "tyrant" is "anyone who exercises power or authority oppressively, despotically, or cruelly," such as "a man . . . who was the greatest of tyrants to his wife and family" (*Oxford*, 1971, p. 3456).

Plants produce thistles. Men produce tyranny. These events are natural and can be regarded as "innate; not acquired or assumed" (*Oxford*, 1971, p. 1899).

Natural though this tyranny may be, Mrs. Adams strongly opposed its expression. Again and again, she argued against authoritarian control—of King George III over the American Colonies, of Europeans over Africans in America, of religious authorities over parishioners, and (especially) of men over women. For her, men were naturally tyrannical in each of these domains, and their actions must be checked or contested.

Just who was this forward-looking woman?

She received no formal schooling, yet she wrote with great skill. In her time, girls were taught just enough reading to study their Bibles, and just enough mathematics to balance their family budgets. Some girls learned these skills in "dame schools," but most were taught at home. Young Abigail may have grown up in this restrictive mold, but she wasn't permanently shaped by it.

Adams broke the gender role mold of her time. Women were expected to be homebodies, but she ran a large family farming business by herself while her husband was gone for years at a time doing his political duties. Even though women were not given formal schooling or allowed to vote, she wrote prolifically about philosophy and politics. While her husband was the second U.S. President (1797–1801), her thinking and writing received much attention—so much so that critics derided her as Mrs. President (*First Lady*, 2009). However, the criticism never weakened her opposition to authoritarianism wherever she saw it.

She caused a ruckus in 1797 when James, a young African freeman who worked for her in the stables, asked to attend a local school to learn "ciphering." Mrs. Adams approved of the idea and enrolled James, but the father of another student came to her house and objected, saying that if James attended, "other lads" would refuse to attend class because he was black. Abigail was angry, and wrote a letter to her husband:

> This Mr. Faxon is attacking the principle of Liberty and equality of Rights. The Boy is a freeman as much as any of the young Men, and merely because his Face is Black, is he to be denied instruction? How is he to be qualified to procure a livelihood? . . . I have not thought it any disgrace to my self to take him into my parlor and teach him both to read and write. (Letter to John Adams, February 13, 1797, in Kaminiski, 2009, p. 124)

Similarly, she opposed authoritarian interpretations of Scriptures found in religious creeds. On January 3, 1818, she wrote a letter to her daughter-in-law, Louisa Catherine Adams, wondering, "When will Mankind be convinced that true Religion is from the Heart, between Man and his creator, and not the imposition of Man or creeds and tests?" Like many other early Unitarians, she refused to accept the authoritarian interpretations of others, instead feeling "assured that those who fear God and work righteousness shall be accepted of him, and that I presume of what ever sect or persuasion" (Kaminiski, 2009, p. 299).

She also wanted men to break out of their own molds and voluntarily give up their naturally authoritarian ways in the new U.S. Constitution. During their deliberations, she drew up a "List of Female Grievances" and sent them to her husband John Adams, one of the delegates. His response: "I cannot but laugh." But she minced no words in responding to him.

> I can not say that I think you are very generous to the Ladies, for whilst you are proclaiming peace and good will to Men, Emancipating all Nations, you insist upon retaining an absolute power over Wives. But you must remember that Arbitrary power is like most other things which are very hard, very liable to be broken—and notwithstanding all your wise Laws and Maxims we have it in our power not only to free ourselves but to subdue our Masters, and without violence throw both your natural and legal authority at our feet. (Letter to John Adams, May 7, 1776, in Kaminiski, 2009, p. 358)

When Abigail Adams died of typhoid fever in 1818, a young boy in England was nine years old. He would grow up and persuade millions that Abigail's theory has a scientific basis. His name was Charles Darwin, and he reported his findings in a densely written book that sparked debate and outrage: *Origin of Species*.

Longevity

Women live longer than men. That reality has been true for a very long time, in every corner of the globe. Longevity for both women and men has increased dramatically in the last century. Longevity is measured as "life expectancy," a term that predicts how long we will live if current mortality rates do not change in our lifetimes.

In 1900, life expectancy in the United States was 46.3 years for men and 48.3 for women. The gap: 2.0 years in favor of women. Just over 100 years later, a man's life expectancy in the United States had increased to 75.9, and a woman's to 80.9 years, the gap widening to 5.0 years. Today,

TABLE 4.1 Longevity Gap Between Males and Females (2011 estimate)

Country	Gap in years	Males	Females
Russia	13.3	59.8	73.1
Brazil	7.3	69.0	76.3
Japan	6.7	79.0	85.7
European Union	6.4	75.7	82.1
Ethiopia	5.2	53.6	58.8
Australia	5.0	79.4	84.4
Israel	4.4	78.8	83.2
Jordan	2.8	78.7	81.5

Source: Central Intelligence Agency World Factbook, 2011 Estimate.

this female advantage appears in every country that produces reliable health statistics (see Table 4.1 for examples).

It is clear that environmental realities affect longevity. A hundred years ago, many people in the United States and Europe pumped water from sometimes impure wells, breathed air filled with smoke, ate many carbohydrates, lived in damp, crowded, and cold houses, and had little recreational time to spend in the few green parks that were available. Today, by contrast, water and sanitation are efficient, and attention is being given to clean air, healthy food, safe housing, adequate leisure time, and environmentally aware construction. These and similar factors offer a reasonable explanation for the longevity jump of 30 years in just one century.

Longevity is not static, nor is the gap between males and females. Currently, it is narrowing, and rather rapidly so. One statistician at the U.S. Centers for Disease Control and Prevention (CDC) examined present trends and predicted the gender gap could disappear entirely by 2035 (Deaths, 2010). That is only two generations from now.

Nevertheless, an important question remains. Why has there been such a pronounced gender gap? It has occurred in all cultures with adequate records and has continued for generations. Have females lived longer because they are biologically superior to men? Or have males died earlier because they work in more hazardous occupations, break more rules of health, and kill each other more often?

Health

Broken down, the longevity gender gap takes on more substance when the actual causes of death are reviewed. We can start by looking at the top five causes of death in the United States, according to the Centers for Disease Control and Prevention (CDC) (see Table 4.2).

Note that the top five causes of death fit into two categories. Most deaths result from chronic diseases, but a substantial number are caused

TABLE 4.2 Top Five Causes and Numbers of Deaths, United States, 2007

Cause of death	Number of deaths
Heart disease	616,067
Cancer	562,875
Stroke (cerebrovascular diseases)	135,952
Chronic lower respiratory diseases	127,924
External factors (accidents, suicides, homicides)	123,706

Source: Fast Stats: Deaths and Mortality, CDC, 2011.

TABLE 4.3 Percentage Distribution of Top Five Causes of Death, by Age Group

Age group	Death by external factors	Death by chronic disease
Ages 1–24	64%	36%
Ages 25–44	39%	41%
Ages 45–64	6%	94%
Ages 65 and older	0%	100%

Source: National Center for Health Statistics, CDC, Data Brief No. 26, December 2009.

by behavior. Over the lifespan, the proportion of deaths attributable to these two factors changes dramatically (see Table 4.3).

Clearly, younger people are substantially more likely to die of external causes than chronic diseases. For both categories, male mortality rates are higher than female rates. A commonly used statistic is the "age-related death rate." This number shows what mortality rates would be if there were no changes in the age composition of the population from year to year. It is a better measure of gender-related deaths than the actual number of deaths because there are more women in the population, and they live longer than men.

For *all* the top 15 causes of death (81.4% of all deaths), the age-adjusted death rate for males is higher than for females. This includes accidents (traffic, firearms, drowning, fire, poisoning, legal interventions), intentional deaths (suicide, homicide, war), and chronic diseases (heart, cancer, stroke, respiratory, Alzheimer's, kidney, septicemia, and Parkinson's).

In part, the disease rate for males is worsened by their higher rates of engaging in harmful behavior, such as smoking, drinking, and drugging. These behaviors contribute directly to higher death rates for men. It is worth noting that these rates are lowering, according to the CDC, not only because of advances in medical technology but also because of changes in controllable behaviors such as smoking fewer cigarettes, using blood pressure medicines, changing dietary habits, and decreasing blood cholesterol levels (Achievements, 1999).

Even so, the overall age-adjusted death rate for men is 40.8% greater for men than for women (Deaths, 2011). The question is, why? Why is the adjusted death rate higher for men than women, all over the world, regardless of culture? Some thoughtful observers stress the biological contributions to these matters. We turn now to those arguments.

SURVIVING AND REPRODUCING: THE EVOLUTIONARY WAY

Natural Selection

On a rainy day in December, 1831, a young man left Plymouth Harbor in England on a ship named after a dog breed, the HMS Beagle. The winds were calm, but 22-year-old Charles Darwin immediately got seasick and second-guessed his decision to do scientific research aboard the vessel. Captain Robert FitzRoy had put together a crew of 73 men with all the supplies they would need for a very long trip. The plan was to sail to South American and survey the coastline for 2 years. That did not happen. The trip extended to 5 years and produced much more than charts.

While the captain mapped the coastline, Darwin spent most of his time on land. He looked closely at geological formations and talked with local residents about ancient history. And he saw things that puzzled him. He found large bones next to modern seashells. On the Galápagos Islands, he discovered that mockingbirds were different from each other on the various islands. He learned that locals could identify which island a tortoise came from by looking at its shell. Darwin collected many specimens and periodically sent some of them back to Cambridge University in England for analysis.

All during his journey, Darwin made meticulous notes about his observations and started scribbling ideas about what they meant. He brought a huge collection of specimens back to England with him—exotic insects, new plant species, fungi, marine creatures and shells, and many bones. The man was obsessive in his note-taking: 18 volumes of field notes, 4 volumes of zoological notes, 3 volumes of geological notes, and 12 catalogues listing all the specimens (Leff, 2011).

On his return journey home, Darwin began organizing his notes and thoughts. In the meantime, scientists had been examining the specimens he had sent them earlier and were amazed at what he had found. By the time he returned to Cornwall, England, in 1836, he had become a scientific superstar. Darwin was just 27 years old. His fame would only grow as his ideas spread. Eventually, he gave his central theory a name: Natural Selection. Not just scientists, but pliers of almost every academic trade were affected by his findings—theologians, politicians, economists, ethicists, geneticists, and eventually psychologists. Not everyone agreed with him, but everyone had to deal with him. Darwin finally finished his *Origin of Species* in 1859, and the first printing of

1,250 copies sold out in one day. The *Origin*, of course, has become one of the two or three most influential books of all time.

Natural Selection is a rather straightforward theory to outline. Although its tenets are widely known, they are worth reviewing as background for our topic. Here is Darwin's own summary of the idea, from the fourth chapter of his *Origin*:

> If during the long course of ages and under varying conditions of life, organic beings vary at all in the several parts of their organisation, and I think this cannot be disputed; if there be, owing to the high geometrical powers of increase of each species, at some age, season, or year, a severe struggle for life, and this certainly cannot be disputed; then, considering the infinite complexity of the relations of all organic beings to each other and to their conditions of existence, causing an infinite diversity in structure, constitution, and habits, to be advantageous to them, I think it would be a most extraordinary fact if no variation ever had occurred useful to each being's own welfare, in the same way as so many variations have occurred useful to man. But if variations useful to any organic being do occur, assuredly individuals thus characterised will have the best chance of being preserved in the struggle for life; and from the strong principle of inheritance they will tend to produce offspring similarly characterised. This principle of preservation, I have called, for the sake of brevity, Natural Selection. (Darwin, 1859/1962, p. 134)

That paragraph changed the way many 19th century humans thought of themselves. The idea was radical at the time: All forms of life have descended from a common ancestry, over very long periods of time.

Darwin later regretted the term Natural Selection, by the way. On a Friday evening in September of 1860, he wrote a letter to his friend Charles Lyell wondering if the term Natural Preservation would have been more accurate. He noted how someone had complained, "Selection was obviously impossible with plants" (Darwin letter 2931, September 28, 1860).

Darwin's theories were accepted rather quickly, in spite of intensely harsh criticism from opponents. Cartoons put his face on the bodies of monkeys, for example. But by the 1950s, a broadly based consensus among scientists had been achieved (Bowler, 2003). Natural Selection is here to stay. The theory, as you may remember from your early life education, consists of four parts. The illustrative beetle example below comes from the University of California Museum of Paleontology's website, Understanding Evolution.

1. Variation. Organisms in all species vary in appearance and behavior.
   Some beetles in a given environment are green, and some are brown.
2. Reproduction. Most populations produce more individuals than the environment can support, so many individuals die without reproducing.
   Green beetles are eaten by birds more often than brown ones, so the brown ones reproduce more than the green ones.

3. Inheritance. Some traits are heritable and get passed on from parent to offspring.
   Brown beetles reproduce more brown beetles because brown is a genetic trait.
4. Survival. Surviving individuals have certain traits that enable their survival. These traits are contributed to the next generation and become more common in the population.
   Over time, all the beetles in the given environment will tend to be brown.

Does this really occur in the natural world? Apparently so. Darwin and his successors have pointed to many examples. A famous early illustration is the finch population on the Galapagos Islands. After drought periods, the finches developed deeper and stronger beaks that allowed them to eat the tougher seeds available in the drought (Grant & Grant, 2002). But countless examples exist and are readily found in biology textbooks.

Sexual Selection

Twelve years after the publication of *Origin of Species*, Darwin finished his second major book on evolutionary theory. This follow-up book provided his first extended comment on a key question left hanging from his first book: Are human beings a production of evolution? Darwin's answer is suggested in the title of this 1871 book: *The Descent of Man, and Selection in Relation to Sex*. He argued that humans, indeed, have descended through a process he called Sexual Selection. Here is the heart of his explanation:

> Sexual selection depends on the success of certain individuals over others of the same sex, in relation to the propagation of the species; whilst natural selection depends on the success of both sexes, at all ages, in relation to the general conditions of life. The sexual struggle is of two kinds; in the one it is between the individuals of the same sex, generally the males, *in order to drive away or kill their rivals* [emphasis added], the females remaining passive; whilst in the other, the struggle is likewise between the individuals of the same sex, in order to excite or charm those of the opposite sex, generally the females, which no longer remain passive, but select the more agreeable partners. (Darwin, 1871/2007, p. 515)

Darwin further argued that these male tendencies are biological. Over time, males have acquired traits that enable them to select the most desirable mates. These traits are then passed on to generations of offspring. In Darwin's words,

> We may conclude that the greater size, strength, courage, pugnacity, and energy of man, in comparison with woman, were acquired during primeval times, and have subsequently been augmented, chiefly through the contexts of rival males of the possession of the females. (Darwin, 1871/2007, p. 506)

The implications of Darwin's ideas for our topic are clear. Over time, certain traits have become embodied in our modern authoritarian males—powerful, dominating, and exploitive. Tyrannical, as Abigail Adams saw it. These characteristics have been "acquired through the law of battle," Darwin argued (p. 499), and are inherited by offspring of the winners of those battles. Thus, concludes Darwin, "there can hardly be a doubt" that these traits "were acquired through sexual selection, and were transmitted to the male sex alone" (Darwin, 1871/2007, pp. 424, 499).

As we just noted, brown beetles would be more likely to survive than green ones because they blend into earthy brown backgrounds. Birds overlook them and spot the lighter green beetles against the same background. Because the color brown is inherited, brown beetles gradually take over the garden. Likewise, powerful and dominant men are more likely to survive because they can use their superior power, strength, and size to defeat weaker males in battle, and those traits are passed on to offspring. Dead men have a hard time propagating.

Darwin's theory has been extended by his successors. Two ideas are of particular interest to us. One is the notion of "inclusive fitness" (Hamilton, 1964). This concept suggests that individuals behave not only to secure their own personal survival but also the survival of other individuals like them. The greater the similarity between two individuals, the greater the likelihood they will help each other survive. This theory explains the tendency of humans to group together and defend themselves against other groups. Egalitarianism is not valued; group superiority is. Hence, we have another explanation of authoritarian behavior. It is adaptive for groups as well as individuals within groups.

Another extension of the theory is the concept of "parental investment" (Trivers, 1972). Briefly, this term refers to any investment of a parent in an offspring that increases the chances of survival. This investment in one baby can be costly to a parent: There is danger from defending the offspring against hungry predators, there is the potential loss of additional mating possibilities, and merely raising offspring creates a time lag until mating can occur again. This idea of parental investment is found in many creatures on the planet—in birds, mammals, fish, amphibians, reptiles, and invertebrates. Parental investment activities are many. Nests must be built, eggs guarded, food provided, and intruders scared off. All for the purpose of turning offspring into functioning adults who can repeat the reproductive process, over and over.

Trivers suggested that the parent most invested in this process will be more discriminating in mate selection than the other parent. That is, if nurturing and protecting the young is done by females, then the females will be selective, and males will compete for access to females. This male–female ratio of investment in parenting is important in understanding the strength of sexual selection that takes place. It should be noted that some observers have challenged Triver's hypothesis, in that parental investment is not apparent in higher primates (Smuts & Gubernick, 1992).

Nevertheless, the concept illustrates how sexual selection can provide hypotheses about the development of authoritarian males.

Evolutionary explanations for individual and group differences can be easily misunderstood. It is not that natural traits alone produce survivability. Rather, social and cultural features of human history interact with inherited traits. Human behavior responds to both variables. The "nature or nurture" question is not relevant. From an evolutionary perspective, the focus is on how the two interact. But the evolutionary principles of natural selection and sexual selection function in guiding the operation of this interaction.

Or so say Darwin and his successors. Have these ideas held up? We can begin with the question of differences between human males and females.

Sex Differences Are Small and Specialized

Janet Hyde reviewed several dozen meta-analyses of differences between women and men and concluded that we are more alike than different. She called her finding "the gender similarities hypothesis" (Hyde, 2005). The differences that do exist vary mostly by age and context. This conclusion followed an extensive analysis of the studies she grouped into six categories of comparison:

- *Cognitive Variables.* Mathematics, reading, vocabulary, perceptual speed, special ability, spelling, verbal reasoning, abstract reasoning, numerical ability, special relations, speech production, mental rotations, and more
- *Communication.* Interruptions in conversation, talkativeness, affiliative and assertive speech, self-disclosure, smiling, facial expression
- *Social and Personality Variables.* Aggression (physical, verbal, psychological), negotiation, helping behavior, sexual behavior, leadership, and the Big Five personality traits
- *Psychological Well-Being.* Self-esteem, depression, life satisfaction, happiness, and coping
- *Motor Behaviors.* Balance, grip, throwing distance, jumping, sprinting, and flexibility
- *Miscellaneous.* Moral, delayed gratification, cheating, computer use and skill, and job preferences

Altogether, 124 effect sizes were calculated, measuring the differences between men and women. The findings: 37 of the differences were near zero, 59 were small, 19 were moderate, and 9 were large or very large.

Important for our thinking at the moment is this finding: The largest differences between men and women are in motor behavior (throwing distance), followed by sexual behavior and aggression. These variables, of course, are rather consistent with the sexual selection theory we have been considering.

Alice Eagly reports that some differences are not as significant as they might seem, at first glance. She reviewed extensive literature examining the sex difference in just one domain—prosocial behavior; that is, actions that are "helping, sharing, comforting, guiding, rescuing, and defending" (Eagly, 2009, p. 644). She reports that men and women are more alike than different on this variable. But there is a sex difference. It is in how prosocial behavior is expressed, not in the overall levels of the behavior. Men help more by offering assistance to strangers and heroically rescuing others; women help more by offering emotional support and transplanted organs.

She explains how these differential expressions might develop. Across nearly all cultures, gender role expectations call for women to be more "friendly, unselfish, concerned with others, and emotionally expressive," while men are expected to be more "masterful, assertive, competitive, and dominant" (Eagly, 2009, p. 645). The result is that women move more into close relational attachments, and men move more into roles involving power, independence, and leadership. These differences lead to different prosocial behaviors. These differences are supported not only by popular conception, but by abundant research.

The end result sets up the differences we have been addressing in this book. "Men's roles in the workplace tend to place them in positions of higher status or power vis-à-vis the women with whom they interact, conveying expectations of dominance and control" (Eagly, 2009, p. 650). She concludes, "The ultimate origins of male and female roles follow mainly from physical differences between the sexes, especially women's reproductive activities and men's greater size and strength, as these factors interact with the demands of the social structure" (Eagly, 2009, p. 651).

Sex Differences Are Important

Like all living organisms, human beings have survived by adapting skillfully to the environments around them. That is, they have developed traits over time that enable them to take control of the resources necessary for two outcomes: survival itself and the production of offspring. Survival has required the control of land and pastures, food, and medicinal supplies. Production of offspring has required mates. Success for males in these endeavors has come from winning competitions with other males for control of these life-sustaining, life-giving resources. Males have developed tools and weapons to help them win these battles. To the winners go the spoils—they live another day, and they reproduce. The losers do not long survive. They do not parent.

David Geary describes how this sexual selection process works from an evolutionary perspective (Geary, 2010). Though males and females are mostly similar, there are some important differences. Males are more likely to use physical aggression and violence, while females focus on mating and parenting. When many males in a culture have the same traits, they tend to join together and form group structures. Social dominance emerges, with groups of males banding together and regarding themselves as superior to other groups (Sidanius & Pratto 1999).

This ingroup dominance is more common among males than females. It transcends generations, political structures, socioeconomic status, and nations. Men simply endorse social dominance of one group over another more often than women—today, about two of every three men endorse this notion more strongly than the average woman. These men also show more willingness to be sexual with multiple women and express less interest in parenting activities (Sidanius, Pratto, & Bobo, 1996).

Survival, then, has been the fight for control over the basic resources that allow some humans to reproduce, thereby preventing others from doing so. Evolutionary theorists suggest these behavioral tendencies still exist. Consider the ways in which contemporary dictators amass wealth and women for themselves in certain cultures. They survive in these roles by controlling the tools of economic and social control, and they reproduce by controlling the women they desire. They survive as long as they do by exerting power, by dominating others, by exploiting resources, by avoiding empathy, and by defining outgroups as inferior.

Hence, men become authoritarian. Geary (2010) describes several "mechanisms" used to achieve this control over resources: psychological capabilities (such as envisioning winning); working memory (recalling previously successful techniques); emotional reinforcement (victory feels thrilling, defeat agonizing); and behavior techniques (such as the male proneness to aggression).

Males and females interact in ways that perpetuate these patterns. Males become jealous of male competitors and aggressive in protecting their females. They become promiscuous because their investment in parenting functions is short-term. They also become more active, independent, and invulnerable in their provisioning and protecting. Females select high-status males who are skilled at providing food and shelter, thus protecting them during the rigors of pregnancy, bearing, lactating, and nurturing. They become more dependent, vulnerable, and communal.

Evolutionary theory holds that these human traits develop in order to ensure survival and produce offspring. Although adaptive mechanisms originally evolved to address survival needs, they now have become influential in defining the different social roles men and women occupy across many cultures.

Does sexual selection offer an explanation of the differential life spans in men and women? Geary (2010) argues that it does. In the animal kingdom, species differ with regard to how much attention males and females give to pregnancy and childcare. Most of the time, females devote more energy to these matters, but not always. When the differences between males and females are greater with regard to childcare—say, females give much more attention than males—then males compete with each other much more strongly for access to females. Males in these species are larger and stronger, more aggressive and violent, and therefore die earlier. In the few species where the reverse is true (males give more attention to childcare), the reverse pattern exists. It is the females who become larger, more aggressive, and have shorter lifespans. Males and females then adjust to these different social roles.

Biosocial Selection

Some evolutionary scholars have looked at the patterns we have just reviewed and drawn slightly different conclusions. Rather than viewing sex differences in behavior as being governed primarily by evolved sexual selection practices, Alice Eagly and Wendy Wood have developed a biosocial approach that broadens the theory (Eagly & Wood, 1999; Wood & Eagly, 2002, 2010). More specifically, their biosocial approach identifies three contributors to the behavioral differences between men and women. One is biological: Men choose certain occupations because of their greater physical strength, women invest in child rearing because of their wombs and lactating breasts, and both are affected by hormonal processes such as oxytocin, cortisol, and testosterone. A second contributor is the set of social expectations a society develops about appropriate male and female behavior: Men are expected to be more dominant, masterful, and agentic; women are expected to be more nurturing and communal. A third is the role played by individual differences in the degree to which a person internalizes gender identity and the dispositional traits that accompany that awareness.

A biosocial approach acknowledges evolutionary factors we have been reviewing, but views them more in concert with other factors. That is not to say other evolutionary psychologists reject social factors. They do not. But biosocial theorists place a stronger emphasis on the interplay among biological, social, and psychological realities.

Biosocial scientists agree that changes have occurred in human communities over time. Early on, division of labor strategies were based on biological differences. Because men were stronger and bigger, they became hunters and protectors. Because women bore children, they became cooks and nurturers. But in modern societies, many men no longer work in jobs that require upper-body strength, and many women choose to have fewer children, if any at all. Social efficiency has become a more important determinate of sex role behavior than adaptive mechanisms. Collaboration between the sexes becomes more possible, as the ancient division of labor standards are no longer as relevant. Therefore, social roles can become proportionally more influential in sex differences.

If closer male–female cooperation is possible, then why does it not occur more broadly? How do men still end up having more status and power? How do they become more controlling? Biosocial theory suggests the answer is more social structural than biological. That is, assignment of power now depends more on a society's values. When a society values male occupations or military heroism more than female childbearing or childcare, for example, then men are going to be given more status and power than women. And if men are given more power, they are going to exercise it through the social and occupational roles they assume.

Voila! Men can become authoritarian! In their higher-status roles, they can use their power: gaining more and more wealth, becoming controlling of their possessions, dominating competitors who threaten their status, and viewing social groups other than their own as inferior. Meanwhile, women are assigned a status commensurate with a society's valuing of their tasks. While men are accommodating to roles requiring independence, strength, and control, women may be moving into roles more communal and subservient. The behavior of both is affected by the social role expectations they separately face.

These differing social roles influence behavior. Over time in a culture, these role expectations may even become reflected in the dispositions and temperaments of boys and girls. Gendered learning takes place early in life. You will be a provider, or you will be a homemaker. You will be a coal miner like your father, or a teacher like your mother. As children develop, sex-typed behavior consistent with these expectations appears.

Social structuralists emphasize the variety in cultures that have occurred across time. Social organizations are not static. They change in response to many challenges—new political or religious realities, imbalances in the ratio of men to women, and technological advancement in tools available for male or female tasks. All along, each society faces the same basic question: How will the social duties be divided optimally between men and women? For many cultures, biosocial theorists point out that the answer lies in the differential division of labor. It is these differences that drive the sex differences in behavior. Men and women grow up aware of these differences, and feel pressure to conform to them.

So sex differences occur from an interaction of three sets of factors: biological differences in strength and reproductive capacities, societal differences in economic and political structures, and individual differences to the degree in which a person conforms to gendered social role expectations.

The two points of view we have just reviewed—sexual selection and biosocial—can look at the same databases and draw somewhat different conclusions. For example, David Buss published a classic study that examined mate preferences in 37 cultures (Buss, 1989). He used two instruments that listed 13 and 18 different characteristics that a person might value in a potential mate; one instrument asked people to rank the items, and the other to rate them on a scale.

Mostly, Buss found similarities between men and women in the cultures. However, he did find an important difference. Men preferred younger women who were attractive and domestic, while women favored older men with good earning potential. Sample items that illustrate these differences include "good earning capacity," "good housekeeper and cook," and "physically attractive." These differences were explained as understandable from an evolutionary perspective. They are consistent with the sexual selection theory we have just summarized.

Eagly and Wood later examined the same data, focusing on the few sex differences found in the study. These differences had been well-established in research previous to Buss's study. Meta-analyses of studies in the United States had demonstrated that men do indeed look for mates who are physically attractive (younger) and offer strong domestic skills, while women prefer older men with promising earning potential (Powers, 1971). These differences have held up in spite of the overall similarities on most qualities men and women use in choosing mates.

These two researchers wondered if these well-known differences in sexual selection criteria would be narrower in societies that promoted more gender equalities. They reexamined the data in Buss's 37 cultures from this perspective. Would men's preference for youthful women with solid domestic skills be reduced in these more egalitarian cultures? And would women be less focused on older men with greater earning capacity? To answerer this question, they ranked the 37 cultures on gender equality, using data from the United Nations. In these UN measures, gender equality was measured in several ways: proportions of women in management, the professions, and politics; relative incomes of women and men; and degree of access women had to health care, education, and wealth.

The results? As gender equality *increased* across 37 cultures, differences in traditional mate selection criteria *decreased*. Women gave less importance to a man's earning potential, and men ranked domestic skills as less important. The study concluded that the contemporary differences in mate selection criteria for men and women may be less about exclusively evolutionary adaptation, and more about the social roles assigned to men and women. If one is to meet social expectations for gender, then one must prefer mates who meet those expectations. Hence, the male preference for someone with domestic skills, and the female preference for a man with earning potential. However, this age-old separation of duties is fading in more egalitarian cultures. In these settings, if women can meet their own economic needs and men do their own cooking, then the need to find these traits in a potential mate diminishes.

SUMMARY

There are only two kinds of perfectly faultless men, the dead and the deadly.

**—Helen Rowland, American columnist
(1922, *A Guide to Men*, p. 76)**

Evolutionary perspectives offer much in our quest to understand authoritarian behavior. Like most theoretical perspectives, there is variety within this tradition of thought. Most emphasize Darwin's theory of natural selection as the starting point. For this revolutionary thinker, there have been two ultimate purposes of human behavior: survive and reproduce.

In order to accomplish these tasks, males developed both survival skills (hunting, warring, adapting) and reproductive strategies (mating, provisioning). The theory of sexual selection suggests that to gain access to desirable females, males had to compete with other males. They had to demonstrate a convincing capacity to provide the resources necessary for females to bear and raise children. Competition for resources ensued. Males needed to control land for housing, food, and medicinal agents. They needed to develop resources (weapons, allies) to defend and protect their assets. Those with the most skills won. They lived, and they reproduced. The result, as Rowland's witty observation notes, is that we have only two kinds of men: those who are deadly and those who are dead.

The skills to survive and reproduce sound much like our modern Authoritarian Man: power over competitors, control over resources, exploiting others, paying little attention to the distress of others, and supporting the superiority of ones own group over lesser groups.

An important variant on this evolutionary explanation is the biosocial model, which suggests that gender role behavior is affected by differences in three variables: physical attributes (male strength, female reproduction, hormones), social role expectations (assignment of tasks based on sex), and individual differences (personal disposition, degree of internalization of gender identity).

Actually, both models can help us understand authoritarian behavior. What they share in common is a valuing of evolutionary biological explanations for modern male behavior. The basic sex differences we now see fit with both evolutionary and biosocial (or social structural) theory. Both offer explanatory power. Evolutionary ideas provide a survival explanation to authoritarianism. In order to survive and reproduce, men depended on the use of power, domination, and exploitation. And they devalue empathy for their individual competitors and define any competing group of male as inferior, if not threatening. And from the biosocial point of view, males are assigned tasks within a culture. In societies that do not value sexual equalities, men will be assigned greater status and power. They then behave in ways designed to sustain and perpetuate that power—leading, once again, to the increased likelihood of authoritarian behavior.

Actually, helpful as these two views are, the complete picture might be even more complex and nuanced. Next, we shall examine social constructivism.

CHAPTER
5
"He Learned From the Best"
Authoritarian as Social Construction

> Consider...the statements, "The sun always moves," and "The sun never moves," which, though equally true, are at odds with each other.
>
> —Nelson Goodman (1978, *Ways of Worldmaking*, p. 2)

THE CORE OF CONSTRUCTIVISM

What is a rose? A flower, you say. Well, the pink object outside my window is certainly *called* a flower. But this object is not the same for everyone. It depends on who is looking at it. Consider the different experiences of a rose-as-object by a landscaper, a toddler, a groom, a botanist, a photographer, a perfumer, and an abstract painter.

Or, what about you? How are *you* regarded? Well, it depends on who is looking at you. To a barber, you may be a head needing a haircut. To a physician, the fractured ribs in room 3. To a researcher, a mere data point.

Welcome to the world as social constructivists see it. Both words in the term matter. "Social" means that we understand objects in the context of social relationships. We *learn* what roses are. We learn who we are from others in social relationships. "Constructive" means that our realities of rose and self are created, built. We assemble our concepts about life based on our social experiences with others. This presents us with the basic assertion of social constructivism. We create our realities within our frames of reference, so that when we look "out there," we see nothing completely separate from ourselves. Everything we observe is seen "back here," in our minds.

Lest you think this is mere philosophical play, consider the ramifications. This perspective suggests that *all* our concepts are constructed (theories, assumptions, explanations, classification systems, philosophies). It goes on to argue that even our prized scientific observations are constructed. Half a century ago, Thomas Kuhn launched a revolution in theoretical science by arguing that "what a man sees depends both upon what he looks at and also upon what his previous visual-conceptual experience has taught him to see" (1962/1970, p. 113). Even the "facts" of science are interpreted by subjective observers. It also suggests that we construct our understandings of human traits, as well. That is, we create categories to explain ourselves to each other—gender, age, personality, role, family, occupation, ethnicity, and so much more.

The implication for our topic is clear. Are the concepts of "authoritarian" and "man" social constructions? Do they come from cultural, familial, political, or religious systems of thought? In this chapter, we will take a closer look at this theory of constructivism, and then apply it to our joining of two concepts: authoritarian and man.

It is challenging to summarize the constructivist perspective, in part because it is so old. It goes back at least 2,500 years, in both Eastern and Western cultures. In the East, Lao Tzu (1999) and the Buddha wrote about the power of the mind to construct. Both men argued that nothing in the universe is permanent. Everything changes. Each moment is new, and then gone. So change is not a possibility, but an inevitability. For these two ancient sages, this ever-changing reality is constructed in the mind. "Mind is the forerunner of all actions. All deeds are led by mind, created by mind" (Buddha, 1995a, p. 1).

In the West, Greek philosopher Heraclitus wrote during the same century as the Buddha and made a similar point. Plato later quoted Heraclitus's now-famous metaphor about never being able to step into the same river twice: "As they step into the same rivers, other and still other waters flow upon them" (Heraclitus, Fragment 41, cited in Kahn, 1979, p. 166). It is not only the water that changes in the river. A man who crosses the river is changed in some way, as well. We always are under construction—deconstructing, reconstructing. Even the most rigid among us is changing. Every 7 years, even our bodies have reconstituted themselves.

In modern times, the list of constructivist thinkers is impressive: Alfred Adler, Albert Bandura, Viktor Frankl, William James, George Kelly, Jean Piaget, and many more. One luminary is my late professor of psychotherapy, Michael J. Mahoney. He suggested that five themes summarize the essence of constructivism.

We Create

Life is not a passive event. It is active. We create the shape and sound of our lives. Every day, we make choices. How will we respond? What will we say? How will we move? We are not pawns; we initiate the moves. This does not mean we are not influenced by outside events. It is quite the opposite. All construction occurs in the context of socializing with others. We assess what we hear and see, make sense of it, and decide how to think or proceed. Some concepts are constructions that affect the lives of large numbers of people. Consider these ideas:

- Might makes right.
- They did it, and all of them are responsible.
- Let us send them food, water, and medicines.
- This island belongs to us, and to us alone.
- We can negotiate a middle ground.
- That government is pure evil.
- All groups should have equal opportunity.
- Women must submit to their husbands' sexual desires.

These ideas reflect the breadth of our human constructs. None of them is inherently true and universally obvious to everyone. We have choices about what we think, and our thoughts lead to actions that create pain or joy, division or reconciliation.

Every day, we add to the creation of our lives. We paint with our thoughts. We sing with our feelings. We dance through our conversations. The result is an ever-expanding panorama. We call the story "My Life." People in the arts understand this connection between art and life. Their observations apply to so much more than their particular artistic skill: acting, writing, painting, or dancing. Consider the words of people highly skilled in those five professions:

- Actor Alan Alda: "The creative is the place where no one else has ever been. You have to leave the city of your comfort and go into the wilderness of your intuition. You can't get there by bus, only by hard work and risk and by not quite knowing what you're doing, but what you'll discover will be wonderful. What you'll discover will be yourself" (*Things I Overheard While Talking to Myself*, 2007. pp. 21–22).
- Writer Henry David Thoreau: "The world is but a canvas to the imagination" (*A Week on the Concord and Merrimack Rivers*, 1849/1985, p. 238).
- Painter Pablo Picasso: "God is really another artist. He invented the giraffe, the elephant, and the cat. He has no real style. He just goes on trying other things" (Richardson, 2007, *A Life of Picasso*, p. 464).

- Dancer Martha Graham: "There is only one of you in all time, this expression is unique. And if you block it, it will never exist through any other medium and it will be lost" (de Mille, *Martha*, 1992, p. 264).

We Organize

We constantly look to make sense of the world, to create order from disorder and patterns from disarray. The sheer volume of incoming information nudges us to organize. As children, we develop rudimentary understandings of how water flows, fathers talk, and clarinets sound. We define concepts such as nationality, sport, and uncle. Subsequent information on these topics is placed in appropriate bins of thought and experience. Once we learn something, we tend to rely on it, defend it. Understandably, our daily thoughts and actions become routine. Some of our realities dip out of current awareness as we tend to new data, new emotions, and new people. But our learning remains in the background, ready to influence our interpretation of whatever we see and hear. Slowly, often with resistance, we fit new experiences into our ever-expanding network of orderly patterns. We organize because we *can*. We are agents that construct.

> First comes thought; then organization of that thought, into ideas and plans; then transformation of those plans into reality. The beginning, as you will observe, is in your imagination.
>
> —Napoleon Hill (1928/2008, *The Law of Success*, p. 210)

We Individuate

Birth only begins the separation process. All through childhood, we are testing our own ideas against those around us. How are my thoughts like yours? How am I different? This is my opinion, what is yours? How much disagreement is there between us? Where are my boundaries? How am I autonomous, unique?

Change in these areas is constant and inevitable, and so we are more process than product, more developing than developed. But the press is toward individuation, identity. We are social, yet we seek individuality in our social worlds. Note again that the change is dynamic and social, not simply solitary. Our sense of self is created in the living context of shared conversations and experiences. What happens around us influences us. What happens to us changes us. Individuation makes sense only in the context of the larger groups in which we love.

When this process works well, we can say what we think to others. We can express what we feel. We know our boundaries. We make decisions. We choose friends carefully. We take in information from many sources: families, teachers, artists and musicians, peers, religious officials, scientists, and sports heroes. Yet we make up our own minds from this wealth of social information. We mull an idea over, test it, and draw conclusions. When this is happening, we are individuating.

None of this is easy. It is a difficult and years-long process. We have everyday terms that describe the goal: becoming our true self, finding our inner self. Not isolating from others, but becoming and remaining an individual while engaging with others.

We Relate

We are born of relationships and never outgrow them. We learn from our interactions, right from the beginning. Every caregiver's glance matters. It becomes part of what is known. New events are interpreted in light of old ones. New learning is layered on old ideas. This construction of ideas, concepts, and theories is a social activity. We draw from the accumulation of experiential knowledge. The well of resources is deep. Over time, it becomes impossible to identify what is unique and original in the immense data mass we possess. Every thought seems colored by what has preceded it. Creativity may be little more than a skillful rearranging of old patterns in new ways. An idea becomes our own, or so we think. But the list of contributors to the concept becomes impossible to acknowledge. So much social information slips into the backstory and goes silent. Not impotent, but silent. It waits until the time is right to help make sense of a new moment or person.

Our learning relies on many social symbols: words, sounds, drawings, and technologies. We really cannot divorce ourselves from these symbols. We relate to others through them. Especially important are the stories we tell. Some of them cross millennia, like the man who can never step into the same river twice. Ethnic and religious groups have used myths in so many ways: to create community cohesion, to sooth children, to warn of risk, and to inspire courageous actions.

Some of the stories are personal and represent our own journeys. We create these stories by putting daily events into clusters. Every incident gets filed in some cluster of similar experiences or incidents. We have the mother cluster, the school cluster, the religion cluster, and so on. Numerous clusters. Together, they form the content of our personal stories. We use many symbols in the story-telling process: visual memories, conversation fragments, song lyrics, fragrances, and narratives. All of them tell us about ourselves by reminding us of our interactions with others we have known.

> Selves can only exist in definite relationships to other selves. No hard-and-fast line can be drawn between our own selves and the selves of others, since our own selves exist and enter as such into

our experience only in so far as the selves of others exist and enter as such into our experience also.

—George Herbert Mead (1934, *Mind, Self, and Society*, p. 164)

We Develop

Every decision and action over the course of life makes sense in some way. Even the odd, harmful, or self-sabotaging action somehow seems like the best thing to do at the moment. Always, we are doing our best as life moves along and changes. Development is not always smooth. There are traps and unexpected pitfalls. Disappointments occur. Losses can disorient. Depression can linger. Sometimes we are resilient, and sometimes not. We constantly make sense of what has happened, find new ways of thinking about it, incorporate the untoward event, and move on. Sometimes this is not so easy. We can become mired in physical pain, emotional flatness, or relational isolation. These conditions can last a long time and debilitate us.

At all times, however, we are looking to move development along: to construct change, organize information, generate independence, strengthen a relationship. We are self-developing and self-evolving all through life. The change process is rarely, if ever, linear. It lurches along, pauses for a while, or drifts sideways. It oscillates. We get stuck. We repeat old habits, hoping for better outcomes. Sometimes we leap ahead with a startling new insight.

Development involves all aspects of our being: our changing body size, our sleeping and eating patterns, our injuries and illnesses, our mating and parenting, and our aging and dying. Not even death, however, is immune from this desire for continued development. We use many symbolic phrases to sustain the hope that we shall continue to develop. We speak of going to heaven, being reincarnated, living on in the memories of our children, or leaving our footprints behind. One man told me, "I have an agreement with my alma mater. I have promised them a large amount of money on one condition. That they hang my picture on the wall of the Department. The agreement even defines the size of the picture, and it will be large."

What does the constructivist perspective contribute to our understanding of authoritarian men? This idea: men *learn* how the world works from their social interactions. Important questions are addressed all through childhood. Will I use my developing power to control others, or to nurture them? Will I manage the world around me by following authorities, or by challenging them? Will I dominate or negotiate? Be manipulative or genuine? Exploitive or empathic? How shall I think about groups different from my own? Answers to all these questions are constructed over time, in social contexts, and in ever-evolving ways.

The rest of this chapter is a constructivist sketch of how this happens: how a boy learns and practices his version of authoritarian/masculine behavior.

CONSTRUCTION OF AUTHORITARIAN TRAITS

The Child is Father of the Man

My heart leaps up when I behold
A rainbow in the sky:
So was it when my life began;
So is it now I am a man;
So be it when I shall grow old,
Or let me die!
The Child is father of the Man;
I could wish my days to be
Bound each to each by natural piety.

—William Wordsworth
(1802, "My Heart Leaps Up When I Behold")

Wordsworth's line is now an adage, but is it true? Does knowing about a boy's childhood really predict anything useful about his adulthood? In a word, yes. Evidence is now abundant. Personality traits identified early in life predict an adult's personality structure. Neurobiological studies have shown that childhood maltreatment results in measurable brain problems and psychiatric symptoms. Developmental studies have shown that abusive parenting interferes with the normal developmental processes of children, while secure and supportive parenting promotes the development of adaptive personality traits (Johnson, Bromley, & McGeoch, 2009). Here are some findings from the research.

Childhood Abuse and Adulthood Personality Disorders

Physical abuse affects personality development. Adults diagnosed with antisocial personality disorder are more likely to report physically abusive childhoods (Bierer et al., 2003; Norden, Klein, Donaldson, Pepper, & Klein, 1995). In particular, these physically abused boys show higher levels of aggressive, criminal, or antisocial behavior as men (Pollock et al., 1990).

Sexual abuse also has an effect on personality development. Adults with histrionic and narcissistic personality disorders report more childhood sexual abuse than would be expected by chance (Norden et al., 1995). They also have more interpersonal problems than others (Browne & Finkelhor, 1986). The levels of histrionic personality disorder traits remained after other variables were controlled, such as parental psychiatric disorders or other forms of abuse.

Emotional abuse is associated with adult personality disorders, too. These children are more likely to become paranoid (Bernstein, Stein, & Handelsman, 1998) and have problems with low self-esteem and suicidality (Mullen, Martin, Anderson, Romans, & Herbison, 1996). The deeply damaging nature of emotional abuse increases the risk for narcissistic, obsessive-compulsive, and paranoid personality disorders, both in adolescence and adulthood (Johnson et al., 2001; Tyrka, Wyche, Kelly, Price, & Carpenter, 2009).

Childhood neglect also correlates with higher levels of problematic personality traits, including antisocial, hostile, paranoid, and self-destructive behavior (Dubo, Zanarini, Lewis, & Williams, 1997). Neglect is associated with more narcissistic and paranoid personality traits (Johnson, Cohen, Brown, Smailes, & Bernstein, 1999).

I've cited several personality traits associated with childhood abuse, especially narcissism, obsessive-compulsiveness, and histrionic behavior. These are not the only personality variables associated with abuse. But they are consistent with other research showing them to be central to the authoritarian profile. I summarized some of that research in Chapter 2, and I will have more to say about it in a moment. First, here is a closer look at a study demonstrating this important link between childhood experiences and adulthood personality traits.

The Dunedin Study

In 1975, researchers divided a group of more than 1,000 New Zealand children into five groups, based on a series of behavioral assessments (Caspi, 2000). The groups were named Undercontrolled, Inhibited, Well Adjusted, Confident, and Reserved. All the children were 3 years old at the time the study began, and they were assessed again when they reached the ages of 5, 7, 9, 11, 13, 16, 18, 21 . . . all the way up to age 32, most recently.

Researchers found that personality traits identified at age 3 predicted personality structure and behavior in early adulthood. For example, the Undercontrolled group was filled mostly with boys. Their "emotional responses" at age three were "impulsive, restless, negativistic, distractible, and labile" (Caspi, 2000, p. 160). At age 18, they described themselves as "reckless and careless (low self-control) and said they enjoyed dangerous and exciting activities (low harm avoidance). They said that they enjoyed causing discomfort to other persons (high aggression), yet they also reported feeling mistreated, deceived, and betrayed by others (high alienation)" (Caspi, 2000, p. 161).

By age 21, these previously undercontrolled 3-year-olds had many problems. Compared to the well-adjusted group, their interpersonal relationships were poor, their social support networks were weak, they were more likely to be unemployed, they had more diagnosed psychiatric disorders, and they were more likely to have engaged in antisocial behavior such as theft, assault, and vandalism (Caspi, 2000).

By the age of 32, this large sample of children had revealed even more impressive links between childhood and adulthood. Poor self-control traits at age 3 predicted problems with "physical health, substance dependence, personal finances, and criminal offending outcomes" (Moffitt et al., 2011, p. 2, 693). These findings endured, regardless of intelligence, social class, or adolescent mistakes.

Other findings from this ongoing series of studies are germane to our interests, all of them demonstrating the strong relationship between identifiable problems in early childhood and documented problems in adulthood.

- Children with "inadequate parenting, neurocognitive problems, and temperament and behavior problems" became adults with higher rates of delinquent behavior (Moffitt & Caspi, 2001, p. 355).
- Children with self-control problems became adults with higher rates of violence toward others, excessive perception of threat, more conduct disorders, more antisocial behavior in general, and more obsessive-compulsiveness (Arseneault, Moffitt, Caspi, Taylor, & Silva, 2000).
- Higher childhood rates of aggression predicted higher rates of male-to-female partner violence (Moffitt & Caspi, 1999) and more violence toward women and children, generally.
- Early childhood antisocial behavior predicted more adult personality problems (impulsive, psychopathic and antisocial), more aggression and property offenses, more mental-health problems, more financial problems, more anxiety and depression, and more social isolation (Moffitt, Caspi, Harrington, & Milne, 2002).
- A diagnosis of childhood conduct disorder predicted more work-related problems as young adults: use of prohibited work materials, conflicts with bosses, arguments and fights at work, committing offenses that could get them fired, stealing money or other items from work, damaging work property, and coming to work drunk or on drugs (Roberts, Harms, Caspi, & Moffitt, 2007).

What sets these findings apart from other studies is that they are prospective. Data was gathered as it occurred throughout childhood, not retrospectively. With more than a touch of irony, the principal author of these studies concludes, "The child thus becomes the father of the man," at the $p < .05$ level (Caspi, 2000, p. 170).

It appears that the memories of authoritarian men I shall cite in a moment are not randomly recalled. Rather, they point to the likelihood that their personality traits began early in life and continued into adulthood. Unless something unusual and emotionally powerful occurs (e.g., serendipitous events, accumulated failures, trauma, or intensive treatment), the likelihood of these personality traits remaining in place appears to be high.

Does the New Zealand study mean personality variables *cannot* change in childhood? No. Caspi notes that some events appear to shift the trajectory of personality development, including "stochastic events," "fortuitous chance encounters," and "differential opportunities." Furthermore, "parental interventions can generate 'lawful' or predictable discontinuities in early development." How can these two ideas be congruent: the enduring nature of personality characteristics and the ever-present possibility of change? "In the early years of life, person–environment covariation occurs because of the joint transmission of *genes and culture* [emphasis added] from parents to offspring" (Caspi, 2000, p. 170).

Childhood Abuse and Adult Relational Problems

We have just reviewed studies that demonstrate a strong link between early life personality traits and adult life relational distress. What accounts for this? Do events in childhood influence this developmental process? The answer appears to be yes. Allan Schore at University of California, Los Angeles has summarized much of this research (about 2,000 studies, in all) in a trilogy of book-length reviews (Schore, 1994, 2003a, 2003b). He summarized a central theme in this work:

> Events that occur during infancy, especially the transactions with the social environment, are indelibly imprinted into the structures that are maturing the first year of life. The child's first relationship ... acts as template, as it permanently molds the individual's capacities to enter into all emotional relationships. (Schore, 1994, p. 3)

Schore's conclusion is reached in a step-by-step review of the literature.

1. **Two brains develop early in life, each with its own function.** Evidence shows that each of the two hemispheres can function on its own and develops its own ability to perceive, to use language, and to engage in motoric activity (Kaplan & Zaidel, 2001). For most people, the left hemisphere deals with conscious behavior and is more verbal in making sense of incoming information. The right side seems to contain more unconscious information and works with more nonverbal and emotional information. Put another way, the left hemisphere creates an explicit version of the self, and the right hemisphere generates an implicit version (Faust, Kravetz, & Nativ-Safrai, 2004). This means that some of our anxieties and hopes regarding our caregivers are conscious, but some are more out of awareness (De Gelder, Morris, & Dolan, 2005).
2. **The right hemisphere dominates the sense of self for approximately the first 2 years.** The right brain is more dominant at the beginning of life and is fully responsible for developing a coherent and ongoing sense of self (Devinsky, 2000). So, the right brain is

the driver from a few weeks prior to birth, all the way until the second year, when the left hemisphere catches up (Trevarthen, 1996). Men, therefore, begin life with strong emotions. In fact, the limbic system dominates the first couple of years of development. These emotions are intense and allow a boy to adapt to the environment. Incoming information comes from outside himself, but also from sensations in his own body. This early version of the limbic system is connected to both the sympathetic and the parasympathetic parts of the autonomic nervous system that generates the body awareness of emotions (Schore, 2006).

3. **An infant's ability to process and manage emotions is learned through interactions with the primary caregiver.** It seems reasonable to argue that a new human being begins life with one paramount task: to learn how to communicate with the outside world. This process is shaped dramatically by the interactions of the young boy with his caregiver. The child learns how to be "in tune" with his mother or other caregiver. Schore (2003a) explains:

> In this mutually attuned dynamic system, the crescendos and decrescendos of the infant's psychobiological state are in resonance with similar states of crescendos and decrescendos, cross-modally, of the mother. Consequently, both experience a state transition as they move together from a state of neutral affect and arousal to one of heightened positive emotion and high arousal. (p. 39)

An infant takes it all in: sounds, gestures, words, facial expressions, types of touch. Everything a caregiver does communicates something. It follows that a caregiver's emotional accessibility becomes crucial in the emotional connection that develops between the two of them. Attachment occurs and functions like a glue that holds together the developing sense of self in the new boy. He is not just an infant. He is an infant-in-relationship (Miller et al., 2001).

This explains how a boy's emotional development occurs. When the attachment process goes well (secure, settled, connected, safe), then his emotional life will proceed normally. When it does not, emotional distress becomes prominent, and the ability of the boy to attach safely with his caregiver is compromised (Bowlby, 1980). The implications are enormous. The more a boy learns to manage his emotions as a child, the broader will be his emotional competence as an adult (LeDoux, 2000).

4. **An infant's ability to regulate emotions is located in the right hemisphere.** Emotional regulation is a neurobiological event. When the newborn–caregiver connection is functioning well, self-regulatory skills develop in identifiable brain circuits that are established and maintained (Ovtscharoff & Braun, 2001). In case you are neurologically interested, positron emission tomography (PET) reveals

that infants as young as 2 months old show activation of the right fusiform gyrus of the inferior temporal cortex (the visual areas that decodes facial patterns) and in the occipital cortex (Tzourio-Mazoyer et al., 2002). Magnetic resonance imaging (MRI) has found corresponding responses in primary caregivers who look at videos of their infants. The right anterior inferior temporal cortex lights up (this is where facial emotional recognition and expression occurs), and also the right occipital gyrus (involved with visual familiarity) (Ranote et al., 2004).

Emotional regulation includes the notion of resilience. Can an infant bounce back from disappointment or frustration? Yes, if the caregiver can model resilience (Fosha, 2003). If a primary caregiver says or does something that distresses the infant, then that same caregiver can repair the disruption, allowing the infant to resume an attuned relationship. This experience is critically important for the infant's development of resilience. "... (R)e-experiencing positive affect following negative experience may teach a child that negativity can be endured and conquered" (Malatesta-Magai, 1991, p. 218).

The emotional connection between caregiver and infant is striking, and it is evident in unexpected behavior. Sieratzki and Woll (1996, 2004) describe a nearly universal preference for mothers to cradle infants on the left. This is true for both hearing and deaf mothers, both right-handed and left-handed. This practice allows the mother's emotional signals to go into the infant's free left ear and become processed by the infant's emotionally attuned right brain. Men, by the way, show no innate preference, but when they become fathers, 80% of them cradle on the left.

5. **Distressful events influence a child's emotional responses well into adulthood.** Chronic childhood distress impairs the ability to develop functional coping skills. Adult mental health problems follow. However, if a child experiences moderate stressors early in life and learns how to deal with them, then his adult life may be protected from some of the adverse effects of these early life events. When this bond works well, emotion regulatory skills are observed and learned, and the chance of stress-related disorders is reduced (Parker, Buckmaster, Schatzberg, & Lyons, 2004).

Effective management of intense emotions for a child requires the presence of a caregiver who can identify with the infant's responses to events, and then be able to respond in ways that sooth the child and meet appropriate needs. In turn, the child learns how to deal with his own stress and manage it with skill (Murray, 1991).

Child–caregiver connections, of course, can be positive or negative. If positive, then a secure and safe attachment forms. But if separation, loss, or other ruptures occur, then the connection can become negative. Either way, emotions create "a permanent trace" in the developing network of a child's neurons. This network can

either improve or limit the functional capacity of the brain to deal with stressors later in life (Helmeke, Poeggel, & Braun, 2001).
6. **Short-term consequences of childhood trauma.** It is now indisputable that early life trauma affects subsequent adult behavior. Schore (2006) defines abuse in more subtle ways than is common. It occurs, for example, when a caregiver does not play with the infant, induces distressing emotions that endure, provides little interactive repair, or exposes the child to others who may be abusive.

Two potential consequences can occur. One possibility is hyperarousal, with strongly increased heart rate, blood pressure, and respiration. When no reassurance or repair occurs in the moment, hyperarousal can escalate into screaming and even vomiting (Beebe, 2000).

The other possible outcome is dissociation, in which the child simply disconnects from the world. All contact seems broken, and the infant looks off into space, apparently paying little attention to surrounding events. This process includes numbing, avoidance, overcompliance, and restricted emotional responsiveness. A metabolic shutdown occurs. The vagal tone increases dramatically, lowering blood pressure and heart rate. This is the defensive strategy of last resort for a child (Beebe, 2000). Damage is more severe when the abuse is inflicted by a caregiver and is repetitive. Then, the child is not only trapped, but without a reliable protector. It is common at that point for a child to disconnect from outer reality and turn inward. Dissociation becomes easy, organized, and functional.

Infants can oscillate between these two states: hyperarousal and dissociation. Long-term consequences are profound. Four of every five infants treated in this way develop an attachment pattern that is insecure, disorganized, and disoriented (Schore, 2006).
7. **Long-term consequences of early life trauma.** One enduring outcome is a person's inability to adequately regulate intense emotions. Early life relational trauma makes it virtually inevitable that a boy-turned-man will have considerable difficulty regulating his emotions. His actions will be more reflexive than reflective. His emotional needs will seem unbearably intense and in need of immediate attention. The absence of emotional self-regulatory skills is present in most psychological disorders. Personality impairments follow naturally (Taylor, Bagby, & Parker, 1997).

If a boy underregulates his emotions in childhood, then the resulting psychological difficulties are more externalizing. When they are overregulated, the disturbances are more internalizing. In either case, the deficit is observed in the inability to emotionally recover from relational stressors in timely and self-soothing ways (Schore, 2006).

These deficits are neurological. The normal developmental process of programmed cell death (apoptosis) is compromised.

Formation of the myelin sheath around nerve fibers may be delayed. Neurogenesis, the process by which new neurons are generated, may be inhibited (De Bellis et al., 2002). These neurological events contribute directly to a man's later inability to regulate his own emotions. Severe personality problems result (Schore, 2006).

8. **Damage from early life relational disruption is severe, but it can be treated.** Much more about this reality will appear in Part II, but for now, the point can be made succinctly. Psychotherapy produces detectable changes to the brain (Etkin, Pittenger, Polan, & Kandel, 2005). This occurs when a secure relationship forms between psychotherapist and an authoritarian man. In this relationship, an authoritarian man can learn to modulate his emotions and develop self-regulatory skills. It now appears that the biological changes occur in the right brain, largely out of the awareness of the client in the relationship. This change is not novel to one type of psychotherapy, as virtually all of them promote some level of emotional management. The salient contributor to therapeutic success is the collaborative relationship itself. That is what activates this learning.

When psychotherapy is working well, the therapist's emotions are expressed clearly, kindly, and respectfully. Conversations are initiated to repair any emotional disruption that may occur between the two of them. This therapeutic connection is the core of emotional change (Horvath & Greenberg, 1994).

In effect, the therapeutic relationship becomes a new attachment for the man. It is often the first secure attachment he has *ever* had. Again, this idea will be developed in much more detail in Chapters 7 and 10.

Authoritarian Childhoods: Some Qualitative Observations

A child's trust
Once lost
Not easily regained
A loving eye
Turned away
How painful to behold
What can be done
To heal
An ever growing rift
Joy and merriment
Now turned to silence
Louder by the day

—Kenneth R. Kaufman
(2010, "Silence," *Families, Systems, & Health*, 28(1), p. 75)

Information in this section brings to life the research just cited. The following clinical observations have emerged over the course of more than 150 therapist-years of experience in working with authoritarian men in two U.S. treatment centers: the Menninger Clinic and the Professional Renewal Center® (PRC), both in Kansas. Each day, our team of professionals at PRC devotes 90 minutes to clinical discussions about the authoritarian men currently in our intensive day treatment program. What are their psychosocial histories? What childhood memories do they recall? Which adult maladaptive behaviors appear in their childhood recollections? What do they see as important during their therapeutic treatments? From literally thousands of hours of these conversations, we have developed an understanding of common patterns and behaviors in the early lives of these men (B. W. Williams, S. Khamphadky-Brown, S. Frieswyk, S. Campbell, R. Krehbiel, J. Burd, P. Parks, J. Lewis, C. Kumar, personal communications, various dates).

We have found three principal commonalities in the childhoods of the authoritarian men we have treated. All describe their interactions with others—their fathers, their mothers, and their peers. One caution at the outset. These memories are typical, but each man's story is his own. Men do offer memories that are more pleasant than those that follow, but happy events typically do not stand out in the larger cascade of their early life memories. Altered slightly to protect identities, these memories are very much true-to-life. They also are tough to read.

Fathers

Virtually without exception, the authoritarian men we treat report deeply troubled relationships with their fathers. The trouble takes many forms. Some describe extended absences: fathers who worked away from home for weeks at a time, spent months in military service in other countries, or temporarily separated from the family because of marital incompatibility. Other men report (often with considerable shame) that their fathers were convicted of crimes that sent them to prison for months or years. A smaller, but significant, number of men were bereaved at an early age when their fathers died unexpectedly. Accidents at work, suicides, or terminal illnesses ended their fathers' lives prematurely.

Stories of paternal abuse are common—physical and emotional. Men also tell stories about the chaos created by fathers with significant addiction histories: the emotional unpredictability, the financial instability, the occasional violence, and the tirades. The overwhelming presence of a disturbed (and unaddressed) relationship with a father is routine in working with these distressed men.

Taken together, the following composite memories create a realistic picture of what authoritarian men routinely acknowledge in treatment. I have heard hundreds of similar stories. Believe me, these 7 samples are representative, not outliers.

- "My father was very religious, and he preceded each beating with the question, 'Why am I punishing you?' I had to give the right answer, word for word: 'You discipline me because God wants me to obey you.' Then the beating could begin. If I didn't say the words just right, the beating was more severe."

- "My father was a police officer who always wore a belt with metal tips around the house. We always kept an eye on him, because the slightest infraction would lead to that belt being whipped into use. Those metal parts would leave welts. I think I spent more of my child wearing those welts than not wearing them. That's what I used to say to my brother. 'Are you still wearing your welts?' It got so I hardly noticed the pain."

- "I used to be terrified at report card time. I had to bring perfect grades home, but they were never good enough for my father. I once brought home a test paper for mathematics with a score of 85%. My God, I thought he would burn the house down. He was furious with me, but also was mad at my mother because she was supposed to make sure I got perfect grades. I felt terrible that my mistakes got her in trouble, too."

- "The verbal lashings for a mistake would go on for days. I once forgot to take my English book to school, and for weeks, he would hide it at home so I had to look for it. He thought that would make me remember. It didn't work, and I grew to hate him for it."

- (This next story was told with much laughter, as though it were a comedy sketch.) "I remember once my father grabbing me and throwing me across the room. My head hit the window and broke it. Then he blamed me for breaking the window. It was hilarious!"

- "My mother apparently had great pain at my birth, and seemed to be in pain all through my childhood. Something was always wrong with her back. My father told me it all started when I was born. He'd tell me that my bad behavior started before I was even born, and my mother was still suffering from it."

Again, although these painful memories about fathers appear universally in our sample, they are not the only experiences men remember. A man will recall his father laughing on a holiday, walking down the street to a candy shop, or attending an occasional school activity. But these happy events are described as exceptional, and often with the plaintive wish that they could have occurred more frequently.

Some men have written intense poems about these experiences. Here is an example of the impact of a father's early death. The author was at the time just 8 years old. Forty years later, he reviewed the impact of this loss:

No Answer

as the sun eclipsed the mood on the day of death:
"my God, my God, why did you leave me?"
but no one answered:
nor the God who made eternal laws
neither his father working with tools in his carpentry shop
and Dad's death
silenced spiritually, emotionally, physically
his youthful sons into:
fragile insecurities
awkward misidentifications
addictive idealizations
guilt and mistrust
pervasive resentments
masturbatory narcissism
with dissociated burdens of inner shame

(Faul, 2009, p. 62)

Mothers

Mothers of our authoritarian men show some similarities, as well. As wives, their task has been to figure out ways of relating to the fathers we have just described. Typically, this has not been an easy task. They have tried to fill in the gaps for the parenting deficiencies of their husbands. We routinely ask men to think carefully about their mothers and recall what it was like to interact with them. The technique for gathering these memories (*Summary of Themes from Early Life*) is described in detail in the chapter on assessment.

To get along with their husbands, these women have engaged in behavior best described as passive, passive aggressive, and dependent. A few are outright aggressive, as well. Above all, they focus their attention on their children. Mothers are recalled by authoritarian men as being doting on them in protective ways, calling them special, and catering to their every need. In some ways, they attach more to their children than their husbands. Memories along these lines are many and sometimes dramatic as the following composite memories demonstrate.

- "My mother dressed me as a prince every Halloween. She sewed a new costume for me each year, but it was only a new version of the same old role. I remember my favorite outfit was a long vest with, tight pants, a sword, and this really cool crown. And that's the way she treated me. I could do no wrong for her, and no matter what I did, she took my side. I think she still has all those costumes hanging in her basement."

- "When I was small, maybe 6 or 8 years old, my bedroom was like something out of a fantasy movie. My mother made everything in that room, paintings on the wall, drapes hanging from the ceiling, and really elaborate spaces where I could hide. I even had my own little cabinet for snacks. I used to hide in there when my father got drunk. My mother and I would play games in there, and read books. It was great. I was the Golden Boy in her life, that's for sure. Life was great when I was around her. It was the rest of life that sucked."

- "My mother was a very anxious woman. I always thought we were together, just the two of us. We both were afraid all the time. We plotted ways to avoid my father's anger. Well, now that I think about it, it was us two against every one else in the world. I could do no wrong at school. If I messed up and got in trouble, my mother always took my side. It didn't matter what I did."

- "My mother died when I was 14 years old. I was devastated. She was all I had, my only protector. My father said funerals were too expensive, and so he got her cremated and he dumped her ashes in a lake. There was no ceremony or anything. No funeral. And that was the end of it. My father never spoke of her again. But I was devastated."

- "My favorite memory of childhood is breakfasts. My father was always asleep at that hour, so Mom and I would talk about happy things. Just the two of us. We never talked about his drinking. She always wanted me to be happy, and said I could do anything I wanted in the world. 'You don't have to be held back by anything,' she would say. I really believed her, too. She loved me more than anything else in the world, even herself, I think."

- "My mother used to hold me and sing songs to me every night. She would make up songs about all my wonderful talents, and how great I would be in the world. I remember the words of one song she made up: 'Born to be the Pres-i-dent, the best one ever sent.' The crazy thing is that I actually believed her for a while."

- "My mother was always my refuge. I went back home last year, and went out to her grave. It was not well maintained, and I got very depressed. This woman saved my life many times, and the cemetery couldn't even keep the grounds nice. But that's the way her life was. She always got the raw end of things in life. I feel so sad for her, now that I've grown up. I never appreciated her when I was young. I just thought she was weak. But she gave me my great self-confidence. She was such a hermit, but paid so much attention to me. I owe all my great success in life to her."

Men in our sample have described their mothers with many metaphors, such as "the only safe blanket I could hold onto as a child," "my great shield against my father's rages," and "the true life of our family." This special treatment has an effect. Men have described themselves with unabashed narcissism. "I am one of the greatest American success stories ever told." "I am a gift from God to my patients." "I am always the smartest person in the room." "I expect my employees to meet my needs, and if they don't,

I throw them out." Comments such as these are made without a trace of hesitation and with no awareness of how they might sound to others.

Not all mothers of authoritarian men have fit this role, of course. Some mothers are themselves authoritarian and distant from their children. A few others are described in ways that suggest minimal disturbance. But by far the prevailing behaviors include passivity, passive-aggressiveness, and dependence. And their sons-who-become-authoritarians are the focus of much devotional attention.

Bullying

Most authoritarian men recall many incidents of being bullied. They remember feeling humiliated, beaten, ridiculed, mocked, shamed, and denigrated. Initially, many of these stories are shared with the treatment team more as a performance, complete with practiced one-liners. Men appear to distance themselves from the abuse in order to avoid the pain that comes from acknowledging the awful realities they have experienced. Again, a few examples animate this picture.

- "I was always the smallest boy in class. I was only 110 pounds when I finished high school, and teased unmercifully. I had panic attacks, and was scared all the time. Even girls would push me around in the hallway. They'd knock my textbooks out of my hands and laugh hysterically. I couldn't help myself because I was so small. The only time I asked a teacher for help he said, 'Boy, you've just got to learn to protect yourself.' The only relief I had was alcohol, which I started using when I was 12 years old. My parents' wine cellar was a real treasure chest."
- "I was ridiculed in junior high school. My body didn't develop as fast as the other boys, and they mocked my size in gym class. They would throw my underwear around the basketball court, trying to make it hang on the basket. It was awful. I ended up staying home all the time when I wasn't at school. I hated to go out of the house because I might see a bully. So I just played a lot of video games. I really liked the games about revenge."
- "I used to like the Curious George books, because he got into so much trouble, yet always came out fine in the end. It never happened that way with me, but I liked the idea that it might happen. My earliest memory of my father is of him chasing my brother and me in the backyard and down the street, waving a paddle he used all the time to hit us. I remember wishing I could run as fast as a monkey."
- "The big thing in my childhood was my glasses. It was great sport for the other boys to try and rip them off and thrown them across the room. The teachers' tried to stop it, but they couldn't watch me all the time. I don't know how many pairs of glasses were broken that way. My parents kept talking to the school about it, but

nothing seemed to change. I starting wearing contacts, and I think I still wear them to get away from those memories."

It is useful to return to the notion of prototypes described in the first chapter. These childhood memories about fathers, mothers, and bullies are representative descriptions of the prototypical authoritarian men in our center. Not every man acknowledges or identifies with these descriptions of distant fathers, overly doting mothers, and mean peers. Some men's stories are closer to these prototypical childhood experiences, and some are out on the edges. Some men minimize the importance of the painful memories and prefer to emphasize the happy ones. That is the nature of qualitative data.

Verification of these patterns comes from both standardized test data and the converging observations of mental health professionals trained in multiple disciplines: psychology, psychiatry, social work, psychiatric nursing, and psychophysiology. How this data is obtained will be summarized in the chapter on assessment.

One critically important caveat must be emphasized: Not every abused boy becomes an authoritarian man. Not by any means. Others become men who withdraw, numb, avoid, or achieve at high levels. Some are resilient. The constructivist explanation is more general: Authoritarian adulthoods are constructed from materials provided in childhood. Very often, those adulthoods are built on experiences such as those we have just reviewed.

The Unhappy Conclusion

What, then, do we make of all this? For just a moment, look through the eyes of a boy in a dysfunctional family. He has learned three lessons, as Virginia Satir (1972) put it: Don't trust, don't feel, and don't talk about it. If a boy cannot *trust* anyone, then why not use coercion and manipulation to control his world? If he cannot acknowledge his own *feelings*, then why should he empathize with emotional distress in others? And if he does *talk* about his inner struggles in ways that leave him feeling understood, then how can he understand others who speak of being harmed by mistreatment or prejudice?

To such boys, authoritarian tendencies become appealing, sometimes with overwhelming force. Nobody will control me. I will not feel vulnerable. People will not take advantage of me. I will not share information others can use to hurt me. These views seem reasonable to wounded boys, if not inevitable. What else can such a boy think? His father is unpredictably violent. His mother cannot protect him. His school is a warzone where he is bullied for years. Life truly is unpredictable and unsafe for him. Missing are the secure relationships from which he can experientially *learn* about trust, emotional competency, empathy, and egalitarian ideals. Without those experiences, he becomes susceptible to joining authoritarian causes that promise revenge or redemption.

CONSTRUCTION OF MASCULINITY TRAITS

> Masculine norms are communicated to males when they observe that other males tend not to wear pink, when they are told that 'big boys don't cry,' and when they observe that male movie stars and sports heroes are tough and respond with violence when challenged.
>
> —Jim Mahalik, psychologist and researcher (2003, p. 3)

These unhappy themes are reinforced by yet another set of social messages. It is time to wade into the world of masculine socialization.

We humans are born male and female, but not masculine and feminine. The former is a biological difference (sex), and the latter is a social distinction (gender). A social constructivist position is that gender is not an inevitable result of sex, but rather it is dependent on historical and relational forces. Masculinity norms, then, are constructed in social contexts. Boys learn what men do by watching them, listening to them, and imitating them.

These gender norms occur as a result of countless choices made by a community of human beings over an extended period of time (Berger & Luckmann, 1966). In this approach, changes in gender norms are expected to occur. As evidence, observers have referred to the dramatic changes in masculinity constructs that have occurred in North American and European cultures in the last several decades. So many communal events have occurred. Men have been expected to fight in world wars, respond supportively to more women in the workplace, participate in easy divorce procedures, and become more emotionally accessible. Options for "being a man" have mushroomed. Just think, for example, of the diverse ways men can father. They can be unmarried fathers, step fathers, divorced fathers, gay fathers, distant fathers, or refrain from fatherhood at all. These gender role choices differ dramatically from those faced by earlier generations of men. The implication is that each adult man may "construct" his own masculinity, thus making active choices about which gender role expectations he will adopt for himself (Levant & Pollack, 1995).

A burgeoning literature has used social constructivist approaches in understanding many aspects of masculinity. Note, for example, the thousands of citations compiled by Flood (2011) and made available online. Nearly 40 categories organize the academic research about men and masculinity—from violence and pornography to culture and epistemology. Highly skilled researchers are examining a wide variety of influences and experiences in men's lives. A division of the American Psychological Association is called the Society for the Psychological Study of Men and Masculinity. The society's scholarly journal, *Psychology of Men and Masculinity*, is winning praise and being cited in many literature reviews for publishing articles from a social constructivist perspective. This rapidly growing body of work demonstrates that multiple masculinities exist because multiple cultures and subcultures exist. Each human community presents its boys with expectations for their behavior, simply because they are male.

Identifying Masculine Social Norms

So what are the socialized expectations men face? Although cultures vary, some themes transcend most ethnicities. Jim Mahalik and his colleagues (2000) identified gender-related social norms among North American men, many of which are prominent in other cultures, as well. A glance at these norms suggests links between socialized masculinity norms and common authoritarian behaviors.

A series of several psychometric studies identified 11 norms: winning, emotional control, risk-taking, violence, dominance, playboy behavior, self-reliance, primacy of work, power over women, disdain for homosexuals, and pursuit of status. Mahalik's group (Mahalik et al., 2003) defined these traits in the Conformity to Masculine Norms Inventory (CMNI). The technical properties of this instrument are strong, and it has been used for many subsequent studies.

Do the masculinity social norms identified in this research have any relationship to our definition of the Authoritarian Man? Yes. Research has correlated the CMNI with the Social Dominance Orientation Scale, the instrument we discussed back in Chapter 2 (Pratto et al., 1994). Results show positive associations between authoritarian Social Dominators and total scores of the CMNI. Authoritarians endorse many of the masculine social norms identified by the CMNI. Which ones, in particular? Their endorsement of the need to maintain emotional control, their justification of violence, their willingness to use power in their relationships with women, and their pursuit of playboy behavior.

The CMNI also correlates positively with the Aggression Questionnaire. Men who score high on aggressiveness also are likely to engage in behavior that emphasizes winning over others, emotional control, power over women, dominance over others, self-reliance, and a disdain for homosexuals. The stronger a man's adherence to these masculinity norms, the more likely he is to be aggressive.

It appears, then, that the pursuit of these culturally derived and sanctioned social norms for men can lead to actions that match our definition of authoritarianism. These men are controlling, aggressive, domineering, and power-directed toward those they regard as weaker (in this case, women and homosexuals).

Costs of Masculine Social Norms

Men who accept these masculine norms pay a price, as they often find themselves in conflict with others. What happens to the emotions they do not express? How can they make friends with other men while avoiding expressions of warmth and fondness? What if they are uncomfortable with the demands to be successful, powerful, and competitive? These questions have been examined. James O'Neil at the University of Connecticut developed the Gender Role Conflict Scale in 1986 (O'Neil, Helms, Gable, David, & Wrightsman, 1986). Men who adhere to the social norms just described struggle with personality problems, nonegalitarian attitudes, relational conflicts, power and control issues, and poor marriages. This literature will be reviewed in more detail in Chapter 8.

Another review of the research by Cochran and Rabinowitz (2000, p. 85) catalogues more details of the gender role strain produced in men who live by these socialized masculinity norms. In a word, they become depressed, but in a uniquely masculine way. Here are some areas in which they may struggle:

- Interpersonal distance and conflict in their interactions with others
- Anger in their relationships
- A tendency to withdraw from social contact
- Problems with self-esteem and self-respect
- Problems created by the misuse of alcohol and other drugs
- An inability to cry when feeling intense emotion
- The development of maladaptive personality traits (especially antisocial, narcissistic, and compulsive patterns)
- Disruptions in their sexual behavior
- A tendency to complain about somatic distress and discomfort
- Numerous conflicts at work
- Difficulties with concentration and motivation

Another important social cost is the pain these men create in the lives of the women who live with them. Traditional social norms for masculinity lead directly to an expectation that women must be subordinate (Yllö, 2007). Above all, men do not wish to appear feminine (O'Neil et al., 1986). Too much emotional sensitivity, vulnerability, or dependency on women produces shame and low self-esteem. This mix contributes to a context in which men can become violent toward women (Jennings & Murphy, 2000). The link is direct. Men who engage in partner violence with women show lower self-esteem and higher dependency needs than men who are not violent. Instead, they confuse the idea of being strong *for* women with being strong *toward* women (Dobash & Dobash, 1998).

Authoritarian behavior is reinforcing. In the short term, a man who engages in aggressive control of women is more likely to get what he wants. His fearful, compliant, and dependent partner tries hard to meet his demands. The problems come when his expectations are not met. His problematic traits emerge: I am in charge. You must do as I say. It is my duty to help you. You are not equal to me.

MEET A SCHOLAR-CLINICIAN

JIM O'NEIL

Jim O'Neil has devoted his entire career to understanding the psychology of men and masculinities. His point of view has been clear. Male describes the sex, and man describes the gender. The former is apparent at birth, and the latter emerges throughout the lifespan. That is because gender role norms are learned, O'Neil asserts. His seminal and much cited paper in 1981 launched a program of research that has examined both the content and impact of traditional masculine ideologies (O'Neil, 1981).

Regarding content, he has defined traditional Western masculinity as a set of core ideas that generate stress for men: avoidance of anything distinctly feminine or homosexual; pursuit of success, power, competition, and control; restriction of emotionality; and the inevitability of conflict between work and family. With regard to impact, O'Neil developed an empirical scale that measures the stress of adhering to these values. The instrument has been used in about 300 separate peer-reviewed studies. The harmful effects of trying to live by these values are well established in this body of literature.

Over his 30-year career, Jim O'Neil has followed his original work with more than 100 articles and books that address aspects of the authoritarian profile identified in this book: abuse of power, psychological violence, partner abuse, men's violence toward women, and emotional restrictiveness. He has continued to offer theoretical pieces that broaden our understanding of gendered social learning; the impact of culture, race, and sex on masculinities; and more.

Because of his social constructionist perspective, O'Neil believes that maladaptive behavior can be changed. What men have learned about gender role norms can be unlearned and relearned. New models of normative masculinity can be identified and practiced. He has developed an empirical measure based on the observation that gender role norms change over time. In his model, a man's "gender role journey" begins with "acceptance of traditional gender roles," and can be followed by "gender role ambivalence, confusion, anger, and fear," and finally by a "personal-professional activism." This latter phase integrates gender role values that directly counter authoritarianism: empathy, egalitarianism, and social justice (O'Neil et al., 1993). O'Neil's expertise in these matters has placed him on the editorial boards of eight different scholarly journals that publish gender-related research.

It might seem that a body of work as influential as Jim's would have been quickly accepted by scholars. It was not.

> There was very little support in my university setting in the late 1970s when I began to explore men's gender role conflicts. Some thought I was gay because I was "interested" in men. Others were threatened because I was exposing the patriarchal system that enslaves us all. Women had mixed reactions to my ideas. Some radical feminists dismissed me without even any dialogue. More moderate feminists, who were able to get past their anger at men, thought there might be some value in men studying themselves. Yet, even these feminists wondered whether I was trying to justify men's sexism and explain away men's violence against women. The opposite was true: I wanted to really understand the sources of men's sexism and violence against women. Those were lonely and difficult days for me, not only for these political reasons, but because I was starting my own gender role journey, discovering my own pain from my sexist socialization. (O'Neil & Good, 2002)

In the context of his prominent and productive role in scholarly circles, Jim's history of generosity and commitment to new scholars is extraordinary. When I first contacted him as a graduate student, academia still depended more on paper documents than electronic attachments. Nevertheless, he sent back to me a 200-page packet listing scholarly references, with articles he thought especially relevant for my research question marked with a yellow highlighter. The thoroughness of his response startled me; I was an anonymous graduate student at a university on the other side of the United States. But since then, I have heard numerous graduate students tell similar stories at national conferences of psychologists. Jim *lives* a new psychology of male behavior: compassionate, collaborative, straightforward, empathic, and egalitarian—the exact converse of authoritarian thought and behavior.

SUMMARY: AUTHORITARIAN AS SOCIAL CONSTRUCTION

What is real in the universe? Social constructivists have a short answer. Reality is *constructed* in the context of our *social* relationships. What we see is truly what we get. Everything from pinecones to politics is seen through our own eyes, and those eyes are influenced by the social worlds in which we live. Construction is accomplished in several ways: We create, organize, individuate, relate, and develop all through life. In every arena, our construction of "what is real" occurs in the context of our social experiences with others. Even the "facts" of science are identified and interpreted in socially constructed ways. What is orthodox for one generation of scientists is challenged, revised, or discarded by the next.

Implication #1: Authoritarian traits are constructed. When boyhoods are damaged by severe mistreatment, adulthoods suffer. Boys can be abused in many ways: physical violence, sexual coercion, emotional torment, and neglect. The results are predictable. Research shows they tend to engage in narcissistic, obsessive, histrionic, or antisocial behavior, as we noted in Chapter 2. They risk becoming authoritarian. These personality traits can be identified very early in life and strengthen through childhood. Social constructivists emphasize the role of social learning in the construction of these personality variables.

Qualitative observations reveal striking similarities in the childhoods of authoritarian men. Their social worlds were not ideal. Most suffered from the fathering, mothering, and bullying they experienced. Typically, their fathers found fathering to be difficult. Virtually all the authoritarian men I have treated recall their son–father relationships as marred in some way—by violence, addictions, extended absences, unresponsiveness, emotional neglect, explosiveness, incapacity, chronic mood problems, suicidal talk or actions, or constant pain. Just one of these patterns is harmful; living with several of them (say, unresponsiveness and explosiveness) makes matters worse.

Authoritarian men recall their mothers as overly protective, excessively doting, emotionally dependent, often passive, and occasionally aggressive. As one man put it, "She thought I hung the moon, and could do no wrong. I could get away with anything." Another recalled, "My mother was closer to me than she was to my father." These boys also suffer bullying at very high rates. Recollections of hurtful incidents come easily and generate agitation, sadness, shame, and anxiety. Evidence that these early life problems linger into adulthood is very strong. Neurological evidence of the long-lasting effects is growing exponentially.

This is the social world in which boys become authoritarian men. They *learn* to be more reactive than responsive, more disconnected than connected, more unsettled than settled, and more insecure than secure. It is not a great start to life. They cope the best way they can, and some of those boyhood attempts become personality traits that reach the level of impairment as adults. Chronically unsuccessful attempts to feel self-confident can lead to narcissism. Growing up feeling unsafe can produce obsessive, controlling, and domineering behavior. Years of resisting unfair boundaries and restrictions can make adult antisocial behavior more likely. Thwarted attempts to express emotions and opinions can lead to histrionic expressions of need.

Implication #2: Masculinity traits are constructed. Boys *learn* how to become men. As they grow up, they make choices about masculine role behaviors they observe—which ones they accept, and which ones they reject. Biological sex differences are present from the beginning, but social norms for gender behavior develop over many years. Men now have multiple options in defining themselves as men. Various masculinity behaviors can be tried out, revised, rejected, or retained. All of these choices are made in the context of a man's social interactions with others—what he admires or despises in other men, what he hears from women, and what he sees portrayed in the arts, business, politics, sports, and religion. Men construct their blueprints for masculinity when they are young, yet retain the right to modify the plans as their lives change in adulthood.

That last point is a good way to end this chapter. Concepts and practices of both "authoritarian" and "man" *can* be altered. Part II offers many suggestions on how this change might be fostered.

Section I Summary

PUTTING IT ALL TOGETHER

What are we to make of these four explanations of authoritarian men? It is my view that these perspectives all contribute important information to clinicians. Each approach seems to describe one important part of the whole. There is no need to view them as mutually exclusive competitors for the title of the "right view." In working clinically with authoritarian men, I have found it useful to keep all four perspectives in the background of my awareness. A brief review of the four literatures we have examined is in order.

The personality literature provides us with useful and measurable descriptions of how authoritarian men think, feel, and behave. Research reveals much about these men. Authoritarian *followers* are conventional in their views of social and political issues, submissive to established authorities in their societies, and likely to be aggressive in support of those views. Authoritarian *leaders* believe superior groups (to which they belong) have a right to control and dominate inferior groups. We reviewed studies that diagnose these men as narcissistic, obsessive, histrionic, and very defensive. And we have identified personality traits in the Five Factor Model associated with both authoritarian followers and leaders.

Some authoritarian men are highly religious. Clinicians can benefit from understanding the rationale that supports their religiosity. Teachings in fundamentalist faith communities around the world share many similarities. They strongly oppose modern thoughts and practices, view most issues as being good or evil, and regard their scriptural language as inerrant. They believe that God has given men special rights and responsibilities. These views provide a divine mandate that supports the authoritarian ideas found in many fundamentalist families and societies: men must be in charge, women must be subordinate to men, and children can be hit as a form of punishment. Think of these thoughts and behaviors as a menu from which religious authoritarians choose, because not every man espouses each of these beliefs.

Evolutionary scientists argue that contemporary male and female behavior is the result of adaptation over time. All behavior has been driven by the motivation to survive, and success in that task requires the ability to control the resources that sustain life. This perspective also offers an explanation for differences between male and female reproductive strategies. Historically, women have selected men who are most able to provide for them and their offspring and who have social high status. This approach protects their vulnerability while they are pregnant and lactating. Simultaneously, males see other males as potential threats and competitors for their females and offspring. Males therefore have become exploitive, willing to take important resources from other men in order to support themselves, their female mates, and their offspring. Males also become controlling of their female mates, restricting their access to power, resources, and sexual activities with other men. While many of these sexual selection strategies may seem less evident or relevant at this point in history, they still fuel tendencies consistent with authoritarian behavior: the pursuit of power, domination of relationships, and nonegalitarian views of outgroups.

The social constructivist literature examines authoritarian behavior in the context of relationships and environments. It is "social" because we learn how to behave in our social interactions with others. It is "constructive" because each man creates his own realities. All human concepts, then, are viewed as social constructions: our theories about life, our social norms, our views of appropriate gender behavior, and our religious and philosophical views. So men learn to be domineering, exploitive, and nonempathic. And they construct lives that demonstrate those behaviors. Social constructivists support their views by referring to positive statistical correlations between childhood abuse and adulthood personality disorders, between early life trauma and brain development, and between troubled childhood experiences with fathers/mothers/bullies and adulthood authoritarian behavior. Social constructionists agree that authoritarian behavior is not intractable. Rather, it can be deconstructed and reconstructed in less authoritarian ways.

How do these four approaches interact? How much of a man's authoritarian behavior is the result of stable factors within him, such as personality traits or evolutionary realities? And how much is influenced by factors in his outside world, such as religious teachings and gender role expectations? Researchers are examining these questions and producing some interesting findings. I will cite just one illustrative study.

One research group examined this question studying a sample of twins born in Canada and Germany (Jang, McCrae, Angleitner, Riemann, & Livesley, 1998). The sample included 618 monozygotic twins (from a single fertilized ovum) and 380 dizygotic twins (from two fertilized ovums sharing the same uterus). Recall that the theory of the Five Factor Model of personality defines 30 facets distributed among the five factors. The theory views the five factors as biologically based tendencies. However, the theory also holds that these tendencies are internal and cannot be measured directly, so they are observed as culturally influenced behaviors such as habits, practices, and preferences. The tendencies are internal factors, and the behaviors are external factors. Therefore, a man's social environment does not instill his genetic tendencies but does affect his thoughts and behavior. Evidence that supports this theory is found in these large groups of twins. Biometric structural equation models were used to estimate how much of a person's total variance comes from genetic influences (directly from parent to child) and from nonshared environmental influences (events experienced by just one child in the family, such as trauma or extended illness). The study examined all 30 facets in the Five Factor Model.

Findings showed that about 25% of the variance in the 30 facets of personality is heritable. The rest comes from nonshared environmental influences, such as differences in the ways parents treat each child or from other events that occur to individual children in the family. So each authoritarian man appears to be influenced by both inherited tendencies and socially constructed views and actions.

The study reported how much of each contribution was found for all 30 facets. For each of the personality traits associated with high scores on authoritarian measures (see Chapter 2), I will cite two numbers from the twin study. The first number refers to the percentage of that trait attributable to genetic influences, and the second is the percentage attributable to nonshared environmental influences. Authoritarian *followers and dominators are low* on being open to: fantasy (.40, .60), aesthetics (.46, .54), feelings (.31, .69), trying new actions (.44, .56), exploring new values (.38, .62), trusting others (.37, .63), and being empathic (.34, .66). In addition, authoritarian *followers (but not dominators) are low* on impulsiveness (.37, .63) and on accepting new ideas (.49, .51). And finally, authoritarian *dominators (but not followers) are low* on relational warmth (.40, .60), straightforwardness (.31, .69), altruism (.27, .73), and compliance (.38, .62).

Notice that for each one of those authoritarian traits, the second number is larger than the first. Translation: Nonshared environmental influences account for more of the traits than additive genetic factors. But both contribute.

John Saxe wrote an English poem published in 1873 that provides a well-known metaphor for thinking about these internal and external influences on men. Six blind men described an elephant based on what they touched. In the language of the poem, they concluded that an elephant "is very like a wall" (side), "very like a spear" (tusk), "very like a snake" (trunk), "very like a tree" (leg), "very like a fan" (ear), and "very like a rope" (tail) (Saxe, 1873, pp. 77, 78). All six men were right. But none saw the entire elephant.

SECTION

II

Managing Authoritarian Men in the Psychotherapy Room

CHAPTER
6

"I Never Wanted to Be This Way"

Up Close and Personal: Two Authoritarian Men

> First of all, people are much more unhappy than one thinks... and then, the fundamental fact is that *there's no such thing as a grown-up person.*
>
> —Andrè Malraux (1968, *Anti-Memoirs*, p. 1)

An Authoritarian Man is not who he thinks he is. He is what he hides: his troubled childhood. Andrè Malraux was an astute observer of the human condition, both as a provocative novelist (*La Condition Humaine*) and as French Minister of Culture under Charles De Gaulle following World War II. The above comment is from Malraux's memoir. He was quoting a parish priest who responded to the question, "What has confession taught you about men?" The priest's answer summarized his 15 years of listening to confessions about the foibles of others: the truly grown-up person is a myth.

After listening to countless men talk about their lives in my psychotherapy room, I think I understand some of what the priest meant. Although adults by age, authoritarian men often relate to others more like children than grown-ups. The priest's comment hints at a reason for this: When men cannot grow up with relational security and emotional awareness, they are unhappy. As men, they remain deeply and steadfastly unhappy. They may have become adults, but they remain unhappy children. Only their bodies have grown up. Troubled boys do have dreams of becoming happy adults. But when they grow up, their dreams may be all they have left—especially the dream of feeling relationally close to another: trusting, secure, and safe.

Dostoevsky published a short story about this disillusionment in 1848. An unnamed and lonely man walks the streets of St. Petersburg at night, imagining friendships that do not exist. Dostoevsky lets us peek inside the thinking of this forlorn man, as he recalls his childhood hopes for meaningful connections with others. His ideals of "manhood" are disappearing:

> They are being shattered into fragments, into dust; if there is no other life, one must build one from the fragments. And meanwhile the soul longs and craves for something else! And in vain, the dreamer rakes over his old dreams, as though seeking a spark among the embers, to fan them into flame, and to warm his chilled heart by the rekindled fire, and to rouse up in it again all that was so sweet, that touched his heart, that set his blood boiling, drew tears to his eyes, and so luxuriously deceived him! (Dostoevsky, 1918, p. 22)

As we noted in Chapter 5, an authoritarian man struggles all his life to build a secure relational life "from the fragments" of his dreams. From the beginning, he has sought stability. But no human connection has felt fully protected and enduring. Nobody can be trusted—not parents, siblings, friends, romantic partners, supervisors, or subordinates. The disillusionment among authoritarian men is intense. They feel cheated, misled, isolated, and resentful. It is their distressing relational history that forms a context in which they form their beliefs about themselves and the world around them, and it leads to their maladaptive behavior.

How do these beliefs translate into presenting problems in the psychotherapy room? I have kept a log of problems presented by these men in my office. One fruitful question has been, "When people comment on problems in your behavior, what do they say? What are some phrases you have heard?" Here are some representative answers. "They say that I . . ."

Have poor emotional control	Don't tolerate incompetence
Would rather fight than negotiate	Am suspicious of others
Am explosive	Yell at subordinates
Think I am always right	Seem grandiose about my accomplishments
Have poor communication skills	Don't listen well
Act like a bully	Am too demanding and impatient
Take things personally	Curse others too much
Treat others unfairly	Act like administration is the enemy
Don't have good self-care	Criticize and demean my subordinates
Work too much	Get too physical, nudging or pushing others

"I Never Wanted to Be This Way"

Do as I please	Blame everyone else for my problems
Make too many assumptions	Ignore people trying to help me
Seem isolated and lonely	Try to control everyone around me
Act like I am owed	Cannot admit my own errors
Drive others away with anger	Don't use support from others well
Am emotionally exhausted	Think nobody is as skilled as me

In this short chapter, I want to introduce you to two men who illustrate the powerful link between childhood experiences and adult authoritarian behavior. We will follow them through their assessment and treatment in the next few chapters. The first man is Ramu, a consummate Tough Guy. The second is David, an aggressive True Believer. Both stories are true-to-life presentations of real events and people, though they are composite rather than case-specific to protect identities.

Case Study 1—Ramu: Tough Guy as Workplace Bully

Identifying Information. Ramu is a 46-year-old executive employed by an international hotel firm. He currently is Chief Financial Officer for a large hotel in a U.S. city.

Presenting Issue. Ramu is referred by his corporate employer to assess behavioral patterns that have become untenable in the workplace. In an introductory letter to the treatment center, Ramu's superiors describe him as a brilliant officer and tactician for the hotel, a man recently viewed as a candidate for promotion to the head office in Europe. However, his promotion is threatened by a pattern of behavior that includes an overly demanding and abusive style with subordinates, a history of angry diatribes that leave others in his department frightened, and a concern that his morbid obesity is reducing his ability to function. The question presented to the assessment team: "Are these behaviors treatable?"

Family Background. Ramu is married to his first wife, a nurse who stays home to manage the family's home and horse farm. The couple has two sons in a private, well-known college. The boys are doing poorly, one for academic reasons and the other for a recent arrest for selling illegal drugs in his university town. Both Ramu and his wife were born in the United States to parents who emigrated from India. His father was an engineer who frequently moved the family to cities in Canada and the United States. Details are unclear, but Ramu's father apparently lost his job several times for alcohol-related absences. When Ramu was in high school, his father quit engineering altogether and started a successful Indian restaurant in a suburban community. Ramu reports the family was "very much middle class," living in a modest home. During Ramu's first year of college, his father died from a massive heart attack following a long history of depression. Ramu is the oldest of three living siblings. A fourth child was hit by an automobile and died at age 6 when Ramu was 13. Today, Ramu's surviving brother is an academic researcher, and his sister is an engineer. They are said to be doing well professionally. Both have been married twice and divorced once. Their mother is aged 64. She never remarried.

Occupational History. After a stellar high school career that ended with his being named valedictorian, Ramu attended a state college and majored in Business. Although he often felt isolated and was once fired from a retail job for yelling at a customer, Ramu performed well academically, getting an accounting internship at a nearby hotel. This led to glowing reference letters that got him hired at an international chain. For the next 25 years, he slowly worked his way up the ladder to his current role as CFO for a large hotel. He works a very demanding schedule, often putting in 80 to 90 hours a week. He reports that he is very intense about his work and doesn't like to fail. "I don't want any mistakes in my department," he says. "I have a hard time dealing with incompetence." This attitude has led to behavior that produced numerous complaints. He admits that he has not been as concerned about these complaints as he should have been.

Many examples of his disruptive behavior are provided to the assessment team. During all-hands meetings of his large department, he often screams obscenities at staff who cannot answer his detailed questions off the tops of their heads. He typically comes late to meetings he chairs, up to an hour late. He once threw a heavy paperweight through the office window of an employee who hadn't met his expectations. When asked about these and other incidents, he minimizes his own responsibilities. "If others would just do their jobs right, none of this would have happened." The only acknowledgment of any inner concerns was offered in response to the question, "How do you understand these complaints about your behavior?" He said simply, "You know, I never wanted to be this way."

Case Study 2—David: True Believer as Zealous Follower

Identifying Information. David is a 38-year-old trial lawyer who practices with a large firm litigating national product liability cases. He represents plaintiffs injured by products with alleged defects in their design or manufacture, and he proudly describes his work as "David holding the Goliaths accountable." He is particularly proud of cases that resulted in additional safety features to products.

Presenting Issue. David is referred for an assessment by his law firm following a series of concerns raised about his ethical behavior. He recently has been censured twice. In one case, he withheld information about a witness he knew had given false testimony. In the other, a judge cited him for continuing his in-court harassment of defendants after being warned to stop. The final straw for his firm was a new accusation that he was trying to materially prejudice a new case by making inflammatory and deceptive statements to the media.

David is described by his firm as an exceptionally gifted attorney, both for his dogged attention to detail in preparing his cases and for his aggressive performances in the courtroom. Financially, he has contributed much to the firm, winning several nationally known cases that produced many millions of dollars and brought much favorable publicity. The partners want to keep him, but they are willing to terminate him for cause if he continues to engage in behavior that brings unwanted attention to the firm. They have become especially concerned about his increasing involvement in the legal aspects of controversial, faith-based political causes. He has been sought as a consultant and spokesperson for groups he believes are "defending the unborn and the terminally ill against euthanasia." These issues bring publicity to the firm that partners increasingly see as distractions that might scare away new clients. The firm's question to the assessment center: "Can David become a team player, or will his religious views always interfere with firm policies?"

Family Background. As a boy, David was raised in a conservative Christian church that banned card playing, rock music, and alcohol. The entire family attended three services each week, two on Sunday and another on Wednesday evening. David joined the church when he was 12 and became a "junior missionary." He would give pamphlets to patrons outside movie theaters when the shows were too risqué, or walk with an adult door to door offering to give Bible studies to neighbors. His father was an "old school" cabinet maker, proud of his reputation as a craftsman. David's father often told him, "You can be much more in life than I am," and, "God has a special plan for you." His father drove David hard regarding school work and punished him severely for a poor grade. Belts and paddles were frequently used for many infractions of family rules, though David wasn't always sure what wrong he had committed. His mother was a housewife who was quiet and anxious most of the time, but she was quite willing to offer strong opinions when it mattered to her. She was active in their local church as a member of the Evangelism Committee when David was young, and she worked full time as a secretary for the church when he started school. David's parents often argued about finances or parenting, but his father won most of those battles, often appealing to his role as "head of the household." David recalled one incident in which his father apparently pushed his mother "who went flying across the room and landed a heap."

As an adult, David and his wife belonged to the same church in which he had been raised. They were married when both were age 22, and they quickly had three boys. Each was given a Biblical name. His wife stayed home full time while David was completing law school and getting started in his career, and then she began her own full-time career as a secretary. Although the couple was active sexually when they were first married, their sexual interactions had become infrequent and pro forma. David's career requires considerable travel, leaving him feeling more and more emotionally distant. The future of the marriage is uncertain.

Occupational History. David's interest in law began early in life. He remembers coping with bullying by escaping into stories of heroes who exacted revenge for the mistreatment of others. His favorite was Iron Man. David was bullied well into high school, though the harassment lessened some after he won a student government office as sergeant-at-arms. He thrived in this role, as it was his duty to issue rulings on procedural matters in Student Council meetings. Occasionally, his rulings were controversial and reactive. A faculty sponsor reminded him multiple times that he must not make rulings based on his own views of the students involved. David majored in psychology in college, even though his parents objected, saying "psychologists don't believe like we do." Although David agreed, he wanted to "understand how unbelievers think" in order to more effectively counter their views. A political science class led him to join a conservative student club that invited speakers to address controversial social issues. His own religious views coincided with many of the ideas in the club, and he decided to apply to law school. At first, David was overwhelmed by the demands and complexities of law school, and he felt isolated and out of place. That changed when he met a faculty member who often was consulted on nationally prominent cases of interest to conservative groups. In an independent study class taught by this faculty member, David sat in on strategy sessions on how to defend a local city's right to hang a plaque of the Ten Commandments in the entryway of its city hall. From that moment on, David knew his destiny: He was going to be a litigator defending the rights of the weak against more heavily funded governments and businesses.

The next few chapters trace the therapeutic journeys of these two men. Many of the assessment and treatment strategies recommended in the following chapters are familiar to seasoned therapists working with other populations. Some are new to the literature. I will cite research from several areas of study: the nature of therapeutic relationship, the psychology of masculinity, the process of human development, the psychology of religion, theories of personality psychology, and the human change processes. In addition to the research, I offer recommendations that have been tried and refined in the psychotherapy rooms of a multidisciplinary team of professionals who work full time with authoritarian men.

Authoritarian behavioral problems are tough to treat. Traits that make men authoritarian challenge the therapeutic relationship itself.

Walking into the psychotherapy room does not end their interest in power, dominance, and manipulation, or increase their interest in empathy or egalitarianism. But over time—much time, sometimes—those tendencies can change. It's a tough job... and someone gets to do it!

CHAPTER
7

"What Does He Need the Most?"
A Healing Relationship: Attunement and Empathy

> I prefer to think of my patients and myself as fellow travelers, a term that abolishes distinctions between "them" (the afflicted) and "us" (the healers).... We are in this together, and there is no therapist and no person immune to the inherent tragedies of existence.
>
> —Irvin Yalom, psychotherapist (2002, *The Gift of Therapy*, p. 8)

Years ago, it was possible to make a modest living as a "piano tuner." In our neighborhood, the tuner was an elderly man who didn't talk much. He found my childhood curiosity about his work to be intrusive and quite bothersome. He would lay out his A-pitched tuning fork and box of tools, hunch over our piano, close his eyes, and grunt a lot. When a key was off pitch, his face cringed slightly, as if he had popped a lemon wedge into his mouth.

As an adult, I now appreciate his scowl. Consider his task: listening to mistuned piano strings, one after another, all day long—each piano giving him 88 new strings, each one requiring countless taps to tune. No wonder he wasn't social and charming. These days, most of his successors use electronic tuning devices, but the old man's nonverbal message remains with me: when something is out of tune, grimace.

ALLIANCE, *n.* \ə-li-ən(t)s\

This section may be tempting to overlook. Most psychotherapists readily acknowledge the importance of the therapeutic alliance and look for something new to learn: a technique, a tool, or a protocol. But I hope you will linger with me on this point. The therapeutic alliance is not just one factor among many that predict success. I believe the relationship is *the central factor.* The literature on this point is impressive. Bruce Wampold reviewed research examining the role of the working alliance in psychotherapy and concluded that "there is no other variable that has been assessed early in therapy that predicts final outcome better than the alliance" (Wampold, 2010, p. 97). He cites findings from numerous studies that speak to this connection.

- The best treatment outcomes occur when the alliance is strong early in the relationship.
- Even though early progress by a client in therapy is related to better outcome, the alliance itself predicts better outcomes independent of early gains.
- The relationship is central to outcome, no matter who rates the strength of the alliance—clients, observers, or therapists—with the highest association occurring when the clients rate the alliance.
- The alliance is related to treatment outcome regardless of the therapist's theories about therapy.
- Therapist characteristics make the largest contribution to outcome, even for within-treatment comparisons.
- The alliance is related to outcome even when the treatment is psychopharmacological.
- Among prescribing psychiatrists, the effect of therapist characteristics on outcome is greater than the effect of the antidepressants they prescribe.
- Here's a provocative finding: "Indeed, the psychiatrists with the highest effects had better outcomes giving the placebo than did the poorer psychiatrists giving the antidepressant!" (Wampold, 2010, p. 101).
- And finally, the average difference in therapist alliance skills completely accounts for the differences in therapist outcomes.

Why is this? Exactly what *is* a therapist–client relationship? Nearly 50 years ago, Ralph Greenson was a psychiatrist for many well-known celebrities, including Marilyn Monroe, Tony Curtis, and Frank Sinatra. But he was much more than that. Greenson also was a brilliant and influential writer and a clinical professor of medicine at University of California, Los Angeles. In the 1960s, he suggested that therapeutic relationships are different from everyday relationships in three ways (1965). First, the relationship is purposive. Quite simply, that purpose is to *work* together.

It is this agreement that calls them together. Otherwise, they would be unlikely to even meet. This aspect might be called the structured side of the relationship. The therapist's role is twofold: to participate in the experience of the relationship and also to observe what is happening (Bordin, 1979).

Second, the relationship is fictive (Shafer, 1982). Not fictional in the sense of being unreal or false, but fictive in that it allows for imagination, exploration, and experimentation. It differs from all other relationships. It is unique in that new ways of engaging can be considered. New versions of the self can be created and "tried out" in the context of the relationship. This might be called the enacted side of the relationship. The therapist becomes a stand-in for others in the man's life. If the therapist is male, the therapist may represent the man's father, brother, or boss. The man can learn about himself by noting these responses to the therapist. These observations can become explicit, after which they can be discussed. Simultaneously, therapists watch for ways in which their clients activate their own previously developed patterns and tendencies. The two are engaged in a conversational dance that includes both content and enactment. It is fictive, but not fictional. Inventive, but not artificial.

Third, the relationship is real (Greenson, 1971; Gelso, 2010). It involves two people being genuine with each other. The man is encouraged to be real and report what he actually is thinking or feeling. The therapist models genuineness by expressing real responses and reflections. Greenson describes how he remained real with his clients:

> I have permitted the patient at times to feel my disappointment in his lack of progress or to see that world events do concern me. I try to restrict the intensity of my reactions, but I do not open the door every day with the same expression on my face, or close the session in the same way. I don't plan these variations. I allow myself to be flexible in such matters. I am of the opinion that it is of importance to demonstrate in certain actions and behavior that the analyst is truly a human being. This includes permitting some of his human frailties to be visible at times. (Greenson, 1978, p. 223)

Now, what therapist behaviors contribute to building this genuine and real therapeutic relationship? Ackerman and Hilsenroth (2003) reviewed 25 studies that examined ways of fostering the therapeutic relationship. Their findings may not be surprising:

> Therapist's personal attributes such as being flexible, honest, respectful, trustworthy, confident, warm, interested, and open were found to contribute positively to the alliance. Therapist techniques such as exploration, reflection, noting past therapy success, accurate interpretation, facilitating the expression of affect, and attending to the patient's experience were also found to contribute positively to the alliance. (Ackerman & Hilsenroth, 2003, p. 1)

Roy Shafer, a psychology professor at Yale, Cornell, and Columbia University in New York, adds other traits to this list: "gentleness, undemandingness, open-mindedness, flexibility, patience, tentativeness, spontaneity, and individuality and a willingness to go along." He then summarizes the relationship with a marvelous metaphor: the therapist is "a seasoned and hardy coexplorer" (Shafer, 1982, p. 26)

Note the contrast between these qualities and the traits of authoritarian men we have identified earlier. Effective therapists are collaborative, empathic, and egalitarian. Authoritarian men lean toward the use of control, exploitation, and power. When these two people meet and begin talking, something critically important happens. The relationally skilled clinician *shows* an authoritarian man a different way of engaging with others. In and of itself, this novelty can produce important new learning for an authoritarian man. This is crucial, especially at the outset of therapy when he may feel vigilant and uncertain about what he's gotten into.

The alliance is important for authoritarian men for an additional reason. As we noted earlier, authoritarian men have long histories of emotionally unsafe relationships with others. Most have never had a secure connection with another human being. They don't know how to develop or maintain one. This deficit is lifelong. Over and over, authoritarian men report variations on this same theme during their assessments in the center where I work with them. As children, they felt isolated, overlooked, puzzled, fearful, and unimportant. They received very little modeling or overt guidance on how to regulate their emotions. Instead, they lived with adults who often were reactive, unsettled, disconnected, and insecure. Boys in these homes coped the best way they could. Some rebelled. Others withdrew, achieved, numbed themselves, or avoided people. But one thing they all learned: The more control they exerted over their worlds, the safer they felt. Power worked. If caregivers do not meet their needs in natural ways, then they can be maneuvered into doing so.

Imagine this relationship-starved man walking into a psychotherapy room. He is unlikely to admit it, or even imagine it, but the most important thing he can learn is that a new way of connecting with others is possible. He must see in his psychotherapist a difficult and new truth. If he wants to be much better than he is, he must cooperate. Not compete. Not manipulate. Not control. But cooperate.

ATTUNEMENT, *n.* \ə-'t(y)ün-mənt\

Attunement is a wonderful single-word description of an effective therapeutic alliance. Attunement occurs when my male client senses that I truly understand him—that I fully and deeply "get it" when he talks. If I am off-pitch, he also senses it and may grimace. When I am attuned to him, he relaxes into the experience. He sees I notice his emotional states. My responses leave him feeling known. He recognizes himself in *my* words and emotions. I am in sync with him, and he can tell it. In a phrase, he "feels felt" (Bruce, Manber, Shapiro, & Constantino, 2010, p. 87). He feels understood in my facial expressions and gestures, in the sounds of my voice and words. In this way, he connects and begins to trust, often for the first time, someone else in his life.

In some ways, a well-tuned working relationship is the *primary* goal of therapy with authoritarian men. Many of the strategies described in following chapters depend on forging such an attuned relationship with the therapist. The assessment and treatment tasks in the next chapters invite men to report very private memories and emotions. Without attunement, this sensitive information is less likely to be revealed. Remember, his historical tendency is to hide personal information in order to avoid feeling vulnerable or being controlled.

Authoritarian men neither expect this attuned experience nor readily understand it. They expect me to be judgmental or even disdainful of their intense distress, their stories of doubt, rage, or trauma. They fear that I will react as others have—with shock, indifference, mocking, or rejection. But if I can hold my client's ideas and emotions in the solid container of my own experience without judgment, then he can feel something unexpected and new. He can begin to feel safe. His fears about disapproving reactions can recede. Over time, this attuned relationship can provide him with a corrective to his earlier mistuned experiences with childhood bullies, distant parents, rejecting lovers, or disloyal friends (Bridges, 2006).

Studies on attunement began with an interest in the infant–caregiver relationship. How does a newborn begin to connect with a caregiver? Stern's research (1985) concluded that attunement requires a series of steps. The parent must accurately read the emotion of the infant. Then the parent must find a way of sharing this awareness with the infant, using both verbal and nonverbal expressions of that awareness. Finally, the male infant must recognize that his own feelings are reflected in the parent's behavior toward him. In this way, he feels in tune with the caregiver. They both sense a oneness—not an enmeshment, but a harmony. An adult version of this process occurs in the psychotherapy room. I must accurately read the experience of my client, whatever it is, and let him see that I know it. He must see his own ideas and feeling states in my responses. When this occurs, we are attuned. Neither of us grimaces.

Therapist Self-Attunement

Attunement with my client begins with thoughts about myself. I must know a lot about the container that is me. This wisdom is ancient, of course. In the 4th century BCE, the phrase "Know Thyself" was carved into Temple of Apollo in Delphi, Greece. A serendipitous sidenote: Apollo was the god of music and the arts, hinting at our use of the word attunement. Plato writes that Socrates interpreted the dictum in the following words, in a portrayal of a conversation between Socrates and Phaedrus:

> I must first know myself, as the Delphian inscription says. To be curious about that which is not my concern, while I am still in ignorance of my own self, would be ridiculous.... Am I a monster... complicated and swollen with passion... or a creature of a gentler and simpler sort...? (Plato, 360 BC/2008, p. 5)

I suspect most therapists readily agree with this prescription. But how to accomplish self-attunement? In recent years, Western psychology has taken a renewed interest in mindfulness as a way of knowing. Mindfulness, however, is still a somewhat foreign notion to Western thinking. Jon Kabat-Zinn, developer of the *Mindfulness-Based Stress Reduction* course, offers this definition: "Simply put, mindfulness is moment-to-moment awareness. It is cultivated by purposefully paying attention to things we ordinarily never give a moment's thought to" (Kabat-Zinn, 2005, p. 2).

Bhante Gunaratana, a Sri Lankan monk with a PhD from American University, describes mindfulness further:

> Mindfulness is mirror-thought. It reflects only what is presently happening and in exactly the way it is happening. There are no biases.... Mindfulness treats all experiences equally, all thoughts equally, all feelings equally. Nothing is suppressed. Nothing is repressed. Mindfulness does not play favorites. (Gunaratana, 2002, pp. 139–140)

Mindfulness may be occurring as you read this paragraph. If it is, you are focused and attentive, not distracted by sounds around you. You may pause in your reading and become attentive to sensations in your body. Or you may suddenly notice that your mind jumped to a side issue, or to your need to buy tomatoes tomorrow. Mindfulness is the immediate and fleeting awareness of an event, sometimes without language. Sometimes, mindfulness precedes language. Sometimes it is prompted by language.

Mindfulness is the ability to observe my own internal state, as it unfolds—thoughts, sensations, images, emotions, and fantasies. It is an in-the-moment awareness that occurs against a carefully constructed backstory of self-understanding. More specifically, it means that I know my own patterns, tendencies, blind spots, triggers, and idiosyncrasies well enough to notice when they are activated by what a client says. At the same time, I am noticing my client's emotional shifts and thought sequences. The challenge is to keep these two dimensions alive at the same time: my own story as a context for listening and the developing story of my client as the focus of my attention. In this way, mindfulness is a skill, as well as an attitude toward the outside world. It can be practiced.

The capacity to be self-attuned also requires that I be compassionate toward myself. Not judgmental, impatient, or frustrated. But open, kindly, and accepting, even of my missteps. I must both know and accept my own disagreeable tendencies and still maintain a deep sense of compassion for myself. This is not easy, sometimes. But it is essential for self-attunement.

> In mindfulness practice, the development of compassion begins with learning to relate to oneself with compassion and kindness. A person systematically attends to his or her experience with kindness and begins to observe the crippling effects of self-judgment. This continued process allows people to cultivate attunement with themselves, which is the first step toward cultivating attunement with others. (Shapiro & Carlson, 2009, p. 22)

This compassionate attitude toward oneself takes much practice—daily. Not only in the psychotherapy room, but everywhere. The idea is to simply observe what occurs in my inner world and not react with hate or spite. Ajahn Sumedho, an abbot at a monastery north of London, put it this way: Compassion is not

> about finding fault with ourselves but about accepting our meanness of heart, our desire for revenge, the pettiness or stupidity we might feel at times. Having (loving kindness) for our own moods, our own emotional habits, enables us to let them be what they are, to neither indulge in them nor reject them, but to recognize, 'This is my mood; this is how it feels.' The attitude is one of patience, nonaversion, and kindness. (Sumedho, 1989, p. 171)

Compassion toward my feelings and thoughts, no matter what their valence, is what sets the stage for an ability to treat the disagreeable behavior of others with a similar compassion. Not, "You did *what?*" But, "Let's understand this, together." In order to do this well, I must experience the self-kindness I imagine my client can find for himself. This explains why my attitudes toward self are so critically important. When I treat myself with kindness, I understand more fully how to treat others in the same way.

Self-attunement includes an awareness of our own intentions. In the foreground: What is my purpose in agreeing to see this man? Why am I sitting here, right now? In the background: What do I believe about human suffering? Why have I become a therapist? Knowing the answers to these questions is crucial. "Your intentions set the stage for what is possible. They remind you from moment to moment of why you are practicing in the first place" (Kabat-Zinn, 1990, p. 32).

Does kindly self-attunement influence psychotherapy? One study examined, in extraordinary detail, videotapes of therapist–client relationships. Researchers rated the therapist's self-concepts, then looked at each comment the therapist made in the psychotherapy sessions to see how much hostility or control was being expressed. The finding: Highly self-critical therapists made more comments to clients rated as critical, controlling, and hostile. Conversely, therapists who were more self-accepting were also more client-accepting. For this latter group, the relationship also included more comments that were overtly supportive of the client (Henry, Schacht, & Strupp, 1990).

Pema Chodron, director of a Buddhist abbey in Nova Scotia, describes the relationship between self-kindness and other-kindness this way:

> In cultivating loving-kindness, we train first to be honest, loving, and compassionate toward ourselves. Rather than nurturing self-denigration, we begin to cultivate a clear-seeing kindness. Sometimes we feel good and strong. Sometimes we feel inadequate and weak. But... without loving-kindness for ourselves, it is difficult, if not impossible to genuinely feel it for others. (Chodron, 2001, pp. 55–56)

Therapists with long-standing self-disparaging habits need not fret. Compassion toward oneself can be learned. For example, strategies have increased self-compassionate behavior with staff at a Veteran's Administration hospital and with graduate students in a counseling psychology program (Shapiro, Astin, Bishop, & Cordova, 2005; Shapiro, Brown, & Biegel, 2007). A key component of the study was training in mindfulness. As professional therapists became more skilled in mindfulness, they were more tolerant, kind, and accepting of themselves.

Self-attunement matters. It makes other-attunement possible. Harvard-trained physician Dan Siegel (2007) explains the connection in this way: "With mindful awareness," our own thoughts and feelings can be "accepted for what they are, and acknowledged with kindness and respect." It is this "*intrapersonal* [emphasis added] attunement that helps us see how mindful awareness can promote love for oneself." And in turn, "this is the kind of *interpersonal* [emphasis added] attunement that promotes love" (Siegel, 2007, pp. 16–17).

Therapist–Client Attunement

> A therapist has to practice being fully present and has to cultivate the energy of compassion in order to be helpful.
>
> —Thich Nhat Hanh (2000, *Path of Emancipation*, p. 153)

Similar to other therapists, I have sat with men who initially doubted I could tolerate their pain. One man put it this way, after sharing his anguish at having been sexually groped by two men (a monk and a psychologist): "I didn't imagine you could tolerate my rage." At some level, he may have feared yet another rejection or judgment. But if a therapist can listen to such intense emotion while remaining attentive and attuned, then the man can find his fears lessening and his trust in another increasing.

It is both difficult and essential to hold an authoritarian man's stories of power, control, and exploitation in a safe place while he talks. As he learns that my responses to his verbal behavior differ markedly from the responses from others in his life, he can begin to think of himself differently. If I can remain attuned with him and be genuinely interested in his stories of hurtful behavior, then he may begin to respect himself. If

I can respect *him* while understanding his behavior, then maybe he can respect himself, too.

Mindfulness allows this level of attunement between therapist and client. In psychotherapy, this means that I am fully tuned to the man in front of me—the subtle muscles movements in his face, the slight change in voice volume or pitch, and the language he is using to examine an idea. My task is to remain open, and take it all in. As his gestures and words speak to me, I respond naturally. My own facial expressions change as I listen. My prosody (the tone and rhythm of my speech) reflects my experience of what he is saying. When this works well, the two of us are attuned. He can hear the sound and intensity of his own emotions in me, even when I don't use words. The slightest glance conveys it. If I am attuned, then my client hears himself in my responses and becomes aware of his own internal states, uncertainties, contradictions, and needs.

Stern (1985) used the term "affect attunement" to describe the emotional connection that occurs. The therapist mirrors the man's emotions by reporting what is sensed and observed. The man may feel overwhelmed but has no language to describe the experience. It becomes my task as the therapist to gently help him understand his own experience more fully. I might say, "You look frightened," or, "Your face seems really sad as you think about this." This ability to be empathically responsive creates an emotional synchrony that is likely novel for an authoritarian man. The newness of this experience need not be terrifying, however. It can be reassuring. The man feels known and connected with the therapist who knows him. In this way, attuned therapists can use their own responses to their clients' presentations as clues to help them understand what the man himself is experiencing. This doesn't mean the man's emotions become the therapist's. Therapists can hold the anger or confusion of a distressed man in the container of their own experiences and not be waylaid by their own anger or confusion. That distinction between client and therapist remains clear. But being emotionally tuned to the experience of the client in ways that the client can detect and appreciate becomes therapeutic, in and of itself. The relationship that results from this attunement becomes the foundation for subsequent therapeutic change.

This relationship holds clear therapeutic possibilities. It can function as a corrective to earlier relationships that were highly problematic. Unproductive or damaging roles may have been assumed for years, all the way back to the beginning of the man's life. He may have been a life-long controller, manipulator, exploiter, rescuer, or avoider. The therapist can create an emotional space in which the man can recognize this and begin to assume a very different role.

The connecting process begins for human beings at birth. Infants connect with their caregivers in emotional ways. The new infant experiences virtually everything in emotional terms: blankets, milk, skin, and sounds. Stern argues that the infant and caregiver spend most of their time trying to find and maintain an emotional attunement. It is an "active mutual regulation of their own and the other's states ...." (Stern et al., 1998, p. 906). This early relational experience can go awry, of course. And when it does, an effective psychotherapy relationship can become a corrective for earlier disrupted connections in life. There is now neurobiological evidence that this occurs, as we noted in Chapter 5.

In the therapy room, I may say something upsetting or hasty. I may lose my attention and inadvertently be hurtful in some way. This need not end attunement. If I can notice the sudden weakening of the connection, I can turn my attention to the rupture itself. In real time, I can address it. Of course, addressing a rupture means that I must notice it when it occurs. Hints of ruptures, however, can be subtle and easily missed. They can occur not only when I say something but also when I fail to say something. Even a glance can create a break.

Clara Hill and her colleagues at the University of Maryland studied 12 breakdowns ("impasses") in actual therapist–client relationships, and found that they have a profoundly negative impact on both client and psychotherapist. They found that deadlocks are provoked in several different ways: by a disagreement about therapeutic goals or tasks, by interference in the therapy from others, and by the therapist's own issues. Examples of therapists' personal problems that contributed to the impasses included difficulty handling the strong emotions of a client, having unresolved family of origin issues, assuming a rescuer-fixer role, and facing personal or family health problems (Hill, Nutt-Williams, Heaton, Thompson, & Rhodes, 1996).

Other suggestions of events that produce therapeutic ruptures include

> (a) the psychotherapist's temptation to respond to patients sharing of negative feelings by defensively expressing his or her own negative feelings, and (b) the tendency to adhere rigidly to a treatment model when confronted with a rupture... For example, a cognitive-behavioral psychotherapist's perseverative insistence that a patient's negative feelings about treatment are the result of distorted thinking.... (Bruce, Manber, Shapiro, & Constantino, p. 90)

It is unfortunate, but research has shown that psychotherapists often miss or overlook these therapeutic ruptures, and don't notice the immediate pullback of the man (Hill, Nutt-Williams et al., 1996).

Awareness of the rupture is one thing. Active repair is another. This requires that the psychotherapist talk about the rift openly, directly, and nondefensively, and then change or modify any problematic behavior (Foreman & Marmar, 1985). Research suggests that if therapists avoid this repair work, they may lose the man as a client (Safran & Muran, 1996). But when they successfully manage a repair, the process itself can actually strengthen the attunement. Most importantly, the man learns that impasses do not end important relationships. He also learns that he might take these reconnecting skills out of the therapy room and address breaches in relationships elsewhere in life.

Alexander and French (1946) argued that significant change occurs when repair occurs in the therapy room, because old and unresolved conflicts are reenacted with different outcomes. New solutions to old problematic patterns are experienced. As these newer behaviors are tried over time, they can gradually replace the older, less effective ways of engaging. Franz Alexander, a physician and pioneer researcher in psychosomatic medicine, coined the now-famous term for this process, "the corrective emotional experience":

> In all forms of etiological psychotherapy, the basic therapeutic principle is the same: to re-expose the patient, under more favorable circumstances, to emotional situations which he could not handle in the past. The patient, in order to be helped, must undergo a *corrective emotional experience* [emphasis added] suitable to repair the traumatic influence of previous experiences. (Alexander & French, 1946, pp. 66–68)

From this perspective, interpersonal attunement can lead to a man's ability to begin and end relationships in new ways. Over time, he can find himself attached to his therapist without feeling his customary ambivalence, and he can consider separating from the therapist without feeling his familiar anxiety or abandonment.

Client Self-Attunement

If a therapist is self-attuned and able to foster an intrapersonal attunement with a male client, then the man can become more self-attuned, as well. That is, the man can notice more of his own internal landscape. He can pay attention to parts of his life previously overlooked, such as his own subtle or vulnerable emotions. For example, he may learn to respect his own sadness, resentment, confusion, or anxiety. Rather than stifle these emotions or morph them into anger, he may allow them to emerge into his awareness.

How might this happen? Each boy begins his life dependent on his primary caregiver for virtually everything, from food to emotional security. Ideally, this dependent state is experienced as a "secure base" (Bowlby, 1988). Winnocott used the term "holding environment" to describe this initial stage in life (Winnicott, 1960, p. 47). When a "good enough" caregiver (Winnicott, 1941/1975, p. 67) is in charge of maintaining this safe and protective environment, and makes the infant a "preoccupation" (Winnicott, 1956/1975, p. 300), then the infant can move away from dependence into relational interdependence and eventually assume an awareness of himself as a separate person (Robertson & Shepard, 2008). This transition "toward emotional object constancy" occurs over time (Mahler, Pine, & Bergman, 1975, p. 58). When he is independent, the boy-become-man combines the "pleasure of his own autonomy and self-esteem" with skills that allow him to engage effectively in "all subsequent human relationships" (Mahler, Pine, & Bergman, 1975, p. 74, 48).

At least, that is the ideal. When the holding environment is secure, the boy is more likely to develop competent relational skills. He can use rather than avoid emotions. He can more readily identify trustworthy people, and he is less likely to misjudge offers of friendship. His social and emotional antennae work. But when the holding environment is not secure, the ideal may not be reached. The early caregiver environment may have been unsafe, neglectful, distant, or damaged by substance abuse. The normal developmental process for the boy is thrown off course. He does not learn the cues that signal safety. He becomes vigilant, suspicious, and isolated (Kohut, 1971; Mahler & Kaplan, 1977). Autonomy may be forced on him, long before he is ready. When this happens, the results range from problematic to severe. He is subject to feeling abandonment, even when it has not occurred. Losses are experienced as catastrophic. Such a man finds himself on his own, but without the ability to create emotional and relational safety for himself. Interpersonal problems are common and often irresolvable (Pollack, 2001). Emotional self-care becomes marginal to nonexistent. Without a secure base from which to trust others, he tries alternative strategies that don't require trust. He uses control, power, exploitation, manipulation. Empathic and egalitarian responses are correspondingly less important.

In the context of a therapeutic relationship, however, emotional competency becomes possible. "Self-efficacy research indicates that emotional competence can be learned" (Diehl & Prout, 2002, p. 262). Corrective emotional connections can undermine previously held views of incompetency. The success of the therapeutic relationship offers convincing new data to the man that he can indeed make emotional connections.

The psychotherapy room, then, becomes a reenacted world. Rather than being the infant in a child–caregiver relationship, he is now a client in a man–therapist relationship. If the therapist can establish a safe holding environment by being attentive, respectful, and consistently supportive, then the man can begin to examine his inner world with more security than he has heretofore experienced. The therapist's ability to foster an attuned relationship with him enables a more mindful awareness of his own life. He can consider his frightening emotions in new ways. Rather than feel overwhelmed and flooded by unwanted events, he can approach them with acceptance and curiosity. He can learn that intense emotions do not necessarily lead to disconnection. He can feel more settled, more reflective.

In time, the male client can begin to emulate the emotional and relational behavior of the therapist. He becomes able to engage in similar behavior with others in his life. He wants to provide that connection because he has discovered what it is like to be the recipient of such stable and kind attention. He knows attunement, even though the word itself may not appear in his everyday lexicon.

Gelso describes this relationship succinctly. It feels genuine ("the ability to be one who truly is, to be non-phony, to be authentic in the here and now") and real ("the experiencing or perceiving of the other in ways that befit him or her") (Gelso, 2002, p. 37). And this relationship predicts positive outcomes in therapy.

EMPATHY, *n.* \'em-pə-thē\

Empathy may be defined as the therapist's identification with the inner experience of the patient. This identification is both vicarious and partial.... The identification is what allows the therapist to both grasp the patient's experience intellectually and participate in the patient's emotional experience. In this sense, empathy may be both cognitive and affective.

—Charles Gelso (2010, *The Real Relationship in Psychotherapy*, p. 81)

Authoritarian men are not empathic. We have established that repeatedly. But if they're going to fundamentally change the way they engage with the world, empathy must emerge.

As a child, Carl Rogers experienced considerable internal distress. He knew what it was like to be teased without mercy. He often felt belittled by his siblings and thought his older brother was more important to his parents than he was (Demorest, 2005). Young Carl grew up with the experience of wishing others could understand him, could empathize with him. Years later, when he sat in the therapist's chair, he readily sensed the suffering of the other person. Perhaps this partially explains the appeal of his definition of empathy, written more than 50 years ago:

> To sense the man's private world as if it were your own, but without ever losing the 'as if' quality—this is empathy, and this seems essential to therapy. To sense the man's anger, fear, or confusion as if it were your own, yet without your own anger, fear, or confusion getting bound up in it, is the condition we are endeavoring to describe. (Rogers, 1957, p. 99)

Empathy alone may not cure a man's authoritarianism, but it does create a context in which change can occur. A man learns that all his emotions and actions are understandable. He can feel hopelessness *and* hopeful. He can blunder *and* succeed. He can feel shameful *and* courageous. He knows that whatever occurs will not be experienced alone. His therapist will follow his reasoning and understand his emotions.

Empathy is a "feel good" word that seems wholly positive...but only at first glance. There are challenges and risks. It is one thing to empathize with confusion, loss, and sadness. Sitting with these more vulnerable emotions comes easily for most therapists. But what about the underbelly of social behavior? What about empathizing with greed, arrogance, violence, and abuse? Authoritarian men can be grandiose, caustic, vicious, and defiant. Empathy means understanding these behaviors, too—not excusing them, but understanding the struggles that spawn them. And, more importantly, empathy means helping a man understand himself. What relational needs is *he* trying to meet with these maladaptive and harmful behaviors? Bringing clarity to these questions takes much time and therapeutic patience.

Psychotherapist Rollo May believed that "one must have at least a readiness to love the other person, broadly speaking, if one is to be able to understand him" (May, 1958, p. 39). But this task can be challenging. For several years earlier in my career, I took referrals from a family court that mandated therapy for perpetrators of domestic abuse. More than one of my colleagues asked, "How in the world can you work with these guys?" After all, they harm their own families. To work with them, I learned to think differently about them. They are not monsters by choice. They are wounded boys whose needs for nurturance and security were not met. As men, they flail about, trying desperately to feel connected, loved, secure. But they have no clue on how to make this happen. Their efforts are primitive, unfocused, and unskilled. They have never seen a mature attachment, so they are unclear about what they are even looking for. The emotional vacuum that results from this deficit is untenable, and so they try forcing others to meet their needs. Coercion, control, and power become the strategies of choice. It is all they know. Forcing a connection never works, but they have no alternative.

From this perspective, each domestic abuser became a new story for me to hear, a new set of wounds to dress. When I was able to be empathic and curious, they could begin making sense of their behavior. Most abusive men are deeply remorseful about their misbehavior. They also are confused. "Why does this keep happening? I don't want to explode, but I keep doing it. Why?"

I found that the answers to those questions lay deep within each wounded man. My task was to become his "seasoned and hardy coexplorer" (Shafer, 1982, p. 26), and accompany his search for his own answers. When I could do that, I learned a lot. I learned that a wounded-to-abusive man was both ready and willing to explore. His motivation was high. His focus was intense. From this perspective, he was not a monster to me. His behavior truly was monstrous, but he was not.

A caution is in order. I have noticed that some beginning therapists are dismayed when their empathy is *not* welcomed. This has been a topic in my supervision conversations with therapists-in-training. Sometimes a man does not welcome empathy. It can feel too intense, too exposing, or uncomfortably erotic. Men who are used to feeling powerful and in charge can suddenly feel "smothered, seduced, pressured" (Shafer, 1982, p. 50) by comments that convey too much understanding. Though genuinely empathic, some observations can feel intrusive, meddling, or disturbing. And men will react accordingly. They will block the empathy.

No matter how open or supportive the therapist is, the empathy will be resisted.

When these moments occur, it can be helpful to see them as inevitable in working with authoritarian men. It also helps to take the long view of therapy and not get mired in feelings of hurt or resentment. When a man resists empathy, he is trying to maintain his independence. That is his norm. Eventually, if the therapist can maintain a steady, grounded, and compassionate presence, the man can learn that empathy need not be threatening. He can feel known without feeling intimidated. Novel though it may be, the experience begins to feel appealing. Not all at once, but gradually, through fits and starts. Again, keeping the long-range goal in mind can sustain a therapist through these challenges. The man *needs* to experience the ups and downs of a corrective relationship as a way of discovering how to handle relationships for himself.

Sometimes the most empathic response is silence. Respectful, patient silence. When a man is thinking, let him think. I have learned this the hard way, at times. When I offer "the perfect" response or interpretation while he is in the middle of a thought, my comment falls flat. Timing is crucial. Keeping a respectful distance can also leave him feeling understood and valued. There will always be a later time for the comment that seems just right.

It also is important to know when *not* to respond with typical empathy. Some tears are calculated. Some appreciation is ingratiating. This is where a therapist's "seasoned" dimension comes into play. Conveying an awareness of the artificiality of these expressions without shaming the man is the goal. Therapeutically, these events are important. The man learns that incongruent expressions feel manipulative. They push people away and do not generate the response he needs. There are other ways to elicit kindness and support from another. The therapist's role is to be empathic with the *need* being expressed but not with the *method* being used. Underneath the incongruent comment, the man is expressing a need. What is it? Helping a man locate that need as the subtext of his crocodile tears or obsequious comment is the larger empathy. Identifying such a comment that is manipulative may not feel empathic in the moment; but helping him understand the underlying purpose of the comment and then brainstorming new ways of addressing the need is empathic indeed.

A final thought about empathy: a little humility is a good thing. We therapists are not always as empathic as we think we are; we do miss things, even the best among us. Nor are we as special as clients sometimes say we are. Yet our compassionate empathy does matter. A lot.

> Compassion and tolerance are not a sign of weakness, but a sign of strength. The various features and aspects of human life, such as longevity, good health, success, happiness, and so forth, which we consider desirable, are all dependent on kindness and a good heart. All major religious traditions carry basically the same message, that is love, compassion, and

forgiveness. The important thing is they should be part of our daily lives. Our prime purpose in this life is to help others. And if you can't help them, at least don't hurt them.

—The Dalai Lama, XIV (2010, *Words of Wisdom, Love, and Compassion*)

SUMMARY

Assessment and treatment do not occur in a relational vacuum, but in the context of a vibrant and safe connection with a therapist. But trusting relationships have been illusive for an authoritarian man. All his life, he has felt alone, inadequate, and vigilant in his interactions with others. Openness and collaboration have been unfamiliar. Instead, he has sought emotional safety by using power, control, and manipulation. Why? How has this come to be?

In a previous chapter, I described prototypical life experiences of authoritarian men based on my work and the research of others. I detailed commonalities in their early life memories. Men recall parental relationships marred by extended absences, emotional unpredictability, unacknowledged grief, addictions, abuse, and shaming. Fast-forward to adulthood, and they report maladaptive behavior and troublesome experiences in their closest relationships: a constant need for acceptance; a lifelong loneliness; a keen awareness of power differences; a view that all relationships are unstable or frightening; a belief that all love is conditional; a fear of rejection; an absence of emotionally close relationships with men; a need to remain in control of others around them; a lack of interest in their own impact on others; and an insatiable need for comfort.

It is evident that the greatest need of an authoritarian man is to experience an entirely new relationship, one marked by attunement and empathy. The opposite has been his norm: disharmony, disconnection, and disrespect. This makes the emergence of a trusting relationship with a therapist a novel experience, but deeply appealing. But if a Tough Guy or True Believer is lucky, he'll find such a connection in a psychotherapy room. His skilled therapist will help him discover that he can be fully known as a man, as a believer. He doesn't just survive; he thrives. How does this happen?

Attunement occurs. The man sees himself reflected in the words, emotions, and demeanor of the therapist. He feels understood. His own distress and disagreeable emotions are held safely in the container of the therapist's steady and stable experience of him. He feels relational and emotional harmony with another human being, often for the first time in his life. Over time, this attunement becomes a corrective for the man's earlier (and often failed) attempts to connect emotionally with trusted others. He begins to wonder if he might experience attunement elsewhere in his life.

Empathy develops. He sees compassion in his therapist, who is moved by his dilemmas and doubts. He notices the therapist's interest in stories he has never told before, stories that reveal pain and confusion. He discovers how it feels to receive empathy. And he also notices how it is conveyed, through the attentive and understanding presence of the therapist. At first, the empathy flows one way: from the therapist to him. But gradually, he discovers what it is like to become empathic himself. In the safety of this working relationship, he learns about the impact his own behavior has on others and how he is experienced by others. Empathy for those harmed by his adult behavior begins to emerge.

Attunement and empathy begin during the very first conversation in the psychotherapy office. They continue when the assessment is qualitative—conversational and insightful.

MEET A SCHOLAR–CLINICIAN

SID FRIESWYK

Some men change the lives of teenage boys—for good. One such man was Sid Frieswyk's uncle. Here is the story. Sid's grandparents were impoverished Dutch farmers and indigent Irish Americans whose fight for survival exhausted their personal resources. Their lives were hard-edged, and they survived using strategies passed down through generations: hard work, for sure, but accompanied by religious rigidity, alcoholic relief, tyrannical control, occasional fits of rage, and nonegalitarian views of minority groups and women. Their gritty and grueling battles permeated young Sid's life. At any moment, a brutal word or act might burst into the air and demand his boyhood attention.

Then adolescence struck, and he met an uncle who treated people differently. Sid describes him as "benign, compassionate, sensitive, aware, principled, and caring." Here was a nonauthoritarian relationship that demonstrated consistent respect, emotional safety, even healing. Young Sid was hooked. He was experiencing a new model of what his own relationships with others might become.

What became appealing in his personal life eventually became a professional interest. Sid became Dr. Frieswyk, the clinical psychologist who has devoted nearly 50 years to fostering therapeutic relationships with patients. He has experienced them, thought about them, researched them, and written about them. Much of this work occurred at the Karl Menninger School of Psychiatry, where he held several clinical, teaching, and administrative posts. Sid was particularly influential as Director of Psychotherapy Training for the Psychiatric Residency Program. In this role, Sid could both model and teach the importance of therapeutic relationships. Trainees could learn *about* healing relationships by reviewing their cases with Sid, and they could learn *from* their own interactions with him.

Every workday of his life, then, Sid has tended to the connections between himself and others: colleagues, students, and patients. He has learned much about therapeutic relationships. I know this because we have talked for countless hours about the intricacies of this unique human interaction. So many ways of thinking about this fictive relationship: reenacting and acting out, trust and fear, power and vulnerability, closeness and eroticism, playfulness and painful work, and shame and rage. Through it all, attunement and empathy sustain the healing process.

Sid's scholarly publications examine these issues. It is overwhelmingly clear to him that the single most important contributor to changing personality disorders is the clinician–patient relationship itself. He published evidence for this belief from a 12-year research project with his Menninger colleagues. A full-length book resulted in 1996: *Borderline Personality Disorder: Tailoring the Psychotherapy to the Patient*. He reported that personality disorders are brewed in the heat of developmental processes that go awry, and that skilled therapeutic relationships can get that process back on track. In more personal terms, Sid found that personality-disordered patients learn about healing relationships the same way he did as a teen: by experiencing them in an attuned and empathic connection with a trusted other. This link changes everything.

Dr. Frieswyk believes an authoritarian man learns much from a noncompetitive relationship with a clinician. Collaboration, trust, and empathy become real. This learning is counterintuitive for him, as he lives in a society that lionizes maladaptive ferocity, unfettered competition, and degrading interactions with others. But psychotherapeutic attunement is an effective countercurrent in the flow of such a man's life. The experience itself can be life altering.

Now past 70 years of age, Sid continues to develop healing relationships with his patients. I see the process unfold daily in the lives of patients we treat in our day treatment facility. One of Sid's patients offered me an unsolicited assessment of what it is like to work with him. "He is a gentle provocateur." Challenging, but safe. That is a healing relationship. That is Sid.

CHAPTER
8
"What Is Wrong With Him?"
A Qualitative Assessment: Collaboration and Insight

Something was deeply wrong with Harry Angstrom. John Updike devoted four novels to exploring the moral and religious confusion of this man, better known as Rabbit. The traditional dualism of many religions—two opposite kingdoms—is a way of understanding Rabbit, a way of knowing ourselves. Simply put, there is light and dark in all of us. We can achieve so much... yet fail so miserably. Rabbit's life reveals human ambiguity as commonplace, not sophisticated. In Updike's words, "I aim in my mind not toward New York but toward a vague spot a little to the east of Kansas" (Updike, 1968). It is a place where a man can milk the cows *and* abuse his sons. Or rescue people from burning buildings *and* flee the scene of his own drunken accident. Rabbit's Pulitzer Prize story portrays the universal haziness of human life.

Implicit in Updike's books is the psychological question, "What is wrong with Rabbit?" That question also hangs in the air as each psychotherapeutic assessment begins. This question is inevitable because we humans are both blessed and plagued by the very same trait: the ability to understand ourselves. And that is the starting point for a qualitative assessment.

ASSESSING READINESS: CONVERSATIONS AND TASKS

Will an authoritarian man really talk openly during an assessment? Yes. As long as he is answering questions relevant to *him*. Not simply from a computer screen or a piece of paper, but from a fully alive person: an interested psychotherapist who conveys respect. Attunement begins with a face-to-face conversation, not a printed protocol. The idea is to talk *with* him. Interact. Explain the reason for the questions he is asked and why his answers will be helpful. Almost always, he'll start thinking and talking.

The least promising way to begin building a relationship is to require him to complete tests and then wait for days before talking with him. That creates a barrier. He will feel probed, not heard. The process will seem mysterious, even mildly threatening. His initial experience of psychotherapy may be an increase in anxiety, helplessness, and suspicion—none of which foster attunement.

Collaborative Conversations

The goal is to make the assessment both collaborative and insightful. Invite him to be a partner in identifying the problems he faces. Encourage him to explain *his* take on his problems. Explain the potential value of the structured assessment tasks. Most men really do want to solve their personal problems, even when they have trouble acknowledging them. An assessment that invites collaboration in developing insights about the sources of his problems breeds confidence and hope. Maybe, just maybe, he'll be ready to work with a therapist to address them.

When a controlling man hears live questions that seem relevant to him, he starts thinking. When the queries are impersonal, he is ready to defend. This difference is crucial in assessments of authoritarian men. The power differential is real for them. They sense it just by walking into the office. The earlier this concern can be respected, the better. Beginning the assessment with a series of structured discussions can help reduce the initial uneasiness that comes from feeling exposed and incapable.

The overt purpose of the assessment is to help him identify information that will launch the therapeutic process. In particular, he needs to understand exactly which behaviors are problematic for him, how they developed, how they affect others, and how others in his life experience him. This self-learning is challenging and difficult, but essential.

The underlying purpose of an assessment is to begin developing an attuned working relationship with him, one in which he starts hearing himself in the therapist's responses to him. An attuned working relationship requires face-to-face conversations. When a man answers questions using only a keyboard or a pencil, his emotional alliance with the therapist is not strengthening. That partnership forms when he engages with the therapist—using what he sees, what he hears, and what he feels. Considered from this perspective, assessment *is* treatment. In these live interactions, self-awareness is already occurring. The treatment alliance is already forming. This process is facilitated by the use of qualitative measures that are conversational, reflective, and respectful.

Once this interactive process has moved along, quantitative measures can be introduced. I have no data to support this hypothesis, but I wonder if standardized defensiveness scores might be lower if quantitative tests are taken after some qualitative conversations about the man's life have already occurred. If those interactions have gone well, he can sense the therapist's concern for him and may be more likely to trust this strange new person and process. He may be willing to answer tough computerized questions more honestly.

More than 60 years ago, legendary statistician Lee Cronbach wrote, "Complete assessment of a personality must be qualitative" (Cronbach, 1948, p. 365). He made this comment at a time when personality research depended on quantitative data based on particular theories of personality. Individual scores were compared to group scores. This approach presented problems for clinicians because the criterion variables might not apply to the man in front of them. Therapists, after all, treat individuals, not averages. Cronbach (1948) illustrated this point by referring to the practice of quantifying a personality trait he called leadership:

> It is a violation of all personality theory to rate men on leadership, and to use such ratings as a "true" picture of their performance. The rating is an approximation to truth only when the situation in which the men act is virtually uniform. A man's effectiveness as a leader depends on the structure of the group he leads, the tasks that are set, the demands placed upon him by his superior, and a number of other factors. (p. 366)

Although it is useful to know a man's spot on a bell curve, that information is broad and general. Person-specific information comes from person-specific questions. With qualitative questions, a clinician learns what *this* man says about *his* experiences and circumstances. "Qualitative criteria are more meaningful and more truthful than ratings or other quantitative criteria" (Cronbach, 1948, p. 373). That is because the data consist of the man's own words and stories. Cronbach went on to describe an approach that included open-ended questions, multiple assessors, and a method for analyzing the information.

Insightful Tasks

In selecting qualitative assessment tasks, it is helpful to look for several attributes.

First, use structured conversations that are task-oriented. Men respond positively to tasks and assignments in psychotherapy. Multiple experts on psychotherapy with men have noted the socialized expectation that men feel a pressure to "do something" when they face a problem. It works at work. In the office or factory, being an effective problem solver is a good thing. Men who are good at it are rewarded, often with recognition or promotions. Men naturally bring this strategy into the psychotherapy room. It is not surprising, then, when these male clients feel exposed and uncertain about participating in nondirective and self-revealing conversations with therapists. Men expect to *do* something (Addis & Mahalik, 2003; Hurst, 1997; Rabinowitz & Cochran, 2002; Robertson & Fitzgerald, 1992).

Second, use strategies that make intuitive sense to the man. The reason for asking the question should be immediately clear to him. This clarity enables him to be both a participant and an observer. For example, if he is asked to remember events from his childhood, it helps him to know why those questions are being asked. It's not just for the sake of gathering history. He and the therapist are together looking for themes and patterns from childhood that may have contributed to difficulties he currently acknowledges. Knowing this purpose can increase his motivation to remember events, even the difficult or painful ones. Using assessment approaches that make sense to the man both encourages participation and leads to constructive discussions.

Third, select approaches that promise to provide the man with greater self-understanding. Use the narcissism he brings into the room. He wants to see himself in the findings. Let him know that his own views of himself will be helpful. Gentle humor helps. Garfield the cat may be obnoxious, cynical, even sadistic, but his amusing self-observations often hit home. In one, Garfield looks in a mirror and says, "You rock!" He then turns away and muses to himself, "It's nice to know I'm here for me" (Davis, 2011). I may be sitting with him, but an authoritarian man often thinks he is the *only* one there for him.

Men do want to know the results of testing and to hear it in language that is clear and detailed. When that language consists of his own words—what he actually said in responding to questions, the impact can be dramatic and unexpectedly emotional. Ideally, the therapist takes the man's language and creates a narrative that summarizes important themes embedded in what he said. I have found that writing a summary of portions of the qualitative assessment can generate high levels of self-awareness rather quickly. He can be provided with a narrative of the information as a draft, for example. Comments can be invited. He can recommend adjustments or corrections in the written narrative. This enlists the man as a collaborator in the assessment process and conveys the message that the therapy is going to be about him. His views will matter. After all, he knows what is problematic and needs to be addressed. In this way, he is not placed in the step-down position that occurs when he thinks the therapist wants to know more about him than he himself knows. Examples of qualitative approaches that meet these criteria appear later in the chapter.

Collaboration and insight can begin with the first questions asked in the assessment. The second-person pronouns below are deliberate because many authoritarian men don't come voluntarily to psychotherapists. They are mandated by courts, spouses, supervisors, or professional licensing boards. It is not their idea at all. This makes the first assessment task clear: What does *he* think about how he has arrived in the office? A good read on this comes from the initial clinical interview. Many questions can initiate this discussion.

- What is *your* view of the reasons you are here?
- Who seems most bothered by your behavior? What do they tell you?
- What do you think the problem really is?
- Is this problem preventing you from doing what *you* would like to do?
- Does this problem create stress for you? How so?
- What makes the stress worse?
- What accounts for this problem not being any worse than it is?
- If this problem did not exist, how would your life be different?

Readiness for change can also be assessed in this way. Again, invite the man to express his own views. It shows respect for the fact that he likely sees issues differently from others in his life. Asking him about his own views begins to convey the therapist's interest in him, in his ideas. This information can come from the initial clinical interview.

- Do *you* want to make any changes in your life?
- Is this something you have ever thought about doing on your own?
- Is there is a question *you* would like answered from this assessment?
- Have you known of anyone else who faced a situation like this? How did it turn out for them?
- What is riding on this assessment for you?
- In completing this assessment, what challenges will we be facing together?

Information about the man's readiness-to-change also can come from a more formal set of questions. The readiness to change literature offers several instruments (McConnaughy, Prochaska, & Velicer, 1983; Prochaska & DeClemente, 1992; Prochaska & Norcross, 2001, 2007). I have found that talking through these questions rather than asking him to answer them on a form produces richer assessment information. Follow-up questions occur naturally and easily. One question that often produces telling information for me is this one: "If you could change anything at all about your life, what would it be?" It is helpful but cautionary when a man answers, "Change my boss," or, "Get people to see that I'm right." Or, "Nothing." A man who responds, "I really need to control my temper" is in a different place.

MEET A CLINICIAN-SCHOLAR

SUPAVAN KHAMPHAKDY-BROWN

Supavan Khamphakdy's interest in authoritarian behavior is both personal and professional. On the personal side, she was born to parents caught in the crossfire of the Laotian civil war at the time of the Vietnam conflict. On one side was the Pathēt Lao (the Laotian equivalent of the Viet Cong in North Vietnam) and the Khmer Rouge in Cambodia. On the other side was the Royal Lao Army, supported by the U.S. and the Hmong. After the United States combat role in Vietnam ceased, the Laotian civil war ended with the formation of a coalition government. However, that new government quickly fell apart. The Pathēt Lao, supported by the occupying forces of the North Vietnamese army, took over Laos in December 1975. The Laotian monarchy was abolished, and the communist Lao People's Democratic Republic was formed.

Prior to the communist takeover, Supavan's father worked for both the United Nations and the Laotian government as a drug enforcement and customs officer, dealing with opium raids and patrolling the borders. After the takeover, he worked for the new Laotian government in a similar role, though he was periodically required to attend "reeducation" camps run by the Pathēt Lao. The camps were set up in the Laotian wilderness and heavily guarded by troops. Internees had to forage for food and build their own bamboo shelters. During the day, they cut wood, built roads, and worked in the fields. In the evenings, they attended indoctrination sessions, complete with public self-criticism. Captives were tightly controlled, never being allowed to settle in one place. Many died of malaria, and some colleagues of Supavan's father simply disappeared.

Supavan was born at home 2 years after her father's "reeducation" began under the Pathēt Lao. Life in their community of Luang Namtha soon became untenable for the family under authoritarian rule, so when Supavan was 3 years old, the family escaped to a refugee camp in Thailand. They eventually arrived in the United States and settled in the State of Missouri. Her family included two sisters and her parents, Sisavath and Chidsuphin Khamphakdee. They were sponsored by a Christian church that helped them find housing, work, and a social support community. All of them became naturalized U.S. citizens in 1986.

Supavan's professional interests are rooted in these family experiences. How does a stressful early life affect a child? How are social norms learned? And is authoritarian behavior changeable? These questions were natural—if not inevitable—for her. She fell in love with psychology as a way to think about these issues. Supavan graduated summa cum laude with degrees in psychology and sociology. Her earliest clinical services were provided to children harmed by authoritarian men who engaged in domestic violence. She worked closely with the children, helping them establish safe routines and healthy expressions of their troubled emotions. She also worked for the State of Kansas as a family advocate, again addressing the connections between painful early life experiences and maladaptive family functioning.

While working on her PhD in counseling psychology from the University of Missouri in Kansas City, Supavan became involved with a free outreach service for refugee families in Kansas City. The agency provided advocacy, counseling, and home visits to displaced families. In so many ways, Supavan's personal experiences as a refugee from an authoritarian regime have become the focus of her professional interests as a psychologist.

More recently, she has been my colleague in working with authoritarian men at the Professional Renewal Center® in Lawrence, Kansas. Our day treatment facility provides treatment to patients who devote many weeks to understanding and regulating their inclinations to be domineering and manipulative. Supavan is an ideal therapeutic companion for men making this journey. Her steady encouragement enables them to confront the impact of painful early life experiences, and her focus on mindfulness gives them skills for managing the emotions associated with these memories. Multiple times each week, she administers the Summary of Themes from Early Life (STEM), an assessment protocol described in this chapter.

ASSESSING AUTHORITARIAN TRAITS

What Is the STEM of Your Current Challenges?

Several luminaries in the history of psychology have written about the therapeutic value of recalling early life memories, including Sigmund Freud and Alfred Adler (Freud, 1899/1989, p. 124; Adler, 1931/1998, p. 73).

Martin Mayman deepened our awareness of the link between childhood memories and adulthood actions. In a career that spanned 50 years, mostly at the University of Michigan, he wrote 28 scientific papers on assessment, many of them becoming classics. He may be best known for his development of the Early Memories Test:

> I hope to show that early memories are not autobiographical truths, nor even "memories" in the strictest sense of the term, but largely retrospective inventions developed to express psychological truths rather than objective truths about the person's life; that early memories are expressions of important fantasies around which a person's character structure is organized; that early memories are selected (unconsciously) by the person to conform with and confirm ingrained images of himself and others around object relational themes... In short, I propose that a person's adult character structure is organized around object-relational themes which intrude projectively into the structure and content of his early memories just as they occur repetitively in his relations with significant persons in his life. (Mayman, 1968, p. 304)

Early memories do not have to be accurate to be useful. Content is what matters. A man's childhood stories provide a rich look at early versions of his adult life: how he thinks of himself, how he relates to others, and how he has adapted to the world around him. Mayman collected memories using a set of 16 questions, such as a person's earliest memory, earliest memory of mother, happiest earliest memory, and memories that bring back feelings of anger, fear, or shame (Mayman, 1968, p. 309). Clinicians then assess each memory's "predominant affect tone" (pleasant versus unpleasant), how it "depicts" others (as benevolent or malevolent), and how early life caregivers are shown (Karliner, Westrich, Shedler, & Mayman, 1996, p. 61). Other approaches to the retrieval of early life memories have been developed, such as using cue words on cards as prompts (Williams, 2003).

Numerous studies have shown that clinically useful findings come from early memories—information about a person's personality, relationship patterns, depression, borderline pathology, aggression, and dependency (cf., Fowler, Hilsenroth, & Handler, 2000); trauma (Parks & Balon, 1995); and even about the roots of a narcissistic personality disorder (Shulman & Ferguson, 1988).

With a colleague at the Professional Renewal Center®, I have developed a public domain tool that enables authoritarian men to recall early life memories. Virtually all men participate in the exercise with curiosity. We call the instrument the Summary of Themes from Early Memories (STEM) as a way to emphasize that the purpose of the activity is to get to the stem of the problem (Robertson & Khamphadky-Brown, 2010). The questionnaire elicits memories of specific events, not general impressions. See Exhibit 8.1.

Exhibit 8.1 Summary of Themes from Early Memories[*]

To the Psychotherapist: The following questions are asked in a face-to-face conversation with the client. Each memory is copied down verbatim. It takes about 60–90 minutes to administer the questions. For *each* question, ask the following follow-up questions:

   a. What is your impression of yourself in the story?
   b. What are your impressions of others in the event?
   c. What is the predominant emotional tone of the memory?
   d. What is the most vivid scene in the memory—a visual snapshot that stands out?

Verbal Instructions to the Client: In this conversation, I'm going to ask you about some events from your life as a child. My hope is that these memories will help both of us understand your current situation better. I am using the word "memory" in a very specific way to refer to a particular incident or event. For example, you might begin with a comment like "I remember one time when..."

   1. What is your earliest memory of anything at all? What is your next earliest memory?
   2. What is your earliest memory of your mother? And your next earliest?
   3. Can you remember a comment your mother made about what she thought of you?
   4. What is your earliest memory of your father? And your next earliest?
   5. Can you remember a comment your father made about what he actually thought of you?
   6. What is your earliest memory of school?
   7. Is there an event you now regard as having had a significant impact on your life?
   8. What was your favorite story or book as a child? What did you like about the story?

---

[*] The *Summary of Themes from Early Life* is copyrighted by J. M. Robertson, 2007. It may be freely used and copied if: (1) the author is identified on all copies, (2) no changes are made to the wording, and (3) it is not sold for profit.

9. What memory illustrates what you thought of yourself as a child?
10. What did you learn about life from your childhood? Life is...

From this information, a tentative set of developmental themes is easily found. It is tentative because it is helpful to review the themes with the man before settling on them as subject matter for therapy. The therapist's task is to step back and reread each early memory as a metaphor. What is the underlying message or the theme in the story? The focus is not on what the story is *about*, but on what the memory *is saying* about what the child is learning. The results reveal patterns that have influenced or governed the man's life ever since.

We now have collected literally thousands of early life memories and find that they can be readily assigned to just four categories: the boy's early self-concepts, his relational patterns, his adaptive strategies, and the lessons he learned about how life works.

Self-Concepts

Memories in this category reveal an authoritarian man's embryonic views of himself. Is he self-critical or self-congratulatory in the story? Does he engage in any self-regulatory behavior? What about his emotional stability or lability? Is his behavior self-caring or self-defeating? How does he use (or see others use) power and control? Does he see himself as superior to others, or equal? Here are some examples that have sprung from our data, worded in the first-person language of the man's own point of view. Some of the self-concepts are rather grandiose, while others reveal underlying distress. Typically, comments that admit vulnerability are not volunteered by authoritarian men in an assessment (there is much more bravado), but uncertainty does appear readily in the indirect task of recalling memories from childhood.

I am always competent.	I am different and don't belong.
I am a special child.	I am self-conscious.
I am superior.	Inside, I feel small, inferior.
I am carefree; others care for me.	I constantly feel fear.
I have important spiritual insights.	I am too emotional.
I am reliable and get things done.	I am unable to defend against danger.
I am self-focused.	I need to be stronger.
I am smart.	I get anxious in social settings.
I am disciplined.	I easily get angry.
I am inquisitive and curious.	I feel trapped, helpless, caught.

Relational Patterns

Another category of memories deals with a boy's earliest relationships. Is he alone in the stories? If others are mentioned, are they prominent or in the background? Are others viewed more with trust or suspicion? Are the interactions marked with warmth and connection, or isolation and insecurity? The following phrases show the breadth of relational themes that we have found in the early life memories. None of them, you will notice, portray secure and stable relationships with others.

I feel insecure in relationships.	I can trick or bully others.
I am afraid of rejection.	I often feel isolated, lonely.
I cannot control my anger.	I cannot trust anyone.
I never seem to feel safe with others.	My parents were absent, unavailable.
I am never good enough for others.	Loss and grief are best ignored.
Love seems to be based on performance.	I am afraid of abandonment.
Relationships are unstable, unpredictable.	Violence seems normal.
Conflict feels frightening.	I feel doted on by others.
I cannot let things go.	Problems are not my fault, usually.

Adaptive Strategies

Other childhood memories of authoritarian men reveal early versions of adult strategies for adapting to problems. How did the boy respond to challenges, expectations, traumas, successes, disappointments, intrusions, or threats? Does he describe himself as active in some way—resilient, defiant, self-sufficient? Or are more passive approaches used—withdrawal, repression, self-neglect? Here are some representative adaptive themes appearing in our collection of developmental memories:

I must depend on myself, not others.	I must be perfect.
I need external behavior controls.	I withdraw, avoid, and ignore.
I escape into fantasy and imagination.	I can laugh my pain away.
I achieve, perform, and accomplish.	I try hard to please.
I bounce back and try again.	I pray when things are desperate.
I escape into work.	I minimize my responsibility.
I become a peacekeeper.	I act emotionally tough.
I suppress or hide emotions.	I ruminate and obsess.
I numb myself with substances.	I seek thrills, risks.
I control things around me.	I learn how to get my way.

Lessons Learned

Other memories reveal what a child learned about life. These long-standing lessons may have become unquestioned truths for the man. When the origins of these lessons are uncovered, understanding follows—how his self-concepts formed, how relationship patterns developed, and how maladaptive behavior got started. His life begins to "make sense" to him. Discussions follow easily. Examples of lessons learned from our data include the following:

Ethnic clashes are normal.	Men are superior to women.
Acting out is acceptable.	Life is unfair.
Men are in control.	Men have no emotions.
The world is a dangerous place.	No friendship lasts.
If you need it, take it.	Everyone manipulates.
Nature is safer than people.	Trauma is inevitable.
Mother is my protector.	Fathers ignore children.
Always be vigilant.	Men must provide, regardless.
Others must praise me.	Hard work wins approval.
Hitting when angry is normal.	Dishonesty works.

Presenting the Findings

It is extremely useful to discuss these themes with the client. To do this, we write a narrative of the themes, including portions of memories that illustrate each theme. We then read the document to him as a draft. When men hear these themes and listen to their memories in their own words, strong emotions can be aroused. Eyes well up, even in emotionally hardened men. They quickly begin to see parallels between their early life experiences and their current adult problems. Listening to their memories enables them to see their presenting issues from a distance, with a broader perspective. To use the language of researchers, they can take a point of view that is longitudinal, not cross-sectional. This leads a man, almost inevitably, to serious reflections about difficulties in his personal history: his negative self-concepts, his unsatisfactory relationships, his ineffective coping skills, or his cynical views about how the world works. Discussions about these matters are immediate. The conversations become intense, reflective, and motivating. Although it is "just the assessment," therapeutic insight has occurred and psychotherapy has begun. More importantly, a new relationship is starting.

Let us catch up on Ramu and David. If you have not read the earlier introductions to these two men, you may want to review the introductions to their stories in the preceding chapter.

Case Study 1—Ramu: A Tough Guy's STEM

SELF-CONCEPTS

I am special. Ramu told several stories that portrayed himself as exceptional and out of the ordinary. His earliest memory is of being told about his birth by his mother. *"Everyone in the family came to see me in the hospital. And that's the way it's always been. My whole family dotes on me. They are all happy to have me in their family, and be their leader."* He also remembers being regarded as an extraordinary student in school. He was called into the principal's office one day and found his parents there waiting for him. *"The principal told my parents how bright I was, and that they should treat me special."* He loved bringing his report cards home, because *"they always were perfect and everyone just loved it."* His mother and grandmother would show the card to others in their Indian American community. *"Everyone knew about me because my high grades happened to so few."* Remembering his student days, he observed, *"I was perfect—just perfect."*

Others dote on me. Ramu smiled as he recalled his mother's devotion to him. *"She thought I could do no wrong, that I was everything."* He felt *"like a king"* when he was around her. *"She met my every need. I mean, she would jump off a bridge for me. She just doted on me, day in and day out. I loved her because she couldn't do enough for the family."* He added, *"She was a great homemaker, too. We could eat off the floor in her kitchen."*

RELATIONAL PATTERNS

I am often alone. None of Ramu's memories included peers or friends. He remembered an early birthday party in which he got a tricycle and learned how to ride it, but the memory didn't include any other children. All his memories were similar in this regard. If others were present, they were on the sidelines, watching him. When this observation was offered to him at the end of the exercise, he readily agreed. *"Yes, I was alone at lot. I think it's because our family moved a lot. My father was looking for the right place to start a restaurant. It's also because I was Indian, I think. Other children didn't like me. I never had a best friend."* He paused, and added, *"Still don't have a best friend, for that matter."*

Some people abuse me without cause. Another theme in his memories is the sense of being victimized. His relatively small high school had a football team, and all the boys were expected to try out for football. His memories of those events were uniformly bad. *"I hated it. There was one guy who was a foot taller than me, and very strong. He attacked me and nobody came to my defense. Not even the coaches. I did nothing to him, and he kept doing it."* With some anger he recalled, *"I was heavy as a kid; well, I was fat. And bigger boys used to punch me in the stomach just to see it jiggle. It was awful."* In a telling comment, he added, "*You know, I still have to watch out for people taking advantage of me. I think that's part of what makes me a good manager. I am not fooled by people.*"

ADAPTIVE STRATEGIES

I must stand up for myself. Ramu recalled that his father was "*very passionate*" about his family, "*maybe too much.*" He saw his father sometimes cry over events that occurred to the family, and Ramu despised him for it. "*I saw it as the sign of weakness that it was.*" When teachers did not protect him in school, he decided to fight back. "*If they couldn't help me, then I had to stand up for myself. That's the way it is in life—sometimes you just have to take things into your hands and not depend on anyone.*" He learned to disable others by "*kicking their knees and moving fast*" to avoid getting hurt.

I must excel academically. Ramu recalls the excitement of learning something new in school. "*It was the only thing that made school worthwhile.*" He remembers the first time he got recognized for being a smart child. "*I was learning to read, and it was great to have the teacher tell everyone I was a good reader.*" He became a voracious reader, even reading randomly from a multivolume encyclopedia in his home. He remembers, "*The harder I worked at school, the more attention I got.*"

I must not express my emotions. He remembers feeling angry at his father for being at the restaurant "*all the time,*" rather than paying attention to him. But "*I didn't show it because I was fearful of what my happen, so I just found a book and read.*" His books became a way of escaping and avoiding emotions. Even though his father cried from time to time, Ramu remembers being told not to. "*I cried once when I fell off my new bicycle. My father said, 'Maybe you are too young to have a bike,' and walked away.*"

WORLDVIEWS

The world is dangerous. Ramu offered several memories that illustrated his childhood view that the world was a dangerous and unpredictable place. His earliest memories were about waking up in the middle of nightmares. In school, he remembers being bullied by other students who not only called him names that were ethnic slurs but also beat him up on the edges of the playground. He reports being severely beaten on several occasions and having his arm slashed on his first day of seventh grade. In addition, he recalls avoiding social events because he was "*too embarrassed about everything. Other kids laughed at me a lot, so I just stayed away from them.*"

The world is unjust. Ramu recalled several examples of mistreatment based on his Indian heritage. "*You wouldn't believe the names I was called, just because my skin was dark. It's not like I was that different from other kids. I was born here, for God's sake. I spoke a lot better

English than they did, and there was no accent, either. Yet I was never treated the same as everybody else."

SUMMATIVE COMMENT

Ramu's early life memories hint at themes that have become dominant in his adult life. He still believes he is special and deserves the instant attention of his staff. When staff cannot meet his immediate need, he rages. Internally, he feels alone and at risk of being abused in the unjust world around him. And so he becomes vigilant, ignores his emotions, and puts all his energy into accomplishing at a high level. He escapes from his inner distress by working very long hours, just as his father did.

Case Study 2—David: A True Believer, STEM of a Zealous Follower

SELF-CONCEPTS

I am inferior and never good enough. As a child, David remembers feeling inferior. He had little confidence in himself. He was smaller than other boys and thought of himself as clumsy, always embarrassing himself. He remembers once urinating in his seat in his Christian elementary school. *"I was too embarrassed to ask the teacher to use the restroom. Just going there called attention to myself. So I just snuck home that day, and felt like a total failure."*

Academically, David remembered never feeling *"good enough."* He was forced to do his homework each evening at the dinner table, where his parents could keep an eye on him to make sure he wasn't *"dawdling."* In spite of his success in school, he regarded himself as slow and *"dumb."* He remembers one assignment in the fourth grade. *"We were supposed to write about ourselves. I just wrote on my paper that I was the dumbest kid in class. I really thought I was."*

I can avoid getting caught. To get attention, David found that he could be a class clown. *"It helped me get away with murder,"* he recalls. He remembers one time when the teacher put him in time-out, and she made him sit by her at the front of the class. *"I tried tickling her leg, to see if she would laugh. But she didn't. She got mad. The other kids laughed, however. And that made it worthwhile."* As a high school student he remembers shoplifting escapades and drinking beer illegally. *"I could do what I wanted, and I didn't have to answer to anyone. I had a lot of fun."* With a smile, he adds, *"I was probably a lot more sneaky than I should have been."*

I act impulsively. David remembers having much trouble regulating his emotions. *"I was impulsive, I'll tell you that. I would just think of doing something, and then do it immediately. I never thought about consequences."* He illustrated this with a story from his junior high years. "*Our gym had a balcony around the edge of it for people to watch basketball games. One day, I just wondered what it would be like to jump. And so I did. It scared people, but I thought it was funny. Now, I think it was stupid, but that's the way I've always done things.*"

RELATIONAL PATTERNS

I am a target. David offered many memories about being bullied by bigger and older children. "*There was something about me that made me a target. I hated it.*" He recalled the glee with which older boys in elementary school stole his lunch, pushed his textbooks on the floor, and ridiculed him in the hallways. In junior high school, he was scorned in gym class for being small and weak. He found the experiences so humiliating that he feigned injuries and illness to avoid the derision.

It is hard to get reassurance from others. David tried hard to win assurance from teachers in his Christian elementary school. "*I remember once we were given an assignment to color in a big elephant going into Noah's ark. I worked really hard on it, trying to stay inside the lines. Other kids finished quickly, but I took extra time to do it right. I hoped the teacher would like it. But all she said was, 'Davey, it's a nice elephant, but you took too much time.' I wanted her to say something nice, and she didn't.*"

David also tried to get his father's approval. "*I worked on a wood project at home in the garage. I cut out the pieces for a birdhouse. I didn't work by any plans or anything. I showed it to my father, and all he said was, 'Birds will get wet in there. Why did you make the crack in the roof so wide?' I felt so hurt. I wanted him to like it, and he didn't.*"

WORLDVIEWS

The world is an evil place. Very early, David decided the world was unsafe and filled with evil. This message came from his parents, the preacher at his church, and the teachers in his Bible school. "*My father was scary. He spanked us kids a lot when we misbehaved.*" But when the boys hit each other in a fight, the message changed. "*He would say, 'Boys, don't hit each other. That's the evil way of the world.' Whenever we did something he didn't like, that's what he said. 'It's the evil way of the world.'*" David added, "*But you know, he was basically right. I respect him for it now.*"

At church, "*My family sat on the second row. It was close enough that I could see the saliva flying out of the preacher's mouth. He talked a lot about sin because everybody is a sinner. He described how hellfire would burn everybody up. He was preaching the truth, but I have to admit it was scary to me as a kid. For a long time, I wanted to know what brimstone was, but I was afraid to ask. Thank God he also talked about salvation, so there was some hope for us boys who were sinners.*"

People don't care about me. In recalling his early memories, David struggled to identify feelings in others. He remembered his own emotions: sad about the death of his dog, angry about being left out of the school play, and embarrassed when girls called him names for being overweight. But the feelings of others were a mystery to him. *"I don't remember paying much attention to other people. I was so focused on my own problems."* He explained, *"I guess that's because people just took advantage of me, all the time."*

God forgives any sins. *"I was taught that only God is good. All human beings are bad. The only cure is forgiveness. So each Sunday, the preacher would tell the sinners to come down to the altar to ask forgiveness from God. No matter what you did, all could be forgiven if you went down to the altar in church, raised your hands to God and prayed."* David added, *"You know what? That still gives me hope. I've made some mistakes in life, but I believe God forgives. I really do. That makes my mistakes not so bad."*

ADAPTIVE STRATEGIES

Fantasy helps me escape. *"As child, I would get lost in my daydreams. I could really get into it. I'd look out the window at school and make up some story of revenge or something. The teacher would ask me a question, and I had no idea what she was talking about. I was not aware of things around me. I can still remember some of those fantasies to this day."* One had him being the sheriff and going to the homes of kids who had bullied him. *"I'd show up, swinging my big stick, and take them to jail. I felt like I was in charge, like anything in life was possible. The make-believe was very real to me as a little kid."* With just a hint of a tear, he added, *"That make-believe world was safe."*

SUMMATIVE COMMENT

Forms of David's early life themes continue into adulthood. He still sees the world as an unsafe place in which *"the little guy"* must be constantly on the alert. His career litigating manufacturers of unsafe products reinforces this view. When those attempts don't go well, he blames himself. He has no memories of feeling emotionally close and secure with either parent.

The mask he created in childhood has only grown thicker. He now has no close friends. He calls himself a *"robot with no emotions."* Other than feeling angry or sexual, he now seems unaware of his emotions. He relies heavily on his religious beliefs to cope with life, especially the divine promise of forgiveness. No matter what he does, he believes in saying a prayer and getting forgiveness. And that ends the matter.

What Can We Learn From Your Imagination?

Early memories are not the only source of instructive stories. The man's own imagination is another important source. The venerable Thematic Apperception Test (TAT) (Murray, 1943, 1965) invites a person to create stories based on a set of drawings on cards. The person is shown the cards, one after another, and asked to write a creative story about the thoughts and feelings of people in the pictures. Each story is to have a beginning, middle, and end. Some men need encouragement to overcome their cautiousness or self-doubt, but the stories are a task, and men do respond to the instructions. The resulting stories lead to conversations that men find both intriguing and instructive.

The use of the TAT with authoritarian men is qualitative. The focus is not on generating a score, but on fostering a conversation about important aspects of a man's life. Comparisons between the TAT stories and their own lives can lead men to unexpected insights during their assessments. Two examples illustrate the immediacy of this connection.

Exhibit 8.2 Thematic Apperception Tests for Ramu and David

Ramu—Tough Guy, Workplace Bully

Ramu wrote his TAT stories rapidly. He plowed ahead, as though finishing the assignment was more important than telling a carefully constructed story. The focus of his stories was on tasks and duties and performing them well. Absent from his stories was any reference to the internal lives of his characters. He did not speak of their motivations, fears, or hopes. Instead, the people in his stories are detached, much as he apparently feels in completing the tasks of his life. Ever so slightly, one character weeps about a loss, but then bravely moves on. His relationships convey no mutual awareness, no emotional force. He uses no emotional vocabulary. His most detailed story is about a man who has withdrawn from the world into a state of intellectual disengagement. Another story is about a man who tries to awaken his partner but gets "no response" from her, and so he remains alone. At the end of the exercise, he is asked about a theme from the stories that comes closest to describing his own situation. He replies, "*The sense of emptiness felt when one accomplishes much in life.*" In that phrase, he illustrates the thread that ties all the stories together: A man feels emotionally "dead" when he is externally driven and has no close connections with others.

David—True Believer, Zealous Follower

David's TAT stories present variations on a central theme: The world is a dangerous place that requires strong actions of self-defense, and when errors are made in this regard they can be forgiven. In one story, he describes a husband who has mistreated his wife. His story suggests that the resolution of her anguish can occur if the man simply says he is sorry. Nothing more than that is required. His characters swing from despair to hope in the instant of a reassuring word or touch. That is all it takes. Asked to reflect on a principle theme that appears across his stories, he says, *"Everyone makes mistakes. God knows I have. But God always forgives. This never fails, so I give Him all the glory when I defeat the big boys in court, and do great things for victims."* Much shows through in that comment—his hunger for justice, if not revenge; his narcissism; and his somewhat casual expectation that divine forgiveness is easy to obtain.

ASSESSING MASCULINITY NORMS: STRENGTHS AND STRESSORS

Can We Talk About Some of Your Strengths... As a Man?

Much of this book addresses the detrimental aspects of authoritarian male behavior. In this section, we flip the coin and briefly look at masculinity norms from a strengths perspective. This inquiry occurs in the context of an upsurge of interest in human strengths (Seligman & Csikszentmihalyi, 2000). Several taxonomies of human strengths have been proposed (e.g., Peterson & Seligman, 2004).

Why talk about strengths during an assessment with authoritarian men? Aren't they already thinking too highly of themselves? Well, yes—at least on the surface. But under that boastful and controlling exterior, they are often self-doubting and self-reproachful. They easily feel anxious, at risk, or inferior. When they walk into the psychotherapy room, they are not feeling their strengths, even though they may try to "take over" an assessment. They are feeling more like a failure than a success.

Research shows that emphasizing strengths does produce benefits (e.g., Lopez, 2008; Lopez & Snyder, 2009). However, a caution is in order. The relationship between personal strengths and masculinity norms is complex. One study probed this connection directly. Joseph Hammer and Glenn Good studied 250 men between the ages of 18 and 79. (Hammer & Good, 2010). They compared a set of personal strengths (grit, personal control, autonomy, endurance, resilience, self-esteem, and life satisfaction) with a list of stereotypical male norms (winning, emotional control, risk-taking, violence, dominance, self-reliance, primacy of work, and pursuit of status). They found that conformity to traditional masculine norms has both positive and negative correlations with various psychological strengths. So, for example, it is not enough simply to identify a man as having high levels of risk-taking or self-reliance. What is the context? Is it a strength for this man, or does it create problems for him?

Identifying Strengths

Some psychologists have proposed that more attention be given to positive aspects of masculinity in working with men. For example, Mark Kiselica and Matt Englar-Carlson have argued that developing a model of male strengths would "enhance our understanding of, and clinical work with, boys and men" (Kiselica & Englar-Carlson, 2010, p. 276). They have proposed the outline of such a model by naming ten strengths. Here are five of them:

- *Male relational styles.* Men connect with each other by doing things together. They share activities that are active, productive, or recreational. The activity becomes the setting in which men talk with each other in friendly, connecting, and often playful ways.
- *Male ways of caring.* Men enact their caring feelings. They show their love by doing things for those they love—building, repairing, and maintaining. They think about ways of protecting family assets.
- *Male self-reliance.* Men see a value in being responsible and in using their own skills and experiences to tackle problems. If given an assignment, they expect themselves to complete it.
- *The worker/provider tradition of men.* Men are expected to work, and most do. It is often regarded as a duty to generate the resource necessary to sustain the lives of those who depend on them. Many benefit from their labor.
- *Humanitarian service.* Men have developed and joined many organizations with a civic or service purpose. Most cities have several such organizations for men in business and the professions. Religious groups of men organize to meet community needs. Much good has been accomplished by these groups.

It should be noted that these strengths are human, not male-specific. The point here is that boys grow up seeing these strengths as appropriate male behavior.

Discussing Strengths

The next question is how to use this information in a qualitative assessment. How can a man be encouraged to think about strengths in a constructive way? The first step is simply to ask an open-ended question (e.g., "What do you think are some of your strengths?"). However, some men cannot produce much of an answer to this question. Or they will cite only their career achievements. But the arrogant exterior an authoritarian man often feels ineffective and incompetent to him. In fact, he may be baffled by a question about his strong points because he genuinely doubts he has any worth mentioning. After all, he is talking with a therapist, which means (at least to him) that he is a failure. So, if he does not respond well to an open-ended question, then handing him a list gives him a chance to identify traits he may not have regarded as pluses. "Here are some strengths common to many men. Which words describes you in some way?" (See Exhibit 8.3)

Exhibit 8.3 Can You Circle Some of Your Strengths?

Brilliant	Creative	Capable	Confident	Reliable	Courageous
Innovator	Likeable	Friendly	Loving	Caring	Considerate
Joyful	Energetic	Playful	Friendly	Forgiving	Calm
Satisfied	Trustworthy	Honest	Sober	Responsible	Powerful
Spiritual	Successful	Wealthy	Thankful	Healthy	Happy

Two types of responses tend to occur. Those heavy on narcissism will circle half the list, if not more. Those more attuned to the self-doubts that commonly underlie narcissism will be more hesitant with this task. Follow-up conversations are crucial. The therapist might ask, "Can you give me an example of how you use this strength?" "Have others commented on this quality?" "Is there any way this ability might help address the reason you are here?"

Another question more directly approaches the assessment task itself: "Is it possible to overuse this strength? If this happens sometimes, what are the consequences?" In this way, a man can begin reporting his version of the problems he needs to address. It is often much easier for a man to talk about his difficulties in terms of overused strengths than to simply admit a series of free-standing deficits. When does the pursuit of success become harmful to oneself? When do playful comments become ridicule? It takes patience and skill to help a man sort these questions out. Is this tendency *really* a strength?

Strength assessment can also be quantitative, of course. Examples of available instruments include the Spiritual Strengths Assessment (Eichler, Deegan, Canda, & Wells, 2006), the Values in Action-Inventory of Strengths (Peterson & Seligman, 2004), and the *Positive Psychological Assessment: A Handbook of Models and Measures* (Lopez and Snyder, 2003), a lengthy volume that evaluates many instruments assessing various strengths. The optimal use of these quantitative assessments is heuristic. When a man can be given a profile of how his answers compare to others, he becomes less defensive and more engaged. He becomes curious. It is the discussion that matters, not the numbers.

Identifying strengths need not mask a man's difficulties. The impact of his maladaptive behavior is still taken very seriously. The idea here is to broaden a man's perspective so that he can include personal strengths among his self-concepts. Motivation can be built, and inner resourcefulness can emerge.

This approach also helps the psychotherapist. It requires finding (at least) one positive thing about the troubled man in the room—giving attention to personal strengths *in addition* to his problematic tendencies, not instead of them. It also helps, I have found, to remind myself that this man wants to be happy and competent, just as I do.

What Are Your Stresses... As a Man?

All human strengths—overused or misused—have costs. The price tag for overusing masculine strengths can be painfully high. In this section, we review some of the costs for men who put all their energies into "being a man." To examine this issue, we need to review two categories of interest: norms and stresses. In the norms category, we are interested in what men believe it is *appropriate* for them to do, to feel, and to think. What do they believe others expect of them, just because they are men? In the stressor category, we want to know about the personal *consequences* of his views of masculinity. Does he feel any pressures, expectations, or judgments about being a man?

Masculine Norms

The first significant attempt to measure contemporary male role norms was produced in 1986 and called the Male Role Norms Scale (Thompson & Pleck, 1986). Several similar instruments have been published since. The one I mentioned in Chapter 5 has been the most useful for me—the Conformity to Masculine Norms Inventory. It was produced by Jim Mahalik and his colleagues at Boston College (Mahalik, Locke, Ludlow, Diemer, Scott, Gottfried et al., 2003).

To identify specific masculine role expectations currently faced by men, Mahalik reviewed the research literature and assembled focus groups that met weekly for 8 months to discuss their daily observations about the "normative messages from the dominant culture that have been identified in the masculinity literature" (Mahalik et al., 2003, p. 6). The group defined several norms and developed descriptive sentences for each norm: Winning ("In general, I will do anything to win"); Emotional Control ("I never share my feelings"); Risk-Taking ("Taking dangerous risks helps me to prove myself"); Violence ("Sometimes, violent action is necessary"); Power Over Women ("In general, I control the women in my life"); Dominance ("I should be in charge"); Playboy ("I would feel good if I had many sexual partners"); Self-Reliance ("I hate asking for help"); Primacy of Work ("I am often absorbed in my work"); Disdain for Homosexuals ("I would be furious if someone thought I was gay"); and Pursuit of Status ("It feels good to be important").

Men's scores vary along these dimensions. Some may score higher on violence, and lower on primacy of work, for example. The variables are continuums. Any man can subscribe to higher or lower levels of each of these constructs. Some variables identify thoughts about masculinity, while others address emotions and behavior.

What does a clinician gain from measuring a man's masculinity norms at an assessment? He gets a quick snapshot of how gender constructs may be justifying his authoritarian behavior. Note again the names of the subscales and how similar some of them are to our definition of authoritarianism: high on power, control, exploitation, and low on empathy and egalitarian views of others.

Masculine Stressors

A second approach to assessing masculinity looks at strains or stresses that might be associated with adhering to traditional masculinity norms. Hundreds of studies have demonstrated strong correlations between trying to live by these norms and reporting mental health difficulties.

Back in Chapter 5, I mentioned Jim O'Neil's work at the University of Connecticut. He developed a widely used instrument to measure masculine role conflict (O'Neil, Good, & Holmes, 1995), the Gender Role Conflict Scale (GRCS) (O'Neil, Helms, Gable, David, & Wrightsman, 1986). The GRCS has now been used in about 300 studies in many countries, including Australia, Ireland, England, Portugal, Korea, Japan, Sweden, Germany, Canada, Hungary, Columbia, Taiwan, Poland, Russia, Tasmania, Costa Rica, South Africa, Malta, and Indonesia. Findings are impressive. O'Neil has summarized the studies in print (O'Neil, 2008) and on his website (http://web.uconn.edu/joneil/). Below, I note some of the studies that examine variables associated with authoritarian behavior. Full references are found in the 2008 review or online.

Men with higher levels of Gender Role Conflict (GRC) are more likely to suffer from problems in the following list. Note how many of these issues describe our Authoritarian Man.

- *Personality difficulties.* They report more narcissism, compulsiveness, emotional instability, hostility, social discomfort, aggressiveness, paranoia, self-assertive entitlement, and anger.
- *Nonegalitarian attitudes.* They acknowledge more bias toward women, gays, and ethnic minorities, and show stronger sex role stereotyping.
- *Relational conflicts.* They report more domineering and rigid interpersonal behavior and more problems with sociability and intimacy. They also have problems with closeness, intimate self-disclosure, and emotional expression.
- *Use of power and control.* Men with high GRC are more likely to be involved with dating violence, hostile sexism, and hostility toward women. They are more likely to accept the rape myth, tolerate sexual harassment, and expect male entitlement. They also are more likely to engage in sexually aggressive behaviors and engage in other abusive behaviors and coercion. The GRCS actually distinguishes coercive from noncoercive men, aggressive from nonaggressive men, and domestic abusers from nonviolent men.

- *Poor marital interactions.* When wives report higher levels of GRC in their husbands, they also report more spousal criticism, more hostile behaviors during marital interactions, and lower levels of marital adjustments in themselves (less happiness, more depression, and more negative affect).
- *Poor coping skills.* Men with high GRC scores use less effective defenses (projection, denial, and isolation) and more often turn against others. They are more prone to self-destructive behavior, have higher suicidal probability, struggle more approach-avoidance conflicts, and have low problem-solving confidence.

And finally, a dissertation at Columbia University's Teacher's College examined the relationship between GRC and authoritarianism directly. William Chamberlin (1994) surveyed 188 airline pilots and found that men with high levels of GRC (feeling the need to be successful, powerful, and competitive) faced several problems. They were more likely to display authoritarian personality attributes, more likely to be unable to express interpersonal warmth to other men, and more likely to experience interpersonal conflict. GRC accounted for 34% of the variance on authoritarian personality attributes.

ASSESSING RELIGIOSITY: ISSUES AND AIDS

This section offers a quick primer of information about assessing religiosity. It begins with some comments about psychotherapists and religion, followed by a summary of the larger religious context in which religious men live in North America and Europe. I then describe in detail a qualitative approach to gathering *clinical* information using a structured conversation about a man's religious memories, concepts, ethics, emotions, rituals, and social experiences.

Issues to Consider

What If the Psychotherapist Is Not Religious?

Good question, because that includes a lot of therapists. Some of the most prominent contributors to the discipline of psychology have written biting and critical words about religion. Freud famously called religion the "universal obsession neurosis of humanity" (Freud, 1927/1989, p. 713). Behaviorist John Watson of Little Albert fame wanted to make religion illegal because it gives people excuses for weakness and failure and represents an obsolete form of social control (Simpson, 2000).

Most contemporary psychologists do not describe themselves as being either spiritual or religious (Bilgrave & Deluty, 2002; Smith & Orlinsky, 2004). Here is how one study summarized a survey of a random sample of members of the American Psychological Association:

> Relative to the general population, psychologists were more than twice as likely to claim no religion, three times more likely to describe religion as unimportant in their lives, and five times more likely to deny belief in God. They were also less likely to pray, to be a member of a religious congregation, or to attend worship.... It appears to be a relatively frequent experience among psychologists to have lost belief in God and disaffiliated from institutional religion. Of psychologists in our sample who ever believed in God, 27% no longer do. Such loss of faith is uncommon in the general population, occurring in less than 4%. (Delaney, Miller, & Bisonó, 2007, p. 542)

That is not to say psychologists are opposed to religion. "The vast majority... regarded religion as beneficial (82%) rather than harmful (7%) to mental health" (Delaney et al., 2007, p. 538). It just appears that their interests are more personal than institutional.

For psychologists, formal training in religious issues is rare. Two thirds of the training directors in clinical psychology graduate programs in the United States "never foresee religious/spiritual training being offered in their program" (Russell & Yarhouse, 2006, p. 434). For psychiatrists, however, two of every three medical schools *do* offer diversity training with modules that address religious and spiritual issues in the practice of medicine (Puchalski, 2004).

This religious uneasiness among some clinicians contrasts sharply with most people's behavior in a crisis. It is useful to remember that a person with severe emotional problems is just as likely to consult with a religious figure as a mental health professional (Weaver, Flannelly, & Oppenheimer, 2003). Among those immediately affected by the September 11 attack on the World Trade Center in the United States in 2001, more people talked with a religious counselor (60%) than a mental health professional (40%) to address their emotional distress (American Red Cross, 2002).

What are the implications of these findings? If many mental health professionals have little religious interest, does that mean they are less likely to ask their clients about religion? It may, but the cost will be high. Too much important information will be missed by not discussing these matters in an assessment.

Why? Why are questions about spirituality so important in an assessment? Because the religious reach is broad, stretching into all aspects of a man's life: education, politics, marriage, ethics, and social community. Therefore, asking men for their views on religious or spiritual matters is always instructive in some way. Sometimes, in unexpected ways.

In 1969, Ninian Smart wrote a book about religious experience that has become a classic. It is still readily available. Smart made two points with much relevance for psychotherapists. The first is his distinction (unusual at the time) between religious studies and traditional theology. They are not the same. Religious studies can be approached as an observer, but theology is typically studied as a person of faith. Therefore,

Smart argued, educators can teach *about* religion without promoting it (Smart, 1968).

Similarly, psychotherapists can discuss religion without expressing agreement. The man's religious views may express anything from abhorrence to adherence. He may be poorly informed or well read. What matters in the assessment is that the therapist show interest in these convictions, whatever they are.

Smart's second point is referenced in his obituary in *The Guardian* in London: "Just as no religion is an island, so Smart also argued that no culture and civilization is without its religion or world view. Failure to realize this can be a threat both to peace and the human imagination" (Gates, 2001). Every male client has a world view, whether formal or not. Even if only tacit or implicit, he has a comprehensive and personal set of ideas about the human experience: how life should be lived, how relationships really function, and how society ought to work. His views on these matters are likely to have a strong influence on his behavior, and those views may appear in his religious concepts.

A more thorny issue is the religious therapist who wants to use religious ideas in therapy. Richards and Bergin offer several cautionary recommendations for this scenario (cited by Shafranske, 2005, p. 508): inform clients at the first psychotherapy session that you may use a theistic perspective, describe spiritual interventions before using them and gain client approval, and never push religious beliefs onto a client.

Religion Does Have Some Benefits for Some Men

Much literature has been developed on the relationship between religion and health. Two handbooks have been published on these connections, one for mental health (Koenig, 1998) and one for physical health (Koenig, McCullough, and Larson, 2001). In an *American Psychologist* article that presented comprehensive review of the literature, Powell, Shahabi, and Thoresen (2003) summarized findings from about a dozen studies of more than 50,000 people. Two conclusions about benefits stand out:

- Regular church attendance is associated with a *25% reduction in mortality*, even when adjusted for covariate risk factors; for example, life expectancy is 7 years longer for those who attend regularly compared with those who never attend.
- Religion or spirituality *does protect against cardiovascular disease;* in particular, practices such as regular church attendance, meditation, yoga mantras, and rosary prayer produced measurable beneficial changes.

The findings also suggest that the most salient religious predictor of benefits is regular attendance at religious ceremonies and programs. Why is that? Several hypotheses have been offered and are worth consideration by psychotherapists with an interest in assessing social support.

The benefits may come from volunteerism among congregants (Musick, Herzog, & House, 1999), or from increased social contact from others who offer meals, financial assistance, childcare, and crisis support (Plante & Sherman, 2001). Others see benefits from the facilitation of positive emotions, an encouragement to rest, and experiences of rejuvenation (Muller, 1999), or from modeling and rewarding of caring and compassionate behavior toward others (Oman & Thoresen, 2003).

Of course, it must also be noted that religion has also been associated with many harmful experiences, as well, such as refusing life-saving medical procedures (blood transfusions, immunizations), failing to seek treatment in a timely way, permitting child abuse, and the fostering of emotional abuse, coercion, and even violence (cf., Koenig, McCullough, & Larson, 2001).

Men May Claim a Religious Preference...

The Baylor Religion Survey reports that 87% of US men claim a religious affiliation (Bader, Froese, Johnson, Mencken, & Stark, 2005). The diversity of religious preference among U.S. men is worth noting. In general terms, U.S. religious men describe themselves as more moderate (34.5%) and liberal (34.4%) than fundamentalist (25.7%) (Davis & Smith, 2008). The percentage of U.S. men stating a religious preference goes up to 95% when they are married and fathers (Mahoney, 2000). This coin has two sides, however. About 20% of men say they are more secular than religious. When asked directly by the American Religious Identification Survey, "When it comes to your outlook, do you regard yours as Secular, Somewhat Secular, Somewhat Religious, or Religious?" just under one fifth (19%) of American men chose one of the secular options (Kosmin, Mayer, & Keysar, 2001, p. 17). Beginning in the early 1990s, more and more U.S. men are identifying themselves as secular (Kosmin, Mayer, & Keysar, 2001, pp. 10–11). Most of those men in the United States are leaving Christianity, as the proportion of Christians has declined from 86% to 77% in the last few years (Kosmin, Mayer, & Keysar, 2001, p. 10).

In Europe, just under half (46%) of a sample of 27,000 people in the European Union say that religion is *not* important to them, though three fourths claim an affiliation. That means one of every four is best described as a nominal member (Eurobarometer, 2005). The same poll found a strong move away from traditional religious affiliation. This move is most pronounced in mostly Protestant countries (e.g., Netherlands, Denmark, Sweden) and in countries with a strong secularist tradition (e.g., France, Belgium). However, religious beliefs remain quite strong in Catholic countries (Poland, Croatia, and Slovakia) (Eurobaromater, 2005, pp. 9–11).

...But Men May Not Belong to The Religion They Prefer

It is not enough simply to ask a man about his religious affiliation during an assessment. That detail tells something, but sometimes not much. In North America, many men who claim religious affiliation never attend services. Only 41.3% of North American men say their religious preference is "strong" or "somewhat strong" (Davis & Smith, 2004). That may explain another finding: Only half (54%) of men who express a religious preference actually belong to their preferred local temple, sangha, church, mosque, or synagogue. This finding covers the largest 22 religious groups that include 92% of adults who identify with a religious group (Kosmin, Mayer, & Keysar, 2001).

In Europe, the opposite situation often exists. Affiliation rates are higher than rates of religious beliefs. In part, this is cultural. In Norway, for example, most children have been registered with the Church of Norway when they are born; the church is headed by the king of Norway. To exit the church rolls, they must make a formal request that involves bureaucratic paperwork. Few make this request because there is little advantage in doing so. The result is that 88% of the population is on the church membership lists. However, the religious beliefs of Norwegians reveal a different picture. A 2006 survey in Norway's largest newspaper, *Aftenosten* (The Evening Post), found that only 29% believe in "a god or deity," 23% believe a higher power without being certain of what that power is, and 22% were in doubt about the question (Demographics, 2010).

Still, other men may describe themselves as spiritual, but not religious. These two words—spiritual and religious—have become joined at the hip and are now used in tandem in public discourse. The distinction between them is important because many men are quite particular about them. They may define themselves as spiritual but not religious, religious but not spiritual, neither, or both. I have asked many authoritarian male clients about their ideas and preferences on this. Spiritual seems to evoke these notions: transcendence, internal experience, personal meaning, universal principles, and harmony with the natural world. Religious focuses more on statements of belief, buildings, membership lists, public rituals, and theism. Currently, 51.2% of U.S. men say they are religious, 33.5% say they are "spiritual but not religious," and only 11.1% say they are neither (Greenberg & Berktold, 2005).

Many Men Espouse Religious Beliefs...

Most men say they agree with many religious teachings. To illustrate, most U.S. men believe in the existence of a place called heaven (77%), literal angels (73%), Satan (67.6%), literal demons (61%), and say they "have no doubts that God exists" (59%) (Bader, Froese, Johnson, Mencken, & Stark, 2005). Most also believe there is life after death (67.5%) (Davis & Smith, 2004).

In Europe, people espouse religious beliefs at much lower levels. In the *Financial Times*/Harris Poll (2006), 12,000 people in five countries were asked about their beliefs in God. The percentages of those who acknowledged believing in "any form of God or any type of supreme being": Great Britain (35%), France (27%), Italy (62%), Spain (48%), and Germany (41%). In the same poll, 73% said yes to the same question in the United States.

... But May Have Little Religious Knowledge

Put more bluntly, North American men know very little about the actual beliefs of the groups they prefer. Professor Stephen Prothero of Boston University wrote a *New York Times* best seller that began with this observation: "Americans are both deeply religious and profoundly ignorant about religion." He continued, "There are Protestants who can't name the four gospels, Catholics who can't name the seven sacraments, and Jews who can't name the five books of Moses" (Prothero, 2007, p. 1). Is the professor correct? Yes, he is.

The Pew Forum on Religion and Public Life produced abundant data on this question (Pew Forum, 2010). The survey asked factual questions about various religions. Examples: Who led the exodus from Egypt? What was Mother Teresa's religion? Other questions concern the Ten Commandments, the Protestant Reformation, and which religion emphasizes nirvana. Basic questions, all of them. But half of North American men do not know the answers to them. The percentage of correct answers was about the same for men, regardless of their religious affiliation. The sample included 1,590 men, whose average score was 16.7 correct answers from the 32 questions (p. 43). Interestingly, higher scores were obtained by those who do *not* believe that Scripture is the literal word of God (their average score was three correct answers higher than those who believed in inerrancy). Similarly, those who do *not* believe in God scored *higher* than those who do believe in God (p. 51).

It is clear that asking a man to identify his religious preference on an intake form will produce some therapeutically useful information, but follow-up conversations can generate a wealth of important data at the assessment.

So What Difference Does Religious Affiliation Really Make?

For many, it matters a lot. The benefits are many, and sometimes the costs are high. Considerable research has examined the varying gains and harms from religious affiliation. Kenneth Pargament, a psychology professor at Bowling Green State University, summarized this large body of literature and drew five conclusions (Pargament, 2002, p. 168):

- First, some forms of religion are more helpful than others. Well-being has been linked positively to a religion that is internalized, intrinsically motivated, and based on a secure relationship with God, and negatively related to a religion that is imposed, unexamined, and reflective of a tenuous relationship with God and the world.
- Second, there are advantages and disadvantages to even controversial forms of religion, such as fundamentalism.
- Third, religion is particularly helpful to socially marginalized groups and to those who embed religion more fully in their lives.
- Fourth, religious beliefs and practices appear to be especially valuable in stressful situations that push people to the limits of their resources.
- Finally, the efficacy of religion is tied to the degree to which it is well integrated into an individual's life.

It is apparent that much more information is needed from a man during his assessment than his announced affiliation. What do his religious experiences, background, and beliefs say about him as a person? How can answering those questions help him understand the benefit of psychotherapy? What does a particular authoritarian man believe?

There are several ways to get answers to these questions, though some may be more clinically useful than others. The most direct approach, of course, is to ask the man as the assessment conversation unfolds. But other resources do exist and can be useful. For example, a clinician may want to quickly find reliable factual information about a religion, or consider ways of including religion into a particular school of psychotherapy. Let's look at resources in both these areas.

Aids to Consult

General References

I will mention a few sources that I've found useful. All can be helpful in providing background to a man's stated religious preference.

The most complete resource is the 15-volume *Encyclopedia of Religion* (Jones, 2005). More than 3,000 articles, many of them lengthy, are included. Topics include religious leaders, beliefs, organizations, values, rituals and practices, sacred spaces and buildings, and historical events. It is useful, but very pricey.

A more affordable resource for American religious groups is *Melton's Encyclopedia of American Religions* (Melton, Beverely, Jones, & Nadell, 2009). It includes information on nearly 2,500 religious groups in America. Entries have introductory and historical essays, and there is also a directory of contact information. Articles quickly orient the reader to some of the major themes that may be in the background when a man identifies a religious preference.

A similar but much smaller book is the annually produced *Handbook of Denominations in the United States* (e.g., Mead, Hill, & Atwood, 2005).

This resource is much less expensive and covers about 200 denominations with brief summaries and a list of readings for further information. Christian, Jewish, Islamic, and many other smaller groups are covered. Another valuable resource is the *Oxford Handbook of Global Religions* (Juergensmeyer, 2006),

Suggestions on therapeutic issues for members of various religions can be found in Richards and Bergin (2000). This edited volume features ideas for psychotherapists working with Roman Catholics, Eastern Orthodox Christians, Mainline Protestants, Evangelicals, Fundamentalists, Pentecostals, Mormons, Seventh-day Adventists, Orthodox Jews, Conservative and Reform Jews, Muslims, Buddhists, Hindus, and various ethnic-centered religious traditions.

Many measurements of religiousness exist. Nearly all of them are quantitative. The questions are standardized and specific and do not appear intended to spark real-time discussions with an administrator. The focus is more on religious content than on psychological information about a person's emotionality or behavior. For a review of many of these questionnaires, see Hill (2005). These tools ask about a person's general level of interest in religion, spiritual well-being, content of religious beliefs, stages of faith development, and so forth. Most feature rating scales and closed questions. If they are used, they can produce much more information when the findings are discussed directly with the client.

The Kansas Spiritual Assessment (KSA)

Next, I will describe a qualitative approach to gathering religious information. The purpose is not to gather religious data per se, but to generate useful clinical observations. On one level, this approach is a structured conversation about a man's religious background, ideas, and experiences. But at a deeper level, it also reveals any authoritarian tendencies he may have. It is an approach I have refined over hundreds of administrations, and it unfailingly provides clinical information that is immediately useful in the assessment. The purpose of the questions is to see a man's life through his eyes and to hear his philosophical views in his own words (Robertson, 2003).

Are men willing to talk about their religious background and experiences? An unqualified "yes." In fact, never has a man refused to discuss the matter. Most are eager to do so, including agnostics and atheists. Even men with little to no exposure to religion seem interested in talking about it.

The KSA (Exhibit 8.4) is structured around Ninian Smart's six "dimensions" common to all major faith communities: myths (stories), doctrines, ethics, rituals, experiences, and social relationships (Smart, 1969). In 1998, he added a seventh dimension, the material (Smart, 1998). The questions are asked in a face-to-face interview, with answers written down verbatim. Following administration, the therapist identifies themes and patterns in the information and writes a narrative. The narrative can be read to the client for review and editing. The ideas that emerge from this exercise inevitably stimulate reflection and discussion about a man's personality, relationship patterns, motivations, emotionality, and ideals.

The story dimension. Over the centuries, religions have used stories for many purposes: to inspire, to warn, and to teach. These stories are not easily or completely forgotten when children become adults. When these childhood religious stories are recalled, the comments are rich with metaphorical meaning and therapeutic value. For example, a man who admires young David's victory over the giant Goliath will later admit that *he* often feels inferior in life. A man who admires Muhammad's companion Umar because he was renowned for being fair later acknowledges that *he* has been treated with gross unfairness. Or a man who admires Dada-Ji, the Hindu leader whose teachings have challenged the caste system in India, later agrees that he has been victimized by casteism. Recalling a religious story from childhood makes it easier for a man to acknowledge his own views and vulnerabilities. When follow-up questions are raised—is this a trait you value in your own life?—the acknowledgement comes quickly and easily.

The conceptual dimension. Much clinical information comes from a man's views on religious teachings about the big questions life, such the existence of supernatural beings, the purpose of human life, and the meaning of suffering. These questions offer clues to a man's understanding of his own struggles or difficulties. Men may regard God as benevolent, distant, authoritative, or critical (Froese & Bader, 2010), and these views reveal much about themselves. Men who can name a book about religion they have liked as adults are quite willing to describe what appealed to them. But a man who is trying to make a good impression may name a book he has heard about, but he suddenly "cannot remember" anything at all about the contents.

The ethical dimension. All major religions have developed brief—and overlapping—codes of ethics that prohibit lying, stealing, killing, and so forth. Men who offer two or three personal ethical guidelines are identifying their behavioral norms in their own words. Many seemed surprised by follow-up questions that ask for examples of how they live by them, or how they respond when they fail to live up to them. Much is revealed in these questions. Can a man even acknowledge he makes mistakes? If he does, how does he cope with the aftermath? Is divine forgiveness cheap and easy? Does he determine not to repeat the behavior? Or does he try to repair any damage he has done?

The ritual dimension. Some men use rituals to make connections with something invisible: a divine presence, nirvana, higher consciousness, or a sacred energy. These rituals can be exceedingly important to some men, and most are quite willing to recall them for the interviewer. When faced with difficult life problems, many authoritarian men do not report finding support from rituals, or from any outside source, including people. They depend solely on themselves. Many simply cite axioms ("Everyone gets tackled in life; what matters is how you get up"), their personal determination ("I just try again"), or their tendency to withdraw from problems ("I go for a walk and just forget about things"). Except for True Believers, most face life's challenges alone.

The experiential dimension. Spiritual experiences are personal and often difficult to describe with language. Yet they have been written about in ways that inspire others. In *The Varieties of Religious Experience*, William James quoted this dramatic report from an unnamed clergyman:

> I remember the night, and almost the very spot on the hilltop, where my soul opened out, as it were, into the Infinite, and there was a rushing together of the two worlds, the inner and the outer. It was deep calling unto deep...reaching beyond the stars. I stood alone with Him, who had made me....The ordinary sense of things around me faded. For the moment nothing but an ineffable joy and exaltation remained. It is impossible fully to describe the experience. It was like the effect of some great orchestra when all the separate notes have melted into one swelling harmony that leaves the listener conscious of nothing save that is soul is being wafted upwards, and almost bursting with its own emotion. The perfect stillness of the night was thrilled by a more solemn silence (James, 1901/1958, p. 67).

Not all religious experiences are sublime, of course. Some are about harm or terror, or contact with "evil spirits." An assessment that overlooks these possibilities may miss hearing about an event that has become pivotal and defining in a man's life.

The social dimension. Most religious groups meet for ceremonies, charitable activities, religious studies, or friendships. These social connections can have great significance for men who have them, especially the True Believers. Answers to questions about involvement in a spiritual community provide a rich context for understanding a man's social world. How active and involved is he? Does he attend frequently or rarely, as an observer or as a leader, openly or with reservations?

Concluding the interview with an open-ended question about concepts or experiences that have not been covered gives him an opportunity to describe what is really important to him.

Exhibit 8.4 Kansas Spiritual Assessment[*]

To the Psychotherapist: The following questions can be asked in a conversational style. As far as possible, write down the responses verbatim. Follow-up questions for clarifications are appropriate. Administration takes between 60 and 90 minutes.

---

[*] The Kansas Spiritual Assessment is copyrighted by J. M. Robertson, 2003. It may be freely used and copied if: (1) the author is identified on all copies, (2) no changes are made to the wording, and (3) it is not sold for profit.

Verbal Instructions to the Client: In this conversation, I am interested in your thoughts on a topic many men find challenging: spirituality and religion. I hope you are willing to talk about this for a few minutes? (PAUSE) My questions are organized around some "big questions" of life, meaning suffering, ethics, and so forth. Some ideas could occupy us for hours, I suppose. But I am going to be writing down your answers, so I am hoping your comments can be succinct and to the point—just the core of your idea, or the heart of the matter.

STORIES

1. One way of beginning our conversation is to think about any religious experiences you may have had early in life. While you were growing up, did you attend any religious activities at all—programs, ceremonies, education, recreation? Can you describe them?
2. Can you give me an example of a religious story you remember hearing as a child—a story about a biblical figure, a saint, a religious leader or founder? What stood out for you in the story? Can you share a second story?
3. Can you name someone you admire from world history? What do you admire?

CONCEPTS

4. What is the most useful or interesting book about religion or spirituality you have read as an adult, if any—other than books regarded as sacred or scriptural? What did you like about the book? If no book has been read: What is the most interesting book you've read on any topic? What did you like?
5. Is there a spiritual idea that has special meaning for you—a saying, a teaching, a text, a story?
6. What is your best understanding of the purpose or function of human life, if you see one?
7. Have you learned anything about life from any personal experiences of suffering you may have had?
8. Do you have a belief in a supreme being or force/energy/intelligence? If so, can you describe this being or force?

ETHICS

9. When it comes to your personal behavior, what are the two or three most important ethical guidelines you try to live by?
10. Can you select any one of these guidelines, and give me an example of something you've done in the last month that illustrates how you live by that value?

"*What Is Wrong With Him?*" 189

11. Over the years, which of your ethical guidelines has been the most challenging for you to follow—that is, which has taken the most energy or effort?
12. When you act contrary to one of your own ethical guidelines, how do you respond?

PRACTICES

13. Over the course of your life, have you ever tried to enhance your life using spiritual activities, rituals, or practices? If so, can you describe them?
14. When life is difficult, what thoughts or activities sustain you?

EXPERIENCES

15. Have you ever had an intense transformational experience—an emotional event that made a strong impact on your life at the time?
16. Do you ever experience a connection with something greater or larger than yourself?
17. In your life, what *experiences* bring you the deepest happiness?
18. Have you ever had an experience with religion that has been harmful to you in some way?

GROUPS

19. Over the course of your life, have you ever used any religious or spiritual groups to help you face problems or difficulties?
20. Currently, are you closely associated with any group that meets regularly—religious or otherwise? If so, what do you gain the most from your involvement with others in the group?

REVIEW

21. Is there anything I have missed? Something about spirituality or religion that is important to you?
22. Let's step back from these questions for a moment. Reviewing all your comments, what stands out? What is most important for you about this topic?

We now return to David and Ramu, and see what their spiritual assessments revealed.

Exhibit 8.5 Spiritual Assessments for Ramu and David

Ramu—Tough Guy, Workplace Bully

Ramu was raised by Hindu parents active in their local faith community. When asked to recall an example of a religious story he heard as a child, Ramu quickly responded, *"The story of Ramayana."* He remembered hearing stories from this ancient epic often, and he learned early in life that his name was a form of the hero's name, Rama. This lengthy poem is familiar to everyone in Ramu's Hindu community. References to it appear often in movies, music, and plays.

The epic portrayed a strong and memorable message to young Ramu: *"Above all, you must do your duty. No matter what the price, do your duty. You must never fail."* In the story, Rama was the perfect son, the ideal husband, the hero in everything he did. He never failed. He was always right. Even though he was the victim of trickery by a conniving stepmother who made it impossible for him to be given his rightful role as king, Rama did the right thing. After years of banishment, Rama's loyalty and wisdom were finally rewarded and he triumphantly returned to the city as king. For centuries, this epic has been celebrated in the Indian Hindu community as the Festival of Lights. It is a much-anticipated festival for children, who get snacks, sweets, and brightly colored balloons. All through his childhood, then, Ramu's namesake, Rama—the hero of the story—was the center of celebration. Always, he was portrayed as a man who demonstrates the eternal truth that right trumps wrong. Many adults commented on the importance of his name, saying he always must live up to the true Rama and always do the right thing.

Ramu cited contemporary men who have lived like Rama, overcoming enormous threats in their pursuit of goodness: Gandhi, King, and Mandela. They knew the right thing to do, and they did it. *"They had to step out of the box to oppose racism, oppression, bigotry, and military occupation in their work."* The work of these men had personal appeal to Ramu as he recalled prejudice and bigotry directed toward him in the small suburban area in the United States where he grew up.

In sum, Ramu portrays in his work setting a strong outward commitment to do his duty. He must always do right. Reports from his worksite confirm this attitude, suggesting he thinks he always has the right answer, the right solution. His given name is Ramu, and he has become a metaphorical Rama, a man whose ideas are inherently correct and not to be doubted.

David—True Believer, Zealous Follower

David attended a conservative Christian church and Bible School all through his childhood. *"It was nondenominational, but very fundamentalist. We never flailed about, because we all knew what we believed."* One memory is particularly telling with regard to the impact of religion on his childhood. While in the 8th grade, David sent a note to one of his friends with the word "bitch" in it. His teacher intercepted the note and gave it to David's mother, who kept him out of school for a month to keep him away from *"evil influences."* He recalls the event was some respect: *"I don't fault her. She had the right ethics, even though I wasn't living up to them myself."*

David does not worry about the larger questions of life: the creation of the universe, the purpose of life, the reason for human suffering, and the possibility life after death. He believes these questions have all been answered, and his job is simply to submit to the Biblical interpretations of his church and to depend on them. When asked to recall favorite stories from his exposure to religious teachings, he mentioned three. All have a metaphorical connection to the issues that brought him to the assessment. The first story was about David's defeat of the giant Goliath. *"I liked the idea that David wasn't going to take the abuse anymore. He was the little guy winning against all odds. You see, the biggest one is not always the right one."* He also mentioned the courage of Daniel whose faith kept him from being eaten by lions, and the forgiveness granted a younger brother who squandered his father's wealth but returned home as the prodigal son. David's mission in life has required these traits, as well: courage to fight large interests in court, a sense of divine protection against adversaries, and forgiveness for overstepping the line in his vigorous defense of his clients.

SUMMARY: ASSESSING AN AUTHORITARIAN MAN

What does all this attention to qualitative assessment produce? Typically, a set of problems a man can acknowledge as his own. When he has felt collaborative in the process, he is more likely to find new insights. He will have thought carefully about his motivations, personality, strengths, masculinity, and religiosity. You will notice I have not mentioned all the variables that may need to be evaluated. Depending on the assessment question to be answered, a psychotherapist also may examine qualitatively a man's history of sexual behavior, use of substances, physical health, and so forth. Formal personality inventories are always used, as well.

The preceding qualitative techniques can be compared with findings from quantitative tests that provide means and standard deviations. Again and again, I have found a convergence of the qualitative and quantitative data. Standardized scores are indispensable—they provide a check on hypotheses and clinical opinions. But in working with authoritarian men, it is the relationship that is primary. And that is best facilitated by the qualitative approaches.

Most men want to know their diagnoses at the end of an assessment. But telling a man he has a disordered personality marked by narcissism, obsessive-compulsiveness, histrionic behavior, and defensiveness is both daunting and distancing (recall from Chapter 2 that these four traits are common in authoritarian men). But the relationship is primary. I have found that language matters greatly in fostering a connection at the end of an assessment. The dimensional approach to personality described by John Oldham and Lois Morris is exceedingly helpful. Consistent with the approaches outlined in this chapter, their presentation of personality problems is easy to read and stimulates much conversation. They present disorders as strengths gone overboard. Narcissism is defined as high levels of Self-Confidence. Obsessive-Compulsiveness is explained as too much Conscientiousness. And Histrionic patterns are described as a Dramatic style (Oldham & Morris, 1990). Using this language facilitates a conversation, not a judgment. A man ends up working *with* the assessment, rather than against it. It is easier to acknowledge having too much of a good thing than to admit to having an outright "personality disorder."

A final question: Does an interactive assessment actually improve treatment outcomes? Yes, it does. A meta-analytic review of 17 studies of assessments that used interactive client feedback found that 66% of the interactive clients scored higher than control groups and comparison groups on both treatment process and treatment outcome variables (Poston & Hanson, 2010).

Most importantly, a collaborative and insightful assessment sets the stage for a treatment relationship that is attuned and empathic, which is an experience both essential and novel for him.

CHAPTER
9

"How Can He Be Helped?"
A Multimodal Treatment: Self-Understanding and Self-Regulation

> When we are no longer able to change a situation—just think of an incurable disease such as inoperable cancer—we are challenged to change ourselves.
>
> —Viktor Frankl, Holocaust survivor (1959/1984, *Search for Meaning*, p. 135)

For years, Mark Twain struggled with how to write his own autobiography. He did not want to make it chronological. That was too predictable. So he ended up talking his memories out loud, as they occurred to him. No pen in hand. Just talking. He first tried speaking into Thomas Edison's newly invented recording device, but he gave that up because it was "as grave and unsmiling as the devil" (Smith, 2010, p. 20). Above all, Twain liked to make people smile, and a companionable stenographer would give him that audience. So he spent much of the next 3 years talking about himself . . . to her. He would sit in his bed surrounded by giant white pillows, or pace the room in his pajamas, telling his stories. Half a million words later, his autobiography was done. He loved the results, as he noted in a letter to his friend William Dean Howells:

> I've struck it! And I will give it away—to you. You will never know how much enjoyment you have lost until you get to dictating your autobiography; then you will realize with a pang, that you might have been doing it all your life.... And you will be astonished (& charmed) to see how like *talk* it is, & how real it sounds... & what a dewy & breezy & woodsy freshness it has.... (Smith, 2010, p. 20)

In spite of their reputation to the contrary, men do like to talk. Especially when they can talk about themselves to someone interested in every word. A skilled psychotherapist helps a man do just that—tell his own story in ways that facilitate deeper self-understanding. The "woodsy freshness" of that understanding can encourage him to think differently about himself and, eventually, to behave differently toward others.

It is useful to think about treatment with authoritarian men as having two parts. The first is self-understanding: helping a man to tell his own story in detail, from the beginning. That means he must take a long view of his life, thinking about his early life, his personality tendencies, his problematic behavior, his defenses. Reaching this level of self-understanding is a tall order, but most men are up to the challenge. It is a task, a project. And it makes use of the narcissism and compulsiveness that are likely part of his personality.

The second focus in treatment is self-regulation: giving him practical skills he can use to manage his thoughts, emotions, and behavior. Skill-based approaches allow him to try specific techniques for improving his life: moderating anger at home, refraining from aggression at work, developing more egalitarian relationships, acting more empathically, and so forth. I am using the word *multimodal* to emphasize the variety of technical strategies that can be used: targeting somatic distress, cognitive blocks, emotional reactivity, and relational limitations.

SELF-UNDERSTANDING

> I can give you nothing that has not already its being within yourself. I can throw open no picture gallery but your own soul. All I can give you is the opportunity, the impulse, the key. I can help make your own world visible. That is all.
>
> —Hermann Hesse, German novelist and poet (1971, *Portrait*, p. 113)

Self-awareness matters. In one study, both clients and therapists ranked it as the most helpful event that occurs in psychotherapy—more than 11 other variables, such as the development of positive views of oneself, problem clarification, relief from symptoms, and even problem resolution (Castonguay et al., 2010).

Self-awareness is also difficult to achieve. Authoritarian men see themselves through a distorted lens. The task of psychotherapy is to help them see those distortions in the lens itself. To put it mildly, this task is challenging.

Can We Work Together?

Ideally, the collaborative spirit that begins in the assessment continues into treatment. This cannot be assumed, however, especially with authoritarian male clients. These men do not move into a trusting relationship easily, as we have noted. All their lives they have tried to be in charge and to manipulate others into subservient roles. That tendency does not vanish when they sit in front of a psychotherapist. Understanding their ambivalence about working *with* therapists (as opposed to *against* them) can make this connection much easier to forge. There is no need to compete with an authoritarian male client. But there is a need to understand his long-practiced reluctance to be open and trusting. Well-timed and respectful comments about his ambivalence can be most helpful. Psychologist Glenn Good and I have written about our own experiences as psychotherapists in this regard, summarizing the reticence we have heard expressed by tough and independent male clients (Good & Robertson, 2010).

The following comments are real and represent an authoritarian man's best attempts to protect himself from risk that feels unmanageable. These thoughts—logical or not—do need to be respected because they represent his best efforts at making sense of his world. At the outset of therapy, these internal objections can make it challenging to begin working together. It helps to anticipate these concerns and to acknowledge them openly when they are mentioned, even if the reference is vague or indirect.

But I solve my problems myself. Male action heroes in the popular media are not weak or helpless. They fix problems by being strong, clever, and competitive. In this social context, who wants to ask for help? Calling a psychotherapist represents a failure. So, vulnerability and resistance walk into the therapist's office with him. An authoritarian man has years of practice masking such fears, so he may not tip his hand in the first session. But if those anxieties are present, they will leak out into the conversation at some point.

Responding skillfully to these hints is an art. It requires a keen sensitivity to the subtle distinction between being reassuring or patronizing. The man wants to be understood without feeling exposed, accepted without feeling undermined. When a man who is mandated for treatment makes a comment that reveals his need to be independent, why not acknowledge it: "I agree. I think you can solve your problems yourself, too. I certainly cannot solve them for you. But you and I do have one thing in common. We are expected to meet together for a while. How do *you* think we should spend our time?"

Why trust someone I don't know? Stories of men who abuse their power are common in popular culture. Every occupational barrel

MEET A SCHOLAR-CLINICIAN

GLENN E. GOOD

Most authoritarian men were bullied as boys. We reviewed that link in earlier chapters. However, not all bullied boys become authoritarian men. Some find a different pathway into adulthood. Glenn Good took a different route and has made parts of his journey public. On the occasion of his election as Fellow of the Society of Counseling Psychology in the American Psychological Association, Glenn told the following story. The bully in the incident is named Miles.

> What I have come to think of as a "defining moment" of my childhood involved Miles. We four boys were playing together at Miles' house. He had a pot of boiling water—I can't recall what he exactly intended to do with it or why he had it. What I recall is that it suddenly ended up being poured down my shoulders and back. I can still recall the searing pain—a pain that caused me to fall to the floor and writhe around seeking to cool my back on the cement slab floor. As I cried out in agony and thrashed, there was a sea of male faces looking down on me: Miles, the other boys, and Miles' teenage brother, the only boy who had more status than Miles himself. "Shut up and quit being a crybaby!" his brother said with a cutting sneer. In an instant, the emotional shame and humiliation of my "childish" and "wimpy" reaction became more prominent than the physical pain in my shoulders and back. I shut down my tears. Later, safely away from Miles and his brother, at the hospital with my parents, I still didn't cry. As the doctors painfully scraped

away the well-intentioned lotion Miles' mother had applied, I didn't make a sound. I didn't cry when I started Kindergarten with my back swaddled in bandages. I didn't cry again for twenty years. (Good, 2001)

Events like these can transform a boy's life. Some convert the shame into rage and become bullies themselves—not only toward other boys, but toward vulnerable adults in later life. Glenn did not walk that road. He became prosocial, not antisocial. He became a researcher and a clinician.

As a scholar, Dr. Good has investigated many aspects of what I am describing as male authoritarian behavior: abuses of power, the tendency to dominate and control, male violence, the objectification of women, racial and sexual prejudice. As a clinician, he has addressed these issues in the psychotherapy room. How did Glenn's interest in these topics arise? In his Fellows Address, he said, "In an odd kind of way, I owe Miles a tribute for shaping both my life and my interests. I have lived a piece of what I research and assist clients with."

Today, Dr. Good is a much honored scholar and mentor. When he was awarded the *William T. Kemper Fellowship for Teaching Excellence*, the inscription described him well: "an extraordinarily sensitive, insightful guide through the potentially troublesome topic of gender issues" (Good, 2005). The award quoted several of his students. One said Glenn "challenged us to push the boundaries of our thinking" in "a safe environment where we could explore the difficult topics of gender roles, race and sexuality." Another felt like a "genuine collaborator," and yet another described Glenn's enjoyment of his work as "both contagious and inspirational."

These warm comments also describe Dr. Good the clinician: safe, genuine, collaborative, inspirational. I have known Glenn well, and I agree with his students. He served as the cochair of my dissertation committee. We have been coauthors and copresenters at professional conferences. And he has been a trusted and valuable friend. Away from work, he rides bicycles, canoes on rivers, swims, and participates in long-distance runs.

A pithy line from the Scottish poet Robert Burns describes Glenn. In the satirical poem, "The Two Dogs," Burns imagines two dogs discussing the strange behavior of humans. One dog—Caesar—describes how the rich and powerful use authoritarian intimidation and mistreatment to control other humans. Burns pokes fun at these ruthless men by turning the tables on them. It is the observant Caesar who is given the honorable title *"the gentleman an' scholar."*

contains some rotten apples. Pharmacists mislabel. Clergy misuse children. Politicians mishandle funds. Teachers manhandle students. And...psychotherapists harm men. True, the vast majority of professionals do not violate their fiduciary responsibilities. But some do. How is a man to know the difference between a safe therapist and a risky one? What if he chooses someone who will harm him? Considered from this perspective, it becomes reasonable to avoid taking unnecessary chances. If a man believes he can solve his problem himself, why try a psychotherapist? Is it not better to try and fail...than to trust and fail? Why give someone else a chance to make things worse?

Inside the therapy room, trust must be earned in all the usual ways. It starts with being present and on time (seriously). It continues with being a real person, with unfeigned interest. It means avoiding false promises of hope, half-hearted expressions of support, and misleading comments of any kind. In a word, it means being genuine. Authoritarian men will test psychotherapists by being pushy, controlling, and challenging. The therapeutic task is to remain steady while keeping the larger objective in view—the development of an attuned relationship.

I'm not sure I really have a problem. The internal monologue goes something like this: "Maybe I am being set up. Maybe my boss needs me to have a problem. Or my wife is just trying to get rid of me. They *say* they want me to get help because I have a problem. But is that true?" Under this defensive stance lies a painful awareness. The man really may not know what he is doing wrong. This uncertainty must be set aside to simply make an appointment. I sometimes wonder if this is one reason so many first appointments for authoritarian men are initiated by someone else—an exasperated boss, a concerned mother, an angry partner, or a defense attorney. These "on behalf of" calls may be driven by compassion, but they also risk perpetuating the man's reluctance to admit having a problem.

For this reason, I prefer talking directly with the man before agreeing to an appointment for an assessment or treatment. I can begin developing a relationship in that first phone call. I can give him an idea of what it will be like to talk with me in the psychotherapy room. He will be making judgments about me, as he must. He will note the sound of my voice, the words I use, and my willingness to negotiate. But at the same time, he tacitly will be taking ownership of his own problem. This is not a hard and fast rule with me; there are some situations that make such phone calls impractical or impossible. But by and large, I want him to have a chance to begin seeing how we might work together. When this first conversation works well, the long process of developing attuned relationship has begun.

Most problems go away on their own. That does seem to be the case, sometimes. Soreness resolves without a medical visit. Anger fades and people seem to forget. It becomes tempting to wonder if ignoring a problem might solve it. Investigating may just stir things up.

Or so it may seem to a man. More precisely, so he hopes. But time does not heal all wounds. Even when they heal, scars remain. This makes it imperative to respect his initial hesitancy to admit having a flaw, yet not let him off the hook. A comment like, "I'm not sure you have a problem, either. I wonder how can we figure this out?" fosters more collaboration than, "Well, this is confusing because everyone around you sees a problem. Why is that, do you think?"

You can't force me to change. Authoritarian men do not wish to be coerced. This is a red-hot button. At all times, they must be in control. This socialized expectation is a social norm for most many men (Mahalik et al., 2003), but it is critically important for authoritarian men. It is one of the defining elements of their style to control situations and people around them. This makes mandated treatment—often the only way they come through the door—so utterly repugnant to them. They will be required to act in ways contrary to their lifelong practices, to their very instincts. They fear having to be vulnerable, cooperative, transparent, and empathic. These tendencies are not natural.

Therapists can respond to this fear by simply acknowledging it when it comes up. "I have no interest in forcing you to change. Others might, but I don't. I'm more interested in how *you* see this situation."

What Might Block Your Self-Understanding?

Most people have some defenses against self-understanding. Some realities are just too tough to admit. Authoritarian men have many such defenses. I have found it helpful to use two separate lexicons for defenses: one for professional settings and one for psychotherapy conversations. The first is professional in the sense that most mental health professionals have studied the defenses in the psychoanalytic literature. These strategies are sometimes called "ego-defense mechanisms," though many of them have become part of the everyday vernacular. The list is familiar: repression, denial, reaction formation, projection, displacement, rationalization, sublimation, regression, introjection, identification, compensation, and ritual. Much ink and electronic memory has been used to explain and debate these defenses against unwanted anxiety. The original idea was that these tactics defend the wounded ego from anxiety and injury, and are not necessarily pathological. They can be quite adaptive in helping a person avoid facing a painful reality by (temporarily) enabling a denial or distortion of some reality that is too difficult to face.

But this professional lexicon is arcane and generates suspicion in many men. Just hearing the term "defense mechanism" sounds pejorative to many men. It feels judgmental to hear they are "in denial" or "regressing." For this reason, I have developed a colloquial lexicon to use in sessions. Instead of labeling these strategies as defenses against anxiety, I have called them "Defenses Against Self-Understanding." This carries a different connotation for men. It feels less intrusive or judgmental, and the words are readily understood. Few men want to admit they do *not* want to understand themselves better. I have listed these colloquial descriptors on a poster and hung it on the wall of the group room in which we work. At least initially, these defenses are easier for men to acknowledge when they are looking at a poster.

Exhibit 9.1 Common Defenses Against Self-Understanding

Glaring	Withdrawing	Theorizing	Analyzing
Threatening	Switching	Criticizing	Attacking
Rationalizing	Just Joking	Minimizing	Contradicting
Mocking	Evading	Moralizing	Assuming
Opposing	Explaining	Generalizing	Grinning
Deflecting	Justifying	Overlooking	Ridiculing
Excusing	Demanding	Misleading	Forgetting
Filibustering	Sarcasm	Blaming	Accusing
Interrupting	Yes-But...	Arguing	Lecturing

In a group session, someone might simply point to the poster on the wall and ask another group member if he is "just joking" or making an important point. When the entire group looks at the list rather than the man who has told a distracting joke, the man feels less threatened. The entire group—including the jokester—can look at the wall for a moment. They are side by side looking at an issue. The discussion that ensues is a joint activity. Together, they work to help a man figure out what he is really doing. In individual psychotherapy rooms, the chart can play a similar role. Together, the two people can think about the word as a possible description of his behavior.

What About Setting Some Goals—Your Goals?

Most authoritarian men respond well to the invitation to set their own goals. It is *his* life, after all. Setting his own goals makes him a partner in the work. He is working *with* his therapist. He is not being told what he must change. This invites the collaboration that is crucial to therapeutic success. Remember, this population of men is independent to a fault. They are quite willing to "take charge" of the goal-setting task. I have encouraged men to write the goals in first-person language. I may encourage him with prompts, if necessary. "Do you want to see anything different in your relationships?" "What skills do you want to strengthen or add to your life?" And so on. The goals need to be specific and focused on learning something or doing something. It also is important to encourage him to define goals in ways that do not sacrifice his masculinity or his religiosity. Notice the I-language in the following objectives written by Ramu and David, whose stories we have been following. See Exhibit 9.2.

Exhibit 9.2 Treatment Goals Developed by Ramu and David

RAMU (TOUGH GUY, WORKPLACE BULLY)
1. I used to do things for fun. I've lost track of what some of those things are. I want to know why I stopped pursuing them, and how to get back to them.
2. What makes me so impatient with the incompetence of others?
3. I need some help with being a father. My sons are not doing well, and I need to try something different.
4. I need to find some guidelines or spirituality that keeps me focused on doing things the right way.
5. At work, I'm too forceful with my points of view. People back away from me. How can I better explain my ideas?
6. Most of all, how did I end up being the way I am: angry, disliked, and working too much? This makes no sense to me.

DAVID (TRUE BELIEVER, ZEALOUS FOLLOWER)
1. I obey strict rules in my faith. But I have broken some professional rules. I need to understand how this happened and what it means.
2. I wonder if all the bullying I experienced as a child has affected me.
3. I have not taken as much time for my family as I should. This confuses me, as I love them more than my clients at work.
4. I've been told I don't pay attention to how my behavior affects others. I need to understand this, but I don't know how to do it.

Given the severity of the problems Ramu and David faced, these objectives might seem to be a stretch. How can they move that far during an assessment? But I have found this is common. Most authoritarian men can become this self-aware during a qualitative assessment, especially when their motivation to return to work with new skills is high. Most take this task seriously and participate fully in the conversation that generates these self-written objectives.

Here Is The Central Task: What Is Your Story?

> There is no psychology; there is only biography and autobiography.
> —Thomas Szasz (1990, *The Untamed Tongue*, p. 195)

This therapeutic task—telling one's own story—takes advantage of an authoritarian man's interest in his own needs and opinions. The assignment is simple. Step back from the immediate situation and take a structured looked at three or four generations of your family background. It is a sizable project and takes several hours outside of sessions to complete. The story that emerges from this project becomes a shared understanding between psychotherapist and client. For the duration of therapy, references to the story become frequent and inevitable.

Of course, this quest for "making sense" of the story of one's life is not novel to authoritarian men, or to men in general. It is a human interest (Angus & McLeod, 2004).

Jennifer Ire (1997) wrote a qualitative dissertation about the actual experiences of those who have written their own stories. She found that people report several benefits. They express their emotions more easily. They shift their understanding of themselves in constructive ways. They change their relational behavior. Participants also noted that creating their life stories clarified problems that needed to be addressed and improved their abilities to work on those problems. They learned things about themselves that were new and unexpected.

I have seen these same benefits for authoritarian men who create their life stories. The task itself has intuitive appeal. The story can be revised over the course of therapy, and often is. The ultimate purpose is to facilitate a man's understanding of the sources of his maladaptive behavior. The point is *not* to label those behaviors as bad (for the tough guy) or evil (for the true believer), but rather to see them as coping strategies that developed early in life and were quite functional. This perspective feels more self-respecting and encourages motivation to make changes.

One useful way to assemble the story is to produce a genogram (McGoldrick, Gerson, & Shellenberger, 1999). This familiar technique is rooted in systems theory (Bowen, 1978) and produces a large poster-sized representation of a man's family, back to his grandparents or great-grandparents. Men nearly always need to make contact with family members to gather this information. They call parents and other relatives, some of whom they may not have seen in years. Constructing his family tree in a genogram format stimulates much reflection and self-understanding. A backstory is created that illumines current tendencies and problems. Men are prompted to review or ask family members about many aspects of life: how conflicts have been managed, how moral or religious values were taught or lived, how children were disciplined, addictions, definitions of success and failure, social norms for gender, and significant physical and emotional health problems. Heretofore unknown family stories may emerge about weddings, separations, and divorces. In this process, a man cannot help but think about ways in which his own interpersonal style has been influenced.

This investigative work makes it clear to a man that the male models in the family may have faced some of the same childhood disadvantages he lived with. Each man across the generations may have grown up only to express a new version of his father's maladaptive behavior. In just a few days of working on this task, men come to see themselves as impacted by ideas and behavior that turned out poorly for their fathers, uncles, and grandfathers. This enlarged awareness can create a Long Reflective Pause for a man. Generational behavior becomes personal. When he begins to see that he has become a new version of his rage-filled father, or that he treats his own children the way he was treated, he is jarred. He knows first-hand what it is like to be treated in ways that are unfair, manipulative, and controlling. The dawning recognition that he is simply repeating a pattern that goes back generations can hit hard. He begins to see his abusive father more empathically because his father was raised as he was. He faced the same challenges. This recognition, when it occurs, deepens motivation. A man may see that his behavior is creating for his children what he himself struggled with as a child. This project quietly encourages a man to begin taking responsibility for his own actions—not because the therapist tells him to, but because he begins to see himself as both harmed and harming.

> I would say that our patients never really despair because of any suffering in itself! Instead, their despair stems in each instance from a doubt as to whether suffering is meaningful. Man is ready and willing to shoulder any suffering as soon and as long as he can see a meaning in it.
>
> —Viktor Frankl (1961, *Logotherapy and the Challenge of Suffering*, p. 5)

SELF-REGULATION

Self-regulation is not a skill; it is a set of skills. This word, by the way, is appealing to men in therapy. Skills are tangible. "Psychobabble is mush," as one man told me. A *set* of skills is needed because we humans are "many-splendored" beings. We have sensations, emotions, thoughts, and relationships. We are an active species. In a word, we experience life multimodally. Managing all these dimensions effectively requires a set of skills.

Managing Somatic Distress

Men learn early to ignore their bodies. When boys are injured in a sport, they hear "Shake it off," "Rub some dirt in it," or "Suck it up." The point is clear. Don't pay attention to your body. Taken seriously, of course, these iconic sayings lead to trouble. A man at midlife can minimize serious chest pain as indigestion, or left arm pain as merely a strained muscle.

Psychophysiologic training. The field of psychophysiology rests on research that demonstrates a close association between physiological and psychological states. Researchers have demonstrated that thoughts and emotions affect many organ systems (Cacioppo, Tassinary, & Berntson, 2007). It has become broadly apparent that humans have significant somatic responses to their own thoughts and events around them. Bodies reveal these responses in ways that can be measured. When men *see* evidence that their thoughts affect skin temperature, for example, they can feel both motivated and rewarded.

The simplest biofeedback tool is a small and inexpensive thermometer that measures skin temperature on the finger. I have invited men to use this device during some psychotherapy sessions, suggesting they glance at changes as the topics of discussion shift. It can be quite startling for a man who thinks he is in total control of himself to see the temperature dropping as he talks about a stressful event. Some men have wanted to wear the device for a week, just to see what thoughts or emotions make their temperature go up or down. The principle benefit is a tangible awareness that their body systems function as accurate signaling devices. This suggests they can train themselves to notice changes in their bodies that warn them of impending risk—which muscle groups tighten the most, where their skin feels hot or cold, and how to sense when their pulses or respiration rates change. This takes practice, but it is a challenge that authoritarian men find appealing. In time, they begin generalizing this awareness into more effective self-regulatory skills. The sooner they can detect rising frustration or anxiety, the more opportunity they have to control their behavior. More expensive equipment can be used as well, such as instrumentation that measures brain wave patterns.

One practical outcome of using this modality is the discovery of which thinking habits are problematic. Bodies tighten when thoughts are rigid, obsessive, or binary. Skin temperature drops when emotions are agitated, sad, critical, or defensive. Men also learn the reverse: Their muscles relax and skin warms when they feel calm, stable, and secure. And so the contrasts emerge. Is he being accepting or argumentative, collaborative or competitive, responsive or reactive?

Mindfulness training. "Without awareness, we are not truly alive" (Bugental, 1999, p. 257). I sometimes ask a man, "Draw three circles on a piece of paper. Make each circle a different size, depending on how much energy and attention you give to three aspects of your life: past events, future events, and undivided attention to the present moment." Nearly all men make the present-tense circle the smallest. Many have just penciled a dot on the paper. This opens a discussion of self-awareness and how little time he spends noticing what is happening right now, this very second.

Self-awareness is a skill. It takes practice. It is worth the effort, because self-awareness is the gateway to self-understanding. This wisdom is ancient. "Yesterday is a memory. Tomorrow is the unknown. Now, is the knowing" (Sumedho, 1989, p. 3). Simple words, but with many implications for psychotherapy. The authoritarian man's past is gone. It is done. He cannot change any events that have already occurred. No mistake can be unmade. In some ways, this is good news for authoritarian men who have harmed their partners. A man will say of his wife, "Why does she keep bringing up the past? I can't change a thing." He's right. He cannot redo what is done. But it is also sobering news for him. Because his wife may be experiencing damage in the present. Even though he cannot change the past, he still must live with the ongoing consequences of his thoughts, words, and actions. He has harmed her in the past, but those memories remain influential in the present.

Similarly, the future has not arrived. When authoritarian men are confronted with the distress they create in others, they can be tempted to make promises. "I'll never do it again, I promise." In this way, attention on the anguish in the moment is deflected to events that have not yet occurred, and may never occur. These declarations of change can lose their impact, of course, if promised reformation never occurs, or lasts only briefly. He can always imagine and plan change. But he cannot live in moments that do not yet exist.

Both these strategies—looking back and looking forward—can be defensive. They enable a man to avoid dealing with the consequences of his own behavior. When he says, "Quit bringing up the past," he may be trying to avoid facing the music his behavior has created. Or when he says, "I'll do better; just watch me," he escapes into a future that does not exist.

This impasse can be broken by learning how to pay attention to what is happening right now, by addressing issues in real time. And that brings us to the word that has developed great cachet among psychotherapists in the last couple of decades: mindfulness.

At the outset, I must acknowledge that some men may *not* be ready to develop mindfulness skills. They may be massively depressed and unable to concentrate on anything. Or they may be suffering from a trauma that needs immediate attention. Some observers have cautioned that personality disorders might be another contraindication for teaching mindfulness. That may be true in some situations, but my own experience in working with hundreds of men with personality disorders in a day treatment clinic indicates otherwise. Narcissistic, compulsive, histrionic, and highly defensive men *can* become more self-observing and self-regulating. This process is not only productive for persons with personality disorders, but essential for change. Until a man can mindfully notice what he and others are *really* experiencing at the moment, he won't know *what* he needs to change. Change becomes unlikely.

It goes without saying that psychotherapists need to know what they are talking about on this topic. Therapists who do not practice mindfulness are unlikely to teach it effectively. I once attended a continuing education seminar on mindfulness taught by a man who acknowledged (when pressed by a participant) he did not have the time to practice the skill himself. It showed. And it will show to clients, as well. Men will have questions about mindfulness that only an experienced practitioner can address. There are many ways clinicians can learn this skill, but the most effective approach is to join groups and attend presentations that provide ample opportunity for practice and discussion. Experienced teachers can become helpful guides.

How is mindfulness a skill? I am defining mindfulness conventionally—as full awareness of the present moment. It is the ability to pay attention, to observe. Internally, mindfulness pays attention to sensations, emotions, and thoughts. Externally, mindfulness notices the environment or the experiences of others. A fuller definition of mindfulness includes several elements (cf., Gunaratana, 2002).

- Mindfulness does not judge. It is an impartial awareness. No assessment. No blame. Just awareness.
- Mindfulness accepts. It gently notices what is happening, right now, in this very moment. It does not reject, avoid, or suppress.
- Mindfulness is curious. It is interested in what is happening, open to examining something as it unfolds. Mindfulness explores, investigates, and discovers.
- Mindfulness looks closely. It assumes nothing. Each sensation, emotion, or sound is taken in, as if for the first time.
- Mindfulness is patient. There is no hurry to get to the next thing. Whatever is occurring right now is of interest. In time, it will shift. The sound will disappear, the sensation will end. New events will emerge. There is no need to speed this along.
- Mindfulness is trusting. It requires a confidence that one's own experience is worthy of attention.
- Mindfulness is reflective. It notices internal tendencies of reacting, patterns of thought that have become habitual, and emotions that have been avoided. Rather than reacting in familiar ways, mindfulness steps back and simply observes the experience in an accepting way. Let the experience be whatever it is; there is no need to "do something" about it.

The point: Mindfulness leads to self-understanding, and that opens the door to self-regulation. Much research and numerous practical applications are presented in the lengthy *Clinical Handbook of Mindfulness* (Didonna, 2009). I also have found Jon Kabat-Zinn's mindfulness textbook (2005) helpful for clients who wish to do some reading about this skill.

How effective is mindfulness in treatment? One review examined 39 studies that used mindfulness in addressing depression and anxiety. Improvement in those groups showed an effect size of .97 for anxiety, and .95 for mood symptoms (Baer, 2003). By any measure, these findings are robust and impressive. (An ES of 1.0, you may remember, is an improvement of exactly one standard deviation above the average score for the control group, and represents an improvement from the 50th to the 84th percentile.)

Why? What does mindfulness accomplish? It is such a simple activity to describe, yet so challenging to practice. Just notice whatever is happening in the moment. Not with judgment. But with curiosity and acceptance. Four potential benefits follow, all of them addressing problems of our authoritarian males.

The first is that mindfulness appears to disable some effects of stressors. Stress can come from an unbalanced focus on past events (regret, rumination, anger, shame) or future events (doubt, dread, confusion). This excessive focus on either the past or future generates chronic distress and often manifests as depression and anxiety. Paying attention to the present moment defuses a depressing review of events that have already occurred, or an anxious anticipation of events that have not yet occurred.

A second benefit is that mindfulness enables a person to respond more reflectively to events, and less reflexively. Pausing to think before acting is not a common practice among men with behavioral difficulties. They see and they act, almost in one motion. Stopping to notice whatever is occurring in the moment—sounds, sensations, and emotions—without immediately reacting to them is in itself a self-regulatory skill.

A third benefit is that mindfulness practice encourages people to accept internal experiences without trying to change them. Simply observe them, their frequencies, intensities, and vividness. Let them be what they are. This reduces the energy that goes into trying to *get* something one does not have, or to *shed* something one does not want. When a person can do this with some skill, it becomes easier to be more deliberative (Hayes, Luoma, Bond, Masuda, & Lillis, 2006).

A fourth factor is more somatic. Slow and easy breathing can itself balance the sympathetic and parasympathetic systems (Kabat-Zinn, 2003). Many researchers are investigating the neurobiological mechanisms that operate during mindfulness (e.g., Stein, Ives-Deliperi, & Thomas, 2008).

There are many "how to" books on mindfulness meditation skills. Three I have found especially useful (and easy to read) include the following:

> Gunaratana, H. (2002). *Mindfulness in plain English* (2nd ed.). Boston, MA: Wisdom.
> Kabat-Zinn, J. (2005). *Where you go, there you are: Mindfulness meditation in everyday life* (10th ed.). New York, NY: Hyperion.
> Kornfield, J. (1994). *A path with heart: A guide through the perils and promises of spiritual life.* New York, NY: Bantam Books.

One final comment on mindfulness: "Meditation takes gumption. It is certainly a great deal easier just to sit back and watch television. So why bother? Why waste all that time and energy when you could be out enjoying yourself? Why? Simple. Because you are human" (Gunaratana, 2002, p. 1).

Breathing Exercises. When feeling unsteady from emotions or memories, men can ground themselves by taking control of their breathing. The in-and-out movement is constant, essential, and mostly automatic. But breathing is not always steady, full, or natural. Our breathing changes when we feel challenged in some way, such as feeling a sustained anxiety, sadness, confusion, or irritation. We may hold onto each breath, take only shallow breaths, gasp the in-breaths, or hyperventilate. These patterns only intensify the unpleasant somatic sensation that accompanies difficult experiences. Taking charge of the breathing for a few moments changes the somatic discomfort, introduces a calmer state, and seems to increase confidence in the ability to manage the stress. The heart rate slows. Muscles begin to relax. Skin warms slightly. Consciousness changes.

Many books offer detailed descriptions of breathing exercises, and they are worth consulting. Training in diaphragmatic breathing is especially helpful. I have found three simple breathing techniques to be immediately appealing to men (see Exhibit 9.3).

Exhibit 9.3 Three Simple Breathing Exercises

THE "LET IT GO" BREATH
1. Sit or stand with your back straight.
2. Balance yourself, so that you do not lean forward, backward, or to the side.
3. Slowly fill your lungs to capacity with a long, full breath.
4. Let go of the breath in a natural way, neither forcing nor holding it.
5. As the breath leaves your body, make a contented sound (such as "Relaaaaaaax" or "Ahhhhhhh").
6. Start the next breath when you feel ready, and repeat the process two or three times.

THE "GIVE IT A BREAK" BREATH
1. Sit or stand up straight, and balance yourself.
2. Fill your lungs to capacity with a slow in-breath.
3. Begin a controlled release of the air—slowly and steadily.
4. Make a slight sound as you exhale. This can be done by pursing your lips and blowing gently, by making the sound of an extended s ("sssssss"), or by barely blowing the sound of the letter h from the back of the open throat.
5. Release the breath slowly, keeping the pace constant by monitoring the sound of the escaping air.
5. When you get to the end of the breath, give yourself and your lungs a break. While the lungs are still empty, silently count 3 to 5 seconds before taking the next in-breath.
6. Allow two or three breaths to flow in and out naturally before taking the next full breath.
6. Repeat two or three times.

THE RHYTHMIC BREATH (cf., Ramacharaka, 2003)
1. Sit straight up, shoulders slightly back and relaxed.
2. Check your pulse rate with your fingers until you can feel the rhythm of beats in your mind. Count the rhythm of the beats silently: 1, 2, 3, 4, etc.

3. With hands in your lap, count six beats as you take in a complete breath through the nostrils.
4. Hold the breath for three beats.
5. Exhale through nostrils, counting six beats.
6. Pause for three beats before beginning the next in-breath.
7. Take the next in-breath on a count of six beats.
8. Repeat a few times, as comfortable.
9. End the exercise with a deep cleansing breath that ends with a sigh.
10 Follow with natural breathing, neither forcing nor holding the breath.

Eye Movement Desensitization and Reprocessing (EMDR). This technique has become a widely used therapy for helping people address the sequelae of trauma (Shapiro, Kaslow, & Maxfield, 2007). Meta-analytic reviews have shown EMDR to be as effective in working with trauma as cognitive behavioral therapy and equivalent to exposure treatments, but with fewer sessions (Norcross, 2003). To men, it seems like a somatic task, as there is bilateral physical movement that appears to influence changes in the brain.

Remember that authoritarian men typically have unaddressed trauma in their earlier lives. Asking about this during the assessment or early in treatment gives men an opportunity to consider using EMDR. Certified users of this approach are identified on the official EMDR website. Again, the tangible nature of this task is appealing to many men.

Learning Emotional Competency

> An intimate friend and a hated enemy have always been indispensable requirements for my emotional life; I have always been able to create them anew, and not infrequently my childish ideal has been so closely approached that friend and enemy coincided in the same person.
>
> —Sigmund Freud (1913, *The Interpretation of Dreams*, p. 385)

Can emotional competency skills be taught? Former American Psychological Association president Norine Johnson says yes (Johnson, 2001). I agree. Men need to begin with a description of emotions—what they are, and what words describe them. They also need ample opportunity to use the new vocabulary in psychotherapy. Benefits are readily apparent. Empathy increases. The need to control lessens. And hostile attitudes of true believers toward outgroups can moderate (Rothschild, Abdollahi, & Pyszczynski, 2009).

So, how is this done?

Present a model. First, men need a therapeutically useful definition of emotional competency. Several models are available in the literature.

For many years, I have facilitated a daily group called the Emotional Competency Group. A model we have developed at our center is rather simple, but it provides a way for group members to begin thinking about emotions they experience in the group itself. A handout explains:

> Emotional competency is a set of skills that can be operationalized. It includes several abilities: (1) *noticing* when emotions are occurring and being able to identify them by name; (2) *understanding* each emotion's adaptive purpose; (3) *using* the emotions constructively in daily life, and (4) effectively *managing* the intensity and expression of emotions toward others. (Robertson, 2004, p. 7)

It also helps to have a shared model of how emotions work. In our group, we again use a simple and brief description: **Antecedent** events occur constantly around us. We see things. We relate to others. We think. If we are alive and awake, there is much to take in. In this vast sea of events, something catches our attention. When that occurs, we are drawn to make an ***attribution*** about what we are noticing. Is this event normal or threatening? Must we respond, or can we ignore it? Typically, these attributions occur quickly. Our interpretation of an event's meaning is highly personal, based on a multitude of factors in our personalities and personal histories. Our conclusion about the event may cause an ***arousal***. Our bodies become alert. The physiology is complex, but may involve any body system: nervous, respiratory, digestive, circulatory, immunological, reproductive, and muscular-skeletal. In this state, we may change the way we stand, sleep, sit, look, eat, sound, breathe, and move. Here is where emotional competency becomes concrete: We give our aroused response a name—curiosity, pleasure, surprise, sadness, anger, disgust, fear, and shame. The function of our newly named emotion is to motivate us to develop an ***appraisal*** of the situation that got our attention in the first place. We then generate options for responding to the event and consider the pros and cons of various behaviors. When this process works well, we then take a constructive ***action*** that makes an adaptive response to the antecedent event.

In this model, *all* emotions have purpose and function. That includes both pleasant and unpleasant emotions. All of them are "tools" that provide us with important social information about the world around us. This perspective makes an emotion more than a discreet event, such as joy or anger. It is more like a cascade of events: attending, attributing, arousing, appraising, and acting in an ongoing fashion, all day long, over and over.

Provide a lexicon. Simply hanging a poster or chart on the wall of a psychotherapy room makes a strong point. Emotions are important in this room. I have developed a chart organized around the central emotional challenges I have observed in authoritarian men. The headings on the chart have emerged from the countless hours of discussing these matters with men. Over the years, I have noticed that as a group, their histories have emotional commonalities: they respond reactively to events, find themselves disconnected from others, often feel unsettled, and have insecure backgrounds. The alternatives are to feel reflective, connected, settled, and secure. Hence, the chart. See Exhibit 9.4.

Exhibit 9.4 Emotions Chart: "Right now, I feel..."

Reflective	Reactive	Connected	Disconnected
Calm	Angry	Accepted	Rejected
Accepting	Frustrated	Involved	Isolated
Attentive	Scattered	Grateful	Unappreciated
Expectant	Bored	Supported	Lonely
Tolerant	Bitter	Wanted	Abandoned
Curious	Critical	Understood	Misunderstood
Open	Defensive	Committed	Untrustworthy
Engaged	Controlled	Nurturing	Hurtful
Pensive	Flooded	Respectful	Disruptive
Peaceful	Stormy	Caring	Indifferent
Contemplative	Irritable	Helpful	Inhibited
Relaxed	Tense	Empathic	Selfish

Settled	Unsettled	Secure	Insecure
Happy	Sad	Safe	Scared
Contented	Dissatisfied	Comfortable	Anxious
Encouraged	Despairing	Protected	Exposed
Relieved	Preoccupied	Trusting	Suspicious
Energized	Weary	Strong	Vulnerable
Motivated	Hopeless	Blessed	Sinful
Forgivable	Burdened	Healthy	Damaged
Resolved	Confused	Satisfied	Embarrassed
Purposeful	Indecisive	Capable	Dependant
Grounded	Adrift	Restored	Guilty
Stable	Labile	Worthy	Ashamed
Joyful	Depressed	Respectable	Scorned

Developed by J. M. Robertson at the Professional Renewal Center, Lawrence, Kansas

Identify emotion-regulation strategies. Men also find it useful to think about the different ways emotions can be managed. Again, the structured approach of a chart or handout is helpful. It provides language that becomes useful in the psychotherapy process. I have adapted the work of Aldao and Nolen-Hoeksema (2010), whose meta-analytic review summarizes the range of emotion-regulation strategies we humans commonly use. Again, I have hung this summary on the wall for ready reference and to underline the importance of tending to emotion regulation strategies.

Exhibit 9.5 Approaches to Regulating Emotions

Rumination	Repetitively focusing on the details of behaviors, thoughts, or emotions that seem unmanageable
Avoidance	Delaying decisions or actions in order to avoid experiencing unwanted or disagreeable emotions
Suppression	Ignoring, stifling, containing, or blocking painful emotions that evoke suffering
Problem Solving	Collaboratively developing and implementing plans to resolve complex problems
Acceptance	Observing and accepting one's own emotions, fantasies, thoughts, and sensations, just as they are
Reappraisal	Reducing emotional distress by being open to new versions of yourself, your current situation, or your future

Adapted at the Professional Renewal Center (Lawrence, Kansas). From Aldao, A. & Nolen-Hoeksema, S., *Clinical Psychology Review*, 30 217–237, 2010.

The emotion regulation strategy most difficult to learn is also the most useful. The idea is to accept the emotion without getting lost in it. That is, I simply notice anxiety...without becoming anxious. I notice my anger...without becoming enveloped or consumed by it. So when irritation emerges, I simply observe it. There is no need to reject it. No need to cling to it, either. Just accept its presence. Pay attention to its somatic sensations. Then let the emotion accomplish its objective, which is to call attention to a situation that needs to be addressed, and then to motivate an action that addresses the problem constructively.

None of this is easy to do, at first. We may have learned to ignore unpleasant emotions and crave pleasant ones. Avoiding both these responses requires several skills: noticing each emotion, accepting it, discerning its purpose, and letting it go. A familiar metaphor for this process is the third eye: the idea of looking within merely to see what is there.

Meditation teacher Sharon Salzberg (2011) quotes one of her teachers who likens managing emotions to the perspective of a compassionate elderly man sitting on a bench, watching children on a safe playground. This experienced man notices the children's emotions as they come and go. Each emotion is important and instructive, but temporary. When a child trips in the sand or loses a toy shovel, the man views the intensity of the child's crisis from a distance. He knows this emotion will pass—not in an uncaring way, but in an experienced way. He keeps a close eye on it, but neither rejects nor clings to it. And he takes action as necessary to address the situation that has given rise to the emotion.

Can emotional skills be measured? Yes. In the *Encyclopedia of Applied Psychology*, Spielberger (2004) reports that the three most popular instruments are the Emotional Intelligence Test (Mayer, Salovey, & Caruso, 2002), the Emotional Competence Inventory (Boyatzis, Goleman, & Haygroup, 2001), and the Emotional Quotient Inventory (Bar-On, 1997).

Identifying Cognitive Blocks

Men can change the way they think. This is not news, but it is worth giving them that message in the psychotherapy room. Even therapists can change, by the way (Goldfried, 2000). When we change our thoughts, internal pressure builds to change our behavior. The very first line of the Buddha's Dhammapada sounds like a quote from modern cognitive therapy: "Mind is the forerunner of all actions" (Buddha, 1995b, p. 1). Consider the behavioral implications from these cognitions:

- "It's not my fault I lose my temper. The working conditions are impossible."
- "People are either saints or sinners. There's no in between."
- "I tried that mindfulness stuff once. I can't do it. It's impossible."
- "I can tell exactly what she's thinking just by looking at her."
- "It's not fair I'm being singled out. I'm just doing what all supervisors do."
- "If someone agrees to run a department, they can't be making mistakes."
- "If *I'm* unhappy, you can bet everyone else feels the same way."
- "I've got to harass people to get anything done."
- "I don't care what you think. I know I'm right. Get with the program."
- "The way I work, I'm due some consideration."

Like many of the rest of us, authoritarian men tell themselves things that sound rational, but are not. We justify our behavior in so many ways. It is difficult for many men starting therapy even to acknowledge the possibility of illogical thinking, let alone engage in actively refuting those negative thought patterns. But slowly, very slowly sometimes, men can learn to replace problematic thinking with more balanced thinking. Conversations are the best setting for this, both with a psychotherapist and in a group.

I have found that giving men readings provides a masculine-friendly way to start addressing these cognitive blocks. Following the leads of Aaron Beck (1976) and David Burns (1980), many authors have written books that are readable, accessible, and practical. In the privacy of their own homes, men can read descriptions of their problematic patterns (logical inconsistencies, cognitive distortions, common defenses, etc.)

without having to immediately respond to a psychotherapist. Reading appears to give many men a sense of managing their own treatment. Workbooks, especially, provide men with the opportunity to respond to the readings in their own language.

In psychotherapy with authoritarian men, I offer several ideas for reading—books, chapters, packets of articles, and website addresses—and let the man make a choice within a relevant cluster. We then discuss any thoughts and emotions that may have emerged from the readings. Naturally, it is important to review *all* the readings ahead of time for clinical relevance, theoretical reliability, and scientific validity.

Several psychotherapeutic purposes are served by reading targeted material: conceptualizing maladaptive patterns in new ways, increasing motivation to experiment with new behavior, feeling collaborative in working with a therapist, examining sensitive or embarrassing issues privately before discussing them, and developing alternative views of long-held self-concepts. Reading and completing assignments also meets the task-oriented expectation that many men bring to the therapy process.

Does it work? Bibliotherapy does seem to help. Studies have found benefits for depression, anxiety, aggression, and much more (cf., Naylor, 2008; Schechtman & Nachshol, 1996).

Changing Relational Patterns

The ideal way to change relational patterns is to practice them in real time with others. This means a group setting. Unfortunately, groups are difficult to form because in many places, third party payers refuse to reimburse the fees of group therapists.

Real-Time Learning. Two critical processes occur in group psychotherapy with authoritarian men. Both contribute enormously to their progress. These processes mirror the outline of the present chapter in this book. The first process is self-understanding. There is no substitute for sitting with a group of experienced peers who know how to give feedback that is clear, kind, and consistent. Members are trained to make observations without being directive. They learn to be reflective, not reactive. They practice thinking and speaking in ways that reflect curiosity, tentativeness, and empathy. This environment enables a man to listen more openly and attentively to observations about his impact on others in the group.

Groups in our center are trained to identify and avoid statements that offer a judgment, ascribe blame, or accuse someone else. When people feel attacked, they typically respond in one of three ways: they defend, they withdraw, or they counterattack. None of these responses is constructive. Put another way, an authoritarian man is thrown into an environment that is completely new for him. Nowhere else in his entire life has he seen conversations this open, this trusting, and this respectful.

It is frankly disorienting for many new members, as they try to figure out the norms in this new arena. They may lead with their customary ways of finding a place in a group: using power statements, being domineering, manipulating, or making disparaging comments about others. None of this works in a group consisting of treatment peers farther down the treatment road than he is. He suddenly finds himself without the skills he needs. But as he listens, he begins to understand himself. He sees his own tendencies in another, and he finds them ineffective. He begins thinking about other relationships in his life.

The second process is self-regulation. As a man sees that different ways of interacting seem to work, he is tempted to try behaving similarly. Instead of challenge, argument, and conflict, he can try the skills he is seeing enacted in front of him. Maybe he can offer just an observation without adding a snide remark. Perhaps he can phrase his next comment with less judgment or interpretation. Maybe he can check to see if he heard another member correctly before reacting to the statement. In these trial-and-error ways, learning is occurring. He is developing a new insight, a new explanation, a new verbal behavior, or a new awareness of an emotional tendency. He is *wanting* to behave differently because he sees the effectiveness of these skills. People become closer to each other. They feel supportive, empathic, and concerned. These are likely new emotions for him. It is common for a man to come into a group and report that he tried using his new talking skills with someone outside the group, and that he experienced a novel (but pleasant) response. Men begin to think of themselves as agreeable and skilled.

These group sessions are both intensely personal and personally intense, with members exploring relational issues with family members, problematic workplace behavior, and other personal matters.

Role Play Learning. Some groups will ask a member to engage in a role play of situations that have ended badly for him: work rages, family arguments, and so forth.

Ramu, our exemplar workplace bully, was asked to role-play the conversation that resulted in him throwing a paperweight through the window of one of his staffers. He explained the context to the group, and then selected someone to play the role of his former target. Ramu did two role plays. In the first, he played his victim, and someone else played his demanding, angry style. He did not like this role, and he at first received feedback that he didn't seem to be paying attention. But with several repetitions, he got more into the role while his role play partner reenacted Ramu's rage with feeling and energy. Suddenly, it was all quite real. Ramu felt the fear, broke down, and cried. "I never imagined I was scaring someone like this," he said. "It reminds me of being bullied as a kid."

Then Ramu traded roles and played himself. Over and over, he tried to express his expectations in ways that were clear, respectful, and facilitative. The first several tries were flops. He just could not say what he truly wanted to say. Emotions from the actual event revisited him and made it difficult for him to try his new skills. Each attempt, however, was just a little more skilled. As he got feedback that was reinforcing, he became more confident and took more risks. These events and similar events can be role-played over many group sessions, as the learning begins to feel more and more familiar.

Authoritarian behavior really can change. Not always. But more often than most psychotherapists might imagine. Each session, each day, choices are made.

> Human freedom involves our capacity to pause between the stimulus and response and, in that pause, to choose the one response toward which we wish to throw our weight. The capacity to create ourselves, based upon this freedom, is inseparable from consciousness or self-awareness.
>
> —Rollo May (1975, *The Courage to Create*, p. 100)

Putting it All Together: What is Your Story... So Far?

> An autobiography is an obituary in serial form with the last installment missing. We think we write definitively of those parts of our nature that are dead and therefore beyond change, but that which writes is still changing—still in doubt.
>
> —Quentin Crisp, (1968, *The Naked Civil Servant*, p. 212)

As described earlier, a genogram starts a man thinking about himself in a larger context. Psychotherapy deepens the initial findings of the genogram, and he begins implementing patterns that will change some of the generations-long trends he has discovered.

Near the end of the treatment, he can write his full story as a narrative. At this point, the story has developed in ways that allow him to address his current problems with an awareness of their origins and power. The story now is filled with his expanding understanding of what he has learned in treatment. The story can be written out and typically takes 10 to 20 pages to tell. A set of questions provides prompts to organizing the story:

- What did you learn about life as a child? How did you see yourself? How did the world around you work, as you saw it? What did you learn about relationships?
- What specific challenges did you face as a child: expectations, distresses, losses, injuries, adversities, deprivations, moves, intrusions, illnesses, interruptions, threats, deaths, etc.?
- How did you adapt to these challenges as a child? Did you withdraw, comply, rebel, fight, numb, achieve, etc.? Or?
- How does this review of early life adaptive strategies help explain your behavior as an adult? Have you continued to use any of your earliest adaptive strategies in ways that are now maladaptive?
- In the long term, what is the new version of yourself that you wish to live?

- What new self-regulatory strategies have you learned and practiced that will help you live this new version? How will you sustain your use of these approaches? What supports will you use? How will you safeguard your progress?

For many years, I have asked men to present this story to the group in which they have lived and learned during treatment. Men take this assignment very seriously. They invest much energy and effort in it. The resulting presentations have been highly creative and profoundly emotional. Some men have written poems about their lives. Others have found music or photographs that capture important moments or themes. Some have drawn or painted artistic depictions of deep emotions or written brief skits of scenes that illustrate what they have experienced or learned.

David, our True Believer, introduced his life story in this way:

> What is my story? It is not filled with tales of death and destruction. No deep tragedy or anguish for Hollywood to portray. No heart-pounding tale for a jury to consider. Nothing entertaining, here. But hold on. This is my story, and I have made some discoveries on this journey. This I can say, because I have heard several of my peers say that it is our *best* efforts that landed us in treatment... not our worst. I know that is true for me. I never intended to break the laws of my profession. But I did. How has this happened? Well, I have looked into the stories of my past, and found much that is not so good. I have a history that explains my present. You see, I have viewed everything as right or wrong, even how my wife folded the towels in the cupboard. And because of what I learned early in life, I have assumed too much. I have assumed people just get over my misbehavior. And maybe they don't. Maybe I injure them in ways that last a lifetime. I have assumed that apologizing ended the matter. But it doesn't, I have learned. There is no justification for violating the ethical codes of my profession. But that is done. It is over. I cannot change what I have already done. But I can turn in my old instruction manual for a new one. I can write new chapters with more understanding. I have learned that I don't have to be the man I was. Instead, I can be more compassionate, like the members of my therapy group. Genuinely compassionate. I can be a man with empathy in every conversation, not just for the nameless victims of my class action suits. In some ways, I am writing the Prelude to my story right in the middle of it. My future is filled with choices. Every moment, I can choose how to respond. I don't know how all of this will end, of course. Or do I? If I continue to pay attention to the views and emotions of others, life will be different. Of that, I am sure. Anyway, here are the details of my story....

"It is through stories that we obtain a sense of our lives changing. It is through stories that we are able to gain a sense of the unfolding of the events of our lives through recent history, and it appears that this sense is vital to the perception of a 'future' that is in any different from a 'present'" (Epston, White, & Murray, 1992, p. 97).

It is not so much that we tell our story. Rather, the story tells us. It reveals our self-concepts, relational patterns, adaptive strategies, and life lessons learned. Research shows that people who tell personal stories with good outcomes ("redemption sequences") score higher on self-report measures of well-being and generativity. That is, they feel more needed, want to pass their knowledge on to others, believe their actions have a positive effect on others, and so on. Those who tell personal stories with bad outcomes ("contamination sequences") score lower on these measures of well-being and generativity (McAdams, de St. Aubin, & Logan, 1993; McAdams, Reynolds, Lewis, Patten, & Bowman, 2001).

MISCELLANEOUS TREATMENT TIPS

Many of the preceding treatment strategies work most effectively with groups. Does that mean that individual therapy with authoritarian men cannot be effective? I do not think so. I have tried many of these approaches in both group and individual psychotherapy rooms. Group work has many advantages. It is intense, immediate, and practical. Immediate feedback from peers can be provided. But individual work can be productive as well. See Exhibit 9.6.

Exhibit 9.6 Treating Authoritarian Men in Individual Outpatient Therapy

CLIENT FACTORS TO CONSIDER

Frequency: Can he be seen more frequently at the outset of psychotherapy—at least twice a week? There is much to assess, and the relationship will need extra time to form during the assessment.

Commitment: Are there external pressures that will keep him from being involved long enough to become hooked into the process for his own reasons?

Gains: Can he describe goals he would like to reach in his relational or occupational life?

Practice: Is he willing to conduct personal experiments between sessions? Is he willing to try new ways of relating to others and report back to you on the results?

Support: Does he have social support from others who will reinforce productive changes?

PSYCHOTHERAPIST FACTORS TO CONSIDER

Steadiness: Can you be clear, kind, and consistent in responding to his practiced use of authoritarian behavior, even when directed at you?

Empathy: Can you be curious about his life story, even when he reports severe early abuse or his adult life mistreatment of others?

> **Relationship:** Are willing to develop a real relationship with a man who has little empathy, and who views persons in other groups as inferior?
> **Blind spots:** Do you know your personal history and limitations well, and how that translates into issues you are prone to miss, overlook, or avoid?
> **Support:** Are you logistically and personally able to participate in regular case conference reviews with other therapists who know you well and can give direct and honest feedback?

On Being "Tough Guy" Friendly

Your client has a hardened look to his face; he seems to fidget in his chair, as if he cannot get comfortable.... You begin to wonder how you will be able to connect with this man. Clearly, something is happening in his life; after all, he is in your office, yet in the present moment he seems like he does not want to be here. You get the sense that unless something changes between now and the end of the session, he will soon be leaving your office, never to return.

—Matt Englar-Carlson & Mark Stevens (2006, *In the Room With Men,* p. 3)

Frankly, this treatment moment is pivotal. The challenge is to recognize his initial awkwardness while beginning to create a space in which he can talk openly about his life, gender pressures, and all. And those pressures are real. But his views on "what it means to be a man" can be difficult to hear. Some of his ideas may have justified behavior that has harmed others. How, then, can a psychotherapist be tough guy friendly? Here are some possibilities.

Think like an authoritarian. Work from a point of view within the authoritarian perspective. Put his shoes on. Imagine facing his current challenges using only the tools he uses every day. So... you use power and try to force others to do the right thing. You need to dominate each relationship, each interaction. You manipulate without even noticing it. You care little about the impact your behavior has on others. And you mistrust virtually everyone who looks, believes, or speaks differently from you.

From inside this world, what do you need? The short answer: someone to think *with* you. The long answer: an emotionally safe experience with your psychotherapist—one that models interest, empathy, and collaboration.

An authoritarian man needs an attuned relationship with his psychotherapist more than he knows. That relationship may be the first emotionally secure, respectful, fully safe alliance he has ever had. When we can think like he does, he can begin to see himself as we see him.

Respect his masculinity. Professor and clinician Gary Brooks (2010) of Baylor University offered several treatment tips based on decades of research and his clinical work with male clients. Clinicians who work well with men have found that practicing these skills makes a difference. They convey respect.

- Minimize the use of psychological terms and jargon. Use everyday language familiar to men, not just therapy language.
- Avoid lengthy intellectual and theoretical presentations.
- Early in therapy, avoid extended silences and passivity.
- Use metaphors and stories from familiar domains (sports, technology, and culture), especially with men who don't express difficult issues with direct language.
- Use humor that is playful and connecting, not edgy.
- Use natural gestures and body language—"a telling nod, a shoulder-grasp, or extended eye contact to convey both recognition of a man's distress and respect for his need to guard his rate of disclosure" (Brooks, 2010, p. 165).
- Create a comfortable space with adequate lighting and angled chair arrangements, avoiding the dimly lit spaces and close face-to-face seating that make many men uncomfortable.
- Share information based on research or experience without giving direct advice, unless lives are at stake.

Good and Robertson (1992) have offered still other suggestions that make therapy masculine friendly: share small-talk stories, be cautious about challenging rationalizations, use rather than fight resistance, be conservative with confrontations, be slow to offer interpretations, and verbally reinforce the alliance as it emerges.

Discuss masculinity norms openly. In an earlier chapter, we referred to social norms that define stereotypical masculinity, particularly the empirically derived norms identified by Jim Mahalik and his colleagues in the Conformity to Masculine Norms Inventory (Mahalik et al., 2003). His group also describes ways in which the inventory can be useful in treatment (Mahalik, Talmadge, Locke, & Scott, 2005). Their suggestions are well worth noting.

Explore with a man both the gains and risks of adhering to the traditional norms identified in the scale, such as dominating others, maintaining emotional control, or asserting power over women. For example, men can be encouraged to consider the cost-benefit question: Does dominating others sometimes result in more long-term losses than gains? Is the price of trying to control women sometimes too high? These questions widen his scope of understanding. True, he may be gaining something from his behavior, but he may be losing other things he wants even more.

If he has high scores on some of the subscales, tell him. Take a man mandated for treatment for sexual harassment, domestic violence, or workplace bullying. Suppose he scores highly on "power over women" and "dominance." His scores on these scales may give him objective evidence that his views are atypical. Compared with other men, he is an outlier. Simply showing him the profile makes him stand out as different. It may be easier to consider conforming to the views of other men than to stick out and be different—especially when the ways he sticks out is criticized widely in the culture.

Pay attention to your own gender. Does a male client require a male psychotherapist to feel respected? No. But the question is not as simple as it seems. Male therapists do have some built-in advantages, as least initially. They likely have experienced the same socializing into manhood. They know first-hand the pressures and expectations of traditional masculinity. If the therapist can create an attuned relationship with a male client that demonstrates empathy, then a real benefit follows. The client then has a male role model for his own attempts to develop closer connections with others.

On the other hand, if a male therapist becomes competitive with his client, or unwittingly resorts to authoritarian strategies himself by becoming controlling, directive, or judgmental, then he will lose any credibility he might have had by virtue of being male. It (almost) goes without saying that this requires a high level of gender self-awareness in male therapists. A male therapist who simply imports his views of masculinity from outside sources without reflection or rigorous assessment will be less likely to create the desirable attuned and respectful relationship with the man sitting in front of him.

Female therapists have a different advantage. Many men are more comfortable revealing their inner worlds to women because talking with men activates shame, competitiveness, or homophobia. Women can speak helpfully from their own perspectives and experiences. They have credibility when they comment on the impact of certain male behaviors on women. They can create a space for empathy by describing how men's use of power, control, and manipulation to create unequal relationships affects women. Women also can offer respect by recognizing some of the strengths their male clients show, such as effective problem-solving skills, a history of providing for others, a commitment to being reliable, or courage in the face of severe challenges.

At the same time, women therapists face particular challenges in working with authoritarian men. They may hear a male client make disparaging comments about women, or find that their expert observations are devalued or ignored just because they are female. They may face expressions of erotic interest, or attempts to control them. Female therapists can model respect by having verbal strategies ready to respond to these behaviors when they appear. That doesn't mean condemning, lecturing, or competing with him. A power struggle is the last thing a female therapist wants with a Tough Guy. The goal is to turn the moment into something therapeutically valuable in the working relationship.

Underneath the blustery and controlling comments of men, there is typically a keen sense of vulnerability. This reality presents female therapists with an opportunity. Norine Johnson (2000) notes that "men are prone to see a woman therapist as someone who will be different and will not taunt or tease a man for his failures (real or imagined)" (p. 698). Effective female therapists walk a fine line as they balance these two tasks: setting limits when power is asserted, yet providing a supportive and inviting space in which to be vulnerable. Johnson suggests that empathy is critically important in this process: "Just as a woman therapist has empathy for the negative effects of societal expectations on women, so does she need to use empathic knowledge about how men have been affected and to be extremely careful about her own biases" (Johnson, 2000, p. 704). She suggests this process can begin at the intake by asking gender-related questions, and sustained during psychotherapy by consultation with male colleagues who have devoted particular attention to gender socialization issues for men.

Give him information he can use. Give him things to read—explanations of skills you want him to use (empathy, assertiveness, collaboration). He may learn more by reading things over and over on his own than by listening to your live presentation. Take the time to find readings that you believe in, that speak his language. Effective readings are concrete, specific, and strategy oriented. Examples: skills that identify emotional competency, behavioral management, interpersonal skills, boundary behavior, and treatment of women. Give him personal experiments to try, tasks to complete.

Encourage imagination. Help him develop a vision of a man he can become, a "possible self." He can do this. He can detail changes he wishes to make. He can visualize these changes. And he can try them out in both psychotherapy and group rooms.

> Possible Selves represent individuals' ideas of what they might become, what they would like to become, and what they are afraid of becoming, and thus provide a conceptual link between cognition and motivation. Possible Selves are the cognitive components of hopes, fears, goals, and threats; they give the specific self-relevant form, meaning, organization, and direction to these dynamics.... Possible Selves function as incentives for future behavior and provide an evaluative and interpretive context for the current view of self. (Markus and Nurius, 1986, p. 954)

Normalize uncertainty. Under all his convictions and pronouncements, he may carry secret doubts about his convictions. Review Bob Altemeyer's (2006) work that documents the trouble he may have with logic. If this client is like other authoritarians, he may struggle with deductive reasoning and the use of empirical data. He may have learned to be dogmatic, or to compartmentalize contradictory information without noticing he is doing so. He may have double standards, engage in hypocritical behavior, and be blind to the implications of his own behavior. Also, he may be highly ethnocentric. But at some level, he may have an uneasy feeling about his logical missteps. Be alert for soft spots in his armor. Invite him to explain his thinking. Be puzzled, without becoming a debater.

Suggest new experiences. Invite him to meet new people, especially folks different from his group. We now know that a man can become less ethnocentric when he meets others from groups he has learned to despise. His nonegalitarian thinking is not necessarily permanent. Help him get there. Expose him to people he neither knows nor understands. His opinions can change (Altemeyer, 2006).

Identify new norms. Authoritarian followers want to be conventional. They prefer the familiar, the tried and true. Try presenting new ideas as conventional. Broaden his understanding of normal masculinity behavior by citing ways in which most men are changing (time spent with children, broader involvement in emotionality, house care, etc.). Demonstrate how broader norms may optimize his chances of reaching larger goals—partner intimacy, parental satisfaction, reduced personal conflict, less stress, and less acting out.

In the meantime, be curious about how he came to his gender norms. As he talks, sustain respect toward *him*, regardless of what he has believed. Model what you want for him: the ability to remain attuned and empathic, no matter what occurs.

Be alert for shame. Just walking into a psychotherapy room can leave a man feeling shamed. All his life, he may have sought respect by being successful, powerful, and in charge of his life. Asking for help in such a public way can leave him feeling disgraced, embarrassed, and humiliated. He may feel failure because he has lost his job, gotten caught driving while drunk, or been threatened with divorce. He is hurt and unhappy, and he hasn't been able to solve his problem himself. All of this leaves him feeling shamed, and therefore cautious and defensive.

What to do? When a man says he is angry about the public attention given his missteps, a therapist might respond, "Who wouldn't feel shame at being put in such a position?" When a man feels his shame is noticed and normalized, then he learns that the therapist does not intend to take advantage of him because of any masculine failures. The relationship strengthens. These and other suggestions about managing shame come from Krugman (1998) and Osherson and Krugman (1990, p. 335).

On Being "True Believer" Friendly

> Religions are systems for healing psychic illness.... That is why patients force the psychotherapist into the role of a priest, and expect and demand of him that he shall free them from their distress. That is why we psychotherapists must occupy ourselves with problems, which strictly speaking, belong to the theologian.
>
> —Carl Jung (1933, *Modern Man in Search of a Soul*, p. 278)

It is an odd metaphor, perhaps—psychotherapists as priests—but the functions of these two professions do have some similarities. People bring the same questions to both. What should I do? How can I manage my life more effectively? How do I deal with emotional pain? Is divorce a good idea? On and on the questions go, and both psychotherapists and clergy hear them.

Psychotherapists risk much by avoiding or (worse) by demeaning the religious tendencies of male clients. True Believers do not miss the subtle facial hints of disapproval in a therapist: the briefly raised eyebrow, the ever-so-slight flinch. Paying full attention to a man's religious ideas and tendencies generates respect. And the information can be gathered easily by asking respectful questions.

In the world of authoritarians, True Believers take a particular view of truth and themselves. Respect for these ideas can be hard to come by for therapists. These men tend to believe they have found the whole truth about life, and that all other views are false. Some think of themselves as chosen by God for a special purpose in history, and most have joined authoritarian organizations directed by leaders regarded as divinely ordained by God. Many donate much time and money to these groups.

It can be a stiff test for therapists with (often radically) different views to feel friendly toward persons from certain fundamentalist groups. Therapists themselves maybe be former members of such groups, or have little interest in religion. Many mental health professionals are not actively religious. At the same time, reviews of the empirical literature show that many mental health professionals *do* hold religious beliefs and value the role religion plays in human life (Shafranske, 1996, p. 159).

The Duke Center for Spirituality, Theology, and Health has an academic interest in how religion affects health. The director is psychiatrist Harold G. Koenig, who has published 300 articles and 40 books on this topic (e.g., Koenig, 1998, 2007). He strongly believes that therapists must respect their clients' religious values, and suggests several reasons for doing so (italics added) (Koenig, 2007, pp. 15–36).

- Many patients are religious or spiritual, and *would like it addressed* in their health care.
- Religion influences the patient's *ability to cope with illness.*
- Patients, particularly when hospitalized, are *often isolated* from their religious communities.
- Religious *beliefs affect medical decisions* and may conflict with medical treatments.
- Religious involvement is associated with both mental and physical health, and likely *affects health outcomes* (one way or another).
- Religion influences health care in the community.

The *American Psychological Association* is the largest scientific organization in the world (c. 150,000 members), and now includes religion as an identifier covered by that organization's multicultural guidelines. Psychologists are constrained to apply the guidelines to issues of "gender, age, sexual orientation, disability, religion/spiritual orientation, educational attainment/experiences, and socioeconomic status" (American

Psychological Association, 2002, p. 16). Six guidelines are then offered on how to demonstrate respect, thereby becoming more religion friendly (American Psychological Association, 2002, pp. 17–62). Three of the guidelines remind psychologists to

- Remember that some of their own "ideas and beliefs" might "detrimentally influence" their work with people "different from themselves";
- "Recognize the importance" of "sensitivity/responsiveness, knowledge, and understanding" of persons from different groups; and
- "Apply culturally appropriate skills in clinical and other applied psychological practices."

The New Handbook of Psychotherapy and Counseling with Men is a two-volume collection of essays by more than 40 scholars and clinicians interested in the psychology of men and masculinities. One chapter addresses the challenges psychotherapist face in counseling men with religious affiliations. The authors (Maples and Robertson, 2000, pp. 834–836) offer several observations about the impact of religion in the psychotherapy room, all designed to foster a respectful relationship with religiously affiliated men.

- Just because a man does not have a religious affiliation does not mean that he has no interest in religious or spiritual ideas or experiences.
- Many religious men experience stresses and expectations different from those faced by religious women.
- It is not enough to know a man regards himself as Jewish, Christian, Islamic, or Buddhist. Each group includes many varieties and expressions.
- Paying attention to ones own religious prejudices or stereotypes increases trust and safety for men uneasy about asking for help.
- Ignoring a man's religious beliefs about his masculine duties may actually harm the psychotherapeutic process.

The Handbook of Psychotherapy and Religious Diversity is published by the American Psychological Association, and edited by two prolific authors (Richards & Bergin, 2000). In this handbook, nearly 30 authors have contributed specific recommendations for working with Christians, Jews, Muslins, Buddhists, and Hindus. An example of the specificity with which the handbook addresses clinical issues is the chapter on Seventh-day Adventists, which identifies several "common clinical issues" brought to psychotherapists by members of this religion: perfectionism, repressed sexuality, projection of anger, fear of dependency, guilt and shame, depression, and forgiveness and difficulty tolerating ambiguity (Rayburn, 2000). Similar information is presented for a dozen other groups.

I can add four more ideas to these recommendations, based on my own work with True Believers. The following approaches do carry risks, but religious views affect so many aspects of a man's life: ethics, recreation, education, science, politics, fathering, work, prayer, divine mandates, and (perhaps) the cataclysmic end of the world. The breadth of religious interests and opinions makes the risks worth taking, it seems to me.

Utilize religious stories. Stories have long been used by major world traditions to teach important ideas. Metaphors, parables, legends, and historical events provide a rich source of illustrations that can be used in therapy. I have found that when a man refers to such a story, he is bookmarking its importance. He has thought a great deal about the idea in the story. Asking follow-up questions conveys curiosity and respect, both of which free him to convey more (and perhaps more sensitive) religious information. Many True Believers are open to stories offered by the psychotherapist, as well. Referencing the right story at the right moment seems to make more impact than a carefully reasoned interpretation or minilecture. Doing this skillfully, of course, means the psychotherapist is well read and able to use stories either familiar or acceptable to the true believer.

Broaden norms. Many True Believers are open to broadening their understanding of what is normal with regard to religious behavior. This does not mean contradicting religious convictions. It rather means widening the range of application of ideas they already espouse. Doing this requires knowledge of the man's religion (history and content), as well as his own interpretations of religious ethical codes. The idea is to extend the reach of what he already believes, rather than challenge or oppose his convictions. If possible, use information from within his religious tradition in an inquiring and tentative way.

Notice commonalities. Some teachings and values are transreligious. That is, they appear in many individual religions. Many True Believers are taught to believe that their own tradition is the only source of truths, so briefly noting that a particular idea is valued in many faiths can be broadening. Again, the timing of these comments matters. They are not offered to proselyte or undermine, but to broaden and increase respect for points of view different from their own. For authoritarian men, these comments can contribute to the larger goal of becoming empathic toward others.

Examples of these ideas appear in several sources. David Lundberg (2010) cites extensive examples of commonalities in seven major faith communities: Christianity, Islam, Judaism, Hinduism, Buddhism, Taoism, and Confucianism. Using quotations from the sacred texts of these traditions, he documents agreement on such ideas hope, gratitude, meditation, compassion, humility, inner peace, moderation, health maintenance, patience, harmlessness, charity, forgiveness, truthfulness, and self-discipline (Lundberg, 2010). All these ideas are relevant in working with authoritarian men.

Consult wisely. Some issues are primarily theological. A man may want to understand more about a particular practice or teaching in his religious group. After thinking about it in the psychotherapy room for a while, he still might have questions and want to consult with a member of the clergy in his faith community. Most of the time, this request seems reasonable. I have found it helps to know a well-placed member of the clergy who can make recommendations of psychologically minded religious sources and teachers in the community.

FINAL THOUGHT

> ... the purpose of psychotherapy is to set people free.
>
> —Rollo May (1981, *Freedom and Destiny*, p. 19)

Free from what? Initially, authoritarian men simply want freedom from the negative consequences of their behavior: judgment, rejection, isolation, numbness, guilt, etc. Ultimately, however, they hunger for much more. They crave respect based on their strengths and virtues. And they want reliable, kind, and open friendships. They yearn for emotionally safe and trusting romantic relationships. Simple goals, perhaps, but illusive to authoritarian men because of their experiences in life. Psychotherapy can help a man reach these goals.

Self-understanding begins with an autobiographical look at his life. He learns that his maladaptive behaviors were highly adaptive in childhood. Gradually, he develops a vision of how new behaviors might be added to his life. He acknowledges a desire to feel reflective, connected, secure, and safe. Goals for change become clear and specific.

Self-regulation teaches him how to reach his goals. He learns to treat his body with respect. He becomes aware of his emotions and their functions. He identifies ideas that are unfounded or irrational. He explores relating to others with kindness, trust, and reciprocation. And he learns how to control behavior that has been damaging to himself and others.

Ideally, all of this develops in an attuned and empathic relationship with a psychotherapist, male or female. Within the security of that connection, deep self-understanding can emerge. Self-regulatory skills are identified and practiced. Psychotherapy is that simple—and that complex.

CHAPTER
10

"Does an Authoritarian Man Really Change?
Human Change: The Processes and the Psychotherapists

> Faced with the choice between changing one's mind and proving that there is no need to do so, almost everyone gets busy on the proof.
>
> —John Kenneth Galbraith (1971, *A Contemporary Guide to Economics...*, p. 50)

If a man's authoritarian behavior is deeply ingrained, can it change? Can *he* change? Regardless of how we explain his behavior (as a personality trait, a religious mandate, an evolutionary adaptation, or social learning), is change really possible? If he cannot change, then psychotherapy is useless and likely unethical. If he can change, what actually changes, and what is the evidence?

We begin with four tough realities (cf., Mahoney, 2003):

1. Many authoritarian men do not change their behavior.
2. Among those who do, the change can be minor or temporary.
3. Many authoritarian men are unlikely to change unless others demand it.
4. Substantial change is gradual, lengthy, painful, and often expensive.

Now, don't stop reading just yet. Four other realities exist. These are just as important as the ones I just mentioned.

1. It is a fact that many authoritarian men want to change.
2. Their determination to change is real.
3. Substantial change does occur.
4. Authoritarian men who do change report deep and lasting benefits.

This chapter is organized around two aspects of change in authoritarian men. One explores the *processes* associated with change. The other reports the *experiences* of change, both in the men who are changing and in the psychotherapists who are assisting them.

THE PROCESSES OF CHANGE

> Things do not change; we change.
>
> —Henry David Thoreau (1854, *Walden*, Volume II, p. 506)

Earlier, I suggested that the most influential variable in psychotherapy is the experience of the relationship itself. All of Chapter 7 explained why this might be the case. Boys who grow up feeling emotionally unsafe in their own homes carry interpersonal deficits into adulthood. They don't know how to trust, respect, and empathize with others. They grew up without these experiences. So when a psychotherapist creates an attuned and empathic relationship with him, he discovers something very new. He notices himself in his therapist's words and feels understood. He sees empathy modeled in ways that tempt him to treat others in the same way. Change becomes possible in the context of this new (and very therapeutic) relationship.

The next questions are vital, and also complex. What actually changes? And how does it occur? Important questions, both of them. And complicated. I will offer my best summary of relevant literature and my own experiences in working with this population. These minisummaries are necessarily brief, as each question warrants book-length consideration. Even in abbreviated form, however, I have found these ideas immensely helpful to keep in the background of my clinical work. They provide tangible reasons for me to be patient, cautious, and respectful of the change process occurring in front of me and within me. These questions have one thing in common: They explore the *processes* of human change.

Malleability: Do Personality Traits Change?

This issue is widely debated, but several trends have emerged from the research.

Continuity of Personality Traits

In reviewing the following findings, it is useful to recall that correlations answer the question of how much we can know about one variable when we know another. In our case, if we measure personality traits early in life, how accurately can we predict those same traits later in life? The higher the correlation (between 0.00 and 1.00), the better our prediction will be. In 1988, Cohen suggested that correlations can be interpreted as *small* (near .10), *medium* (near .30), and *large* (.50+) (Cohen, 1988, pp. 77–81).

A correlation of .50 on personality continuity over time is not reached very often. One review of 76 clinical and laboratory studies found that only 2 of them reached .50 (Anderson, Lindsay, & Bushman, 1999). James Hemphill (2003) divided correlations from 380 meta-analytic studies into thirds. The lowest third reported correlations of less than .20. The middle third fell between .20 and .30. And the highest third was above .30.

I offer these numbers as a context for interpreting the following findings. How much continuity is there in personality traits? You decide. Here are the numbers:

- One study measured personality traits of a group of children, and again when they were much older. Correlations between the two measurements range between .1 and .3 (Caspi & Silva, 1995; Roberts, Wood, & Caspi, 2008).
- Another study compared traits in a group of architects over a period of 50 years. The average correlations were between .2 and .4, depending on the trait measured (Feist & Barron, 2003).
- Still another study measured a single variable, emotional stability, called neuroticism in the Big Five theory of personality traits. The average consistency of emotional instability over 40 years was about .2 (Fraley & Roberts, 2005).
- People with more socially acceptable personality traits show more continuity over time than those with lower amounts of these traits. One study reported consistencies of .21 for Traditionalism (endorses high moral standards), .14 for Harm Avoidance (prefers safe activities even if they are tedious), .25 for Self-Control (is reflective, cautious, careful, rational, and planful), and .21 for Social Closeness (likes people and turns to others for comfort) (Roberts, Caspi, & Moffitt, 2001, p. 677).

So there is evidence of a continuity of personality traits over the course of life. Using Cohen's guideline, the correlations range from small to moderate. Practically speaking, however, these findings suggest that "we might not recognize the 70-year-old from what we knew when he or she was 20" (Roberts, Wood, & Caspi, 2008, p. 379).

Change in Personality Traits

There also is evidence that substantive personality change occurs:

- A meta-analysis of 92 longitudinal studies showed that personality traits change over time in predictable ways. As we get older, both men and women become more socially dominant, more agreeable, more conscientious, and more emotionally stable. Simultaneously, aging predicts a drop in extraversion and in openness to experience (Roberts, Walton, & Viechtbauer, 2006).
- In general, people show increases in assertiveness, self-control, responsibility, and emotional stability between the ages of 20 and 40 (Roberts, Walton, & Viechtbauer, 2006).
- Even modest changes in personality traits produce significant changes in physical health. For example, when the trait of hostility increases, people show higher levels of obesity and social isolation; when neuroticism increases, mortality increases by 32% (cf., Roberts, Walton, & Viechtbauer, 2006).

When personality change does occur, how does it happen? The short answer: within relationships. There now is much evidence that personalities are systems of traits influenced by interactions with others in the environment. Research indicates that personality changes occur in several settings, all of them involving other people (Roberts, Walton, & Viechtbauer, 2006). Personality traits change

- When people change roles in life, thereby changing their social environments
- When they see that change results in different responses from others
- When they imitate the behavior of others
- When they are given feedback that contradicts views they have of themselves and describes how they should change
- When changes are reinforced

These findings are consistent with what I have seen in working with authoritarian men. Both group work and individual work produce changes in personality. In groups, as men discover new responses to their new behavior, they begin to change. Other group members reinforce change. Members give positive feedback to a man who shows that he is listening more, showing more respect, demonstrating empathy, and becoming less judgmental. These changes, when sustained over the course of intensive treatment (8 hours a day for several weeks), are carried into life following treatment. When authoritarian men return to the workplace following treatment, their newly developed personality traits are rewarded. These positive experiences at work are associated with increases in emotional stability (Roberts & Chapman, 2000; Scollon & Diener, 2006).

Similarly, personality traits change in individual psychotherapy. The evidence is abundant. Generally, higher levels of relationship security predict increases in conscientiousness, and higher levels of relationship dependency are associated with decreases in neuroticism (Lehnart & Neyer, 2006). When men experience something new in a therapeutic relationship—namely, stability, empathy, attunement, and respect—and when they like what they experience, they become motivated to change. Add into the mix the normal developmental changes that occur in personality over time (we all tend to become more agreeable, more conscientious), and it becomes clear that change can occur. "Social contexts can and do affect personality trait change" (Roberts, Walton, & Viechtbauer, 2006, p. 388).

Want more evidence?

- Researchers using the Reliable Change Index (RCI) have found a greater than average chance that psychotherapy changes personality traits (Robins, Fraley, Roberts, & Trzesniewski, 2001). Changes have been documented for childhood, adolescence, young adulthood, and old age (cf., Roberts, Walton, & Viechtbauer, 2006). The RCI defines *reliable change as a move of more than two standard errors* on a trait—an incredibly high bar to define change.
- Another study followed a group of substance users for a year. They were given intensive outpatient help with vocational, coping, and spiritual issues. Researchers found not only symptom change in those areas but also changes in personality traits. Positive changes occurred on *all five* of the Five Factors that measure personality. *Changes ranged between one quarter and one half of a standard deviation* (Piedmont, 2001).
- One other study examined people being treated for depression. The sample was large (599 patients). In just 6 months, emotional instability scores dropped by half of one standard deviation (De Fruyt, Van Leeuwen, Bagby, Rolland, & Rouillon, 2006). Emotional stability is the neuroticism personality trait in the Big Five model.

And here is a remarkable finding from several studies. Although some personality change occurs naturally across the lifespan (as noted earlier), psychotherapy speeds up that change. "Through 6 months of therapy, people can achieve change equal to 20 years of natural progression in personality development" (Roberts, Walton, & Viechtbauer, 2006, p. 388).

The research can be summed in just four words: Personality traits can change!

Staying Power of Personality Changes

Do personality changes last? The answer is, "Yes, when..." In the population of professionals I serve, changes can be sustained when they are supported by the man's environment. When men in our intensive outpatient facility complete treatment, they are not left on their own. They are asked to support the changes that have occurred by working with a therapist in their local community. Typically, they also return to the intensive treatment process three or four times during the next year and stay for a week. If the problematic authoritarian behavior has occurred in the workplace, then the man may agree to anonymous satisfaction surveys, to develop a mentoring relationship, to join a therapeutic group, or to attend recovery support groups. Each aftercare plan is person specific.

Several studies report on the outcome of this approach. Intensive treatment and strong aftercare produce low rates of relapse. One study (Knight, Sanchez, Sherritt, Bresnahan, & Fromson, 2007) found that 74% of patients in programs structured in this way did not relapse into problematic behavior for 2 years, and 75% of those with substance abuse aftercare contracts did not relapse. The success rate for substance abusers went up to 84% when there was involvement of the professional's licensing board. Other studies of similar programs have reported success rates over 2 years as high as 80% (Angres, Delisi, Alem, & Williams, 2004).

An interesting side note is that those who observe the man back in his professional working environment report lower relapse rates than even the clinicians involved in their cases (Waterhouse, Roback, Moore, & Martin, 1997). This is worth repeating: Fellow workers who observe men on the job following treatment see fewer relapses back into disruptive behavior than the psychotherapists the men are seeing once a week in follow-up treatment!

One caveat: The licensed professionals we serve at our center (physicians, dentists, attorneys, pharmacists, clergy, etc.) are arguably more highly motivated than other authoritarian men might be. Their professional licensing hangs in the balance. Even so, if personality change could *not* occur, then they would not be displaying long-term personality trait changes back in their work environments.

Neuroplasticity: Does Psychotherapy Change the Brain?

Neuroscientists study the brain and nervous system in several academic specialties: anatomy, physiology, biology, chemistry, pharmacology, linguistics, psychology, and more. All these groups address different aspects of the same question: How much plasticity is there in the central nervous system? That is, how does the brain acquire the new neural pathways that influence emotion and behavior? Much has been learned so far, and more findings are being published every month. This section is barely a primer, but it does offer some useful ideas for clinicians.

We humans have two brains, not one. The brain we call "the right hemisphere" is better than the left at receiving and expressing emotional information. The right brain does not discriminate between emotions that are pleasant or unpleasant. It processes all of them. This brain also is superior to the left when it comes to interpreting aspects of emotional communication, such as attentiveness, attunement, and empathy. To put it mildly, the effectiveness of a man's emotional processor influences how he is coping with his environment.

The speed with which the brain processes emotional information is startling. It takes just 30 milliseconds for one brain to detect and respond to the emotion of another brain. That's 30/1,000th of a second (Schore, 2003b). This means that emotional recognition occurs before we are even aware of it, long before words can be found to express what we are experiencing. Allan Schore of the School of Medicine at UCLA (University of California Los Angeles) notes the implication of this neurobiological reality for therapy: therapist and client communicate emotions to each other almost instantly, *without the use of words* (Schore, 2001, 2002, 2003b).

Donald Marcus, MD, PhD, puts it this way: The clinician "by means of reverie and intuition, listens with the right brain directly to the... right brain" of the client (Marcus, 1997, p. 238). It is no wonder, then, that attunement is such a powerful experience for both client and clinician. It is very much an "intense affective engagement" (Kantrowitz, 1999, p. 72), as the right brains of both participants are attempting to resonate with each other.

The rapidity and intensity with which these emotional responses are exchanged makes mindfulness all the more important. When the therapist is fully attentive, the entire experience of the client is taken in. Not just the words, but all of the message: the vocal sounds, facial adjustments, gesturing hands, and eye movements. The entire being is expressing an emotion, moment by moment, during the entire therapeutic conversation. This exchange occurs both ways. The client's right brain is also absorbing subtle and overt emotions from the therapist. Simultaneously, then, the two right brains are engaged in an ongoing emotional dance. Back and forth they speak, without words but with great meaning. When these joint experiences are being read accurately, the result is resonance between the two of them. Attunement is occurring.

Schore reviews hundreds of studies that examine this concept further. For example, when considered from this neurobiological perspective, psychotherapeutic "corrective emotional experiences" may be occurring at an out-of-awareness level in the limbic system of the right brain (Mesulam, 1998). Some have suggested that this tacit learning of new relational knowledge may actually form the core of all enduring therapeutic change (Stern et al., 1998). This seems quite reasonable. In an attuned relationship, trust, constancy, and security develop. These experiences may be quite new for the client. As they occur, former relational patterns of suspicion, abandonment, and insecurity are challenged and weakened.

Another important implication is that emotional self-regulation skills can be learned by adults, even when their early life experiences did not include such learning. Posner and Rothbart argue this point directly, saying that self-regulation patterns learned early in life "may be open to change in adult life, providing a basis for what is attempted in therapy" (1998, p. 1925). Self-regulatory skills, then, are not learned only from a book or from therapist explanations. They are learned in real time, in their right brains, without language, in the heart of their interactions with the therapist.

The part of the brain involved in these actions is the orbitofrontal system, including both its cortical and subcortical connections. This is where emotions are regulated and where we process our cognitive-emotional interactions with others (Schore, 2003b). It is where emotions are given meaning. Several fMRI studies (functional magnetic resonance imaging) studies show that the right prefrontal cortex is where we modulate our emotional responses to others (Hariri, Bookheimer, & Mazzoitta, 2000).

It has become increasingly evident that the brain itself changes in psychotherapy. Andreasen (2001) summarizes this link between brain function and emotional management: "We are steadily recognizing that the effectiveness of psychotherapy is a consequence of the ability to affect 'mind functions' such as emotion and memory by affecting 'brain functions' such as the connections and communications between nerve cells" (p. 31). Most schools of psychotherapy acknowledge the importance of the therapeutic alliance and the critical role played by emotions in this relationship. *What is now known is that underlying neural activity during psychotherapy alters the structure of the brain itself.*

This neurobiological information adds weight to the assertion made in Chapter 7: The nature of the therapeutic alliance is the most salient predictor of outcome. It accounts for more of the change in treatment than any technique or protocol that is used. I learned in graduate school that medicines change the brain while psychotherapy changes the mind. That distinction is no longer orthodox. Psychotherapy changes brain function. Research has shown that a new maxim now must be used: "Change the mind and you change the brain" (Pacquette et al., 2003, p. 401).

This section concludes with a list of direct implications of these neurological findings for treatment. I will mention just 6 of the 20 conclusions Daniel Schore (2003b, pp. 279–281) proposes in his Regulation Theory. Effective psychotherapy includes the following:

- *Attunement* between therapist and patient is "a requirement." That means that the "therapist's right brain-driven autonomic states must be in resonance with similar states of crescendos and decrescendos... of the patient's right brain."
- *Mindfulness* is a "a moment-to-moment tracking of content-associated subtle and dramatic shifts in arousal and state in patient narratives."
- "*Interactive repairs*" are important therapeutic events.

- *Therapist emotional tolerance* "is a critical factor determining the range, types, and intensities of emotions that are explored or disavowed..."
- *Empathy* is important in treatment, "not so much a match of left brain verbal cognitions but as a right brain nonverbal psychobiological attunement."
- *Self-regulation* is the central purpose of treatment.

We now have neuroscientific evidence that a boy's early life experiences with his primary caregiver create important neural pathways that predict his adult relationship tendencies. Reviews of studies counted in the thousands provide abundant evidence of the critical importance of the first 2 to 3 years of life in setting the direction of a person's relational history (Schore, 1994, 2003a, 2003b). "Events that occur during infancy, especially transactions with the social environment, are indelibly imprinted into the structures that are maturing the first year of life. The child's first relationship (with a caregiver) acts as a template, as it permanently molds the individual's capacities to enter into all later emotional relationships" (Schore, 1994, p. 3).

We also now know that these early life events create pathways that are subject to change. Our brains retain a lifelong ability to adapt, based on new experiences. New learning creates new neural pathways. More to our point, new experiences inside an authoritarian man's attuned and empathic psychotherapy relationship produce new brain functions. The operative word is *neuroplasticity*.

Cognition: Can Authoritarian Thinking Change?

Back in Chapter 2, I summarized Bob Altemeyer's career-long research on authoritarian leaders and followers. It is time to return to his work as we address the question of change.

The first question: How do authoritarians think? Altemeyer (2006) documented that they make more errors in logic than nonauthoritarians. Specifically, they are more likely to

- Make incorrect inferences from syllogisms
- Consult only authorities with whom they already agree
- Hold inherently contradictory views on a topic
- Use double standards in judging people's behavior
- Ignore information that is critical of their views
- Divide the world into "us and them"
- View their theories as so overwhelmingly true that they could never question them

Authoritarians simply are more likely to make these thinking errors than nonauthoritarians. What this means is that uncritical thinking processes are used to justify authoritarian beliefs about others and the need to control them. Exploitation and manipulation can be supported by arguments with logical inconsistencies.

The next question follows naturally. Given this reality, are changes in authoritarian thinking even possible? Yes. Altemeyer tested this with a study of changes in authoritarian beliefs in college. He found that authoritarian scores drop by about 10% during education at public universities (Altemeyer, 2006). Apparently, education stimulates changes in thinking. Campus life does offer students multiple opportunities to examine the views they bring from home. When they meet respectable people with ideas different from their own, they must grapple with those differences. They may have grown up with the idea that members of certain groups are wrong, dangerous, or immoral, but when they meet people in those groups who belie those stereotypes, they must make sense of it. This process changes the way some authoritarians think.

In a classic study, William Perry (1970) developed a schematic that maps these cognitive changes in college students. A typical student begins college with a dualistic perspective on life, believing that all questions are right or wrong and that authorities know which is which. Then they meet peers and professors with diverse views that spring from within and are not simply drawn from familiar authorities. This nudges them to wonder if all beliefs must be considered with regard to their relevance and context. Finally, many students commit themselves to larger truths that transcend narrow applications.

Authoritarian views of the world change in college. But what happens after graduation? Altemeyer found that *the most* authoritarian first-year college students changed the most by graduation. And the older they got, the more they changed. After 12 years, their authoritarian scores dropped 5%. By 8 years, the drop was 9%. After 27 years, the decrease was 27%. Even more interesting, he found that authoritarian scores of people who were not parents dropped 20% by the time they were 45 years old. Altemeyer (2006) concludes, "Higher education matters, and its effect lasts a long, long time" (p. 69). Of course, many authoritarians do not change their thinking over time, but a significant proportion can, and do.

There also is evidence that personal experiences can change beliefs about outgroups. To illustrate, a person who grows up with judgmental and harsh views of homosexuality tends to moderate those views when he meets gay people who defy the stereotypes he has learned. Same is true for meeting members of different ethnic and religious groups. When we know someone personally, our views of the group to which that person belongs can change. Unfortunately, authoritarians commonly do not go searching for people in groups they do not like. Yet, when they do meet such a person along the way, their views of that person's group later differ from the views of other authoritarians who have not met members from that group (Altemeyer, 2006). Personal contact has been shown to reduce harmful views of outgroups such as sexual minorities (Horn & Romeo, 2010), immigrants (Pagotto, Voci, &

Maculan, 2010), the homeless, persons with AIDS, and even murderers (Batson et al., 1997). So new information and personal experiences can change thinking.

Psychotherapy changes thinking, too. Rice and Greenberg quote several clients who describe shifts in their cognitions. This next comment was made by a patient about the therapist's role in changing thinking:

> Because he really put together all the different pieces that I was talking about and it made sense to me, it helped me to see it in a different way.... Putting it that way made it where I could understand it, made me see that I have tremendous conflict there.... My response was [that] that was something for me to think about, it was a new idea that I hadn't had before. It was something I could take home.... It made me feel good about the session and about doing it, [that] there was a purpose. I felt relieved. (Rice & Greenberg, 1984, pp. 266–267)

Autopoiesis: What Changes—Self or System?

It is a fancy word, but useful. Two biologists in Chile invented the term in the 1970s to describe living systems: cells, organisms, corporations, etc. Humberto Maturana and Francisco Varela combined two Greek words—*"auto"* means self, and *"poiesis"* means creation. So autopoiesis literally means self-creation (Maturana & Varela, 1987; Varela, Maturana, & Uribe, 1974). A variant expression is "self-organization." Two dimensions of this concept are relevant for us.

We Self-Create Within Systems

A function of the family is to raise helpless children. To achieve this end, a family becomes a living system, a unit. It is autonomous and produces what it needs from within. It is therefore a self-creating system. Outside events may impinge on it, but the unit itself determines how it responds. The family has all it needs to adapt and continue its functioning. In effect, it is recursive. This is a time-consuming process, because human infants take more time and must travel more developmental ground than any other species on the planet.

Implications for human development are clear. Early on, a young boy discovers which behaviors prompt others to meet his needs, and which don't. These behaviors settle into familiar routines and practices. If he is raised in a system that functions poorly, *he* fares poorly. He is part of the system. Suppose his parents are rejecting of him. Acts of rejection become normative and actually maintain the family system. Because the developing boy is part of this system, the rejection affects him. Certain consequences are more likely to occur. He concludes that he is not worth much. He feels like he is not fully accepted by the system and is not wanted. He *wants* to belong, but he knows he does not.

And so our boy is confronted with difficult challenges. How shall he get his needs met? How can he forge his way in the world? One way (among others) is to anticipate mistreatment, thereby gaining more time to generate a defense. Anxiety develops, even vigilance. Another strategy is to fight. If the system does not meet his needs, he may force it to respond. Power, domination, and control are tried, and learned. People pay attention to him. At the same time, he shows little interest in the needs and experiences of others, because they have shown little acceptance of him.

So, a boy's family is more than the sum of its member parts. It is an independently functioning system that influences his development. He learns that some of his personality tendencies are more effective than others. The more he uses them, the stronger they become. Others are less effective and become weaker by disuse. In these ways, a boy becomes a self-creation, much as cells, organisms, and even corporations do.

Yet, there is a paradox here. While the boy gradually becomes more self-creating, he also depends on the system in which he is becoming more self-determined. Hence, we broaden the concept.

We Co-Create With Others

Our social networks are living, dynamic systems. The family is a system, but it interacts with larger systems to which it belongs—ethnic, national, and religious. The interaction between two systems affects them both. So the structural relationship of living systems matters greatly. Put more strongly, living systems are determined by their structures—both their constituent components and their interactions with other systems.

From this perspective, it is useful to think of psychotherapy as a structure. It is a two-person structure in which interactions change both members. Changes that occur in the client are manifestations of this structural coupling. This is an important point. Change is not caused by the therapist. It is not caused by protocols or techniques. Change is a function of structural interactions. It is the relationship that matters, not the transmission of information by the therapist. True, a man self-creates, as we just noted. But he does so in the context of interacting with a therapeutic other. So he really is co-creating his change. Two self-creating systems meet in the psychotherapy room.

As this two-person structure interacts, several forces are at work. The client struggles to maintain a balance between two tendencies. One is to act, think, and relate as he always has. Even though he knows these patterns have been problematic, he feels internal pressures to do what is familiar. The other tendency is to try something new: a new understanding, narrative, or response to others.

A delicate dance ensues. How can he balance the familiar with the novel, the known with the unknown? As these questions are answered in real-time interactions with the psychotherapist, he engages in change. He gradually discards old and ineffective patterns (deconstructs them). He slowly changes the core elements of his being: how he uses power, what is valuable to him, how he defines himself, and how he attaches to others (reconstructs himself). This notion harks back to our Chapter 5 discussion of "constructivist" explanations of authoritarian behavior. From this perspective, problematic behaviors are constructed, deconstructed, and reconstructed in social environments. We construct in childhood, deconstruct in crises, and reconstruct in psychotherapy. Through all these processes, we *learn* how to engage with others.

I just used the word *crises*. When the usual ways of doing business no longer work, a crisis appears. As a boy's lifelong strategies for getting his needs met no longer work (say, the use of control and domination), he becomes distressed. The more ineffective his interactions are, the deeper the distress. This internal emotional pressure pushes him toward deconstruction. Some of his core processes are shaken—his sense of power, what is valuable, and how attachments work. These crises prime him for change. They set him up for a leap forward.

Note again that change is co-created. It is the man's ineffective interactions with others that motivate his change, and his effective interactions in psychotherapy that nurture his changes. More formally, the social environment triggers structural change in a man's internal system, and his system responds in ways that spark changes in the environment. This living process continues, back and forth. Maturana and Varela offer a wonderful metaphor to describe these interactions. The foot is always adjusting to the shoe, and the shoe is simultaneously always adjusting to the foot.

Therapeutic Interactions: What Works? What Hinders?

This question has been the subject of much research. So much, that a division of the American Psychological Association commissioned a task force to review the literature and draw conclusions about which relationship factors promote psychotherapeutic change and which ones slow or harm progress. Results of the first round of reviews were published in 1999 and later appeared in book-length form (Norcross, 2002). The task force updated its work in 2011 in a special issue of the division's journal. I shall summarize these findings briefly, but encourage you to obtain a copy of the full journal report. It is well worth the time to read (*Psychotherapy*, Volume 48, Number 1).

What Is Demonstrably Effective

Strengthening the alliance (in individual therapy). A review of more than 200 research studies that provided more than 14,000 treatments found an effect size of +.275 between the strength of the alliance and treatment outcome. This finding is significant at the $p < .0001$ level.

More than 30 different measures of the psychotherapy alliance were used in these studies, but most of them assessed some aspect of a variable loosely called a "confident collaborative relationship."

Fostering cohesion (in group therapy). For group psychotherapy, a meta-analysis of 40 studies found a correlation of .25 between group relationship quality and outcome. Several variables were used to define group relational cohesion. One was the perception of group members toward a leader's competence, genuineness, and warmth. Another was the nature of each group member's relationships with others in the group. Still other variables included task cohesion (the degree to which group members are drawn into the group process in accomplishing tasks or goals), and emotional cohesion (reflecting how much group members feel connected to each other because of the social support they experience).

Showing empathy. A review of nearly 60 studies involving nearly 3,600 clients found a correlation of .31 between empathy and psychotherapy outcome (Elliot, Bohard, Watson, & Greenberg, 2011, p. 43). Some researchers see a growing consensus on a neurobiological definition of empathy. It includes (a) an "emotional simulation" that takes place in the limbic system and reflects or mirrors the emotional experiences of the other person; (b) a "perspective-taking process" that is "localized in parts of the prefrontal and temporal cortex," and (c) an "emotion-regulation process" that soothes a client's distress, pain, or discomfort, and produces compassion. This process apparently occurs in the orbitofrontal, prefrontal, and right parietal cortex parts of the brain.

Asking for feedback. Not all clients improve in psychotherapy. Somewhere between 5% and 14% get worse, and psychotherapists are not always able to detect this deterioration. One strategy has been shown to cut this number in half: Ask for feedback. Three feedback instruments have been used most widely, and their findings are similar. The correlation between using a feedback system and therapy outcome ranges from .23, .25, and .33 using these measures. There also is evidence that using these feedback measures in psychotherapy predicts treatment failures (cf., Lambert & Shimokawa, 2011).

What Is Probably Effective

Reaching goal consensus and developing collaboration. A review of 15 studies involving 1,302 people found an effect size of .34 between goal consensus and treatment outcome. Collaboration has been measured as a sense of mutual involvement, patient cooperation and role involvement, and patient completion of homework. For collaboration, 19 studies sampling 2,260 patients showed a correlation of .33 between collaboration and psychotherapy outcome. At the practical level, Tryon and Winograd (2011) suggest that several psychotherapist behaviors can be based on these findings: Don't start treatment until you have an agreement on goals, don't push your own agenda, ask for patient input, encourage homework completion, and be adaptive as feedback comes in.

Showing positive regard. A meta-analysis of 18 studies between 1979 and 2006 showed an effect size of .27 between measures of positive regard and psychotherapeutic outcome. Implications of this finding are several: Clients benefit from explicit comments from psychotherapists that portray positive regard, sometimes positive regard alone may be sufficient to produce change, and regard reinforces clients for their progress and strengthens confidence in their capacities for change.

What Appears to be Effective, but Needs More Research

Genuineness means there is no hiding behind the mask of the therapist's role. Rather, it is "the ability to and willingness to be what one truly is in the relationship" (Gelso & Carter, 1994, p. 297). When measured, a meta-analytic review of 16 studies found an effect size of .24 between congruence and treatment outcome. Implications for therapists: Model the congruence you want to see in clients, be authentic and consistent, and notice when incongruities arise.

Rupture repair. Not all therapy moments are congruent, collaborative, or empathic. Breaks occur, some minor, some major. Two meta-analyses of this interaction have been calculated. One showed a correlation of .24 between rupture-repair and treatment outcome, and the other showed that training in rupture repair techniques by therapists actually changes their behavior (z-score of .65). Recommendations: Watch for subtle hints of a rupture, comment on differences of experience that may occur, respond to ruptures with openness, and draw parallels between the therapeutic ruptures and other ruptures in the client's life (Safran & Muran, 1996; Safran, Muran, & Eubanks-Carter, 2011).

Managing countertransference. However this term is defined (therapist acting-out behavior, all therapist responses, complementary interactions between the two), one meta-analysis found that successfully managing countertransference leads to better therapy outcomes ($r = .56$) (Hayes, Gelso, & Hummel, 2011). The recommendation for clinicians: Use self-insight, self-investigation, and self-integration.

What Interactions Hinder Psychotherapy?

The same issue of *Psychotherapy* (Norcross & Lambert, 2011) also lists several therapist actions that do *not* work. There is no evidence that any of the following strategies produce positive psychotherapeutic change (Norcross & Wampold, 2011).

- A confrontational style does not help. One review of 12 studies in the addiction field found confrontation to be consistently ineffective.

- Comments that are "hostile, pejorative, critical, rejecting, or blaming" (Norcross & Wampold, 2011, p. 101) are to be avoided at all costs. Not surprisingly, the evidence shows that attacking the person we are trying to help does not work.
- It does not help to assume we know what a client is thinking about the treatment experience, about our behavior, or the degree of progress being made. Not to inquire about these matters increases the chance of premature termination.
- We are better off relying more on the client's view of psychotherapy progress than our own. The reason: Research shows it is a better predictor of psychotherapy outcome.
- We are less effective when we are rigid and inflexible about how to structure treatment or move the change process forward. These efforts often produce ruptures.
- One size does not fit all clients. If we do the exact same thing with each client, we will not get the exact same outcome. Use what works, and skip what doesn't.

Higher-Level Change: Is it Possible?

British anthropologist Gregory Bateson and his wife Margaret Mead drew several conclusions about human change from their observations of development in other cultures (Bateson & Mead, 1951). Over time, Bateson developed a theory of human change that includes multiple levels (Bateson, 1973).

- Learning 0 is the direct experience of something. A swig of salt water tastes disgusting. The learning is reactive.
- Learning I is when we generalize from multiple direct experiences. Apparently, salt water is always disgusting to drink—from any container or in any location. Therefore, I will avoid drinking salt water. The learning is reflective.
- Learning II adds perspective to our understanding of direct experiences and our conclusions about them. We might learn that salt water is sometimes useful, as in intravenous infusions or nasal irrigations. The learning now is reflective and contextual. Paul Watzlawick described Learning II as "second order change" (Watzlawick, Weakland, & Fisch, 1974).
- Learning III takes multiple Learning II experiences and draws broader conclusions about the universe—such as the nature and purpose of oceans in sustaining life on earth. Learning III may be more existential or spiritual.

The higher the level of learning, the less we understand about it. These changes are more profound, and also feel more difficult to manage. Our views and experiences are altered at a fundamental level. Changes at this level are enormously demanding. We are not talking about lower-level changes, such as managing anger with assertiveness or breathing techniques (helpful as though changes are). Rather, we are addressing the underlying and defining aspects of a man's sense of himself and the world.

Michael Mahoney suggested that only a small handful of questions address these higher-level changes, which he calls "core ordering processes" (Mahoney, 1991, p. 179). He suggests there are four such processes, defining what a man believes is real, what he views as good, how he thinks of himself, and how he understands his personal power (Mahoney, 2003, p. 50). I believe a fifth domain might be added: how he understands his attachments. Each of these domains can be phrased as questions of interest that might be addressed in talking with authoritarian men in treatment.

- *Realities*: What does he believe about the world? Core beliefs respond to the big questions of life. What are this man's most important realities in life? What exists to him, and what does not? What is authentic, genuine? What provides him meaning, and what does not? How does the world work? What sort of God is out there, if there is one?
- *Values*: What matters most to him? What does a man value? How does he guide his life? What does he find right and wrong, moral and immoral? Which behaviors are appropriate or inappropriate? What emotions must be expressed or avoided?
- *Identity*: Who is he? And who is he not? Identity consists of a man's self-concepts about his physical traits, social group membership, characteristic behavior, psychological characteristics, relational skills and deficits, and religious or spiritual beliefs.
- *Abilities*: What is he able to do? This question is about personal power and the use of power. What is he able to do? What are his abilities, skills, and talents? How does he manage himself at work? What can he control? How does he use his interpersonal skills? What can he acknowledge he does *not* do well?
- *Attachment*: With whom has he felt deeply connected? What did he experience in his attached relationships with his parents? In his relational history with women? With his children? With others?

When changes in any of these five domains begin, the consequences are profound. A man thinks of himself and others differently. He is not simply changing how he talks to people; he changes his very understanding of who others are. Not just less anxiety, but an understanding of the sources of his anxiety. Not just new skills, but new realities, values, and relationships. The balance between familiarity and novelty tilts toward the novel.

A metaphor makes another point about change. Oscilloscopes measure change in electrical signals. Auto mechanics use them to measure changes in the ignition system, and cardiologists have used them to measure changes on an electrocardiogram. Similarly, human change is

MEET A SCHOLAR-CLINICIAN

MICHAEL J. MAHONEY

Scholars study topics that interest them—not simply academically, but personally. Over and over, researchers examine ideas that emerge from their own personal experiences. That is certainly true of Michael Mahoney and his study of human change processes.

More than most scholars, he changed his own views during his professional life. His theoretical journey began as a behaviorist in the Skinner tradition. But he later shifted into a leading role in the cognitive revolution, and finally became a major contributor to constructivist psychology. He wrote much at each of these stages (e.g., Mahoney, 1974, 1995). So when Michael writes about human change (as he did late in his career), he is reporting on experiences important in his own life.

In some ways, Michael was as much philosopher as psychologist. His reading and writing took him into worlds other psychologists rarely visit. He wrote cogently on the history of ideas, the nature of science, evolutionary epistemology, and transpersonal experience. Simultaneously, his personality took him into personal relationships that represent a Who's Who of modern psychology: Milton Erickson, B. F. Skinner, Victor Frankl, Vittorio Guidano, Sophie Freud, Carl Thoresen, Aaron Beck, Friedrich Hayek, and many others.

Much of his impact, however, came from his personal influence—both as a professor and a psychotherapist. His emotions ran deep, and he profoundly affected his students and patients. I have multiple memories of sitting in his classroom, lights dimmed, while he invited his students to move to the edges of their personal awareness. Psychology for him was not simply about ideas; it was about the experience of being human. He cared much about the mind-body-spirit connection. He took on philosophical challenges, for sure, but he also pushed his body. Though smallish in size, he lifted heavy weights as a competitive hobby. He won eight gold medals in the U.S. National Masters Championships in Olympic weightlifting and placed high in three World Masters Championships.

Change was constant in Michael's life. In reviewing modifications in his thinking during the early phases of the cognitive revolution, he said, "I felt myself to be changing at a rate that felt like it would leave stretch marks" (Mahoney, 2000, p. 195). He also changed as a psychotherapist. Six years before his death, he reviewed those changes:

> How have I changed as a therapist and teacher and supervisor? Probably in many more ways that I realize. The ones that come to mind, however, are that I am more patient now, and much more tolerant of ambiguity. I am not in as much of a hurry to change clients' presenting concerns (which often evolve into other concerns as our work together continues).... I am less technique oriented, and feel much more comfortable working in the lived moment (with its many unknown challenges and trajectories). I have a deeper respect for individual differences, for human resilience and resourcefulness, and for the importance of relationships in the quality of our lives. I now view emotions as healthy and adaptive processes rather than as part of the problem. (Mahoney, 2000, p. 198)

Michael Mahoney was prolific. During the last 15 years of his life, he wrote six books and about 60 book chapters and articles on various aspects of human thinking and change. For me, his magnum opus was his 1991 book, *Human Change Processes*, the influence of which is evident in the final chapter of this book. No topic was more important to him. As he put it, "Change has been the most constant theme in my life work" (Mahoney, 2000, p. 183).

up and down, expanding and contracting. Sometimes there is more, sometimes less. Rarely is it linear. Because higher-order change is complex and far-reaching, the pace varies widely. It is not the steadiness or amount of change that is most important. It is the direction, the trend.

Rate of change matters. I have noticed that most enduring higher-order changes occur gradually. In the short term, change is up and down. But in the longer term, most lasting change develops slowly. Not always, however. An insight that comes from intense feedback in a group psychotherapy session can spark an immediate shift in understanding. Moments can become turning points. But over the long haul, enduring change at the higher levels is not rapid.

A final comment underlines the importance of emotionality in change. Most men learn early to minimize or ignore signals from their limbic systems. This cuts them off from a major source of relevant information about themselves and others. When men see that emotions are more like tools than runaway trains, they open themselves up to a primary driver of change. Intense and unpleasant emotions demand attention. Emotions both initiate and sustain higher-order change (e.g., Greenberg, 2008; Greenberg & Safran, 1987; Wilkinson, 2010).

THE PSYCHOTHERAPISTS WHO CHANGE

The double meaning of that heading is intentional. Psychotherapists not only facilitate change; they themselves change. To stretch the ancient metaphor of Heraclitus just a little: A psychotherapist never steps into the same session twice. Each conversation is different. That is because the interaction between an authoritarian man and his psychotherapist changes both of them. Neither remains unmoved or unchanged. So, the psychotherapeutic process is dynamic, fluid, and adaptive. No session is an exact copy of a preceding one. Therapists who use a manual to structure each session risk missing this reality of the change process. They are not doing psychotherapy. They are conducting classes. Both can be useful, but the two are not the same. Personality change, as we shall see in a moment, requires more than class work.

Fostering change may be healing for the client, but it is also stressful for the therapist. Simply stepping into the raging rivers of an authoritarian man's life takes a toll. Even though the relationship is defined by roles, it is genuinely emotional. Therapists feel, often deeply. Attunement and empathy require much energy. Over time, such relationships can drain a therapist's stamina for attentiveness and responsiveness. It requires uncommon patience to truly participate in the change processes of a man who is driven by power, control, and manipulation, and who is neither empathic nor egalitarian.

The therapist's own life becomes part of this therapeutic process. If these personal issues are not addressed, psychotherapy is harmed. How? Let me be blunt. When psychotherapists minimize or ignore their *own* experiences with trauma, power, defensiveness, stereotypy, or sexism, healthy change in the man becomes less likely. I say that as respectfully as I can. We ignore the interaction of our personal and professional spheres at our own peril, and we thereby reduce our psychotherapeutic effectiveness.

Psychotherapist Stressors

We psychotherapists suffer, too. Daily, we listen to stories of tragedy, mistreatment, and injustice. Moreover, authoritarian men treat us as they treat everyone else. Initially, they look to control, dominate, or manipulate us. When we nurture the sort of relationship we have been talking about—attuned, empathic, respectful—then we are affected by what happens, as well. The cost of these stressors can be high. The following sources of potential psychotherapist stress are compiled from my own observations, as well as the writings of Farber (1983), Mahoney (1991), and Norcross and Guy (2007).

Workplace Stressors

- Professional tensions with other practitioners
- Demands of paperwork: notes, reports, reimbursements, licenses, malpractice, and continuing education
- Long days, long weeks, and few holidays
- Working without knowledgeable consultation or peer support
- Finding and trusting colleagues to provide backup care when we are indisposed
- Not enough help from support staff—reception, filing, billing, and secretarial
- Reporting professional misconduct by colleagues
- Interference by governmental regulations, audits, and policies
- Reimbursement not commensurate for the training, demands, and risks
- Externally imposed limits on session frequency or length of treatment

Authoritarian Pressures

- Responding to the use of power and manipulation in the psychotherapy room
- Hearing stories of violence, illegal behavior, or threats of harm
- Frustration with the slow pace of change
- The constant threat of being sued for malpractice by authoritarian men
- The constancy and severity of narcissistic, histrionic, obsessive, and defensive behavior
- Missed sessions, late arrivals, refusal to pay for services
- Listening daily to misplaced rage, unresolved trauma, and broken dreams
- Prolonged exposure to intense resistance
- Responding to personal attacks, devaluation, and disparagement

Emotional Fatigue

- Emotional exhaustion from always being "on" (attentive, focused, empathic)
- Difficulty leaving intense emotions at the office
- Questions about self-efficacy when the change process stagnates
- Secondary trauma from listening to shocking stories of abuse, neglect, and bullying
- Overidentifying with victims of authoritarian behavior
- Lack of recognition or appreciation for the intensity of this work
- Feeling responsible for the behavior of patients
- Developing skewed views of men
- Sustaining empathy when it is largely one-way
- Impact on self-esteem when positive outcomes are delayed, minimal, or nonexistent
- Emotionally drained by work and therefore less available to family and friends

Psychotherapist Life Changes

- Family: financial reversals, marital distress, divorce, separation, death, pregnancy, and children leaving home
- Personal: injury, illness, sexuality, aging, spiritual crises, legal problems, and loss of friends or social network
- Professional: job loss, relocating to new office or city, problems with professional licensing, and sudden notoriety

Many of these stressors represent losses that can feel like "sandpaper on the soul" (Norcross & Guy, 2007, p. 42). They hurt deeply, and for a long time. Unattended, any of them can harm us. We become unhappy, disconnected, and dissatisfied with our work. And yet, we continue to work. Surveys of psychologists have shown that 62% of us acknowledge having worked when we knew we were too distressed to be effective (Pope, Tabachnick, & Keith-Spiegel, 1987). Yet 37% admit that the quality of our work is lessened when we are distressed. This happens, even though such behavior is widely understood as an ethical issue (Pope, Tabachnick, & Keith-Spiegel, 1987).

The final tragedy is psychotherapist suicide. Among U.S. psychologists, the rate is 7.8 completed suicides for men and 7.6 for women, per 100,000 population per year. Average age of death is 47.9 years (Phillips, 1999). How much better to recognize the warning signs and take action to protect ourselves.

Warning Signs

- Cognitive: Problems with memory, concentration, indecisiveness, clarity of thought, processing speed, racing thoughts, and rumination

- Somatic: Problems with headaches, insomnia, dizziness, gastrointestinal functioning, muscle tension, weight changes, and sexual interest
- Behavioral: Problems with appetite, excessive sleep, use of alcohol, overuse of anxiolytics, procrastination, avoidance, and poor judgment
- Emotional: Feeling overwhelmed, lonely, misunderstood, undervalued, impatient, anxious, pessimistic, fearful, bored, trapped, and on edge
- Spiritual: Loss of interest in aesthetic, philosophical, or spiritual issues, reducing others to religious labels, and blurring the distinction between a man and his beliefs

One problem merits its own paragraph: the risk of secondary stress. Working with authoritarian men is demanding, intense, and stressful. Stories of early life trauma are frequent and tragic. Over time, even the most compassionate among us can suffer as a result. Various terms have been given to this process: secondary victimization, vicarious traumatization, secondary survivor, and secondary traumatic stress (e.g., Harrison & Westwood, 2009). Whatever it is called, the result is a weakening of compassion. Simply having the problem makes it difficult to acknowledge and therefore to treat.

Psychotherapist Survival Kit

What can therapists do to protect themselves? One study asked this question of therapists who have devoted at least 10 years of their professional lives to working with traumatized clients (Harrison & Westwood, 2009). This group of healers had worked with survivors of childhood abuse and with people living under the intense strain of poverty, racism, substance abuse, suicidal ideation, and occupational risk. The study was qualitative, as respondents were asked to answer a series of questions about their lives. The central question: "How do you manage to sustain your personal and professional well-being, given the challenges of your work with seriously traumatized clients?" Findings provide much direction for psychotherapists working with authoritarian men. Here is a summary of what these highly stressed but self-caring treaters actually do.

Counter isolation. Effective therapists join informal peer groups that meet regularly. They get formal supervision where they work. Or they pay consultants to work with them directly. Peer case conference groups have been especially helpful. I cannot emphasize the importance of this enough. If you are going to work with intense and demanding clients, then finding a mutual support group is critical. I know I could not do this work without the regular emotional support of peers who know exactly what the stressors are.

This group of therapists also reported significant interactions with caring others in their personal lives. They intentionally developed strategies and schedules that enabled them to laugh, to feel joy, and to restore their sense of perspective in the world. They go to the theater, listen to musical performances, and watch sporting events. Not every man is authoritarian!

Spiritual connections reduce isolation, as well. High-stress clinicians find relief in thinking about the larger questions of life: What is meaningful, relevant, and purposive? They spend time with others who are *not* helpers and think together about human resilience, growth, suffering, and community. Most spend time in the natural world, paying attention to flowers, animals, trees, sunsets, and stars. They experience the much larger awareness that comes from stepping back and thinking about the scale, endurance, and persistence of life.

Embrace ambiguity. This work exposes clinicians to multiple sides of the human condition. We see both pain and progress. We listen to tales of suffering, rage, and blame. But we also see relief and forgiveness. Sometimes men are confused and uncertain. Or they assert beliefs that harm themselves or others. The challenge is to hold all these factors in the same therapeutic container. In the course of a single day, a clinician might hear intense expressions of fear, hopelessness, dramatic relief, revenge, acceptance, trust, and so much more. Acknowledge them all! Express the full range of emotions, whatever they are. Understand them without trying to stop them. Hold them all in solution, as the authoritarian man reaches for self-awareness and self-understanding.

Maintain optimism. Healers believe in healing. Those who deal effectively with difficult clients find that optimism is particularly important. They find ways of remaining optimistic, even in the face of exploitation, manipulation, loss, and injustice. They find ways to see themselves as good enough to do the work, to trust the human change processes of psychotherapy, and to see the beauty that exists in the world. They look for opportunities to see beauty in the arts and the natural world. The focus is forward-looking and optimistic.

Care for personal needs. Effective trauma clinicians pay attention to their physical health: what they eat, how they sleep, whether they exercise, and the intimacy of their primary relationships. They tend to their emotional lives by talking about them with friends and partners, by attending continuing education and training events on maladaptive emotionality, by engaging in personal therapy when necessary, and by learning how to manage their intense and unpleasant emotions such as anger, distress, and helplessness. They find ways to address spiritual issues, such as developing their own understanding of life and its purpose, immersing themselves in the natural world, and celebrating the beauty, joy, and survivability of life.

Distinguish sympathy from empathy. Clinicians who work with deeply troubled men know the difference and keep the boundary clear. Sympathy is about a merger, a fusing of two people. It is a sameness of feeling. The other person's feeling becomes my feeling. Empathy is the ability to hear another person's suffering, but to do so in ways that are partial, vicarious, and limited. It means conveying an accurate understanding of the suffering, but not joining directly in the suffering itself. The challenge is to understand without becoming, to support without merging. One therapist in the study used a marvelous metaphor that captures this therapeutic stance.

> I try to think of myself as a screen door, where the wind blows through and doesn't attach to the screen. It's an image that I find particularly helpful. I see their story as the wind and I'm the screen. They will have stories that could, if forceful like a gale wind, be dangerous and something to be contended with, but if my door is solid and my screen allows for air to move through it, then even a gale force wind can pass through my screen door. (Harrison & Westwood, 2009, p. 213)

Create meaning. Psychotherapeutic work must be meaningful, or it becomes impossible to continue. Effective therapists actively think along these lines. They put their work in a larger context. The experienced trauma therapists in the Harrison and Westwood study were not opining on what they ought to do. They were reporting on what they actually were doing and found helpful. Their views are both instructive and inspiring.

Warning: No Self-Care, Much Self-Harm

Research reveals the high cost of being a psychotherapist. The following factors come from many studies and provide a warning label for those of us to work with difficult clients, especially authoritarian men (Bermak, 1977; Farber, 1983; Guy & Liaboe, 1986; Kilburg, Nathan, & Thoresen, 1986; Looney, Harding, Blotcky, & Barnhart, 1980; Pope & Feldman-Summers, 1992; Pope & Tabachnick, 1993a, 1993b; Thoreson, Nathan, Skorina, & Kilburg, 1983; Weingarten, 2010).

- One study of psychotherapists showed that 73% suffer from anxiety, and 58% suffer from depression associated with their work.
- Another study found that more than 90% of psychiatrists experience a wide range of emotional problems as a result of providing psychotherapy.
- It appears that the emotional and cognitive impact of conducting psychotherapy may be related to the high rates of alcoholism and suicide among psychotherapists.
- More than half of psychotherapists report that providing psychotherapy reduces their own emotional involvement with their families.
- Some therapists say that providing psychotherapy reduces their abilities to be genuine, spontaneous, and comfortable with their friends. Those practicing for ten years or more experienced a notable reduction in the number of friends in their lives.

- About one third of therapists who work with traumatized persons have trauma histories of their own, which may continue to resurface as problems for them to address.
- Another study of therapists found evidence for extreme distress and discontent. As many as 84% had sought psychotherapy themselves—some for clinical depression (61%), some for suicidal ideation (29%), and a few for actually attempting suicide (4%).
- Fears are frequent and justified. A U.S. study of psychologists found that 97% have feared the suicide of a client, 91% have worried that a patient would get worse, 89% feared that a client would attack someone else, and 83% have feared being attacked directly by a client. And 18% report they have been physically attacked by a patient.
- Formal licensing or malpractice complaints have been lodged against 12% of U.S. psychologists, and 3% have obtained a weapon in order to protect themselves from a potentially violent patient.
- Some psychotherapists face intense problems themselves. One study of nearly 300 psychologists found that many had been sexually abused as children: 26% of the men and 39% of the women. Just over one third report some form of sexual harassment in adulthood.

Clearly, psychotherapists do have their own issues to address. But what does this have to do with therapeutic change? A lot. Again, the most accurate predictor of change is the working relationship, period. By role, the therapist is supposed to be the healer, and the patient the wounded. When the psychotherapist is wounded and emotionally bleeding, therapy is going to be less effective. Change may still occur, but it must transcend the wounds of the therapist in order to do so.

Therefore, much self-care, less self-harm. If need be, get help. It is interesting that the type of psychotherapy preferred by psychotherapists is not related to symptom reduction. It is the approach we have been describing for authoritarian men, as well. Therapists want to be understood, to feel cared about, and to increase their self-understanding. So they want treaters who are caring, open, flexible, and able to foster the development of a real relationship with them (Buckley, Karasu, & Charles, 1981; Grunebaum, 1983).

THE EXPERIENCE OF CHANGE

Client Experiences

Canadian researchers Laura Rice and Leslie Greenburg asked people in psychotherapy to describe how therapeutic interventions affected them. What did they notice? What was important as they changed? Several themes appear in answers to these questions (Rice & Greenburg, 1984, p. 279ff.) (italics added).

- People experience a sense of *newness*. Their perspective changes in some fundamental way: a new awareness, a new idea, understanding, or connection.
- A sense of *relief* emerges. People feel more confident, less anxious, less pressured.
- An emotional *alliance* with the psychotherapist forms. As a result, people feel more trusting of the therapist, and feel more emotionally valued. Camaraderie develops.
- People are *stimulated to think* differently. They find themselves visualizing situations differently, devoting more time to personal reflection, and applying their thinking in new ways.
- Some therapeutic observations become *important insights*. These memorable ideas become turning points, and stimulate an entirely new way of "making sense" of some aspect of life.
- A sense of *connection develops*. Links are made between childhood and adulthood, between events that previously seemed isolated or unrelated. A plausible and coherent explanation of life's conundrums occurs.
- Psychotherapist *accuracy* is important. Professionals must "get it right." They must convey an accurate understanding of the man's emotions, thoughts, and patterns. They must be able to share these observations in ways that resonate with him. He must be able to say, "Yes, that's me. That is really me."

Many men have written about the experience of change, some with the clarity and imagery that comes only in poetry. Their words are haunting, memorable, and inspiring. I want to share a sample of the work that I have seen. It is one thing to write *about* change (which I have tried to do), and quite another to *sense* the experience of change in others. Perhaps it is time for a listen to the latter for a few moments.

The first lines are written by Brett Krablin (2006), a physician in his day job. He describes the common—but often unexpressed—feeling in men who arrive in my psychotherapy room for our first conversation.

The Least of These

"Lord, when did we clothe you?"

It is a universal dream,
The one where you find yourself
All of a sudden in your underwear,
And that is all,
In front of the class
Or at the library.
And the crowd in one form or another
Studies you in staid silence,
Unmoving as you stand there
In your almost nakedness.

> For once it would be nice
> If from the mute gathering
> Someone might step out and say,
> I remember what it was like
> To stand their alone,
> To feel naked,
> To be naked,
> Then hand you their coat
> Just in time for you to wake up.

John Faul (2009, p. 68) has very few memories of his father who died when John was just 8 years old. Nevertheless, some recollections remain. Now an accomplished physician, he writes movingly about what he wanted from his father. But his words also speak indirectly of the needs men bring into the psychotherapy room.

> Dad dressed well
>
> his maroon tie knotted
> with the Pure Wool emblem on his mid chest
> under a sport coat
> complimented by his felt Fedora
>
> but inwardly he was clothed in silence
> tongue tied and unable to say how he felt
> his absence was inherited
> and deceptively presented as masculine strength
>
> I just wanted a little conversation
> about recognition
> and confirmation
> of me
> as his son.

What begins as a need for "a little conversation" can mushroom into a trusting, attuned, empathic, and healing relationship.

Rick Belden (1990) has written an entire book of poems about his own experiences with personal change. In one, he alludes to his childhood fascination with the comic book hero, Iron Man, who stayed alive because of his electrically powered chest plate of armor. Belden experienced the process of change in this way (Belden, 1990, p. 100):

LEARNING TO BREATHE

I'm learning to breathe again
  but it's painful.

when I breathe I feel
  the pressure of my sorrow
  the weight of 10,000 uncried tears.

> when I breathe I feel
>   the power of my shame
>   a jagged chunk of black ice lodged
>   deep in my throat.
>
> when I breathe I feel
>   the animal life
>   animal fear + animal sadness
>   animal panic + animal loss.
>
> when I breathe I feel
>   the screws in my chest beginning to loosen
>   + the life I've known for so long
>   coming to an end.

In another poem called *release*, Belden writes of the liberation that comes as wounds heal. The last stanza is a celebration of both the joy and pain of change (Belden, 1990, p. 101):

> I lay down my axes
>   and let go the clouds
> I dance with the wind
>   and sing with the rain
> I laugh with the sun
>   and cry with the moon.
>
> I live and give thanks for joy and pain
>   another day.

Psychotherapist Experiences

Like most psychotherapists, I have heard the snide remarks about those who enter our profession. "They're just trying to figure out their own problems!" "Why do you think they call them shrinks?" And so on. We are the target of comedy sketches and client diatribes. We are said to be wounded, weak, and unable to help ourselves. The experience of being a psychotherapist includes listening to these critiques. But are they accurate? Are most psychotherapists incompetent or unhappy? The answer is no. Evidence supports this. Most psychotherapists do *not* come from destructive families and were *not* abused as children. Most of us are quite healthy and satisfied with the lives we live (Elliot & Guy, 1993; Orlinsky et al., 2005). We may not be so satisfied with our bodies, but that is true more broadly in Western culture (Radeke & Mahoney, 2000).

All through this book, I have noted the unique and stiff challenge we face in working with Tough Guys and True Believers. They are the toughest of the tough. But that is not all they are. They are wounded and want relief. They are angry and want understanding. They are confused and want clarity.

Being able to respond to these needs is more than an honor, it is a sacred gift. In contemporary culture, the psychotherapist has assumed roles previously held only by members of the clergy. We hear confessions of misbehavior. We offer relief. We offer new ways of thinking and relating. We facilitate the development of meaning and purpose. We mourn loss and celebrate success. We repair ruptures. We demonstrate faith in change. Always, we proffer hope.

A FINAL NOTE: FROM ONE PSYCHOTHERAPIST TO ANOTHER

Dear Fellow Psychotherapist:

With some hesitation, I offer some final tips and hints for helping authoritarian men change. These observations are perhaps more personal than prescriptive. All are based on my own experiences in working with this difficult population. Use what you can, and discard the rest. I am keenly interested in your own observations about this work. If you wish to share your thoughts or experiences—either similar or different from mine—I would be happy to hear from you. Thanks for listening.

—JMR

1. I find that when I begin listening just before a session begins, I hear more. I try to envision the man sitting in his accustomed chair just before I invite him into the space we shall share for our conversation.
2. When I can accept a man's maladaptive or harmful behavior as his best attempt to cope with life, I seem to respect him so much more.
3. His life story may be complicated, and his story-telling convoluted. His defenses may be persistent, and his motivation wavering. When I can acknowledge the complexities of his life, I am hesitant to offer pat answers. Sometimes it is more productive for me to stand back and wait than to jump in and act.
4. I notice I am more effective when I admit my limits. When I consult with my fellow psychotherapists about my blind spots, I have other eyes looking for what I do not see easily.
5. When I engage regularly in activities very different from psychotherapy, my professional energy and attention are easier to sustain. Playing has mattered in my life—bicycles, handballs. I find it is easy to overlook this during times filled with heavy psychotherapeutic conversations.
6. Pace, pace, pace. I always regret intervening too early in a man's change process. Even though I can see where he might land in 6 months, I have learned it is best not to hurry him. I want him to

discover change in his own way, on his own schedule. When I get into a "telling" mode, his authoritarian tendencies kick in, and he tends to resist my attempts to be his self-appointed teacher. Sometimes the best way to help him is to stop trying to help him.
7. Sometimes I am tempted to draw conclusions too early. I remind myself he has lived decades, and I have listened for hours. I only know as much as he has told me... so far.
8. I try to remember the meaning of compassion: *com* meaning "with," and *passio* meaning "suffering." When he pours out the pain he has bottled up, I want to catch it in the container of my own experience. When he senses I can sit *with* his suffering, he reports feeling understood and wanting change.
9. Supportive virtues, to the extent I have them, do seem to help. Can I be reassuring? Can I broaden his thinking without disparaging him? Puzzle over his inconsistencies without shaming him? Offer alternatives without talking down to him?
10. And finally, if I can keep one eye on his resilience and sufficiency, then I am less blinded by his suffering and have more energy for the rest of my life.

Ex Animo

Personal benefits do come from working with wounded men. Our own self-awareness increases. We celebrate *with* others their hard-won triumphs. Their resilience can inspire *us*. We become more respectful of pain, more tolerant of differences, more understanding of maladaptive behavior, and more patient with change. In short, we are drawn to live our own lives with more skill. It is no wonder, then, that psychotherapists report more enrichment than impairment in their work (Mahoney & Fernández-Alvarez, 1998; Radeke & Mahoney, 2000).

Here is my attempt to convey some of the experience in doing this work.

Into The Waters of Heraclitus

We begin with presumed roles, you and I
You the wounded man
I the wounded healer

Each conversation another step into the ever-changing river
You pushed by relentless rush of icy water
I tugged by vicarious pain of your limbic flooding

Together we forge a crossing
Your eyes darting/searching... trusting fear, learning trust
Our traction hard/soft • stepping • slipping • stepping again

Wading cautiously/curiously into ever deeper currents
Cloudy *and* Clarifying • Swirling *and* Stabilizing
Together exiting the still-flowing torrent • Grounded • Parting Ways

Never to be the same. Either of us.

CREDITS

Excerpts from the poems "learning to breathe" and "release" are reprinted by permission of the author, Rick Belden, from *Iron Man Family Outing: Poems About Transition Into a More Conscious Manhood*, copyright 1990 by Rick Belden, http://rickbelden.com.

The poems "No Answer" and "Dad Dressed Well" are reprinted by permission of the author, John Faul, from *A/void*, copyright 2009 by John Faul, johnfaul@shaw.ca.

The poem "The Least of These" is reprinted by permission of the author, Brett Krablin, from *Counting the wide open spaces*, copyright 2006 by Brett Krablin, Bkrablin@pldi.net.

The poem "Into the Waters of Heraclitus" is reprinted by permission of the author, John M. Robertson, copyright 2011.

Photographs of Martin E. Marty, James M. O'Neil, Sid Frieswyk, Supavan Khamphadky-Brown, and Glenn E. Good are reprinted with their individual permissions for use only in this book.

Selection from the *Lawrence Daily Journal-World* of March 25, 1911, is used by permission of the *Lawrence Journal-World*, Lawrence, KS.

Excerpt from "Terry Preaches Theocratic Rule" reprinted by permission of The News Sentinel, Fort Wayne, IN.

The poem "Silence" by Kenneth R. Kaufman is copyright 2010 by the American Psychological Association (APA). Reproduced with permission. The original citation appears in *Families, Systems & Health*, *28*(1), 75. The use of APA information does not imply endorsement by APA.

Permission to quote from the symphonic oratorio, Parable, composed by Robert Aldridge with text by Hershel Garfein, granted by C. F. Peters Corporation, Glendale, New York.

REFERENCES

Achievements. (1999, August 6). Achievements in Public Health, 1900–1999: Decline in deaths from heart disease and stroke—United States, 1900–1999. Centers for Disease Control and Prevention. *Morbidity and Mortality Weekly Report, 48*(30), 649–656.
Ackerman, S. J., & Hilsenroth, M. J. (2003). A review of therapist characteristics and techniques positively impacting the therapeutic alliance. *Clinical Psychology Review, 23*, 1–33.
Adams, A. (2004). Braintree, 31 March, 1776. In F. Shuffleton (Ed.), *The letters of John and Abigail Adams.* New York, NY: Penguin Books.
Adams, S. (1996). *The Dilbert principle: A cubicle's-eye view of bosses, meetings, management fads & other workplace afflictions.* New York, NY: HarperCollins Publishers.
Adams, S. (2002). *What do you call a sociopath in a cubicle? Answer: A co-worker.* Kansas City, MO: Andrews McMeel Publishing.
Addis, M. E., & Mahalik, J. R. (2003). Men, masculinity, and the contexts of help seeking. *American Psychologist, 58*(1), 5–14.
Adherents. (2011). *Major religions of the world ranked by number of adherents.* Available at http://www.adherents.com/Religions.
Adler, A. (1931/1998). Analyzing early memories. In C. Brett (Ed., Trans.), *What life could mean to you.* Center City, MN: Hazeldon.
Adorno, T. W. (1938/1982). On the fetish character in music and the regression of listening. In A. Arato & E. Gephardt (Eds.), *The Essential Frankfurt School Reader* (pp. 270–299). New York, NY: Continuum International Publishing Group.
Adorno, T. W. (1951/1974). In E. F. N. Jephcott (Trans.), *Minima moralia. Reflections from damaged life.* London: New Left Books.
Adorno, T. W. (1991). *The culture industry.* London: Routledge.
Adorno, T. W. (1970/1997). In Hullot-Kentor (Trans.), *Aesthetic theory.* Minneapolis: MN: University of Minnesota Press.
Adorno, T. W. (2002). On popular music. In R. Leppert (Ed.), S. H. Gillespie (Trans.), *Essays on music* (pp. 437–469). Berkeley, CA: University of California Press.
Adorno, T. W., Frenkel-Brunswik, E., Levinson, D. J., & Sanford, R. N. (1950). *The authoritarian personality.* New York, NY: The American Jewish Committee & Harper & Row.
Akrami, N., & Ekehammar, B. (2006). Right-wing authoritarianism and social dominance orientation: Their roots in Big-Five personality factors and facets. *Journal of Individual Differences, 27*(3), 117–126.

Aldao, A., & Nolen-Hoeksema, S. (2010). Emotion-regulation strategies across psychopathology: A meta-analytic review. *Clinical Psychology Review, 30,* 217–237.

Alda, A. (2007). *Things I overheard while talking to myself.* New York, NY: Random House.

Aldridge, R. (composer), and Garfein, H. (text). (2010). Parables. In *Hear it live! Music for Northeast Kansas, the Topeka Symphony Orchestra, 2009–2010 season* (pp. C-18–C-25). Glendale, NY: C. F. Peters Corporation.

Alexander, F., & French, T. M. (1946). *Psychoanalytic therapy: Principles and application.* Oxford, England: Ronald Press.

Almond, G. A., Sivan, E., & Appleby, R. S. (2004a). Fundamentalism: Genus and species. In M. E. Marty & R. Scott Appleby (Eds.), *The Fundamentalism project: Vol. 5. Fundamentalisms comprehended* (pp. 399–424). Chicago, IL: University of Chicago Press.

Almond, G. A., Sivan, E., & Appleby, R. S. (2004b). Fundamentalisms explained. In M. E. Marty & R. Scott Appleby (Eds.), *The fundamentalism project: Vol. 5. Fundamentalisms comprehended* (pp. 425–444). Chicago, IL: University of Chicago Press.

Almond, G. A., Sivan, E., & Appleby, R. S. (2004c). Examining the cases. In M. E. Marty & R. Scott Appleby (Eds.), *The fundamentalism project: Vol. 5. Fundamentalisms comprehended* (pp. 445–482). Chicago, IL: University of Chicago Press.

Altemeyer, B. (1996). *The authoritarian specter.* Cambridge, MA: Harvard University Press.

Altemeyer, B. (2003). Why do religious fundamentalists tend to be prejudiced? *International Journal for the Psychology of Religion, 13*(1), 17–28.

Altemeyer, B. (2004). Highly dominating, highly authoritarian personalities. *The Journal of Social Psychology, 144*(4), 421–447.

Altemeyer, B. (2006). *The authoritarians.* On-line only publication. Retrieved on October 21, 2009, from http://members.shaw.ca/jeanaltemeyer/drbob/TheAuthoritarians.pdf.

Altemeyer, B., & Hunsberger, B. (1992). Authoritarianism, religious fundamentalism, quest, and prejudice. *International Journal for the Psychology of Religion, 2,* 113–133.

Altemeyer, B., & Kamenshikov, A. (1991). Impressions of American and Soviet behaviour: RWA images in a mirror. *South African Journal of Psychology, 12*(4), 255–260.

American Bar Association. (2010). *Model rules of professional conduct.* Center for Professional Responsibility. Available online: http://www.abanet.org/cpr/mrpc/mrpc_toc.html.

American Psychiatric Association. (1952, 1968, 1987, 1994, 2000). *Diagnostic and statistical manual of mental disorders.* Washington, DC: American Psychiatric Association.

American Psychiatric Association. (2011). *DSM-5 development.* Available at http://www.dsm5.org/Pages/Default.aspx.

American Psychological Association. (2002). *Guidelines on multicultural education, training, research, practice, and organizational change for psychologists.* Washington, DC: American Psychological Association.

American Red Cross. (2002). *The lifecycle of a disaster: Ritual and practice: Understanding the impact of the 9/11 terrorist attacks on faith communities and their leaders.* New York, NY: American Red Cross.

Anderson, C. A., Lindsay, J. J., & Bushman, B. J. (1999). Research in the psychological laboratory: Truth or triviality? *Current Directions in Psychological Science, 8,* 3–9.

Andreasen, N. C. (2001). *Brave new brain.* New York, NY: Oxford University Press.

Angres, D., Delisi, S., Alem, D., & Williams, B. W. (2004). A programmatic approach to treating physicians with a dual diagnosis. *Psychiatric Annals, 34*(10), 776–780.

Angus, L. E., & McLeod, J. (2004). *The handbook of narrative and psychotherapy.* Thousand Oaks, CA: Sage.

Anonymous (2008, January 9). *Quotes from women who survived emotionally abusive relationships.* Available online at http://blogs.myspace.com/index.cfm?fuseaction=blog.view&friendId=312011405&blogId=345838556.

Armstrong, K. (2000). *The battle for god.* New York, NY: Random House.

Arseneault, L., Moffitt, T. E., Caspi, A., Taylor, P. J., & Silva, P. A. (2000). Mental disorders and violence in a total birth cohort: Results from the Dunedin study. *Archives of General Psychiatry, 57*(10), 979–986.

Asch, S. E. (1956). Studies of independence and conformity: A minority of one against a unanimous majority. *Psychological Monographs, 70,* 9.

"Authoritative" (2010a). *Dictionary.com unabridged.* Random House, Inc. Retrieved June 10, 2010, from http://dictionary.reference.com/browse/authoritative.

"Authoritarian" (2010b). *Dictionary.com unabridged.* Random House, Inc. Retrieved June 10, 2010, from http://dictionary.reference.com/browse/authoritarian.

Bacote, V., Miguelez, L. C. & Okholm, D. L. (Eds.). (2004). *Evangelicals and scripture: Tradition, authority, and hermeneutics.* Downers Grove, IL: InterVarsity Press.

Bader, C. D., Froese, P., Johnson, B., Mencken, F. C., & Stark, R. (2005). *The Baylor religion survey.* Waco, TX: Institute for Studies of Religion, Baylor University.

Baer, R. (2003). Mindfulness training as a clinical intervention: A conceptual and empirical review. *Clinical Psychology: Science and Practice, 10,* 125–143.

Ballou, A. (1846). *Christian non-resistance, in all its important bearings, illustrated and defended.* Philadelphia, PA: J Miller M'Kim, Merrithew & Thompson.

Bar-On, R. (1997). *The Bar-On Emotional Quotient Inventory (EQ-i): A test of emotional intelligence.* Toronto, Canada: Multi-Health Systems.

Bassman, E. S. (1992). *Abuse in the workplace: Management remedies and bottom line impact.* Westport, CT: Quorum.

Bateson, G. (1973).) *Steps to an ecology of mind.* London: Paladin.

Bateson, G., & Mead, M. (1951). A Balinese family. In video series, *Character formation in different cultures.* Distributed by Penn State Media Sales, University Park, PA.

Batson, C. D., Polycarpou, M. P., Harmon-Jones, E., Imhoff, H. J., Mitchener, E. C., Bednar, L. L., Klein, T. R., & Highberger, L. (1997). Empathy and attitudes: Can feeling for a member of a stigmatized group improve feelings toward the group? *Journal of Personality and Social Psychology, 72*(1), 105–118.

Beasley, R., & Stoltenberg, C. D. (1992). Personality characteristics of male spouse abusers. *Professional Psychology: Research and Practice, 23*(4), 310–317.

Beck, A. T. (1976). *Cognitive therapies and emotional disorders.* New York, NY: New American Library.

Beebe, B. (2000). Coconstructing mother-infant distress: The microsychrony of maternal impingement and infant avoidance in the face-to-face encounter. *Psychoanalytic Inquiry, 20,* 412–440.

Beit-Hallahmi, B., & Nevo, B. (1987). "Born-again" Jews in Israel: The dynamics of an identity change. *International Journal of Psychology, 22,* 75–81.

Belden, R. (1990). *Iron man family outing: Poems about transition into a more conscious manhood.* Self-published: sabazuma@yahoo.com.

Benson, P. L., Williams, D. L., & Johnson, A. L. (1987). *The quicksilver years: The hopes and fears of early adolescence.* Search Institute. San Francisco, CA: Harper & Row.

Berger, P. L., & Luckmann, T. (1966). *The social construction of reality.* Garden City, NY: Doubleday.

Berke, M. (1996). God and gender in Judaism. *First Things, 64,* 33–38.

Bermak, G. E. (1977). Do psychiatrists have special emotional problems? *The American Journal of Psychoanalysis, 37*(2), 141–146.

Bernstein, D.P., Stein, J. A., & Handelsman, L. (1998). Predicting personality pathology among adult patients with substance use disorders: Effects of childhood maltreatment. *Addiction Behaviors, 23*(6), 855–868.

Bierer, L. M., Yehuda, R., Schmeidler, J., Mitropoulou, V., New, A. S., Silverman, J. M., & Siever, L. J. (2003). Abuse and neglect in childhood: Relationship to personality disorder diagnoses. *CNS Spectrums, 8,* 737–754.

Bilgrave, D. P., & Deluty, R. H. (2002). Religious beliefs and political ideologies as predictors of psychotherapeutic orientations of clinical and counseling psychologists. *Psychotherapy: Theory, Research, Practice, Training, 39*(3), 245–260.

Board, B. (2005, May 11). Tipping point. *New York Times.* Available online at http://www.nytimes.com/2005/05/11/opinion/11board.html?_r=2&th&emc=th&partner=USERLAND.

Board, B., & Fritzon, K. (2005). Disordered personalities at work. *Psychology, Crime, & Law, 11*(1), 17–32.

Boeri, M. W. (2002). Women after the utopia: The gendered lives of former cult members. *Journal of Contemporary Ethnography, 31*(3), 323–360.

Bordin, E. D. (1979). The generalizability of the psychoanalytic concept of the working alliance. *Psychotherapy, Theory, Research & Practice, 16*(3), 252–260.

Bouchard, T. J., & McGue, M. (2003). Genetic and environmental influences on human psychological differences. *Journal of Neurobiology, 54,* 4–45.

Bowen, M. (1978). *Family therapy in clinical practice.* Northvale, NJ: Jason Aronson.

Bowlby, J. (1981). *Loss, sadness, and depression, Vol. 3 of Attachment and loss.* London: Hogarth.

Bowlby, J. (1988). *A secure base.* London, England: Routledge.

Bowler, P. J. (2003). *Evolution: The history of an idea* (3rd ed.). Berkeley, CA: University of California Press.

Boyatzis, R. E., Goleman, D., & HayGroup (2001). *The Emotional Competence Inventory (ECI).* Boston, MA: HayGroup.

Boyce, M. (2001). *Zoroastrians: Their religious beliefs and practices.* New York, NY: Routledge.

Bridges, M. R. (2006). Activating the corrective emotional experience. *Journal of Clinical Psychology/In Session, 62,* 551–568.

Brooks, G. R. (2010). *Beyond the crisis of masculinity: A transtheoretical model for male-friendly therapy*. Washington, DC: American Psychological Association.
Brousse, G., Fontana, L., Ouchchane, L., Boisson, C., Gerbaud, L., Bourguet, D., Perrier, A., Schmitt, A., Llorca, P. M., Chamoux, A. (2008). Psychopathological features of a patient population of targets of workplace bullying. *Occupational Medicine, 58*(2), 122–128.
Browne, A., & Finkelhor, D. (1986). Impact of child sexual abuse: A review of the research. *Psychological Bulletin, 99*, 66–77.
Bruce, N. G., Manber, R., Shapiro, S. L., & Constantino, M. J. (2010). Psychotherapist mindfulness and the psychotherapy process. *Psychotherapy Theory, Research, Practice, Training, 47*(1), 83–97.
Buck, C. (2004). The eschatology of globalization: Baha'u'llah's multiple-messiahship revisited. In M. Sharon (Ed.), *Modern religions, religious movements and the Babi-Baha'i faiths* (pp. 143–178). Boston, MA: Brill Leiden.
Buddha (1995a). *The middle length discourses of the Buddha: A new translation of the Majjhimia Nikaya* (Original trans. by B. Nanamoli, and rev. by B. Bodhi). Kandy, Sri Lanka: Buddhist Publication Society.
Buddha (1995b). *The Dhammapada* (A. Maitreya, trans., R. Kramer, rev.). Berkeley, CA: Parallax Press.
Buckley, P., Karasu, T. B., & Charles, E. (1981). Psychotherapists view their personal therapy. *Psychotherapy: Theory, Research & Practice, 18*(3), 299–305.
Bugental, J. F. T. (1999). *Psychotherapy isn't what you think: Bringing the psychotherapeutic engagement into the living moment*. Phoenix, AZ: Zeig Tucker & Theisen.
Burns, D. D. (1980). *Feeling good: The new mood therapy*. New York, NY: New American Library.
Burns, J. F. (2007, November 30). British Muslim leaders propose 'code of conduct.' *New York Times*. Retrieved October 29, 2011 from www.nytimes.com/2007/11/30/world/europe/30britain.html
Buss, D. M. (1989). Sex differences in human mate preferences: Evolutionary hypotheses tested in 37 cultures. *Behavioral and Brain Sciences, 12*, 1–14.
Cacioppo, J. T., Tassinary, L. G., & Berntson, G. G. (Eds.). (2007). *Handbook of psychophysiology* (3rd ed.). New York, NY: Cambridge University Press.
Caspi, A. (2000). The child is father of the man: Personality continuities from childhood to adulthood. *Journal of Personality and Social Psychology, 78*(1), 158–172.
Caspi, A., Silva, P. A. (1995). Temperamental qualities at age three predict personality traits in young adulthood: Longitudinal evidence from a birth cohort. *Child Development, 66*(2), 486–498.
Castonguay, L. G., Boswell, J. F., Zack, S. E., Baker, S., Boutselis, M. A., Chiswick, N. R. et al. (2010). Helpful and hindering events in psychotherapy: A practice research network study. *Psychotherapy Theory, Research, Practice, Training, 47*(3), 327–344.
Cather, W. (1921). Interview by Latrobe Carroll in *Bookman*, May 1921. Cited in W. M. Curtin (Ed.), *The world and the parish, Willa Cather's articles and reviews, 1893–1902*. Lincoln, NE: University of Nebraska Press.

Chamberlin, W. C. (1994). Gender role conflict as a predictor of problem solving, leadership style, authoritarian attributes, and cockpit management attitudes. *Dissertation Abstracts International: Section B: The Sciences and Engineering*, p. 6708. (Doctoral dissertation, Columbia University, 1993). *Dissertation Abstracts International, 52*, 844.

Chicago Statement on Biblical Inerrancy. (1978). Retrieved March 19, 2010 from http://www.bible-researcher.com/chicago1.html.

Chodron, P. (2001). *The places that scare you. A guide to fearlessness in difficult times*. Boston, MA: Shambhala.

Cochran, S. V, & Rabinowitz, F. E. (2000). *Men and depression*. San Diego, CA: Academic Press.

Cohen, J. (1988). *Statistical power analysis for the behavioral sciences* (2nd ed.). Hillsdale, NJ: Erlbaum.

Colleen (2009, December 9). I was singled out. *Sexual harassment support: A support community for anyone who has experienced sexual harassment*. Available online at http://sexualharassmentsupport.org/speakupse/page/2/.

Collinsworth, L. L., Fitzgerald, L. F., & Drasgow, F. (2009). In harm's way: Factors related to psychological distress following sexual harassment. *Psychology of Women Quarterly, 33*(4), 475–409.

Commission on Professional and Hospital Activities. (1968, 1986, 1991). *The international classification of diseases*. Ann Arbor, MI: Edwards Brothers.

Costa, P. T., Jr., & McCrae, R. R. (1992). Normal personality assessment in clinical practice: The NEO Personality Inventory. *Psychological Assessment, 4*, 5–13.

Crisp, D., & Stanko, B. (2000, January). Reducing domestic violence…What works? Monitoring costs and evaluating needs. *Crime reduction research series*. London, England: Home Office Research, Development and Statistics Directorate.

Crisp, Q. (1968). *The naked civil servant*. Originally published in Great Brittan: Jonathan Cape. Republished in 1997, New York, NY: Penguin Group.

Cronbach, L. J. (1948). A validation design for qualitative studies of personality. *Journal of Consulting Psychology, 12*(6), 365–374.

Dacia (2002). Story #2. Retrieved from http://www.jaredstory.com/dacias_homework.html.

Dalai Lama, XIV. (2010). *Words of wisdom, love, and compassion*. Retrieved online at http://www.tibetanlife.com/dalai-lama-quotes.html.

Dansky, B., & Kilpatrick, D. (1997). Effects of sexual harassment. In W. O'Donohue (Ed.), *Sexual harassment: Theory, research, and treatment* (pp. 152–174). New York, NY: Allyn & Bacon.

Darwin, C. (1859/1962). *Origin of species*. Toronto, Canada: Collier Books.

Darwin, D. (1871/2007). *The descent of man, and selection in relation to sex*. Republished by Forgotten Books: www.fortottenbooks.org.

Davenport, N., Distler, S. R., & Pursell, E. G. (1999). *Mobbing: Emotional abuse in the American workplace*. Ames, IA: Civil Society Publishing.

Davis, J. (2011, January 6). Garfield. *Lawrence Journal World*, p. 9A.

Davis, J. A., & Smith, T. W. (2004, 2008). *General social survey*. Storrs, CT: The Roper Center for Public Opinion Research.

Davis, M. H. (1996). *Empathy: A social psychological approach*. Boulder, CO: Westview Press.

Deaths: Final Data for 2007. (2010, May 20). *National Vital Statistics Report*, *58*(19), 1–135. Hyattsville, MD: Centers for Disease Control and Prevention: U.S. Department of Health and Human Services.

De Bellis, M. D., Keshavan, M. S., Shifflett, H., Iyengar, S., Beers, S. R., Hall, J., & Mortiz, G. (2002). Brain structures in pediatric maltreatment-related post-traumatic stress disorder: A sociodemographically matched study. *Biological Psychiatry, 52*, 1166–1078.

Declaration of Baha'u'lah (2010). Retrieved March 31, 2010 from the Bahai Library at http://bahai-library.com/file.php?file=davidmerrick_holydays_declarationofbaha.

De Fruyt, F., Van Leeuwen, K., Bagby, R. M., Rolland, J.-P., & Rouillon, F. (2006). Assessing and interpreting personality change and continuity in patients treated for major depression. *Psychological Assessment, 18*(1), 71–80.

De Gelder, B., Morris, J. S., & Dolan, R. J. (2005). Unconscious fear influences emotional awareness of faces and voices. *Proceedings of the National Academy of Sciences of the USA, 102*, 18,682–18,687.

Delaney, H. D., Miller, W. R., & Bisonó, A. M. (2007). Religiosity and spirituality among psychologists: A survey of clinician members of the American Psychological Association. *Professional Psychology: Research and Practice, 38*, 538–546.

de Mille, A. (1992). *Martha: The life and work of Martha Graham*. New York, NY: Vintage Books.

Demographics (2010). *Demographics of atheism*. Wapedia. Available online at: http://wapedia.mobi/en/Demographics_of_atheism.

Demorest, A. (2005). *Psychology's grand theorists: How personal experiences shaped professional ideas*. Mahwah, NJ: Lawrence Erlbaum.

Department of Education and Skills, United Kingdom. (2006). *Bullying around racism, religion and culture*. Sherwood Park, Annesley, Notthingham: England.

DeSouza, E. R., & Cerqueira, E. (2009). From the kitchen to the bedroom: Frequency rates and consequences of sexual harassment among female domestic workers in Brazil. *Journal of Interpersonal Violence, 24*(8), 1264–1284.

Devinsky, O. (2000). Right cerebral hemisphere dominance for a sense of corporeal and emotional self. *Epilepsy & Behavior, 1*, 60–73.

DeVoe, J. F., Kaffenberger, S., & Chandler, K. (2001). *Student reports of bullying: Results from the 2001 school crime supplement to the National Crime Victimization Survey*. National Center for Education Statistics, U.S. Department of Education Sciences. Available at http://nces.ed.gov/pubs2005/2005310.pdf.

Didonna, F. (Ed.) (2009). *Clinical handbook of mindfulness*. New York, NY: Springer.

Diehl, A. S., & Prout, M. F. (2002, April). Effects of posttraumatic stress disorder and child sexual abuse on self-efficacy development. *American Journal of Orthopsychiatry, 72*(2), 262–265.

Diener, M. S., Erhard, F. K., Fischer-Schreiber, I. (1991). *The Shambhala dictionary of Buddhism and Zen* (M. H. Kohn, trans.). Boston, MA: Shambhala Publications.

Di Vesta, F. J. (1966). A developmental study of the semantic structures of children. *Journal of Verbal Learning and Verbal Behavior, 5*, 249–259.

Di Vesta, F. J. (1973, February). *Improving instruction in the 1970's: Alternative views*. Invited Address presented at the annual convention of the American Educational Research Association, New Orleans, LA.

Dobash, R. E., & Dobash, R. P. (1998). *Rethinking violence against women*. Thousand Oaks, CA: Sage.

Dombeck, M. (2006). *Mental health professions ethical codes*. Retrieved from www.mentalhelp.net/poc/view_doc.php?type=doc&id=9150&cn=145

Donnelly, M., & Straus, M. A. (Eds.). (2005). *Corporal punishment of children in theoretical perspective*. New Haven, CT: Yale University Press.

Dostoevsky, F. (1918). *White nights and other stories by Fyodor* (C. Garnett, Trans). New York, NY: Macmillan.

Dubo, E. D., Zanarini, M. C., Lewis, R. E., & Williams, A. A. (1997). Childhood antecedents of self-destructiveness in borderline personality disorder. *Canadian Journal of Psychiatry, 42*, 63–69.

Duckitt, J. (1989). Authoritarianism and group identification: A new view of an old construct. *Political Psychology, 10*(1), 63–84.

Duckitt, J., Wagner, C., Du Plessis, I., & Birum, I. (2002). The psychological bases of ideology and prejudice: Testing a dual process model. *Journal of Personality and Social Psychology, 83*, 75–93.

Due, P., & Holstein, B. E. (2008). Bullying victimization among 13 to 15 year old school children: Results from two comparative studies in 66 countries and regions. *International Journal of Adolescent Medicine and Health, 20*(2), 209–221.

Eagly, A. H. (2009). The his and hers of prosocial behavior: An examination of the social psychology of gender. *American Psychologist, 64*(8), 644–658.

Eagly, A. H., & Wood, W. (1999). The origins of sex differences in human behavior: Evolved dispositions versus social roles. *American Psychologist, 54*(6), 408–423.

Eichler, M., Deegan, G., Canda, E. R., & Wells, S. (2006). Using the spiritual strengths assessment to mobilize spiritual resources. In K. B. Helmeke & C. F. Sori (Eds.), *The therapist's notebook for integrating spirituality in counseling: Homework, handouts and activities for use in psychotherapy. Haworth practical practice in mental health* (pp. 69–76). New York, NY: Haworth Press.

Elliot, D. M., & Guy, J. D. (1993). Mental health professionals versus non-mental-health professionals: Childhood trauma and adult functioning. *Professional Psychology: Research and Practice, 24*, 83–90.

Equal Employment Opportunity Commission (EEOC). (2010). *Sexual harassment charges EEOC & FEPAs combined: FY 1997–FY 2009*. Available online: http://www.eeoc.gov/eeoc/statistics/enforcement/sexual_harassment.cfm.

Elliot, R., Bohard, A. C., Watson, J. D., & Greenberg, L. S. (2011). Empathy. *Psychotherapy, 48*(1), 43–49.

Ellison, C. G., Bartkowski, J. P., & Segal, M. L. (1996). Do conservative Protestant parents spank more often? Further evidence from the National Survey of Families and Households. *Social Science Quarterly, 77*(3), 663–673.

Ely, G. E., & Flaherty, C. (2009). Intimate partner violence. In J. T. Andrade (Ed.), *Handbook of violence risk assessment and treatment: New approaches for mental health professionals* (pp. 157–177). New York, NY: Springer.

Englar-Carlson, M., & Stevens, M. A. (2006). An invitation: Bringing the reader into the book. In M. Englar-Carlson & M. A. Stevens (Eds.), *In the room with men: A casebook of therapeutic change* (pp. 3–12). Washington, DC: American Psychological Association.

Epston, D., White, M., & Murray, K. (1992). A proposal for a re-authoring therapy: Rose's revisioning of her life and a commentary. In S. McNamee & K. J. Gergen (Eds.), *Therapy as social construction* (pp. 97–115). Thousand Oaks, CA: Sage.

Etkin, A., Pittenger, C., Polan, H. J., & Kandel, E. R. (2005). Toward a neurobiology of psychotherapy: Basic science and clinical applications. *The Journal of Neuropsychiatry and Clinical Neurosciences, 17*(2), 145–158.

Eurobarometer (2005). *Social values, science, and technology.* Directorate General Research. European Commission. Available online at http://ec.europa.eu/public_opinion/archives/ebs/ebs_225_report_en.pdf

Evans, P. (2010). *The verbally abusive relationship: How to recognize it and how to respond.* Avon, MA: Adams Media.

Faley, R. H., Knapp, D. E., Kustis, G. A., & Dubois, C. L. Z. (1999). Estimating the organizational costs of sexual harassment: The case of the U.S. Army. *Journal of Business and Psychology, 13*(4), 461–484.

Farber, B. A. (1983). The effects of psychotherapeutic practice upon the psychotherapists. *Psychotherapy: Theory, Research, and Practice, 20,* 174–182.

Faul, J. (2009). *A/void.* Canada: Artbookbindery.com.

Faulkner, K., & Stoltenberg, C. (1988, August). *Are individuals in physically abusive relationships pathological, non-pathological, or both?* Paper presented at the 96th Annual Convention of the American Psychological Association, Atlanta, GA.

Faust, M., Kravetz, S., & Vativ-Safrai, O. (2004). The representation of aspects of the self in the two cerebral hemispheres. *Personality and Individual Differences, 37*(3), 607–619.

Fehr, B., & Russell, J. A. (1984). Concept of emotion viewed from a prototype perspective. *Journal of Experimental Psychology: General, 113*(3), 464–486.

Feist, G. J., & Barron, F. X. (2003). Predicting creativity from early to late adulthood: Intellect, potential, and personality. *Journal of Research in Personality, 37*(2), 62–88.

Fekkes, M., Pijpers, F. I. M., Fredriks, A. M., Vogels, T., & Verloove-Vanhorick, S. P. (2006). Do bullied children get ill, or do ill children get bullied? A prospective cohort study on the relationship between bullying and health-related symptoms. *Pediatrics, 117*(5), 1568–1574.

Feldman, S. (2003). Enforcing social conformity: A theory of authoritarianism. *Political Psychology, 24,* 41–74.

Ferrell-Smith, F. (2009). Bullying puts teens at risk. In C. Watkins (Ed.), *Teens at risk, opposing viewpoints* (pp. 51–59). Farmington Hills, MI: Greenhaven Press/Gale Cengage Learning.

Financial Times/Harris Poll. (2006, December 20). *Religious views and beliefs vary greatly by country, according to the latest Financial Times/Harris Poll.* Financial Times/Harris Interactive. Retrieved February 9, 2011 from www.harrisinteractive.com/NEWS/allnewsbydate.asp?NewsID=1130

First Lady Biography: Abigail Adams. (2009).The National First Ladies' Library, Education and Research Center, Canton, OH. http://www.firstladies.org/biographies/firstladies.aspx?biography=2

Fitzgerald, L. F. (2000). Sexual harassment. In A. Kazdin (Ed.), *Encyclopedia of psychology, Vol. 7* (pp. 251–254). Washington, DC: American Psychological Association & Oxford University Press.

Louise F. Fitzgerald: Award for Distinguished Contributions to Research in Public Policy. (2003). *American Psychologist, 58*(11), 913–924.

Fitzgerald, L. F., Drasgow, F., Hulin, C. L., Gelfand, M. J., & Magley, V. J. (1997). Antecedents and consequences of sexual harassment in organizations: A test of an integrated model. *Journal of Applied Psychology, 82*(3), 578–589.

Fitzgerald, L. F., Gelfand, M. J., & Drasgow, F. (1995). Measuring sexual harassment: Theoretical and psychometric advances. *Basic & Applied Social Psychology, 17*, 425–427.

Fitzgerald, L. F., Shullman, S. L., Bailey, N., Richards, M., Swecker, J., Gold, Y., Omerod, M, & Weitzman, L. (1988). The incidence and dimensions of sexual harassment in academia and the workplace. *Journal of Vocational Behavior, 32*(2), 152–175.

Flood, M. (2011). *The men's bibliography*. Available online: http://mensbiblio. xyonline.net/.

Foreman, S. A., & Marmar, C. R. (1985). Psychotherapist actions that address initially poor therapeutic alliances in psychotherapy. *American Journal of Psychiatry, 142*(8), 922–926.

Fosha, D. (2003). Dyadic regulation and experiential work with emotion and relatedness in trauma and disordered attachment. In M. F. Solomon & D. J. Siegel (Eds.), *Healing trauma: Attachment, trauma, the brain and the mind* (pp. 221–281). New York, NY: Norton.

Fowler, J. C., Hilsenroth, M. J., & Handler, L. (2000). Martin Mayman's early memories technique: Bridging the gap between personality assessment and psychotherapy. *Journal of Personality Assessment, 75*(1), 18–32.

Fox, S., & Stallworth, L. E. (2009). Building a framework for two internal organizational approaches to resolving and preventing workplace bullying: Alternative dispute resolution and training. *Consulting Psychology Journal: Practice and Research, (61)*3, 220–241.

Fraley, R. D., & Roberts, B. W. (2005). Patterns of continuity: A dynamic model for conceptualizing the stability of individual differences in psychological constructs across the life course. *Psychological Review, 112*(1), 60–74.

Frankl, V. E. (1959/1984). *Man's search for meaning: An introduction to Logotherapy*. Boston, MA: Beacon Press.

Frankl, V. E. (1961). Logotherapy and the challenge of suffering. *Review of Existential Psychology and Psychiatry, 1*(1), 3–7.

Freud, S. (1899/1989). Screen memories. In *The Freud reader* (P. Gay, trans.). New York, NY: Norton.

Freud, S. (1913). *The interpretation of dreams*. New York, NY: Macmillan.

Freud, S. (1927/1989). The future of an illusion. In P. Gay (Ed.), *The Freud reader* (pp. 685–721). New York, NY: Norton.

Froese, P. & Bader, C. (2010). *America's four Gods: What we say about God—and what that says about us*. New York, NY: Oxford University Press.

Garrett, J. L., Jr., Hinson, E. G., & Tull, J. E. (1983). *Are southern baptists "Evangelicals?"* Macon, GA: Mercer University Press.

Gastic, B. (2008). School truancy and the disciplinary problems of bullying victims. *Educational Review, 60*(4), 391–404.

Gates, B. (2001, February 2). Roderick Ninian Smart: A life devoted to studying world religions for the common good. *The Guardian*. Available online at http://www.guardian.co.uk/news/2001/feb/02/guardianobituaries.

Geary, D. C. (2010). *Male, female: The evolution of human sex differences.* Washington, DC: American Psychological Association.

Gelfand, M. J., Fitzgerald, L. F., & Drasgow, F. (1995). The structure of sexual harassment: A confirmatory analysis across cultures and settings. *Journal of Vocational Behavior, 47,* 164–177.

Gelso, C. J. (2002). The real relationship: The "something more" of psychotherapy. *Journal of Contemporary Psychotherapy, 32*(1), 35–40.

Gelso, C. J. (2010). *The real relationship in psychotherapy: The hidden foundation of change.* Washington, DC: American Psychological Association.

Gelso, C. J., & Carter, J. A. (1994). Level of generality and clear thinking in theory construction and theory evaluation: Reply to Greenberg (1994) and Patton (1994). *Journal of Counseling Psychology, 41*(3), 313–314.

General Conference of Seventh-day Adventists (2009). *Statement of confidence in the spirit of prophecy.* Retrieved November 25, 2009, from http://www.adventist.org/beliefs/statements/main_stat24.html.

Glozier, N., & Grunstein, R. (2009). Losing sleep over work? Does it matter? Commentary on Niedhammer et al. "Workplace bullying and sleep disturbances: Findings from a large scale cross-sectional survey in the French working population." *Sleep: Journal of Sleep and Sleep Disorders Research, 32*(9), 1115–1116.

Goldfried, M. R. (Ed.). (2000). *How therapists change: Personal and professional reflections* (pp. 183–200). Washington, DC: American Psychological Association.

Good, G. E. (2001, August 25). *Me & Miles.* Division 17 New Fellows Address, Society of Counseling Psychology, at the annual conference of the American Psychological Association, San Francisco, CA.

Good, G. E. (2005). *Glenn E. Good.* William T. Kemper Fellowships for Teaching Excellence. Columbia, MO: University of Missouri.

Good, G. E., & Robertson, J. M. (1992). *Therapy with men: New developments for old issues.* Three-hour workshop presentation to the annual convention of the Kansas Psychological Association, Wichita, KS.

Good, G. E., & Robertson, J. M. (2010). To accept a pilot? Addressing men's ambivalence and altering their expectancies about therapy. *Psychotherapy Theory, Research, Practice, Training, 47*(3), 306–315.

Goodman, N. (1978). Ways of worldmaking. Indianapolis, IN: Hackett.

Goodman, L. A., Koss, M. P., & Russo, N. F. (1993). Violence against women: Physical and mental health effects: Part I. Research findings. *Applied & Preventive Psychology, 2,* 79–89.

Gradus, J. L., Street, A. E., Kelly, K., & Stafford, J. (2008). Sexual harassment experiences and harmful alcohol use in a military sample: Differences in gender and the mediating role of depression. *Journal of Studies on Alcohol and Drugs, 69*(3), 348–351.

Grant, B. R., & Grant, P. R. (2002). Unpredictable evolution in a 30-year study of Darwin's finches. *Science, 296,* 707–711.

Grasmick, H.G., Bursik, R.J., Jr., & Kimpel, M. (1991). Protestant fundamentalism and attitudes toward corporal punishment of children. *Violence and Victims, 6*(4), 283–298.

Greenberg, A., & Berktold, J. (2005). *Faith and family in America, 2005. Summary reported in association of Religion Data Archives (ARDA)*. Retrieved on November 25, 2007 from http://www.TheArda.com/Archive/Files/Descriptions/FAITHFAM.asp.

Greenberg, L. S. (2008). Emotion and cognition in psychotherapy: The transforming power of affect. *Canadian Psychology/Psychologie Canadienne, 49*(1), 49–59.

Greenberg, L. S., & Safran, J. D. (1987). *Emotion in psychotherapy*. New York, NY: Guilford.

Greenson, R. R. (1965). The working alliance and the transference neurosis. *Psychoanalytic Quarterly, 34*, 155–181.

Greenson, R. R. (1971). The "real" relationship between the patient and the psychoanalyst. In M. Kanzer (Ed.), *The unconscious today: Essays on Max Schur* (pp. 213–232). New York, NY: International Universities Press.

Greenson, R. R. (1978). *Explorations in psychoanalysis*. New York, NY: International Universities Press.

Grunebaum, H. (1983). A study of therapists' choice of a therapist. *The American Journal of Psychiatry, 140*(10), 1336–1339.

Gullotta, T. P., & McElhaney, S. J. (Eds.). (1999). *Violence in homes and communities: Prevention, intervention, and treatment*. Thousand Oaks, CA: Sage.

Gunaratana, B. H. (2002). *Mindfulness in plain English*. Somerville, MA: Wisdom Publications.

Gutek, B. A. (1985). *Sex and the workplace*. San Francisco, CA: Jossey-Bass.

Gutek, B. A., & Koss, M. P. (1993). Changed women and changed organizations: Consequences of and coping with sexual harassment. *Journal of Vocational Behavior, 42*, 28–48.

Guttman, D. (2008). *Divinity and inerrancy of the Torah and the dispassionate scholar*. Retrieved on March 23, 2010 from http://yediah.blogspot.com/2008/04/divinity-and-inerrancy-of-torah-and.html.

Guy, J. D., & Liaboe, G. P. (1986). The impact of conducting psychotherapy on psychotherapists' interpersonal functioning. *Professional Psychology: Research and Practice, 17*(2), 111–114.

Hamberger, L. K., & Hastings, J. (1986). Personality correlates of men who abuse their partners: A cross validation study. *Journal of Family Violence, 1*, 763–770.

Hamberger, L. K., & Hastings, J. (1988, November). Cognitive and personality correlates of men who batter: Some continuities and discontinuities. In A. Holtzworth-Monroe (Chair), *Research on marital violence: What we know, how we can apply it*. Symposium presented at the Meeting of the Association of Behavior Therapy, New York, NY.

Hamilton, W. D. (1964). The genetical evolution of social behaviour, I and II. *Journal of Theoretical. Biology, 7*, 1–52.

Hammer, J. H., & Good, G. E. (2010). Positive psychology: An empirical examination of beneficial aspects of endorsement of masculine norms. *Psychology of Men & Masculinity, 11*(4), 303–318.

Hanh, T. N. (2000). *Path of emancipation*. Berkeley, CA: Parallax Press.

Hariri, A. R., Bookheimer, S. Y., & Mazziotta, J. C. (2000). Modulating emotional responses: Effects of a neocortical network on the limbic system. *NeuroReport, 11*, 43–48.

Harned, M. S. (2000). Harassed bodies: An examination of the relationships among women's experiences of sexual harassment, body image, and eating disturbances. *Psychology of Women Quarterly, 24*, 336–348.

Harned, M. S., & Fitzgerald, L. F. (2002). Understanding a link between sexual harassment and eating disorder symptoms: A meditational analysis. *Journal of Consulting and Clinical Psychology, 70*(5), 1170–1181.

Harris, W. H., & Levey, J. S. (Eds.). (1975). *The New Columbia Encyclopedia*. New York, NY: Columbia University Press.

Harrison, R. L., & Westwood, M. J. (2009). Preventing vicarious traumatization of mental health therapists: Identifying protective practices. *Psychotherapy Theory, Research, Practice, Training, 46*, 203–219.

Hassan, S. (1988). *Combating cult mind control*. South Paris, ME: Park Street Press.

Hassan, M. K., & Khalique, A. 1981. Religiosity and its coordinates in college students. *Journal of Psychological Research, 25*, 129–136.

Hathcoat, J. D., & Barnes, L. L. B. (2010). Explaining the relationship among fundamentalism and authoritarianism: An epistemic connection. *International Journal for the Psychology of Religion, 20*(2), 73–84.

Hauge, L. J., Skogstad, A., & Einarsen, S. (2009). Individual and situational predictors of workplace bullying: Why do perpetrators engage in bullying others? *Work & Stress, 23*(4), 349–358.

Hayes, J. A., Gelso, C. J., & Hummel, A. M. (2011). Managing countertransference. *Psychotherapy, 48*(1), 88–97.

Hayes, S. C., Luoma, J. B., Bond, F. W., Masuda, A., & Lillis, J. (2006). Acceptance and commitment therapy: Model, processes and outcomes. *Behaviour Research and Therapy, 44*, 1–25.

Heim, A. & Westen, D. (2009) Theories of personality and personality disorders. In J. Oldham, A. E. Skodol, & D. S. Bender (Eds.), *Essentials of Personality Disorders* (pp. 13–34). Washington, DC: American Psychiatric Association.

Helmeke, C., Poeggel, G., & Braun, K. (2001). Differential emotional experience induces elevated spine densities on basal dendrites of pyramidal neurons in the anterior cingulated cortex of Octodon degus. *Neuroscience, 104*, 927–931.

Hemphill, J. F. (2003). Interpreting the magnitudes of correlation coefficients. *American Psychologist, 58*(1), 78–79.

Henry, W. P., Schacht, T. E., & Strupp, H. H. (1990). Patient and therapist introject, interpersonal process, and differential psychotherapy outcome. *Journal of Consulting and Clinical Psychology, 58*, 768–774.

Herman, J. (1992). Complex PTSD: A syndrome in survivors of prolonged and repeated trauma. *Journal of Traumatic Stress, 5*(3), 377–391.

Hesse, H. (1971). In B. Zeller, *Portrait of Hesse: An illustrated biography*. New York, NY: Herder and Herder.

Hill, N. (1928/2008). *The law of success*. New York, NY: Penguin.

Hill, P. C. (2005) Measurement in the psychology of religion and spirituality: Current status and evaluation. In R. F. Paloutzian & C. L. Park (Eds.), *Handbook of the psychology of religion and spirituality* (pp. 43–61). New York, NY: Guilford.

Hill, C. E., Nutt-Williams, E., Heaton, K. J., Thompson, M. J., & Rhodes, R. H. (1996). Psychotherapist retrospective recall impasses in long-term psychotherapy: A qualitative analysis. *Journal of Counseling Psychology, 43,* 207–217.

Hinduism Today. (2007). Hinduism's code of conduct: Twenty keys for spiritual living in contemporary times. In *What is Hinduism? Modern adventures into a profound global faith.* Kapaa, HI: Himalayan Academy.

Hirst, D. (2003). *The gun and the olive branch: The roots of violence in the Middle East.* New York, NY: Avalon.

Hoffer, E. (1951). *The true believer: Thoughts on the nature of mass movements.* New York, NY: Harper and Row.

Horn, S. S., & Romeo, K. E. (2010). Peer contexts for lesbian, gay, bisexual, and transgender students: Reducing stigma, prejudice, and discrimination. *The Prevention Researcher, 17*(4), 7–10.

Horvath, A. O., & Greenberg, L. S. (Eds.). (1994). *The working alliance: Theory, research, and practice.* Oxford, England: Wiley.

Huang, G. (Writer & Director). (1994). *Swimming with sharks.* United States: Cineville.

Hunsberger, B. (1995). Religion and prejudice. The role of religious fundamentalism, quest, and right-wing authoritarianism. *Journal of Social Issues, 51,* 113–129.

Hurst, M. A. (1997). The best fit in counseling men: Are there solutions to treating men as the problem? *Dissertation Abstracts International: Section B: The Sciences and Engineering, 58*(3-B), 1534.

Hyde, J. S. (2005). The gender similarities hypothesis. *American Psychologist, 60*(6), 581–592.

Ike's favorite author (1956, June 12). *Look: America's Family Magazine, 20,* 40–42.

Indian Health Service, Behavioral Health (2005). *Warning signs of domestic violence.* Washington, DC: US Department of Health and Human Services. Available online: http://www.ihs.gov/medicalprograms/mch/V/DV11.cfm.

Ire, J. (1997). Autobiographical writing as part of therapy: A tool for self-understanding and change. *Dissertation Abstracts International: Section B: The Sciences and Engineering.* December 1997, p. 3339.

James, W. (1901/1958). *The varieties of religious experience: A study in human nature.* New York, NY: The New American Library.

Jang, K. L., McCrae, R. R., Angleitner, A., Riemann, R., & Livesley, W. J. (1998). Heritability of facet-level traits in a cross-cultural twin sample: Support for a hierarchical model of personality. *Journal of Personality and Social Psychology, 74*(6), 1556–1565.

Jennings, J. L., & Murphy, C. M. (2000). Male–male dimensions of male–female battering: A new look at domestic violence. *Psychology of Men & Masculinity, 1*(1), 21–29.

Jewish Publication Society (2000). *Isaiah.* Philadelphia, PA: Jewish Publication Society.

Jill (2010, January 2). You won't tell, would you? In *Sexual harassment support: A support community for anyone who has experienced sexual harassment.* Available online at http://www.sexualharassmentsupport.org/speakupse/

John, O. P., Srivastava, S. (1999). The Big Five Trait taxonomy: History, measurement, and theoretical perspectives. In L. A. Pervin & O. P. John (Eds.), *Handbook of personality: Theory and research* (2nd ed., pp. 102–138). New York, NY: Guilford.

Johnson, J. G., Bromley, E., & McGeoch, P. G. (2009). In J. M. Oldham, A. E. Skodol, &. D. S. Bender (Eds.), *Essentials of personality disorders* (pp.143–157). Washington, DC: American Psychiatric Association.

Johnson, J. G., Cohen, P., Brown, J., Smailes, E. M., & Bernstein, D. P. (1999). Childhood maltreatment increases risk for personality disorders during early adulthood. *Archives of General Psychiatry, 56,* 600–606.

Johnson, J. G., Cohen, P., Smailes, E. M., Skodol, A. E., Brown, J., & Oldham, J. M. (2001). *Comprehensive Psychiatry, 42*(1), 16–23.

Johnson, N. G. (2001). Women helping men: Strengths and barriers to women therapists working with men clients. In G. R. Brooks & G. E. Good (Eds.), *The new handbook of psychotherapy and counseling with men: A comprehensive guide to settings, problems, and treatment approaches* (Vol. 2, pp. 696–719). San Francisco, CA: Jossey-Bass.

Joint Commission on Accreditation of Healthcare Organizations (2008, July 29). Behaviors that undermine a culture of safety. *Sentinel event alert.* Retrieved from www.jointcommission.org.

Jones, L. (Ed.). (2005). *The encyclopedia of religion, second edition.* Detroit, MI: Macmillan Reference USA.

Judd, C. H. (1910). Evolution and consciousness. *The Philosophical Review, XVII,* 77–97.

Judd, C. H. (1932). Charles H. Judd. In C. Murchison (Ed.), *A history of psychology in autobiography, Volume II,* (pp. 207–235). Worcester, MA: Clark University Press.

Jung, C. (1933). *Modern man in search of a soul.* New York, NY: Harcourt, Brace.

Juergensmeyer, M. (Ed.). (2006). *Oxford handbook of global religions.* New York, NY: Oxford University Press.

Kabat-Zinn, J. (1990). *Full catastrophe living: Using the wisdom of your mind to face stress, pain and illness.* New York, NY: Dell Publishing

Kabat-Zinn, J. (2003). Mindfulness-based interventions in context: Past, present, and future. *Clinical Psychology: Science and Practice, 10,* 144–156.

Kabat-Zinn, J. (2005). *Full catastrophe living.* New York, NY: Bantam Dell.

Kahn, C. H. (1979). *The art and thought of Heraclitus.* New York, NY: Cambridge University Press.

Kaminiski, J. P. (2009). *The quotable Abigail Adams.* Cambridge, MA: Massachusetts Historical Society and the President and Fellows of Harvard College.

Kantrowitz, J. L. (1999). The role of the preconscious in psychoanalysis. *Journal of the American Psychoanalytic Association, 47,* 65–89.

Kaplan, J. T., & Zaidel, E. (2001). Errors monitoring in the hemispheres: The effect of lateralized feedback on lexical decision. *Cognition, 82,* 157–178.

Karliner, R., Westrich, E. K., Shedler, J., & Mayman, M. (1996). The Adelphi Early Memory Index: Bridging the gap between psychodynamic and scientific psychology. In J. Masling & R. Bornstein (Eds.), *Psychoanalytic perspectives on developmental psychology* (pp. 43–67). Washington, DC: American Psychological Association.

Kennedy, R. F. (1964). *The pursuit of justice.* New York, NY: Harper & Row.

Khomeini, R. (1942). Cited in A. Taheri (1987), *Holy terror: Inside the world of Islamic terrorism*. Bethesda, MD: Adler & Adler.

Kilburg, R. R., Nathan, P. E., & Thoresen, R. W. (Eds.). (1986). *Professionals in distress: Issues, syndromes, and solutions in psychology*. Washington, DC: American Psychological Association.

Kiselica, M. S., & Englar-Carlson, M. (2010). Identifying, affirming, and building upon male strengths: The positive psychology/positive masculinity model of psychotherapy with boys and men. *Psychotherapy Theory, Research, Practice, Training, 47*(3), 276–287.

Kivimäki, M., Elovainio, M., & Vahtera, J. (2000). Workplace bullying and sickness absence in hospital staff. *Occupational and Environmental Medicine, 57*, 656–660.

Knight, J. R., Sanchez, L. T., Sherritt, L., Bresnahan, L. R., & Fromson, J. A. (2007). Outcomes of a monitoring program for physicians with mental and behavioral health problems. *Journal of Psychiatric Practice, 13*(1), 25–32.

Koenig, H. G. (Ed.). (1998). Handbook of religion and mental health. San Diego, CA: Academic Press.

Koenig, H. G. (2007). *Spirituality in patient care: Why, how, when, and what*. Conshohocken, PA: Templeton Press.

Koenig, H. G., McCullough, M. E., & Larson, D. B. (2001). *Handbook of religion and health*. New York, NY: Oxford University Press.

Kohut, H. (1971). *The analysis of the self: A systematic analysis of the treatment of narcissistic personality disorders*. New York, NY: International Universities Press.

Kosmin, B. A., Mayer, E., & Keysar, A. (2001). *American religious identification survey*. New York, NY: The Graduate Center of the City University of New York.

Koss, M. P., Goodman, L., Browne, A., Fitzgerald, L. F., Keita, G., & Russo, N. (1994). *No safe haven: Violence against women at home, at work, and in the community*. Washington, DC: American Psychological Association.

Krablin, B. (2006). *Courting the wide open spaces*. Kingfisher, OK: Privately published.

Krugman, S. (1998). Men's shame and trauma in therapy. In W. S. Pollack & R. F. Levant (Eds.), *New psychotherapy for men* (pp. 167–190). Hoboken, NJ: John Wiley & Sons.

Kuhn, T. S. (1962/1970). *The structure of scientific revolutions*. Chicago, IL: University of Chicago Press.

Kruse, M. (2010, January). Constellations. *The Sun, Issue 409*. Chapel Hill, NC: The Sun Publishing Company.

Laband, D. N., & Lentz, B. F. (1998). The effects of sexual harassment on job satisfaction, earnings, and turnover among female lawyers. *Industrial and Labor Relations Review, 51*(4), 594–607.

LaHaye, T., & Jenkins, J. B. (1999). *Are we living in the end times?* Carol Stream, IL: Tyndale House.

Lalich, J. (1997). Dominance and submission: The psychosexual exploitation of women in cults. *Cultic Studies Journal, 14*(1), 4–21.

Lalich, J. (2004) *Bounded choice: True believers and charismatic cults*. Berkeley, CA: University of California Press.

Lambert, M. J., & Shimokawa, K. (2011). Collecting client feedback. *Psychotherapy, 48*(1), 72–79.

Lao Tzu. (1999). *Tao Te Ching: An illustrated journey* (S. Mitchell, Trans.). London, England: Francis Lincoln Limited.

Laythe, B., Finkel, D. G., & Kirkpatrick, L. A. (2001). Predicting prejudice from religious fundamentalism and right-wing authoritarianism: A multiple regression approach. *Journal for the Scientific Study of Religion, 40,* 1–10.

Layton, D. (1998). *Seductive poison: A Jonestown survivor's story of life and death in the People's Temple.* New York, NY: Random House.

Leape, L. L., & Fromson, J. A. (2006). Problem doctors: Is there a system-level solution? *Annals of Internal Medicine, 144,* 107–115.

LeDoux, J. E. (2000). Emotion circuits in the brain. *Annual Review of Neuroscience, 23,* 155–184.

Leff, D. (2011). *How Darwin organized his data.* AboutDarwin.com.

Lehnart, J. & Neyer, F. J. (2006). Should I stay or should I go? Attachment and personality in stable and instable romantic relationships. *European Journal of Personality, 20*(6), 475–495.

Levant, R. F., & Pollack, W. S. (Eds.). (1995). *A new psychology of men.* New York, NY: Basic Books.

Liftin, R. J. (1961/1989). *Thought reform and the psychology of totalism.* Chapel Hill, NC: University of North Carolina Press.

Lindsey, H. (1970). *The late great planet earth.* Grand Rapids, MI: Zondervan.

Looney, J. G., Harding, R. K., Blotcky, M. J., & Barnhart, F. D. (1980). Psychiatrist's transition from training to career: Stress and mastery. *The American Journal of Psychiatry, 137*(1), 32–36.

Lopez, S. J. (Ed.). (2008). *Positive psychology: Exploring the best in people, Vol. 1: Discovering human strengths.* Westport, CT: Praeger/Greenwood.

Lopez, S. J., & Snyder, C. R. (Eds.). (2003). *Positive psychological assessment: A handbook of models and measures.* Washington, DC: American Psychological Association.

Lopez, S. J., & Snyder, C. R. (Eds.). (2009) *Oxford handbook of positive psychology* (2nd ed). New York, NY: Oxford University Press.

Lund, R., Nielsen, K. K., Hansen, D. H., Kriegbaum, M., Molbo, D., Due, P., & Christensen, U. (2009). Exposure to bullying at school and depression in adulthood: A study of Danish men born in 1953. *European Journal of Public Health, 19(1),* 111–116.

Lundberg, C. D. (2010). *Unifying truths of the world's religions: Practical principles for living and loving in peace.* New Fairfield, CT: Heavenlight Press.

Lundberg-Love, P. K., & Wilkerson, D. K. (2006). Battered women. In P. K. Lundberg-Love & S. L. Marmion (Eds.), *"Intimate" violence against women: When spouses, partners, or lovers attack* (pp. 31–45). Westport, CT: Praeger/Greenwood.

Mahalik, J. R. (2000, August). *A model of masculine gender role conformity. Symposium—Masculine gender role conformity: Examining theory, research, and practice.* Paper presented at the 108th Annual Convention of the American Psychological Association, Washington, DC.

Mahalik, J. R., Locke, B. D., Ludlow, L. H., Diemer, M. A., Scott, R. P. J., Gottfried, M., & Freistas, G. (2003). Development of the conformity to masculine norms inventory. *Psychology of Men and Masculinity, 4*(1), 3–25.

Mahalik, J. R., Talmadge, W. T., Locke, B. D., & Scott, R. P. J. (2005). Using the Conformity to Masculine Norms Inventory to work with men in a clinical setting. *Journal of Clinical Psychology, 61*(6), 661–674.

Mahler, M. S., & Kaplan, L. (1977). Developmental aspects in the assessment of narcissistic and so-called borderline. In P. Hartocollis (Ed.), *Borderline personality disorders* (pp. 71–86). New York, NY: International Universities Press.

Mahler, M. S., Pine, F., & Bergman, A. (1975). *The psychological birth of the human infant: Symbiosis and individuation.* New York, NY: Basic Books.

Mahoney, A. (2000). *U.S. norms on religious affiliation, self-reported importance, and church attendance of mothers and fathers of children and adolescents: Secondary analyses of 1995 Gallup poll.* Unpublished manuscript, Bowling Green State University.

Mahoney, M. J. (1974). *Cognition and behavior modification.* Cambridge, MA: Ballinger.

Mahoney, M. J. (1991). *Human change processes.* New York, NY: Basic.

Mahoney, M. J. (Ed.). (1995). *Cognitive and constructive psychotherapies: Theory, research, and practice.* New York, NY: Springer.

Mahoney, M. J. (2000). Behaviorism, cognitivism, and constructivisim: Reflections on persons and patterns in my intellectual development. In M. R. Goldfried (Ed.), *How therapists change: Personal and professional reflections* (pp. 183–200). Washington, DC.: American Psychological Association.

Mahoney, M. J. (2003). *Constructive psychotherapy: Theory and practice.* New York, NY: Guilford.

Mahoney, M. J., & Fernández-Alvarez, H. (1998). La vida personal del psicoterapeuta/The personal life of the psychotherapist. *Avances en Psicologia Clinica Latinoamericana, 16,* 9–22.

Malatesta-Magai, C. (1991). Emotional socialization: Its role in personality and developmental psychopathology. In D. Cicchetti & S. L. Toth (Eds.), *Internalizing and externalizing expressions of dysfunction: Rochester symposium on developmental psychopathology* (Vol. 2, pp. 203–224). Hillsdale, NJ: Erlbaum.

Malraux, A. (1968). *Anti-Memoirs* (T. Kilmartin, trans.). New York, NY: Holt, Rinehart & Winston.

Maples, M. R., & Robertson, J. M. (2000). Counseling men with religious affiliations. In G. R. Brooks & G. E. Good (Eds.), *The new handbook of psychotherapy and counseling with men: A comprehensive guide to settings, problems, and treatment approaches* (Vol. 2, pp. 816–843). San Francisco, CA: Jossey-Bass.

Marcus, D. M. (1997). On knowing what one knows. *Psychoanalytic Quarterly, 66,* 219–241.

Markus, H., & Nurius, P. (1986). Possible selves. *American Psychologist, 41,* 954–969.

Martin, J. (1984). *Adorno.* Cambridge, MA: Harvard University Press.

Martin, W. (2003). *Kingdom of the cults.* Bloomington, MN: Estate of Walter Martin & Bethany House Publishers.

Marty, M. E. (1970). *Righteous empire: The Protestant experience in America.* New York, NY: Dial Press.

Marty, M. E. (2005). *When faiths collide.* Carolton, Victoria, Australia: Blackwell.

Marty, M. E. (2007a). *The mystery of the child.* Grand Rapids, MI: Eerdmans.

Marty, M. E. (2007b, August 17). Bill Moyers talks with historian Martin E. Marty. *Bill Moyers Journal.* Arlington, VA: Public Broadcasting System.

Marty, M. E. (2010). *Building cultures of trust.* Grand Rapids, MI: Eerdmans.

Marty, M. E., & Appleby, R. S. (Eds.). (1991). *The fundamentalism project: Fundamentalisms observed, Vol. 1.* Chicago, IL: University of Chicago Press.

Marty, M. E., & Appleby, R. S. (Eds.). (1993). Hardacre, H., Mendelsohn, E., & Tehranian, M. (Associate Eds.). *The fundamentalism project: Fundamentalisms and society, reclaiming the sciences, the family, and education, Vol. 2.* Chicago, IL: University of Chicago Press.

Marty, M. E., & Appleby, R. S. (Eds.). (1996). Garvey, J. H., Kuran, T. & Rapoport, D. C. (Associate Eds.). *The fundamentalism project: Fundamentalisms and the state, remaking polities, economies, and militance, Vol. 3.* Chicago, IL: University of Chicago Press.

Marty, M. E., & Appleby, R. S. (Eds.). (2002). Almond, G. A., Appleby, R. S. & Silvan, E. S. (Associate Eds.). *The fundamentalism project: Strong religion, the rise of fundamentalisms around the world.* Chicago, IL: University of Chicago Press.

Marty, M. E., & Appleby, R. S. (Eds.). (2004a). Ammerman, N. T., Frykenberg, R. E., Heilman, S. C., & Piscatori, J. (Associate Eds.). *The fundamentalism project: Accounting for fundamentalisms, the dynamic character of movements, Vol. 4.* Chicago, IL: University of Chicago Press.

Marty, M. E., & Appleby, R. S. (2004b). *The fundamentalism project: Fundamentalisms comprehended, Vol. 5.* Chicago, IL: University of Chicago Press.

Maturana, H. R. & Varela, F. J. (1987). *The tree of knowledge: The biological roots of human understanding.* Boston, MA: Shambhala.

Mavor, K. I., Macleod, C. J., Boal, M. J., & Louis, W. R. (2009). Right-wing authoritarianism, fundamentalism, and prejudice revisited: Removing suppression and statistical artifact. *Personality and Individual Differences, 46*(5–6), 592–597.

May, R. (1958). The origins and significance of the existential movement in psychology. In R. May, E. Angel, & H. F. Ellenberger (Eds.), *Existence: A new dimension in psychology* (pp. 3–36). New York, NY: Basic Books.

May, R. (1975). *The courage to create.* New York, NY: Norton.

May, R. (1981). *Freedom and destiny.* New York, NY: Norton.

Mayer, J. D., Salovey, P., & Caruso, D. (2002). *Mayer-Salovey-Caruso emotional intelligence test (MSCEIT), Version 2.0.* Toronto, Canada: Multi-Health Systems.

Mayman, M. (1968). Early memories and character structure. *Journal of Projective Techniques and Personality Assessment, 32,* 303–316.

McAdams, D. P., de St. Aubin, E., & Logan, R. L. (1993). Generativity among young, midlife, and older adults. *Psychology and Aging, 8*(2), 221–230.

McAdams, D. P., Reynolds, J., Lewis, M., Patten, A. H., & Bowman, P. J. (2001). When bad things turn good and good things turn bad: Sequences of redemption and contamination in life narrative and their relation to psychosocial adaptation in midlife adults and in students. *Personality and Social Psychology Bulletin, 27*(4), 474–485.

McCloskey, M. S., Kleabir, K., Berman, M. E., Chen, Y. Y., & Coccaro, E. F. (2010). Unhealthy aggression: Intermittent explosive disorder and adverse physical health outcomes. *Health Psychology, 29,* 324–332.

McConnaughy, E. A., Prochaska, J. P., & Velicer, W. F. (1983). Stages of change in psychotherapy: Measurement and sample profiles. *Psychotherapy, 20,* 368–375.

McFarland, S. (2010). Authoritarianism, social dominance, and other roots of generalized prejudice. *Political Psychology, 31*(3), 453–477.

McGoldrick, M., Gerson, R., & Shellenberger, S. (1999). *Genograms: Assessment and intervention* (2nd ed.). New York, NY: Norton.

McKim, D., & Lasseter, J. (Producers), & Anderson, S. (Director). (2007). *Meet the Robinsons*. United States: Walt Disney Pictures.

McNeel, S. P., & Thorsen, P. L. (1985). A developmental perspective on Christian faith and dogmatism. *The High School Journal, 68,* 211–220.

Mead, F. S., Hill, S. S., & Atwood, C. D. (2005). *Handbook of denominations in the United States*. Nashville, TN: Abingdon Press.

Mead, G. H. (1934). *Mind, self, and society: From the standpoint of a social behaviorist*. Chicago, IL: University of Chicago Press.

Melton, J. G., Beverely, J., Jones, C., & Nadell, P. S. (Eds.). (2009). *Melton's Encyclopedia of American Religions* (8th ed.). Detroit, MI: Gale Research, Inc.

Mesulam, M.-M. (1998). From sensation to cognition. *Brain, 121,* 1013–1052.

Miller, B. L., Seeley, W. W., Mychack, P., Rosen, H. J., Mena, I., & Boone, K. (2001). Neuroanatomy of the self. Evidence from patients with frontotemporal dementia. *Neurology, 57,* 871–821.

Mills, J. (1979). *Six years with god: Life inside Rev. Jim Jones's people's temple*. New York, NY: A & W Publishers.

Moffitt, T. E., Arseneault, L., Belsky, D., Dickson, N., Hancox, R. J., Harrington, H. Houts, R., Poulton, R., Roberts, B. W., Ross, S., Sears, M., R., Thomson, W. M., & Caspi, A. (2011). A gradient of childhood self-control predicts health, wealth, and public safety. *PNAS Proceedings of the National Academy of Sciences of the United States of America, 108*(7), 2693–2698.

Moffitt, T. E., & Caspi, A. (1999). Findings about partner violence from the Dunedin Multidisciplinary Health and Development Study. *National Institute of Justice: Research in Brief* (pp. 1–12). Washington, DC: US Department of Justice National Institute of Justice.

Moffitt, T. E., & Caspi, A. (2001). Childhood predictors differentiate life-course persistent and adolescence-limited antisocial pathways among males and females. *Development and Psychopathology, 13*(2), 355–375.

Moffitt, T. E., Caspi, A., Harrington, H., & Milne, M. J. (2002). Males on the life-course-persistent and adolescence-limited antisocial pathways: Follow-up at age 26 years. *Development and Psychopathology, 14*(1), 179–207.

Momen, M. (1985). *An introduction to Shii Islam*. New Haven, CT: Yale University Press.

Mullen, P. E., Martin, J. L., Anderson, J. C., Romans, S. E., & Herbison, G. P. (1996). The long term impact of the physical, emotional, and sexual abuse of children: A community study. *Child Abuse & Neglect, 20,* 7–21.

Muller, W. (1999). *Sabbath: Restoring the sacred rhythm of rest*. New York, NY: Bantam Books.

Murray, H. A. (1943). *Thematic apperception test manual*. Cambridge, MA: Harvard University Press.

Murray, H. A. (1965). Uses of the thematic apperception test. In B. I. Murstein (Ed.), *Handbook of projective techniques* (pp. 425–432). New York, NY: Basic Books.

Murray, L. (1991). Intersubjectivity, object relations theory, and empirical evidence from mother-infant interactions. *Infant Mental Health Journal, 12*(3), 219–232.

Murray-Swank, A., Mahoney, A., & Pargament, K. I. (2006). Sanctification of parenting: Links to corporal punishment and parental warmth among biblically conservative and liberal mothers. *The International Journal for the Psychology of Religion, 16*, 271–287.

Musick, M. A., Herzog, R., & House, J. S. (1999). Volunteering and mortality among older adults: Findings from a national sample. *Journals of Gerontology Series B: Psychological Sciences and Social Sciences, 54*, S173–S180.

Naime, G. (2003). *The Workplace Bullying Institute (WBI) 2003 report on abusive workplaces.* Retrieved online from http://www.workplacebullying.org/res/2003results.pdf.

Naime, G. (2007). *U.S. workplace bullying survey, September, 2007.* Bellingham, WA: The Workplace Bullying Institute.

Naismith, J. (1941). *Basketball: Its origin and development.* New York, NY: Association Press.

Nansel, T., Overpeck, M., Pilla, R. S., Ruan, W. J., Simmons-Morton, B., & Schmidt, P. (2001). Bulling behaviors among US youth. *Journal of American Medical Association, 285*, 2095–2100.

National Center for Health Statistics (2009). *Health, United States, 2009: With special feature on medical technology.* Hyattsville, MD: Centers for Disease Control and Prevention: U.S. Department of Health and Human Services.

Naylor, E. V. (2008). A five-minute bibliotherapy prescription as a physician-delivered treatment for depression. *Dissertation Abstracts International: Section B: The Sciences and Engineering, 69*(4-B), 2635.

New International Version (1984). *Holy Bible.* Grand Rapids, MI: Zondervan.

Newman-Carlson, D., Horne, A. M., & Bartolomucci, C. L. (2000) *Bully busters: A teacher's manual for helping bullies, victims, and bystanders.* Champaign, IL: Research Press.

Norcross, J. C. (2002). Empirically supported therapy relationships. In J. C. Norcross (Ed.), *Psychotherapy relationships that work: Therapist contributions and responsiveness to patients* (pp. 3–16). New York, NY: Oxford University Press.

Norcross, J. (2003). Sociopolitical and psychohistorical factors in acknowledging the effectiveness of EMDR. Paper presented at the Annual Conference of the American Psychological Association (111th, Toronto, Canada, August 7–10, 2003).

Norcross, J. C., & Guy, J. D. (2007). *Leaving it at the office.* New York, NY: Guildford.

Norcross, J. C., & Wampold, B. E. (2011). Evidence-based therapy relationships: Research conclusions and clinical practices. *Psychotherapy, 48*(1), 98–102.

Norden, K. A., Klein, D. N., Donaldson, S. K., Pepper, C. M., & Klein, L. M. (1995). Reports of the early home environment in DSM-III-R personality disorders. *Journal of Personality Disorders, 9*(3), 213–223.

Norris, G. (2005). *The authoritarian personality in the 21st century.* Doctoral dissertation submitted to Bond University, Queensland, Australia. Available online from epublications.bond.edu.

Oberst, C. (2002). Bowl of oranges. On the album *Gone Fishin'...3 years later*, by Bright Eyes. London, England: Wichita Recordings.

O'Connor, B. P., & Dyce, J. A. (2002). Tests of general and specific models of personality disorder configurations. In P. T. Costa and T. A. Widiger (Eds.), *Personality disorders and the five-factor model of personality* (2nd ed., pp. 223–246). Washington, DC: American Psychological Association.

Office of Violence Against Women (2009, March). *About domestic violence*. Retrieved from http://www.ovw.usdoj.gov/domviolence.htm.

Oldham, J. M., & Morris, L. B. (1990). *The personality self-portrait*. New York, NY: Bantam.

Olweus, D. (1993). *Bullying at school: What we know and what we can do*. Malden, MA: Blackwell Publishing.

Oman, D., & Thoresen, C. E. (2003). Spiritual modeling: A key to spiritual and religious growth? *International Journal for the Psychology of Religion, 13(3),* 149–165.

O'Neil, J. M. (1981). Male sex-role conflicts, sexism, and masculinity: Implications for men, women, and the counseling psychologists. *The counseling psychologist, 9(2),* 61–80.

O'Neil, J. M. (2008). Summarizing 25 years of research on men's gender role conflict using the gender role conflict scale: New research paradigms and clinical implications. *Counseling Psychologist, 36,* 358–445.

O'Neil, J. M., Egan, J., Owen, S.V., & Murry, V.M. (1993). The gender role journey measure (JRJM): Scale development and psychometric evaluations. *Sex Roles, 28,* 167–185.

O'Neil, J. M., & Good, G. E. (2002, August 23). *Gender-role conflict research: Empirical studies and 20-year summary*. Symposium presented at the annual convention of the American Psychological Association, Chicago, IL.

O'Neil, J. M., Good, G. E., & Holmes, S. (1995). Fifteen years of theory and research on men's gender role conflict: New paradigms for empirical research. In R. F. Levant & W. S. Pollack (Ed.), *A new psychology of men* (pp. 164–206). New York, NY: Basic Books.

O'Neil, J. M., Helms, B. J., Gable, R. K., David, L., & Wrightsman, L. S. (1986). Gender-role conflict scale: College men's fear of femininity. *Sex Roles, 14,* 335–350.

Orlinsky, D. E., Rønnestad, M. H., Gerin, P., Davis, J. D., Hansruedi, A., Davis, M. L., Dazord, A., Willutzki, U., Aapro, N., Botermans, J-F., & Schröder, T. A. (2005). The development of psychotherapists. In D. E. Orlinsky, D. E. Rønnestad, & M. Hedge, *How psychotherapists develop: A study of therapeutic work and professional growth* (pp. 3–13). Washington, DC: American Psychological Association.

Osherson, S., & Krugman, S. (1990). Men, shame, and psychotherapy. *Psychotherapy: Theory, Research, Practice, Training, 27(3),* 327–339.

Osipow, S. H. (1990). Careers: Research and personal; or how I think an individual's personal and career life intertwine: A personal example. *The Counseling Psychologist, 18,* 338–347.

Ovtscharoff, W. Jr., & Braun, J. (2001). Maternal separation and social isolation modulate the postnatal development of synaptic composition in the infralimbic cortex of *octodon degus*. *Neuroscience, 104,* 33–40.

Oxford English Dictionary (1971). *The compact edition of the Oxford English Dictionary: Complete text reproduced micrographically, Volume I: A–O, Volume II: P– Z*. London: Oxford University Press.

Pacquette, V., Levesque, J., Mensour, B., Leroux, J-M., Beaudoin, G., Bourgouin, P., & Beauregard, M. (2003). "Change the mind and you change the brain." Effects of cognitive-behavioral therapy on the neural correlates of spider phobia. *NeuroImage, 18*, 401–409.

Pagotto, L., Voci, A., & Maculan, V. (2010). The effectiveness of intergroup contact at work: Mediators and moderators of hospital workers' prejudice towards immigrants. *Journal of Community and Applied Social Psychology, 20*(4), 317–330.

Palmieri, P. A., & Fitzgerald, L. F. (2005). Confirmatory factor analysis of post-traumatic stress symptoms in sexually harassed women. *Journal of Traumatic Stress, 18*(6), 657–666.

Papers alter Israeli cabinet photo (2009, April 3). *BBC News*. Retrieved on May 1, 2010, from http://news.bbc.co.uk/2/hi/middle_east/7982146.stm.

Pargament, K. I. (2002). The bitter and the sweet: An evaluation of the costs and benefits of religiousness. *Psychological Inquiry, 13*, 168–181.

Parker, K. J., Buckmaster, C. L., Schatzberg, A. F. Lyons, D. M. (2004). Prospective investigation of stress inoculation in young monkeys. *Archives of General Psychiatry, 61*(9), 933–941.

Parks, E. D., & Balon, R. (1995). Autobiographical memory for childhood events: Patterns of recall in psychiatric patients with a history of alleged trauma. *Psychiatry, 58*(3), 199–208.

Pascal, B. (1669/1958). *Pensées* (W. F. Trotter, trans.). New York, NY: Dutton.

Patterson, A. (2009, December 12). Lawsuit threatened over atheist councilman. *Lawrence Journal World*, p. 5A.

Paul VI. (1965). *Dogmatic constitution on divine revelation, Dei Verbum, solemnly promulgated by his Holiness, Pope Paul VI, on November 18, 1965*. Retrieved March 16, 2010 from http://www.vatican.va/archive/hist_councils/ii_vatican_council/documents/vat-ii_const_19651118_dei-verbum_en.html.

PDM Task Force (2006). *Psychodynamic diagnostic manual*. Silver Spring, MD: Alliance of Psychoanalytic Organizations.

Pentecost, J. D. (1976). *Things to come: A study in biblical eschatology*. Grand Rapids, MI: Zondervan.

Perry, William G., Jr. (1970) *Forms of intellectual and ethical development in the college years: A scheme*. New York, NY: Holt, Rinehart, & Winston.

Peterson, C., & Seligman, M. E. P. (2004). *Character strengths and virtues: A handbook and classification*. New York, NY: Oxford University Press.

Pettegrew, L. D. (1982, Fall). Will the real fundamentalist please stand up? *Central Testimony, 26*(2). Plymouth, MN: Central Baptist Theological Seminary of Minneapolis.

Pew Forum on Religion & Public Life (2010). *U.S. religious knowledge survey*. Available online at: http://pewforum.org/Other-Beliefs-and-Practices/U-S-Religious-Knowledge-Survey.aspx.

Phillips, S. M. (1999). U.S. psychologists' suicide rates have declined since the 1960's. *Archives of Suicide Research, 51*(1), 11–26.

Pickthall, M. M. (1953). *The meaning of the glorious Koran. An explanatory translation*. New York, NY: New American Library of World Literature.

Piedmont, R. L. (2001). Cracking the plaster cast: Big five personality change during intensive outpatient counseling. *Journal of Research in Personality, 35*(4), 500–520.

Plante, T. G., & Sherman, A. C. (Eds.). (2001). *Faith and health: Psychological perspectives*. New York, NY: Guilford Press.

Plato (360 BC/2008). *Phaedrus* (B. Jowett, trans.). Forgotten Books.com.

Pollack, W. S. (2001). "Masked men": New psychoanalytically oriented treatment models for adult and young adult men. In G. Brooks & G Good (Eds.), *The new handbook of psychotherapy and counseling with men* (pp. 282–308). New York, NY: Wiley.

Pollock, V. E., Briere, J., Schneider, L., Knop, J., Mednick, S. A., & Goodwin, D. W. (1990). Childhood antecedents of antisocial behavior: Parental alcoholism and physical abusiveness. *American Journal of Psychiatry, 147*, 1290–1293.

Pope, K. S., & Feldman-Summers, S. (1992). National survey of psychologists' sexual and physical abuse history and their evaluation of training and competence in these areas. *Professional Psychology: Research and Practice, 23*(5), 353–361.

Pope, K. S., & Tabachnick, B. G. (1993a). Therapists as patients: A national survey of psychologists' experiences, problems, and beliefs. *Professional Psychology: Research & Practice, 25*, 247–258.

Pope K. S., & Tabachnick, B. G. (1993b). Therapists' anger, hate, fear, and sexual feelings: National survey of therapist responses, client characteristics, critical events, formal complaints, and training. *Professional Psychology: Research and Practice, 24*, 142–152.

Pope, K. S., Tabachnick, B. G., & Keith-Spiegel, P. (1987). Ethics of practice: The beliefs and behaviors of psychologists as therapists. *American Psychologist, 42*, 993–1006.

Posner, M. I., & Rothbart, M. K. (1998). Attention, self-regulation, and consciousness. *Philosophical Transactions of the Royal Society of London B, 353*, 1915–1927.

Poston, J. M., & Hanson, W. E. (2010). Meta-analysis of psychological assessment as therapeutic intervention. *Psychological Assessment, 22*, 203–212.

Powell, L. H., Shahabi, L., & Thoresen, C. F. (2003). Religion and spirituality: Linkages to physical health. *American Psychologist, 58*(1), 36–52.

Powers, E. A. (1971). Thirty years of research on ideal mate characteristics: What do we know? *International Journal of Sociology of the Family, 1*, 207–215.

Pratto, F., Sidanius, J., Stallworth, L. M., & Malle, B. F. (1994). Social dominance orientation: A personality variable predicting social and political attitudes. *Journal of Personality and Social Psychology, 67*(4), 741–763.

Prochaska, J. O., & DiClemente, C. C. (1992). Stages of change in the modification of problem behavior. In M. Hersen, P. M. Miller, & R. Eisler (Eds.), *Progress in behavior modification* (Vol. 28, pp. 184–218). New York, NY: Wadsworth.

Prochaska, J. O., & Norcross, J. C. (2001). Stages of change. *Psychotherapy: Theory, Research, Practice, Training, 38*(4), 443–448.

Prochaska, J. O., & Norcross, J. C. (2007). *Systems of psychotherapy: A transtheoretical analysis*. Belmont, CA: Thomson.

Prothero, S. (2007). *Religious literacy: What every American needs to know—and doesn't*. New York, NY: HarperCollins.

Puchalski, C. (2004). Spirituality in health: The role of spirituality in critical care. *Critical Care Clinics, 20*, 487–504.

Rabinowitz, F. E., & Cochran, S. V. (2002). *Deepening psychotherapy with men*. Washington, DC: American Psychological Association.

Radeke, J. T., & Mahoney, M. J. (2000). Comparing the personal lives of psychotherapists and research psychologists. *Professional Psychology: Research and Practice, 3*(1), 82–84.
Rahula, W. (1974). *What the Buddha taught.* New York, NY: Grove.
Ramacharaka, Y. (2003). *Hindu Yogi breathing exercises.* Whitefish, MT: Kessinger Publishing.
Ranote, S., Elliott, R., Abel, K. M., Mitchell, R., Deakin, J. F. W., & Appleby, L. (2004). The neural basis of maternal responsiveness to infants: An fMRI study. *NeuroReport: For Rapid Communication of Neuroscience Research, 15*(11), 1825–1829.
Raskauskas, J. (2010). Text-bullying: Associations with traditional bullying and depression among New Zealand adolescents. *Journal of School Violence, 9*(1), 74–97.
Rayburn, C. A. (2000). Psychotherapy with Seventh-day Adventists. In P. S. Richards & A. E. Bergin (Eds.), *Handbook of psychotherapy and religious diversity* (pp. 211–234). Washington, DC: American Psychological Association.
Raynor, C. (1997). The incidence of workplace bullying. *Journal of Community & Applied Social Psychology, 7*(3), 199–208.
Reed, M. E. (2003, August). Numbers and voices: Content validity of the sexual experiences questionnaire. *Sexual experiences Questionnaire: What it can and can't do (yet).* Symposium conducted at the meeting of the American Psychological Association, Toronto, Canada.
Reed, M. E. (2005). The psychological impact of sexual harassment and previous sexual victimization in a sample of class action litigants. *Dissertation abstracts International: Section B: The sciences and engineering,* p. 6057.
Rice, L. N., & Greenberg, L. S. (1984). *Patterns of change: Intensive analysis of psychotherapy process.* New York, NY: Guilford.
Richards, P. S., & Bergin, A. E. (2000). *Handbook of psychotherapy and religious diversity.* Washington, DC: American Psychological Association.
Richardson, J. (2007). *A life of Picasso: The triumphant years.* New York, NY: Knopf.
Rigby, K. (2001). Health consequences of bullying and its prevention in schools. In J. Juvonen & S. Graham (Eds.), *Peer harassment in school: The plight of the vulnerable and victimized* (pp. 310–331). New York, NY: Guilford Press.
Rigby, K., & Slee, P. (1999). Suicidal ideation among adolescent school children, involvement in bully-victim problems, and perceived social support. *Suicide and Life-Threatening Behavior, 29*(2), 119–130.
Roberts, B. W., Caspi, A., & Moffitt, T. E. (2001). The kids are alright: Growth and stability in personality development from adolescence to adulthood. *Journal of Personality and Social Psychology, 81*(4), 670–683.
Roberts, B. W., & Chapman, C. N. (2000). Change in dispositional well-being and its relation to role quality: A 30-year longitudinal study. *Journal of Research in Personality, 34*(1), 26–41.
Roberts, B. W., Harms, P. D., Caspi, A., & Moffitt, T. E. (2007). Predicting the counterproductive employee in a child-to-adult prospective study. *Journal of Applied Psychology, 92*(5), 1427–1436.
Roberts, B. W., Walton, K. E., & Viechtbauer, W. (2006). Patterns of mean-level change in personality traits across the life course: A meta-analysis of longitudinal studies. *Psychological Bulletin, 132*(1), 1–25.

Roberts, B. W., Wood, D., & Caspi, A. (2008). The development of personality traits in adulthood. In O. P. John, R. W. Robins, & L. A. Pervin (Eds.), *Handbook of personality psychology: Theory and research* (3rd ed., pp. 375–398). New York, NY: Guilford.

Robertson, J. M. (1994). Tracing ideological perspectives through 100 years of an academic genealogy. *Psychological Reports, 75*, 859–879.

Robertson, J. M. (2003). *Kansas Spiritual Assessment*. Unpublished assessment instrument. Lawrence, KS: Professional Renewal Center. Available upon request from JRobertson@sunflower.com.

Robertson, J. M. (2004). *Emotional competency group*. Unpublished handout. Lawrence, KS: Professional Renewal Center.

Robertson, J. M., & Khamphadky-Brown, S. (2010). Early life memories: A male-friendly approach to developing couple collaboration. In D. Shepard (Ed.), *Working successfully with men in couples counseling: A gender-sensitive approach*. New York, NY: Routledge.

Robertson, J. M. & Fitzgerald, L. F. (1992). Overcoming the masculine mystique: Preferences for alternative forms of assistance among men who avoid counseling. *Journal of Counseling Psychology, 39*(2), 240–246.

Robertson, J. M., & Shepard, D. S. (2008). The psychological development of boys. In M. S. Kiselica, M. Englar-Carlson, and A. M. Horne (Eds.), *Counseling troubled boys: A guidebook for professionals* (pp. 3–29). New York, NY: Routledge.

Robertson, J. M., & Williams, B. W. (2010). "Gender Aware Therapy" for professional men in a day treatment center. *Psychotherapy Theory, Research, Practice, Training, 47*(3), 316–326.

Robertson, P. (1991). *The new World order.* Dallas, TX: Word.

Robins, R. W., Fraley, R. C., Roberts, B. W., & Trzesniewski, K. H. (2001). A longitudinal study of personality change in young adulthood. *Journal of Personality, 69*(4), 617–640.

Rogers, C. R. (1957). The necessary and sufficient conditions of therapeutic personality change. *Journal of Consulting Psychology, 21*(2), 95–103.

Rokeach, M. (1960). *The open and closed mind.* New York, NY: Free Press.

Rowland, H. (1922). *A guide to men: Being encore reflections of a bachelor girl.* New York, NY: Dodge Publishing.

Rosch, E. H. (1973). Natural categories. *Cognitive Psychology, 4*(3), 328–350.

Rothschild, Z. K., Abdollahi, A., & Pyszczynski, T. (2009). Does peace have a prayer? The effect of mortality salience, compassionate values, and religious fundamentalism on hostility toward out-groups. *Journal of Experimental Social Psychology, 45*(4), 816–827.

Rubinstein, G. (1996). Two peoples in one land: A validation study of Altemeyer's right-wing authoritarianism scale in the Palestinian and Jewish societies in Israel. *Journal of Cross-Cultural Psychology, 27*, 216–230.

Russell, S. R. & Yarhouse, M. A. (2006). Religion/spirituality within APA-accredited psychology predoctoral internships. *Professional Psychology: Research and Practice, 37*, 430–436.

Safran, J. D., & Muran, J. C. (1996). The resolution of ruptures in the therapeutic alliance. *Journal of Consulting and Clinical Psychology, 64*, 447–458.

Safran, J. D., Muran, J. C., & Eubanks-Carter, C. (2011). Repairing alliance ruptures. *Psychotherapy, 48*(1), 80–87.

Salzberg, S. (2011, June 24). *How to bring meditation tools to clients.* Workshop presented in Lawrence, KS.
Salzinger, S., Rosario, M., Feldman, R. S., & Ng-Mak, D. S. (2008). Aggressive behavior in response to violence exposure: Is it adaptive for middle-school children? *Journal of Community Psychology, 36*(8), 1008–1025.
Sartre, J.-P. (1943/1992). *Being and nothingness: A phenomenological essay on ontology* (H. E. Barnes, trans.). New York, NY: Washington Square Press.
Satir, V. (1972). *Peoplemaking.* Palo Alto, CA: Science and Behavior Books.
Savage, M. (2005, January 5). *Savage on the tsunami: "I wouldn't call it a tragedy...We shouldn't be spending a nickel on this."* Retrieved on line from http://mediamatters.org/research/200501050006.
Saxe, J. G. (1873). *The poems of John Godfrey Saxe, complete edition.* Boston, MA: James R. Osgood and Company.
Schechtman, Z., & Nachshol, R. (1996). A school based intervention to reduce aggressive behavior in maladjusted adolescents. *Journal of Applied Developmental Psychology, 17,* 535–551.
Schernhammer, W. (2005). Taking their own lives—The high rate of physician suicide. *The New England Journal of Medicine, 352*(24), 2473–2476.
Schneider, K. T., Swan, S., & Fitzgerald, L. F. (1997). Job-related and psychological effects of sexual harassment in the workplace: Empirical evidence from two organizations. *Journal of Applied Psychology, 82*(3), 401–515.
Schore, A. N. (1994). *Affect regulation and the origin of the self: The neurobiology of emotional development.* Hillsdale, NJ: Lawrence Erlbaum.
Schore, A. N. (2001). Minds in the making: Attachment, the self-organizing brain, and developmentally-oriented psychoanalytic psychotherapy. *British Journal of Psychotherapy, 17,* 299–328.
Schore, A. N. (2002). Neurobiology and psychoanalysis: Convergent findings on the subject of projective identification. In J. Edwards (Ed.), *Being alive: Building on the work of Anne Alvarez* (pp. 57–74). London: Brunner-Routledge.
Schore, A. N. (2003a). *Affect dysregulation and disorders of the self.* New York, NY: Norton.
Schore, A. N. (2003b). *Affect regulation and the repair of the self.* New York, NY: Norton.
Schore, A. N. (2006, April, May). *Affect regulation and the repair of the self.* Conference presentation for mental health professionals, University of Kansas. Lawrence, KS.
Schwartz, J. P., Hage, S. M., Bush, I., Burns, L. K. (2006). Unhealthy parenting and potential mediators as contributing factors to future intimate violence: A review of the literature. *Trauma, Violence, & Abuse, 7*(3), 206–221.
Scollon, C. N., & Diener, E. (2006). Love, work, and changes in extraversion and neuroticism over time. *Journal of Personality and Social Psychology, 91*(6), 1152–1165.
Sealy, J. R. (2002). Physician sexual misconduct. *Sexual Addiction & Compulsivity, 9,* 97–111.
Seligman, M. E. P., & Csikszentmihalyi, M. (2000). Positive psychology: An introduction. *American Psychologist, 55,* 5–14.

Sexual Harassment Support. (2010). Harasser patterns. *sexual harassment support: A support community for anyone who has experienced sexual harassment.* Available online at: http://www.sexualharassmentsupport.org/TypesOfHarassers.html.

Shabak, I., & Mezvinsky, N. (1999). *Jewish fundamentalism in Israel.* London: Pluto Press.

Shafer, R. (1982). *The analytic attitude.* New York, NY: Basic Books.

Shafranske, E. P. (1996). Religious beliefs, affiliations, and practices of clinical psychologists. In E. P. Shafranske (Ed.), *Religion and the clinical practice of psychology.* Washington, DC: American Psychological Association.

Shafranske, E. P. (2005). The psychology of religion in clinical and counseling psychology. In R. F. Paloutzian & C. L. Park (Eds.), *Handbook of the psychology of religion and spirituality* (pp. 496–514). New York, NY: Guilford.

Shakir, M. H. (trans) (1983) *The holy Qur'an,* New York, NY: Tahrike Tarsile Qur'an, Inc.

Shapiro, S. L., & Carlson, L. D. (2009). *The art and science of mindfulness.* Washington, DC: American Psychological Association.

Shapiro, F., Kaslow, F., & Maxfield, L. (Eds.). (2007). *Handbook of EMDR and family therapy processes.* Hoboken, NJ: Wiley.

Shulman, D. G., & Ferguson, G. R. (1988). Two methods of assessing narcissism: Comparison of the Narcissism-Projective (N-P) and the Narcissistic Personality Inventory (NPI). *Journal of Clinical Psychology, 44*(6), 857–866.

Sibley, C. G., & Duckitt, J. (2008). Personality and prejudice: A meta-analysis and theoretical review. *Personality and Social Psychology Review, 12,* 248–279.

Sidanius, J., & Pratto, F. (1999). *Social dominance: An intergroup theory of social hierarchy and oppression.* New York, NY: Cambridge University Press.

Sidanius, J., Pratto, F., & Bobo, L. (1996). Racism, conservatism, affirmative action and intellectual sophistication: A matter of principled conservatism or group dominance? *Journal of Personality and Social Psychology, 70,* 476–490.

Siegel, D. (2007). *The mindful brain: Reflection and attunement in the cultivation of well-being.* New York, NY: Norton.

Sieratzki, J. S., & Woll, B. (1996). Why do mothers cradle babies to the left? *Lancet, 347,* 1746–1748.

Sieratzki, J. S., & Woll, B. (2004). The impact of maternal deafness on cradling laterality with deaf and hearing infants. *Journal of Deaf Studies and Deaf Education, 9*(4), 387–394.

Simpson, J. C. (2000, April). It's all in the upbringing. Pioneers of scholarship. *Johns Hopkins Magazine,* 50th Anniversary Edition. Online edition available at: http://www.jhu.edu/~jhumag/0400web/.

Skovill, N. B. (2011). *The liberation of women in religious sources.* Milwaukee: WI: The religious consultation on population, reproductive health and ethics. Available online at http://www.religiousconsultation.org/liberation.htm#Judaism.

Smart, N. (1998). *Dimensions of the sacred: An anatomy of the world's beliefs.* Berkeley, CA: University of California Press.

Smart, R. N. (1968). *Secular education and the logic of religion.* New York, NY: Humanities Press, 1968.

Smith, A. E., & Walton, F. (Eds.). (1896, November 7). Notes and queries. *The Outlook: A family paper,* volume 54, 844.

Smith, H. E. (2010). Introduction. In H. E. Smith (Ed.), *Autobiography of Mark Twain, Volume 1*. Berkeley, CA: University of California Press.

Smith, E. P., & Orlinsky, D. E. (2004). Religious and spiritual experience among psychotherapists. *Psychotherapy: Theory, Research, Practice, Training, 41*(2), 144–151.

Smuts, B. B., & Gubernick, D. J. (1992). Male-infant relationships in non-human primates: Paternal investment or mating effort? In B. S. Hewlett (Ed.), *Father–child relations: Cultural and biosocial contexts* (pp. 1–30). Hawthorne, NY: Aldine de Gruyter.

Society for Social Research (1925). *Institute for Social Research at the University of Frankfurt*. Frankfurt, Germany: Frankfurt on the Main.

Son Hing, L. L., Bobocel, D., R., & Zanna, M. P. (2007). Authoritarian dynamics and unethical decision making: High social dominance orientation leaders and high right-wing authoritarianism followers. *Journal of Personality and Social Psychology, 92*(1), 67–81.

Spielberger, C. (Ed.). (2004). *Encyclopedia of applied psychology*. San Diego, CA: Academic Press.

Srabstein, J., & Piazza, T. (2008). Public health, safety and educational risks associated with bullying behaviors in American adolescents. *International Journal of Adolescent Medicine and Health, 20*(2), 222–233.

Stein, D. J., Ives-Deliperi, V., & Thomas, K. G. F. (2008). Psychobiology of mindfulness. *CNS Spectrums, 13*(9), 752–756.

Steinem, G. (1983). *Outrageous acts and everyday rebellions*. New York, NY: Holt, Rinehart, and Winston.

Stern, D. N. (1985). *The interpersonal worm of the infant: A view from psychoanalysis and developmental psychology*. New York, NY: Basic Books.

Stern, D. N., Sander, L. W., Nahum, J. P., Harrison, A. M., Lyons-Ruth, K., & Morgan, A. C. (1998). Non-interpretive mechanisms in psychoanalytic therapy: The "something more" than interpretation. *International Journal of Psychoanalysis, 79*, 903–921.

Stern, D. N., Bruschweiler-Stern, N., Harrison, A. M., Lyons-Ruth, K., Morgan, A. D., Nahum, J. P., Sander, L., & Tronick, E. Z. (1998). The process of therapeutic change involving implicit knowledge: Some implications of developmental observations for adult psychotherapy. *Infant Mental Health Journal, 19*, 300–308.

Stop Bullying in SA: *A collaborative effort of the interagency roundtable on workplace bullying* (2008). Adelaide, South Australia: Department of the Premier and Cabinet, Government of South Australia. Available online at http://www.stopbullyingsa.com.au/whatis.asp.

Sumedho, A. (1989). *Now is the knowing*. Hertfordshire, England: Amaravati Publications.

Swiggart, W., & Starr, K. (2002). Sexual boundaries and physicians: Overview and educational approach to the problem. *Sexual Addiction & Compulsivity, 9*, 139–148.

Szasz, T. (1990). *The untamed tongue: A dissenting dictionary*. Chicago, IL: Open Court.

Taylor, G. J., Bagby, R. M., & Parker, J. D. (1997). *Disorders of affect regulation: Alexithymia in medical and psychiatric illness*. Cambridge: U.K.: Cambridge University Press.

Tepper, B. J. (2000). Consequences of abusive supervision. *Academy of Management Journal, 43*(2), 178–190.

Terry, R. (1993, August 16, First Section). In B. Caylor, Terry preaches theocratic rule: "No more Mr. Nice Guy Christian" is the pro-life activist's theme for the 90's. First section, *The News Sentinel*. Fort Wayne: IN.

The Commandments. (2010). *Keep the Sabbath day holy*. Retrieved on April 8, 2010 from http://www.mormon.org/mormonorg/eng/basic-beliefs/the-commandments/keep-the-sabbath-day-holy.

Thompson, E. H., Jr., & Pleck, J. H. (1986). The structure of male role norms. *American Behavioral Scientist, 29,* 531–543.

Thoreau, H. D. (1849/1985). *A week on the concord and Merrimack rivers*. New York, NY: Library of America.

Thoreau, H. D. (1854). *Walden, or life in the woods, Volume II*. Boston, MA: Tichnor & Fields.

Thoreson, R. W., Nathan, P. E., Skorina, J. K., & Kilburg, R. R. (1983). The alcoholic psychologist: Issues, problems, and implications for the profession. *Professional Psychology: Research and Practice, 14*(5), 670–684.

Tomkins, C. (1968). *Eric Hoffer: An American odyssey*. New York, NY: Dutton.

Torrey, R. A., Dixon, A. C., & Others (1917, 1996). *The Fundamentals: A testimony to the truth*. Grand Rapids, MI: Baker Book House.

Trevarthen, C. (1996). Lateral asymmetries in infancy: Implications for the development of the hemispheres. *Neuroscience and Biobehavioral Reviews, 20,* 571–586.

Trivers, R. L. (1972). Parental investment and sexual selection. In B. Campbell (Ed.), *Sexual selection and the descent of man, 1871–1971* (pp. 136–179). Chicago, IL: Aldine.

"True Believer." (2010). In *Merriam-Webster online dictionary*. Retrieved March 3, 2010, from http://www.merriam-webster.com/dictionary/true believer

Tryon, G. S., & Winograd, G. (2011). Goal consensus and collaboration. *Psychotherapy, 48*(1), 50–57.

Tyrka, A., Wyche, M., Kelly, M., Price, L., & Carpenter, L. (2009). Childhood maltreatment and adult personality disorder symptoms: Influence of maltreatment type. *Psychiatry Research, 165*(3), 281–287.

Tzourio-Mazoyer, N., De Schonen, S., Crivello, F., Reutter, B., Aujard, Y., & Mazoyer, B. (2002). Neural correlates of woman face processing by 2-month old infants. *Neuroimage, 15,* 454–461.

Underwood, L. G., & Teresi, J. A. (2002). The Daily Spiritual Experience Scale: Development, theoretical description, reliability, exploratory factor analysis, and preliminary construct validity using health-related data. *Annals of Behavioral Medicine, 24*(1), 22–33.

Updike, J. (1968, Winter). John Updike: The art of fiction No. 43. Interviewed by C. T. Samuels. *The Paris Review, 45*. Available online at http://www.theparisreview.org/interviews/4219/the-art-of-fiction-no-43-john-updike

Van Leeuwen, M. S. (2004). Is equal regard in the Bible? In D. Blankenhorn, D. Browning, & M. S. Van Leeuwen (Eds.), *Does Christianity teach male headship? The equal regard marriage and its critics* (pp. 13–22). Grand Rapids, MI: Eerdmans.

Varela, F., Maturana, H., & Uribe, R. (1974). Autopoiesis: The organization of living systems, its characterization and a model. *BioSystems, 5,* 187–196.

Vartia, M. A-L. (2001). Consequences of workplace bullying with respect to the well-being of its targets and the observers of bullying. *Scandinavian Journal of Work, Environment & Health, 27*(1), 63–69.

Von Marees, N., & Petermann, F. (2010). Bullying in German primary schools: Gender differences, age trends and influence of parents' migration and educational backgrounds. *School Psychology International, 31*(2), 178–198.

Wallace, W. R. (1896, September 5). What rules the world? *The Critic, 26*(759), 151.

Wampold, B. E. (2010). *The basics of psychotherapy: An introduction to theory and practice.* Washington, DC: American Psychological Association.

Watchtower Bible and Tract Society of Pennsylvania. (1991). *Pay attention to yourselves and to all the flock.* Brooklyn, NY: International Bible Students Association.

Waterhouse, G. J., Roback, H. B., Moore, R. F., & Martin, P. R. (1997). Perspectives of treatment efficacy with the substance dependent physician: A national survey. *Journal of Addictive Diseases, 16*(1), 123–138.

Watzlawick, P., Weakland, J. H., & Fisch, R. (1974). *Change: Principles of problem formation and problem resolution.* Oxford, England: Norton.

Weaver, A. J., Flannelly, K. J., & Oppenheimer, J. E. (2003). Religion, spirituality, and chaplains in the biomedical literature: 1965–2000. *International Journal of Psychiatry in Medicine, 33*(2), 155–161.

Weber, M. (1946). The sociology of charismatic authority. In H. H. Gerth & C. W. Mills (Ed.), *From Max Weber: Essays in sociology* (pp. 196–244). New York, NY: Oxford University Press.

Weber, M. (1978). *Economy and society: An outline of interpretive sociology* (E. Fischoff et al., trans.). Berkeley, CA: University of California Press.

Weingarten, K. (2010). Intersecting losses: Working with the inevitable vicissitudes in therapist and client lives. *Psychotherapy: Theory, Research, Training, 47*(3), 371–384.

Wertheimer, A. (2008). Exploitation. In *Stanford encyclopedia of philosophy.* Open access online encyclopedia entry retrieved from http://plato.stanford.edu/entries/exploitation/.

Wiler, R. J. (2006, November). *The Olweus bullying prevention program.* Training presented in the Lawrence Public Schools, Unified School District 497, Lawrence, KS.

Wilhelm, K., & Lampsley, H. (2000). Disruptive doctors: Unprofessional interpersonal behavior in doctors. *Medical Journal of Australia, 173*, 384–386.

Wilkinson, M. (2010). *Changing minds in therapy: Emotion, attachment, trauma, and neurobiology.* New York, NY: Norton.

Williams, J. M. G. (2003). *Autobiographical memory test scoring manual.* Unpublished manuscript.

Williams, B. W., & Williams, M. V. (2008). The disruptive physician: A conceptual organization. *Journal of Medical Licensure and Discipline, 94*, 12–20.

Winnicott, D. W. (1941/1975). The observation of infants in a set situation. In D. W. Winnicott, *Through paediatrics to psycho-analysis: Collected papers* (pp. 52–69). London: Hogarth.

Winnicott, D. W. (1956/1975). Primary maternal preoccupation. In D. W. Winnicott, *Through paediatrics to psycho-analysis: Collected papers* (pp. 300–305). London: Hogarth.

Winnicott, D. W. (1960). The theory of the parent–infant relationship. *International Journal of Psychoanalysis, 41*, 585–595.

Wood, W., & Eagly, A. H. (2002). A cross-cultural analysis of the behavior of women and men: Implications for the origins of sex differences. *Psychological Bulletin, 128*(5), 699–727.

Wood, W., & Eagly, A. H. (2010). Gender. In S. T. Fiske, D. T. Gilbert, & G. Lindzey (Eds.), *Handbook of social psychology* (Vol. 1, 5th ed., pp. 629–667). Hoboken, NJ: Wiley.

Woodruff, A. D. (1962). *Basic concepts of teaching.* San Francisco, CA: Chandler.

Wright, S. A. (1991). Reconceptualizing cult coercion and withdrawal: A comparative analysis of divorce and apostasy. *Social Forces, 70*(1), 125–145.

Wundt, W. (1907). *Outlines of psychology* (3rd ed., C. H. Judd, Trans.). Leipzig: Engelmann.

Wundt, W. (1916). *Elements of folk psychology: Outlines of a psychological history of the development of mankind* (E. L. Schaub, trans.). London: MacMillan. (Original work published 1912)

Yahya, H. (2001). *Miracles of the Qur'an.* Toronto, Canada: Al-Attique Publishers.

Yalom, I. (2002). *The gift of therapy: An open letter to a new generation of therapists and their patients.* New York, NY: HarperCollins.

Yllö, K. A. (2007). Gender, diversity, and violence: Extending the feminist framework. In S. J. Ferguson (Ed.), *Shifting the center: Understanding contemporary families* (3rd ed., pp. 611–622). New York, NY: McGraw-Hill.

Zapf, D., & Einarsen, S. (2005). Mobbing at work. Escalated conflicts in organizations. In S. Fox & P. E. Spector (Eds.), *Counterproductive work behavior: Investigations of actors and targets* (pp. 237–270). Washington, DC: American Psychological Association.

INDEX

A

Adams, Abigail, 75–78
Adaptation, 75–91
   Alzheimer's disease, 80
   blood cholesterol levels, 80
   cancer, 80
   categories of comparison, 85
   causes of death, 80
   chronic lower respiratory diseases, 80
   cognitive variables, 85
   dietary habits, 80
   external factors, 80
   genders, contrasting, 75–81
      health, 79–81
      longevity, 78–79
   heart disease, 80
   inheritance, 83
   kidney disease, 80
   longevity, gender differences, 79
   motor behaviors, 85
   Parkinson's disease, 80
   psychological well-being, 85
   reproduction, 81–90
      biosocial selection, 88–90
      natural selection, 81–83
      sexual selection, 83–88
   respiratory disease, 80
   septicemia, 80
   sexual selection, gender differences, 85–88
   smoking, 80
   social variables, 85
   stroke, 80
   suicide, 80
   survival, 83

Adaptive strategies, 164–165, 168, 171, 216, 218
Adler, Alfred, 94, 162
Adorno, Theodor W., 33–38
Affiliation, religious, 183–184
Agreeableness, 44–45
Alcohol, problems created by, 115
Alda, Alan, 95
Alexander, Franz, 145
Alliance, 136–138, 156–157, 219–220, 236, 241–242, 255
Altemeyer, Bob, 38–41
Altruism, 45
Alzheimer's disease, 80
Ambiguity, 68, 155, 225, 247, 252
   embracing, 252
American Bar Association's Center for Professional Responsibility, 12
American Psychiatric Association, 34
Anger in relationships, 115
Anguine, 33
Anti-egalitarianism, 42
Anti-intraception, 37
Approval, divine, 68–72
   hitting children, 71
   nonegalitarian views of women, 70–71
   religious empathy, 71–72
   taking charge, 69–70
Attachment, 103–106, 148, 245
Attunement, 135, 139, 141–146, 150, 152–153, 156, 233, 235–237
   relationship, 135–153
Australia, 79
Authoritarian followers, dominators, FFM traits, 44

The Authoritarian Personality, 33–34, 37–38, 43, 46, 52, 55
"The Authoritarian Personality," 34–38
Authoritarian triad, 46–49
"The Authoritarians," 38–41
Autopoiesis, 239–241
  co-creation with others, 240–241
  self-creation within systems, 239–240
Avoidance, 100, 105, 116, 212, 251

B

Bandura, Albert, 94
Behavior, 9–16, 18–22, 24–27
Behavior codes, 66–67
Belden, Rick, 256–257
Beliefs, religious, 182–183
Benefits of religion, 180–181
Biosocial selection, 88–90
Blind spots, 140, 219, 258
Blocks, cognitive, identifying, 213–214
Blood cholesterol levels, 80
Blood pressure, 10, 17, 80, 105
Borderline Personality Disorder Tailoring Psychotherapy to Patient, 152
Boss, 49
  tyrannical, 9–11
Boundaries, 63–64
Boys, authoritarian, 5–8
  behavior, 5–6
  financial impact, 7–8
  impact, 6–8
  social impact, 7–8
  victim impact, 7
Brain, right hemisphere, 102–103
Brain hemisphere, 102–103
Brazil, 79
Breathing exercises, 208–209
  "Give it a break" breath, 208
  "Let it go" breath, 208
Bullying, 5–10, 111–112, 118, 132, 201, 220, 250
Bullying Checklist, 9
Buss, David, 89

C

C-PTSD. *See* Complex Posttraumatic Stress Disorder

Callousness, 48
Cancer, 8, 80, 193
Caring, male ways of, 174
Categories of comparison, 85
Causes of death, 80
Caveats, 68
Cerebrovascular disease, 80
Change, 229–260
  autopoiesis, 239–241
    co-creation with others, 240–241
    self-creation within systems, 239–240
  client experiences, 254–257
  cognition, 237–239
  cohesion in group therapy, fostering, 242
  countertransference, 243
  empathy, 242
  experience of change, 254–260
  feedback, 242
  goal consensus, reaching, 242–243
  higher-level change, 244–248
  individual therapy, strengthening, 241–242
  malleability, 230–234
    change in personality traits, 232–233
    continuity of personality traits, 231
    personality changes, 233–234
  neuroplasticity, 234–237
    emotional tolerance of therapist, 237
    interactive repairs, 236
  positive regard, exhibiting, 243
  processes of change, 230–248
  psychotherapist, 248–254
    ambiguity, embracing, 252
    meaning, creation of, 253
    optimism, maintaining, 252
    personal needs, caring for, 252
    psychotherapist survival kit, 251
    self-care, 253
    sympathy, empathy, distinguished, 252–253
  psychotherapist experiences, 257–258
  rupture repair, 243
  stressors for psychotherapist, 249–251
    emotional fatigue, 250
    pressures, authoritarian, 249

Index

psychotherapist life changes, 250
  warning signs, 250–251
  workplace stressors, 249
 therapeutic interactions, 241
  interactions hindering, 243–244
Charm, 19
The Child is Father of Man, 99
Childhood
 conduct disorder, diagnosis of, 101
 qualitative observations, 106
 trauma, 105
  short-term consequences, 105
Childhood rates of, 101
Choleric personality, 33
Cholesterol levels, 80
Christianity, 63, 70–72, 181, 226
Chronic lower respiratory diseases, 80
Cicero, 3
Client experiences, 254–257
Client self-attunement, 146–147
Co-creation with others, 240–241
Codes of behavior, 66–67
Cognition, 237–239
Cognitive blocks, identifying, 213–214
Cognitive variables, 85
Cohesion in group therapy, 242
 fostering, 242
Collaboration, 88, 150, 153, 155–156, 159, 199–200, 219, 222, 242
 developing, 242–243
Collaborative conversations, 156–157
Commitment, 24, 117, 190, 218, 221
Commonalities, 107, 150, 210, 226
Communication, 25, 61, 85, 128, 235
Competency, emotional, 209–213
Complex Posttraumatic Stress Disorder, 47
Compulsive patterns, 115
Concealing documents, 12
Concentration, difficulties with, 115
Confession, 25, 127
Construction of authoritarian traits, 99, 102–106
Constructivism, 93–99
Consult aids, 184–191
 religiosity, 184–191
Consulting, 208, 227
A Contemporary Guide to Economics, 229
Continuity of personality traits, 231

Control of others, 28, 42, 150
Conventionalism, 22, 37, 39
Coping skills, 104, 166, 178
Costa, Paul, 43–46
Countertransference, 243
The Courage to Create, 216
Creativity, 95–96
Crisp, Quentin, 216
Criticism of job performance, 9
Cynicism, 37

D

Dalai Lama, 150
Darwin, Charles, 81
Dawson, Karen, 68
Defenses against self-understanding, 200
Defining authoritarian personality, 33–43
Destroying work materials, 9
Destructiveness, 37
Development, 98–99
Diagnosing authoritarian man, 46–52
 authoritarian triad, 46–49
 partner abusers, 50
 personality diagnoses, authoritarian prototypes, 49–51
 workplace bullies, 49–50
 zealous followers, 51
Dietary habits, 80
Dilatory practices, 12
Disabled persons, actions towards, 12
Discomfort, somatic, complaints of, 115
Disruptive professional, 11–13
Distress, somatic, 203–209
Divine mandate, authoritarian as, 55–74
 behavior codes, 66–67
 boundaries, 63–64
 caveats, 68
 chosen, 65
 divine approval, 68–72
  hitting children, 71
  nonegalitarian views of women, 70–71
  religious empathy, 71–72
  taking charge, 69–70
 dualism, 61–62
 fundamentalism, 57–58
 inerrancy, 64–65

male leaders, authoritarian, 67–68
messianism, 62–63
reactivity, 60
selectivity, 61
Document alteration, 12
Domination, 42
Drugs, problems created by, 115
Dualism, 61–62
Dunedin study, 100–102

E

Early life trauma, 105, 122, 251
long-term consequences, 105–106
Edgerton, H.K., 61–62
EEOC. *See* U.S. Equal Employment Opportunity Commission
Egalitarianism, 23, 30, 43, 71, 74, 84, 117, 133
EMDR. *See* Eye movement desensitization and reprocessing
Emotion-regulation strategies, 211–213
Emotional competency, 209–213
Emotional fatigue, 250
Emotional tolerance of therapist, 237
Emotions chart, 211
Empathy, 135–153, 242
sympathy, distinguished, 252–253
Englar-Carlson, Matt, 174, 219
Enumeration, 173–176
Equal Employment Opportunity Commission, 14
Ethics, 186
Ethiopia, 79
European Union, 61, 79, 181
Experience of change, 254–260
Experiential dimension, 187
Exploitation, 14, 27, 29, 41–43, 177, 238, 252
External factors, 80
Extraversion, 44
Eye movement desensitization and reprocessing, add;209

F

Faces, prototypical, authoritarian men, 46–47

Failures, seeing as others' fault, 19
Families, Systems & Health, 106–113
Fathers, 107–109
Fatigue, emotional, 250
Faul, John, 256
Feedback, 192, 214–215, 218–219, 232, 243, 248
FFM. *See* Five Factor Model
Findings, presenting, 166–171
Fitzgerald, Louise F., 15–16
Five Factor Model, 43–46
personality traits, 45–46
Flexibility, lack of, 19
Frankl, Viktor, 94, 193, 203, 246
Freud, Sigmund, 162, 178, 209, 246
Frieswyk, Sid, 151–153
Frivolous claims, 12
Fundamentalism, 51, 56–62, 64–68, 121
behavior codes, 66–67
boundaries, 63–64
caveats, 68
chosen, 65
dualism, 61–62
inerrancy, 64–65
male leaders, authoritarian, 67–68
messianism, 62–63
reactivity, 60
selectivity, 61
The Fundamentalism Project, 57, 68

G

Galbraith, John Kenneth, 229
Galen, 33
Gelso, Charles, 137, 147, 243
Gender differences
contrasting, 75–81
role conflict, 115
sexual selection, 85–88
Genuineness, 137, 242–243
The Gift of Therapy, 135
"Give it a break" breath, 208
Goal consensus, 242
reaching, 242–243
Goal setting, 200–201
Good, Glenn E., 196–197
Goodman, Nelson, 17, 93
Graham, Martha, 96
Greek philosophers, 33, 94

Index

A Guide to Men, 90–91
Gunaratana, H., 140, 206–207

H

The Handbook of Psychotherapy and Religious Diversity, 225
Hanh, Thich Nhat, 142
Harassment, 12–13
Health, contrasting genders, 79–81
Heart disease, 20, 80
Heim, Amy, 34
Heraclitus, 94
Hesse, Hermann, 194
Higher-level change, 244–248
Hill, Napoleon, 96, 144, 184–185
Hinduism, 66, 70, 72, 226
Histrionic personality, 34, 47, 49–50, 53, 99, 121, 192, 205, 249
Hitting children, 71
Homicide, 80
Humanitarian service, 174

I

Identity, 26, 40, 47, 53, 65, 88, 91, 96, 245
Imagination, 172–173
Impulsiveness, 44
In Room With Men, 219
Inability to cry, 115
Inadequate parenting, children with, 101
Incompetent persons, actions towards, 12
Individual outpatient therapy, 218–219
Individual therapy
  alliance in, 241
  strengthening, 241–242
Individual's story, relating, 201–203, 216–218
Individuation, 96–97
Inerrancy, 64–65
Infants
  ability to process, 103
  ability to regulate emotions, 103–104
Inheritance, 83
Insightful tasks, 157–161
Instructions, verbal, to patient, 163–164
Insults, 9
Interpersonal distance, 115

The Interpretation of Dreams, 209
An Invitation to Social Construction, 68
Islam, 21, 63–64, 70–72, 226
Isolation, 19, 25, 98, 227, 232, 251–252
Israel, 57, 79

J

James, William, 94
Japan, 79, 177
Jealousy, 19
Jordan, 79
Judaism, 63–64, 66, 70, 72, 226
Jung, Carl, 223

K

Kabat-Zinn, J., 140–141, 206–207
Kansas Spiritual Assessment, 185–191
Kaufman, Kenneth R., 106–113
Kelly, George, 94
Kennedy, Robert, 55
Khamphakdy-Brown, Supavan, 160–161
Kidney disease, 80
Kierkegaard Construction of Aesthetic, 36
Knowledge, religious, 183
Kornfield, J., 207
KSA. *See* Kansas Spiritual Assessment

L

Lack of empathy, 14, 27, 48, 50
Language loading, 26
Lao Tzu, 94
The Law of Success, 96
"Let it go" breath, 208
Logotherapy and Challenge of Suffering, 203
Longevity
  contrasting genders, 78–79
  gender differences, 79
Lower respiratory diseases, 80

M

Mahalik, Jim, 113
Mahoney, Michael J., 94, 246–247
Maladaptive personality traits, 115

Male leaders, authoritarian, 67–68
Malleability, 230–234
    change in personality traits, 232–233
    continuity of personality traits, 231
    personality changes, 233–234
Mandate, divine, 55–74
    behavior codes, 66–67
    boundaries, 63–64
    caveats, 68
    chosen, 65
    divine approval, 68–72
        hitting children, 71
        nonegalitarian views of women, 70–71
        religious empathy, 71–72
        taking charge, 69–70
    dualism, 61–62
    fundamentalism, 57–58
    inerrancy, 64–65
    male leaders, authoritarian, 67–68
    messianism, 62–63
    reactivity, 60
    selectivity, 61
Man's Search for Meaning, 193
Marty, Martin E., 58–59
Masculinity strengths, 173–178
    caring, male ways of, 174
    enumeration, 173–176
    humanitarian service, 174
    identifying, 174
    provider tradition, 174
    self-reliance, 174
    worker tradition, 174
Masculinity stress, 176–178
    coping skills, 178
    gender role conflict, 177
    marital interactions, 178
    masculine norms, 176–177
    relational conflicts, 177
Masculinity traits, 113–117
    masculine social norms
        costs of, 114–117
        identifying, 114
May, Rollo, 216
McCrae, Robert, 43–46
MCMI. *See Million Clinical Multiaxial Inventory*
Mead, George Herbert, 98, 184, 244
Meaning, creation of, 253

Melancholic personality, 33
Messenger from God, true believer as, 23–27
Messianism, 62–63
Milieu control, 25–26
Million Clinical Multiaxial Inventory, 46, 50
Mills, Jeannie, 24
Mind, Self, and Society, 98
Mindfulness, 140–143, 161, 204–207, 213, 235–236
    training, 204–207
Mindfulness in Plain English, 207
Minimalist definition of personality, 34
Mistakes, seeing as others' fault, 19
Model Rules of Professional Conduct, 12
Modern Men in Search of a Soul, 223
Mothers, 109–111
Motivation, difficulties with, 115
Motor behaviors, 85
"My Heart Leaps Up When I Behold," 99
Mystical manipulation, 25

N

The Naked Civil Servant, 216
Narcissistic personality disorder, 48, 50–52, 162
Natural selection, 81–83
Need to be right, 19
Negative attitude about women, 19
NEO Five-Factor Inventory, 43
NEO Personality Inventory, 43
Neuroplasticity, 234–237
    emotional tolerance of therapist, 237
    interactive repairs, 236
Neuroticism, 44, 49
The New Handbook of Psychotherapy and Counseling with Men, 225
The New World Order, 60
Non-empathic responses, 42
Non-religious psychotherapist, 178–180
Nonegalitarian attitudes, 115, 177
Nonegalitarian views of women, 70–71

O

Obsessive-compulsive personality disorder, 48–49, 100

Obsessive personality, 34, 47–49, 53, 81, 118–119
O'Neil, Jim, 116–117
Openness, 44
Optimism, maintaining, 252
Organization, 96
Origin of Species, 78, 81–83
Outpatient therapy, 218–219
Outrageous Acts and Everyday Rebellions, 41

P

PAI. *See Personality Assessment Inventory*
Parkinson's disease, 80
Partner abusers, 18–21, 50
Pascal, Blaise, 27
Path of Emancipation, 142
A Path with Heart: A Guide Through Perils and Promises of Spiritual Life, 207
Patterns, relational, 165
Perfectionism, 48, 225
Personal needs, caring for, 252
Personality, minimalist definition, 34
Personality Assessment Inventory, 46
Personality diagnoses, authoritarian prototypes, 49–51
Personality disorders, 99–100
Personality traits, 45–46
 change in, 232–233
 continuity of, 231
Personality type, 33–53
 agreeableness, 44–45
 altruism, 45
 anguine, 33
 anti-egalitarianism, 42
 anti-intraception, 37
 authoritarian followers, dominators, FFM traits, 44
 "The Authoritarian Personality," 34–38
 "The Authoritarians," 38–41
 callousness, 48
 choleric personality, 33
 compliance, 45
 defining authoritarian personality, 33–43
 destructiveness, 37
 diagnosing authoritarian man, 46–52
 authoritarian triad, 46–49
 partner abusers, 50
 personality diagnoses, authoritarian prototypes, 49–51
 workplace bullies, 49–50
 zealous followers, 51
 extraversion, 44
 Five Factor Model, 43–46
 personality traits, 45–46
 histrionic personality, 47
 minimalist definition of personality, 34
 narcissistic personality disorder, 48, 50–52, 162
 neuroticism, 44
 non-empathic responses, 42
 obsessive-compulsive personality disorder, 48–49, 100
 obsessive personality, 47
 perfectionism, 48, 225
 phlegmatic personality, 33
 projectivity, 38
 prototypical faces, authoritarian men, 46–47
 psychopathic type, 48
 rigidity, 48, 151
 "Social Dominators," 41–43
 straightforwardness, 44
 submission, 37
 superstition, 37
 Trait Anger, 50
 warmth, 44
 workplace bosses, 49
Personality variables, 85
Phlegmatic personality, 33
Piaget, Jean, 94
Picasso, Pablo, 95
Plato, 3, 94, 139–140
Positive regard, exhibiting, 243
Possessiveness, 19
Pratto, Felicia, 41–43
Preference, religious, 181
Presenting findings, 166–171
Pressures, authoritarian, 249
Problem solving, 195, 212
Processes of change, 230–248

Projectivity, 38
Prototypes, 3–31
   abusive partner, 18–21
   boys
      authoritarian, 5–8
      behavior, 5–6
      financial impact, 7–8
      impact, 6–8
      social impact, 7–8
      victim impact, 7
   charm, 19
   concealing documents, 12
   confession, 25, 127
   conventionalism, 22, 37, 39
   criticism of job performance, 9
   destroying work materials, 9
   dilatory practices, 12
   disabled persons, actions towards, 12
   egalitarianism, 30
   emotional consequences, 17
   flexibility, lack of, 19
   frivolous claims, 12
   harassment, 12
   insults, 9
   jealousy, 19
   lack of empathy, 14, 27, 48, 50
   language loading, 26
   manipulation, 29
   milieu control, 25–26
   mistakes, seeing as others' fault, 19
   mystical manipulation, 25
   negative attitude about women, 19
   purity, demand for, 25
   rumors, spreading, 9
   selfishness, 19
   sexual harassment, impact of, 17
   threats of, 9
   true believer
      as messenger from God, 23–27
      as zealous follower, 21–23
   U.S. Equal Employment Opportunity Commission, 14
   violent household, growing up in, 19
   warning signs, controlling behavior, 19
   work meetings, exclusion from, 9
   workplace bully, 8–18
      behavior, 9–27
      Bullying Checklist, 9
      disruptive professional, 11–13
      impact, 10–13, 17–18, 20–21, 27
      sexual harassment, 13–18
      tyrannical boss, 9–11
Prototypical faces, authoritarian men, 46–47
Provider tradition, 174
Provider tradition of men, 174
Psychological well-being, 85
Psychopathic type, 48
Psychophysiologic training, 203–204
Psychotherapist, 248–254
   ambiguity, embracing, 252
   meaning, creation of, 253
   optimism, maintaining, 252
   personal needs, caring for, 252
   psychotherapist survival kit, 251
   self-care, 253
   sympathy, empathy, distinguished, 252–253
Psychotherapist experiences, 257–258
Psychotherapist factors, 218–219
Psychotherapist life changes, 250
Psychotherapist stressors, 249–251
   emotional fatigue, 250
   pressures, authoritarian, 249
   psychotherapist life changes, 250
   warning signs, 250–251
   workplace stressors, 249
Psychotherapist survival kit, 251
Punitive action, or violence, threats of, 9
The Pursuit of Justice, 55
Put-downs, 9

Q

Qualitative assessment, 155–192
   masculinity strengths, 173–178
      caring, male ways of, 174
      enumeration, 173–176
      humanitarian service, 174
      identifying, 174
      provider tradition, 174
      self-reliance, 174
      worker tradition, 174
   masculinity stress, 176–178
      coping skills, 178
      gender role conflict, 177
      marital interactions, 178

masculine norms, 176–177
relational conflicts, 177
readiness assessment, 156–161
    collaborative conversations, 156–157
    insightful tasks, 157–161
religiosity, 178–191
    affiliation, religious, 183–184
    beliefs, religious, 182–183
    benefits of religion, 180–181
    consult aids, 184–191
    ethics, 186
    experiential dimension, 187
    Kansas Spiritual Assessment, 185–191
    knowledge, religious, 183
    non-religious psychotherapist, 178–180
    preference, religious, 181
trait assessment, 162–173
    adaptive strategies, 165
    case studies, 167–171
    findings, presenting, 166–171
    imagination, 172–173
    relational patterns, 165
    self-concepts, 164
    STEM, challenges, 162–171
    verbal instructions, 163–164

R

Readiness assessment, 156–161
    collaborative conversations, 156–157
    insightful tasks, 157–161
The Real Relationship in Psychotherapy, 137, 147, 243
Real-time learning, 214–215
Regulating emotions, approaches to, 212
Relatedness, 97–98
Relational disruption, 106
Relational patterns, 164–168, 170, 214–216, 218, 235
Relationship attunement, 135–153
Religiosity, 178–191
    affiliation, religious, 183–184
    beliefs, religious, 182–183
    benefits of religion, 180–181
    consult aids, 184–191
    ethics, 186
    experiential dimension, 187
    Kansas Spiritual Assessment, 185–191
    knowledge, religious, 183
    non-religious psychotherapist, 178–180
    preference, religious, 181
Religious empathy, 71–72
Religious stories, 186, 226
    utilizing, 226
Reproduction, 81–91
    biosocial selection, 88–90
    natural selection, 81–83
    sexual selection, 83–88
        gender differences, 85–88
Respiratory disease, 80
Rhythmic breath, 208–209
Right hemisphere, brain, 102–103
Rigidity, 48, 151
Ritual, 9, 24, 186–187, 199
Role play learning, 215–216
Romans, 33, 65, 69, 100
Rowland, Helen, 90–91
Rumination, 207, 212, 250
Rumors, spreading, 9
Rupture repair, 243
Russia, 39, 79, 177

S

Sacred science, 25–26
Schore, Allan, 102
SDO. *See* Social Dominance Orientation
Selectivity, 61
Self-attunement of therapist, 139–142
Self-care, 253
Self-concepts, 33, 141, 164, 166–167, 169–170, 175
Self-control problems, children with, 101
Self-creation within systems, 239–240
Self-esteem, lack of, 115
Self-regulation, 193–194, 203–218, 227
    cognitive blocks, identifying, 213–214
    emotional competency, 209–213
    relational patterns, 214–216
    somatic distress, 203–209
    story of individual, 216–218
Self-reliance, 173–174, 176
Self-respect, lack of, 115

Self-understanding, 194–203
  defenses against, 200
  goal setting, 200–201
  self-understanding, 199–200
  story of individual, 201–203
  working together, 195–199
Selfishness, 19
Septicemia, 80
Sexual behavior, 13–14, 30, 41–42, 75, 83–91
  disruptions in, 115
Sexual Experiences Questionnaire, 14, 16
Sexual harassment, 13–18
  impact of, 17
Sexual selection, 83–88
  gender differences, 85–88
Shakespeare, William, 52
Sidanius, Jim, 41–43
Six Years With God, 24
Smoking, 80
Social construction, 93–119
  aggression, childhood rates of, 101
  alcohol, problems created by, 115
  anger in relationships, 115
  authoritarian as, 118–119
  childhood conduct disorder, diagnosis of, 101
  childhood trauma, short-term consequences, 105
  concentration, difficulties with, 115
  construction of authoritarian traits, 99, 102–106
    bullying, 111–112
    The Child is Father of Man, 99
    childhood, qualitative observations, 106
    Dunedin study, 100–102
    Families, Systems & Health, 106–113
    fathers, 107–109
    mothers, 109–111
    personality disorders, 99–100
  constructivism, 93–99
    creativity, 95–96
    development, 98–99
    individuation, 96–97
    organization, 96
    relatedness, 97–98

  drugs, problems created by, 115
  early life trauma, long-term consequences, 105–106
  gender role conflict, 115
  inability to cry, 115
  inadequate parenting, children with, 101
  infant
    ability to process, 103
    ability to regulate emotions, 103–104
  interpersonal distance, 115
  maladaptive personality traits, 115
  masculine social norms
    costs of, 114–117
    identifying, 114
  masculinity traits, 113–117
  motivation, difficulties with, 115
  "My Heart Leaps Up When I Behold," 99
  relational disruption, 106
  right hemisphere, brain, 102–103
  self-control problems, children with, 101
  self-esteem, lack of, 115
  sexual behavior, disruptions in, 115
  social construction, authoritarian as, 118–119
  social contact, withdrawal from, 115
  somatic distress, complaints of, 115
  work conflicts, 115
Social contact, withdrawal from, 115
Social Dominance Orientation, 42
"Social Dominators," 41–43
Social norms, masculine
  costs of, 114–117
  identifying, 114
Social variables, 85
Socrates, 3, 139
Somatic distress, 203–209
  complaints of, 115
Steadiness, 218, 247
Stealing work materials, 9
Steinem, Gloria, 41
STEM, challenges, 162–171
Stereotyping, 37
Stevens, Mark, 219
Story of individual, 201–203, 216–218
Straightforwardness, 44

Stress, 176–178, 249–251
  coping skills, 178
  gender role conflict, 177
  marital interactions, 178
  masculine norms, 176–177
  relational conflicts, 177
Stroke, 80
Submission, 22–23, 28, 37, 39–40
Suicide, 5, 13, 17, 80, 250, 253–254
Summary of themes from early life. *See* STEM
Superstition, 37
Suppression, 212
Survival, 83–84, 86–87, 91, 151, 251
Survival kit, for psychotherapist, 251
Swimming with Sharks, 8
Sympathy, 29, 252
  empathy, distinguished, 252–253

T

Terry, Randall, 21
Theodor W. Adorno Award, 36
Therapeutic interactions, 241
  interactions hindering, 243–244
Therapist, self-attunement, 139–142
Therapist-client attunement, 142–145
Thoreau, Henry David, 95, 230
Trait Anger, 50
Trait assessment, 162–173
  adaptive strategies, 165
  case studies, 167–171
  findings, presenting, 166–171
  imagination, 172–173
  relational patterns, 165
  self-concepts, 164
  STEM, challenges, 162–171
  verbal instructions, 163–164
Trait construction, 99, 102–106
  bullying, 111–112
  The Child is Father of Man, 99
  childhood, qualitative observations, 106
  Dunedin study, 100–102
  Families, Systems & Health, 106–113
  fathers, 107–109
  mothers, 109–111
  personality disorders, 99–100

True believer
  as messenger from God, 23–27
  as zealous follower, 21–23
True believer friend, 223–227
Twain, Mark, 193
Tyrannical boss, 9–11

U

U.S. Equal Employment Opportunity Commission, 14

V

Values, 16, 37–39, 116–117, 184, 202, 224, 245
Venus and Adonis, 52
Verbal instructions to patient, 163–164
Violence, threats of, 9
Violent household, growing up in, 19

W

Walden, 230
Warmth, 44
Warning signs, controlling behavior, 19
Ways of Worldmaking, 17, 93
Westen, Drew, 34
Wherever You Go, There You Are: Mindfulness Meditation in Everyday Life, 207
Women, negative attitude about, 19
Words of Wisdom, Love and Compassion, 150
Wordsworth, William, 99
Work conflicts, 115
Work materials, stealing, 9
Work meetings, exclusion from, 9
Worker tradition, 174
Working together, 195–199
Workplace bosses, 49
Workplace bully, 8–18, 49–50
  behavior, 9–27
  Bullying Checklist, 9
  case study, 129–130
  disruptive professional, 11–13
  family background, 129–132
  impact, 10–13, 17–18, 20–21, 27
  occupational history, 130, 132

presenting issue, 129–131
   sexual harassment, 13–18
   tyrannical boss, 9–11
Workplace stressors, 249
Worldviews, 168–171

Y

Yalom, Irving, 135

Z

Zealous follower
   case study, 130–132
   true believer as, 21–23